East Meets West

*

East Meets West

HUMAN RIGHTS AND DEMOCRACY
IN EAST ASIA

*

DANIEL A. BELL

PRINCETON UNIVERSITY PRESS

PRINCETON, NEW JERSEY

Library of Congress Cataloging-in-Publication Data
Bell, Daniel (Daniel A.)
East meets West: human rights and democracy in East Asia / Daniel A. Bell.
p. cm.
Includes bibliographical references and index.
ISBN 0-691-00507-9 (alk. paper)—ISBN 0-691-00508-7 (pbk.: alk. paper)

1. Human rights—East Asia 2. Democracy—East Asia. I. Title.
JC599.E18 B45 2000
320.95—dc21   99-048077

This book has been composed in New Baskerville

The paper used in this publication meets the minimum
requirements of ANSI/NISO Z39.48-1992 (R1997)
(*Permanence of Paper*)

http:/www.princeton.edu

Printed in the United States of America

1   3   5   7   9   10   8   6   4   2
(Pbk.)
3   5   7   9   10   8   6   4
ISBN -13: 978-0-6910-0508-9 (pbk.: alk. paper)

FOR JULIEN SONG BELL

*

∗ Contents ∗

* Acknowledgments *

THIS BOOK dates from a proposal submitted in 1994 for an application to the University Center for Human Values, Princeton University. Luckily, the proposal was accepted, and I would like to thank the other Laurance S. Rockefeller fellows—Hilary Bok, Chris Bobonich, Samuel Fleischacker, Kent Greenawalt, and Yael Tamir—for helping me to develop and refine my ideas, as well as Elizabeth Kiss and George Kateb, who participated in the fellows' seminars. Special thanks to Stephen Macedo, my liberal friend and adversary.

I would like to thank the following friends and colleagues for comments, discussions, and papers that helped to shape this book: Fred C. Alford, Abdullahi Ahmed An-Na'im, Roger Ames, Gary Bell, Jacques Bertrand, David Brown, Jonathan Chan, Chan Sin Yee, Phyllis Chang, Chee Soon Juan, Albert Chen, Melanie Chew, Ken Christie, Chua Beng Huat, Ci Jiwei, Robert Dahl, Michael Davis, Maria Serena Diokno, Jack Donnelly, Donald Emmerson, Neil Englehart, Chris Fraser, N. Ganesan, Fawaz Gerges, Yash Ghai, Nathan Glazer, Laurence Goldstein, Roger Goodman, Hahm Chaibong, Hahm Chaihark, David Hall, Han Sangjin, Jonathan Hecht, Geir Helgesen, Lusina Ho, Mab Huang, Hashbat Hulan, Inoue Tatsuo, Patrick James, Kanishka Jayasuriya, James Jesudason, Jomo K.S., David Martin Jones, Kang Jung-in, Kim Byung-Kook, Benedict Kingsbury, Chandran Kukathas, Kwok Kian Woon, Rowena Kwok, Lam Peng Er, Joe Lau, Lew Seok-Choon, Lily Ling, Chris Lingle, Michael Martin, David Miller, Mo Jongryn, Tim Moore, Julius Moravscik, Chandra Muzaffar, Andrew Nathan, Masa Okano, Onuma Yasuaki, Norani Othman, Thomas Pogge, Eugene Qian, M. Ramesh, Garry Rodan, Denny Roy, Amartya Sen, Ming Sing, Hari Singh, Tom Smith, Dorothy Solinger, Genevieve Souillac, Gopal Sreenivasan, Tracy Strong, Sulak Sivaraksa, Kevin Y.L. Tan, Charles Taylor, Julia Adeney Thomas, Tu Weiming, Wang Hao, Wang Siyuan, Daniel Weinstock, Dick Wilson, Benjamin Wong, Xia Yong, Xin Chunying, Yasuda Nobuyuki, and Yokota Yozo. Thanks are also due to the kind and supportive administrative staff at the University of Hong Kong's Department of Philosophy: Vivian Chu, Ping Lau, and Loletta Wan.

I owe a special debt to the following individuals: Joanne Bauer, my collaborator on the project that inspired many of the ideas in Part I; Daniel Bell (the distinguished American sociologist), who went beyond the call of distant kinship to read and provide detailed comments on Parts II and III of this book; Joseph Chan, my colleague and friend who helped to clarify many of the arguments in this book; Amitai Etzioni, communitarian comrade and insightful contributor to the international dialogue on human rights; Amy Gutmann, for helpful comments on Part II and for sharing the joys of deliberating about the pros and cons of deliberation; Will Kymlicka, referee for Princeton University Press, who provided lengthy and constructive comments on the manuscript; and Michael Walzer, who inspired this project with his approach to social criticism and subsequently read and commented on the whole manuscript.

Layla Asali, Kristin Gager, Molan Chun Goldstein, Ian Malcolm, and Anita O'Brien facilitated the publication process at Princeton University Press. Editor-in-chief Ann Wald showed faith in the work and helpfully identified the parts that needed to be improved.

I am particularly grateful for the interventions of my most ruthless critic, Song Bing. Our relationship is proof that the "clash of civilizations" can peacefully coexist, even within the same family. Bing normally takes the "Western" side, and I normally take the "Eastern" side, but more often than not we manage to hammer out a workable consensus by bedtime.

I am also grateful to family members in Canada, France, China, Japan, and the United States for supporting this work over the years. I apologize for lengthy periods of absence, and I look forward to the day when intraplanetary travel will be cheap, fast, and free of the effects of jet lag.

Finally, I would like to thank a lovely five-year-old boy named Julien Song Bell, to whom this book is dedicated.

East Meets West

*

* Introduction *

A SMALL SET OF crucial human rights are valued, at least in theory, by all governments in the contemporary world. The most obvious are the prohibitions against slavery, genocide, murder, torture, prolonged arbitrary detention, and systematic racial discrimination. These rights have become part of customary international law[1] and they are not contested in the public rhetoric of the international arena. Of course, many gross human rights violations occur off the record, and human rights groups such as Amnesty International have the task of exposing the gap between public allegiance to rights and the sad reality of ongoing abuse. This is largely practical work, however. There is not much point writing or deliberating about the desirability of practices that everyone condemns at the level of principle.

But political thinkers and activists around the world can and do take different sides on many pressing human rights concerns that fall outside the sphere of customary international law. This gray area of debate includes criminal law, family law, women's rights, social and economic rights, the rights of indigenous peoples, and the attempt to universalize Western-style democratic practices. Some of these issues are contested on cultural grounds, others are a matter of how rights are prioritized in developing nations, and sometimes the question is whether or not to employ the language of rights in the first place. Not all human rights values and practices typically endorsed by Western countries are automatically accepted elsewhere, and dialogue between interested parties is needed to identify areas of commonality and justifiable difference.

This should not be too controversial. The problem, however, is that many prominent voices in the West seem to foreclose the possibility of a constructive dialogue with "the rest."

---

[1] These rights, in other words, cannot be displaced by agreements of states or in any other way. See Oscar Schacter, *International Law in Theory and Practice*, 337–338, and Ingrid Detter, *The International Legal Order*, 304–305.

West-centric Perspectives

Liberal democratic ideals and institutions command almost universal allegiance in Western societies. This phenomenon is to be understood in light of the West's shared history and culture. In what seems like an all too obvious theoretical mistake, however, it is often assumed without argument that liberal democracy also meets the deeper aspirations of the rest of the world. Needless to say, we have moved beyond the brief moment of euphoria that followed the collapse of communism in the Soviet bloc. It is now widely recognized that brutal ethnic warfare, crippling poverty, environmental degradation, and pervasive corruption, to name some of the more obvious troubles afflicting the "developing" world, pose serious obstacles to the successful establishment and consolidation of liberal democratic political arrangements. But these are seen as unfortunate (hopefully temporary) afflictions that may delay the "end of history" when liberal democracy has finally triumphed over its rivals. They are not meant to pose a challenge to the *ideal* of liberal democracy.[2] It is widely assumed that liberal democracy is something that all rational individuals *would* want if they could "get it."[3]

---

[2] It is worth noting, however, that Francis Fukuyama, who coined the term "end of history" as a reference to the ultimate (and presumably final) triumph of liberal democracy, is not an uncritical advocate of the dominant value system in Western liberal democracies. For example, he suggests that Asian-style personalism and "relational contracting" may be particularly appropriate in a sophisticated economy, and that these "Asian values" cannot be blamed for Asia's recent economic decline ("Asian Values and the Asian Crisis," 26). Still, Fukuyama does not to my knowledge argue that Asian *political* values that differ from liberal democratic norms may be appropriate in a modern polity.

[3] Not everyone, of course, holds this viewpoint. But the most prominent political thinker who recognizes that there may be justifiable alternatives to Western-style liberal democracy—Samuel Huntington, author of the notorious article "The Clash of Civilizations"—focuses more on the threat posed by the "other" and the need to build walls between civilizations and prepare for the possibility of military conflict by rearming the West. As he puts it in a follow-up article, the task is "to preserve and renew the unique qualities of Western civilization" by, for example, "controlling immigration from non-Western societies" ("The West Unique, Not Universal," 46, 45). However, Huntington seems to express a rather

More concretely, this blind faith in the universal potential of liberal democracy takes the form of a U.S. government policy to promote human rights and democracy abroad, regardless of local needs, habits, and traditions. As President Bill Clinton argues, "America's interests require the United States to lead an effort to build a world order shaped by U.S. values."[4] Of course, critics on the left point out that there is a large gap between the rhetoric and the reality—that commercial and security interests frequently override human rights concerns in United States foreign policy—but few question the normative premise that the United States *ought* to promote its values abroad.

More surprisingly, perhaps, even critics of U.S.-style human rights discourse—which identifies civil and political rights with human rights in general—often seem to rule out the possibility that there may be something to learn from the non-Western world. It is a widespread view within the international human rights community that the U.S. government (and public, to a substantial extent) tends to regard freedom from the arbitrary powers of the state as most important, with a concomitant reluctance to accept economic, social, and cultural rights as human rights. The leading human rights theorist Jack Donnelly, for example, is critical of U.S.-style "civil and political rights centrism." Instead, he upholds as a universal ideal the more comprehensive set of rights endorsed in West European social democratic states, and he argues that the task of the human rights activist is to implement this ideal in the developing world.[5] But he seems to rule out the possibility that "international" human rights principles can be modified in response to more input by non-Western peoples.

---

different sentiment in his book-length treatise on the topic. He does not repeat the ugly comment about the need to limit the immigration of non-Westerners, and he ends the book by quoting Lester Pearson on the need for different civilizations "to learn to live side by side in peaceful interchange, learning from each other, studying each other's history and ideals and art and culture, mutually enriching each other's lives" (*The Clash of Civilizations and the Remaking of World Order*, 321).

[4] See Christopher Layne and Benjamin Schwarz, "American Hegemony without an Enemy," 7.

[5] Jack Donnelly, "Post–Cold War Reflections of the Study of Human Rights," 97, 112, 116.

The situation is scarcely better in the field of normative political theory. The most influential Anglo-American political philosophers today still seem compelled by a tradition of universalist moral reasoning that proposes one final solution to the question of the ideal polity yet paradoxically draws only on the moral aspirations and political practices found in Western societies. The case of Brian Barry is not atypical. Barry opens his widely cited book *Justice as Impartiality* by boldly affirming the universality of his theory: "I continue to believe in the possibility of putting forward a universally valid case in favor of liberal egalitarian principles."[6] Barry does recognize that a theory of justice must be anchored in substantive moral considerations, but his normative horizon seems to be limited to the values and practices of liberal Western societies.[7] For example, Barry does not draw on anything worthwhile from the Chinese political tradition: his discussion of "things Chinese" is confined to brief criticisms of the Cultural Revolution and the traditional practice of foot-binding.[8]

In short, these West-centric outlooks pose serious obstacles to constructive cross-cultural dialogue. On the one hand, they block the development of a truly international human rights regime that can fully accommodate the needs of non-Western peoples. On the other hand, they fail to allow for the possibility that there may be areas of justifiable difference between political values in the West and "the rest."

---

[6] Brian Barry, *Justice as Impartiality*, 3. Barry portrays himself as a member of an embattled minority of universalists, but in fact his view is far more mainstream among contemporary Anglophone political philosophers than he suggests (e.g., Ronald Dworkin, Thomas Nagel, and Tim Scanlon—to name just some of the leading lights in the field—also defend a universalist account of liberal egalitarianism). Of course, many contemporary political theorists have written at length about multiculturalism, but this does not usually translate into explicit recognition of the possibility that there may be non-Western values of normative importance. And even fewer Western political theorists have written book-length works that seriously engage with non-Western political values and models of political organization.

[7] See my review essay, which develops this criticism of Barry's "parochial universalism" ("The Limits of Liberal Justice," esp. 565–568).

[8] One might consider the reaction to a Chinese intellectual who puts forward a universal theory of justice that draws on the Chinese political tradition for inspiration and completely ignores the history of Western societies, except for brief criticisms of slavery and imperialism.

The East Asian Challenge to Liberal Democracy

The most widely publicized challenge to Western liberal democracy has emerged from the East Asian region.[9] This debate has revolved primarily around the notion of "Asian values," a term devised by several Asian officials and their supporters for the purpose of challenging Western-style civil and political freedoms. Asians, they claim, place special emphasis upon family and social harmony, with the implication that those in the "chaotic and crumbling" societies of the West should think twice before intervening in Asia for the sake of promoting human rights and democracy. As Singapore's senior statesman Lee Kuan Yew put it, Asians have "little doubt that a society with communitarian values where the interests of society take precedence over that of the individual suits them better than the individualism of America."[10] Such claims attracted international attention primarily because East Asian leaders seemed to be presiding over what a recent U.N. human development report called "the most sustained and widespread development miracle of the twentieth century, perhaps all history."[11] In 1997–98, however, the East Asian miracle seemed to have collapsed. And it looks like Asian values was one casualty of the crisis.

But it would be a mistake to ignore East Asian perspectives on human rights and democracy. For one thing, the region accounts for nearly half the world's population. Moreover, as Amartya Sen notes, "even though the evident thrill in the power of Asian values has somewhat diminished with the financial and economic troubles that the East Asian economies have faced during 1997–98, enough has been achieved in the region—both absolutely and in relation to the record of other regions—to make it legitimate to continue to celebrate the economic performance of East Asia over the decades."[12] In most Asian countries, the economic fundamentals—"high savings rates, a well-educated labor force, high levels

---

[9] For purposes of this book, I define East Asia as including Northeast and Southeast Asia.

[10] Quoted in the *International Herald Tribune*, 9–10 November 1991.

[11] Quoted in Barbara Crossette, "U.N. Survey Finds Rich-Poor Gap Widening," *New York Times*, 15 July 1996.

[12] Amartya Sen, "Human Rights and Economic Achievements," 89.

of technology and an outward orientation"[13]—remain in place, and the region may well reemerge "meaner and leaner" in a few years time. China in particular looks set to become an economic and political heavyweight with the power to seriously challenge the hegemony of Western liberal democratic values in international fora. Thus, failing to engage seriously with East Asian political perspectives risks widening misunderstandings and setting the stage for hostilities that could otherwise have been avoided.

From a theoretical point of view, however, it must be conceded that the official debate on Asian values has not provided much of a challenge to dominant Western political outlooks. The main problem is that the debate has been led by Asian leaders who seem to be motivated primarily by political considerations, rather than by a sincere desire to make a constructive contribution to the cross-cultural dialogue on political values. Thus, it was easy to dismiss—rightly so, in most cases—the Asian challenge as nothing but a self-serving ploy by government leaders to justify their authoritarian rule in the face of increasing demands for democracy at home and abroad.

Still, it would be a mistake to conclude that nothing of theoretical significance has emerged from East Asia. The debate on Asian values has also prompted critical intellectuals in the region to reflect and debate over how they can locate themselves in a debate on human rights and democracy in which they had not previously played a substantial part. Neither wholly rejecting nor wholly endorsing the values and practices ordinarily realized through a liberal democratic political regime, these intellectuals are drawing on their own cultural traditions and exploring areas of commonality and difference with the West. Though often less provocative than the views of their governments, these unofficial East Asian viewpoints may offer more lasting contributions to the debate.

Part I of this book consists of my reflections on several dialogues (primarily conferences and workshops) on human rights (chapter 1) and democracy (chapter 2) between Western and East Asian intellectuals. It draws upon arguments made by East Asian intellectuals who are not likely to be motivated by a desire to justify authoritarian rule (in fact, many have been actively involved with

[13] See Joseph Stiglitz (Senior Vice President and Chief Economist, The World Bank), "Road to Recovery," *Asiaweek*, 17 July 1998, 67.

nongovernmental organizations and opposition groups in seeking political change). This section attempts to get beyond the rhetoric that has dogged the Asian values debate and to identify relatively persuasive East Asian criticisms of traditional Western approaches to human rights and democracy. The ultimate aim is to argue for the need to take into account the meanings and priorities East Asians typically attach to a set of political standards that have been largely shaped by the Western experience.

Taking Culture Too Seriously

Having said all this in the name of cultural sensitivity, it is worth noting an opposite tendency that overestimates the social and political importance of traditional cultural values in contemporary societies. It is not unusual these days to find books and articles that engage in systematic comparisons of Eastern and Western philosophies. These comparisons can be interesting, particularly when they help to shed light on philosophical issues neglected or underemphasized in particular cultures. The problem occurs when attempts are made to draw political implications in modern Asian societies on the basis of traditional cultural values.

Such political efforts usually take the form of systematic comparisons between liberal democracy and Asian traditions such as Confucianism. The Singaporean scholar/diplomat Bilahari Kausikan is appropriately skeptical of such attempts: "In its more learned manifestations, this argument involves attempts to recover from ancient Asian texts references that purport to prove that traditional Asian cultures professed democratic, or at least quasi-democratic, values. The charm of these erudite games is that they can be played endlessly without uncovering anything with practical relevance to current concerns. Most Asian societies have such long histories and rich cultures that it is possible to 'prove' nearly anything about them if the context of the recovered references is ignored."[14]

Conversely, however, it is worth noting that cultural defenders of authoritarianism often recover references from ancient Asian texts in order to "prove" that Asians favor restrictions on demo-

[14] Bilahari Kausikan, "Governance That Works," 30.

cratic rule (dozens of my own students from Singapore and Hong Kong have made such arguments over the years). These arguments can also be refuted simply by showing that such values do not have any practical relevance given current normative outlooks and political concerns.

If the aim is to bridge the gap between political philosophy and political reality, it is important to distinguish between traditional values that are still relevant today and others that have been relegated to the dustbin of history. Rather than combing through ancient texts for the purpose of determining the (in)compatibility of two whole political traditions, it is far more useful to limit one's focus to particular traditional values that continue to have widespread impact on people's political behavior in contemporary societies.[15] Once these are identified, the next step is to proceed with a normative argument explaining why such values *ought* to remain influential.[16] As well, it must be recognized that modern East Asian societies are characterized by different mixtures of Confucian, Buddhist, Western, and other values,[17] and that Asian societies may not all share the same set of pressing social needs and political concerns. Thus, it is important to specify both the traditional values that are still relevant (from a political and normative point of view) and the particular context for one's political analysis.

Part II is an attempt to construct a case for democracy in a contemporary Singaporean context. While it is recognized that some Western arguments for democracy may not resonate with the hab-

[15] Ideally, this would be combined with a historically informed argument that shows how such values came to be transmitted from generation to generation. Such an investigation, however, is beyond the scope of this book.

[16] One should also leave open the possibility that it may be desirable to try to resuscitate some marginal traditional values that resonate at a "deeper," not fully conscious level.

[17] Confucianism, which is not a religion with an organized membership, seems to be particularly "compatible with and complementary to religions that are not strictly exclusionistic. Often the adjectival 'Confucian' can be attached to 'Buddhist' or 'Christian' to designate a particular style of being religious" (Tu Weiming, ed., *Confucian Traditions in East Asian Modernity,* 188). In South Korea, for example, "even those who identified themselves as Christians and adhered to Christian values and practices were very much inclined to Confucian values and practices as well . . . This confirms the statement of a well-known Christian theologian, who said, 'Our Christians are Confucians dressed in Christian robes'" (Koh Byong-ik, "Confucianism in Contemporary Korea," 199).

its and politically influential traditions of Singaporeans (chapter 3), prodemocracy forces may have more success by appealing to the continuing influence of traditional "communitarian" commitments to the family and the nation (chapter 4). But these arguments also need to be backed up with detailed knowledge of social realities and political concerns in Singapore.

Part III (chapter 5) is an attempt to construct a case for a distinctively Chinese approach to democracy. It is argued that the Confucian value of respect for rule by an intellectual elite continues to have widespread influence in China and that this value can also be justified with reference to contemporary sociopolitical concerns. On this basis, one can defend a political institution that aims to realize this value in the contemporary Chinese context.

In short, parts II and III are attempts to argue for culturally sensitive interpretations of political values in two Asian societies without falling into the trap of taking culture too seriously. Part II is an argument for extending Western-style democracy to Singapore on the basis of local cultural and political concerns, and part III is an argument that points to an area of justifiable difference (using Western-style liberal democracy as the benchmark) in the Chinese context.

OUTLINE OF THE BOOK

This book is written in dialogue form. This form is meant to be reader-friendly, and it also has the advantage of allowing for a relatively systematic treatment of two contrasting positions.[18] More specifically with respect to the debate on extending human rights and democracy to non-Western societies, this form vividly illustrates the need for cross-cultural social critics concerned with practical effect to actually understand and engage in respectful dialogue with members of other cultures. The medium, in this case, is part of the message.

The main character of this book is named Sam Demo.[19] Demo is the East Asia program officer for a fictitious U.S.-based nongov-

[18] See also the other advantages of the dialogue form as described in my earlier book, *Communitarianism and Its Critics*, 21–23.

[19] Sam Demo is named after "Mr. Democracy," the heroic (fictitious) figure of the May 4, 1919, student movement in Beijing and "Demo," Robert Dahl's fictitious character in his book *Democracy and Its Critics*.

ernment organization named the National Endowment for Human Rights and Democracy (NEHRD). The NEHRD is meant to resemble such groups as the Ford Foundation and the Open Society, which send activists abroad with the mission of promoting human rights and democracy in the long term, alleviating poverty, and building up civil society. These groups often work with official and semi-official organizations, and they need to be aware of local ways and cultural habits in order to develop and maintain working relationships with local partners. (In contrast, human rights groups such as Amnesty International and Human Rights in China that criticize governments for engaging in gross human rights violations have less of a need to understand and respect local ways because they tend to rely more on confrontational tactics, independent research, and nameless informants.) Moreover, program officers for "long-term" human rights groups often take public positions on such issues as democratic elections, family law, criminal law, minority rights, social and economic rights, and human rights education—precisely the sorts of controversial rights where there may be publicly articulated differences between "international" norms and East Asian viewpoints (including official and independent voices). This kind of human rights activist, one hopes, may benefit from a discussion on East Asian approaches to human rights and democracy.

In this book, Demo visits three East Asian societies: Hong Kong, Singapore, and mainland China. The book is therefore divided into three parts, and in each location Demo engages in a dialogue on human rights and democracy with a prominent member of the society under question. In Hong Kong, Demo engages with a human rights activist and business consultant; in Singapore, he engages with a leading politician; and in mainland China, he engages with a political philosopher. The aim here is to create three plausible, situated characters that express three different viewpoints, thus rendering vivid the fact that there are a plurality of thought-provoking voices involved in the debate on human rights and democracy in East Asia. Of course there are many other viewpoints in the East Asian region, but this multiple-voices approach is arguably a better starting point than most works on the topic.

In part I, Demo converses with a Hong Kong businessman and human rights activist named Joseph Lo.[20] This section (as noted above) consists of my critical reflections on several dialogues between Western and East Asian intellectuals concerning human rights and democracy in East Asia, and it is divided into two chapters.

Chapter 1, presents and defends relatively persuasive East Asian criticisms of traditional Western approaches to the subject. It is made explicit at the outset that the debate turns on the merits of publicly contested rights that fall outside the sphere of customary international law. The interlocutors then discuss three separate East Asian challenges: (1) the argument that situation-specific justifications for the temporary curtailment of particular human rights can only be countered following the acquisition of substantial local knowledge; (2) the argument that East Asian cultural traditions can provide the resources to justify and increase local commitment to practices that in the West are typically realized through a human rights regime (as opposed to the claim that human rights ideas and practices are distinctive products of the Western liberal tradition); and (3) the argument that distinctive East Asian conceptions of vital human interests may justify some political practices that differ to some extent from human rights regimes typically endorsed in Western liberal countries. The main point of this chapter is to show that the current West-centric human rights regime needs to be modified with input from East Asian voices.

Chapter 2, draws on the same three East Asian challenges to traditional Western approaches to human rights, though it focuses more specifically on the question of extending democratic rights to the East Asian region. The chapter begins by noting that most East Asian governments do not try to justify the most egregious instances of authoritarianism, such as the jailing of political dissi-

[20] It is worth noting that the Hong Kong setting for part I is largely incidental, since Lo is primarily the mouthpiece for some of my reflections on political dialogues between East Asian and North American intellectuals. (This part is set in Hong Kong simply because many examples are drawn from the Hong Kong context.) In that sense, Lo is less "situated" than the local characters in parts II and III.

dents without trial and the sacking of opposition members from their jobs. The interlocutors then discuss three separate, publicly articulated East Asian challenges to dominant Western notions of democracy: (1) specific trade-off arguments for the curtailment of democratic elections (as in the Hong Kong case) that can only be refuted with the help of local knowledge; (2) the argument that justifications for democratic rights can vary from context to context (which sets up part II on Singapore); and (3) the argument that there may be legitimate constraints on democratic rule and that these constraints may vary from context to context (which sets up part III on democracy in China). The main point of this chapter is that democracy activists should be well informed about the local situation before making up their minds about the desirability of promoting publicly contested democratic rights in the East Asian context.

This part of the book, in sum, is meant to affirm the importance of local knowledge for defenders of contested human rights. East Asian governments and especially intellectuals have raised some plausible doubts about the universal validity of rights that fall outside the sphere of customary international law, and it is impossible to engage with their arguments without the help of local knowledge. This gray area of debate includes the attempt to universalize Western-style democratic practices, and there are powerful reasons for cross-cultural critics to refrain from firm judgments regarding the desirability of democracy in particular East Asian countries prior to local knowledge. This means more than the claim that democratic political systems can be implemented only under certain social conditions, and hence that the prodemocracy activist concerned with effectiveness should understand those conditions before prescribing the desired democratic outcome. Cross-cultural critics, it is argued, should also leave open the possibility of revising their political ideals in response to an engagement with the local culture.

So if there is a case to be made for democracy in East Asia, it will not be made by relying on the abstract and unhistorical universalism that often disables contemporary Western liberal democrats. Rather, it will be made from the inside, from specific examples and argumentative strategies that East Asians themselves use in everyday moral and political debate. This insight is applied to the cases of Singapore and mainland China in parts II and III of this book.[21]

Part II is a discussion between Demo and elder statesman Lee Kuan Yew on the pros and cons of democracy in Singapore. This section attempts to present and evaluate (what I take to be) Lee's most plausible arguments against democracy, understood in the minimal sense of free and fair competitive elections for political rulers. Lee is one of the world's most brilliant politicians (he scored a rare double first at Cambridge), and his views on international relations and economics are widely reported in the international media.[22] More relevant for our purposes, Lee is Singapore's founding father, and he has been willing to articulate his case and attempt to justify his policies to the Singaporean public and the world at large. Moreover, he is famous for speaking his mind, and what he says in public does seem to reflect his "true" thoughts. Hence, it is generally sufficient to rely on Lee's actual speeches to make my points, though I occasionally add my own remarks for the purpose of illustrating his arguments and maintaining the flow of the dialogue.

Why is it important to take Lee's views so seriously? One reason is that his arguments often set the terms for political debate in Singapore. More surprisingly, perhaps, his antidemocratic views are often endorsed by well-intentioned, educated Singaporeans (including many of my former students at the National University of Singapore), and as a consequence they form part of the ideological apparatus that helps to sustain nondemocratic rule. In other words, he expresses the sorts of politically influential arguments that cross-cultural critics need to take into account as a pre-

[21] Why did I choose these two case studies? The main reason is that I am most familiar with these two countries, having lived and worked in each country. Naturally I apply my "culturally sensitive" method to those societies I know best. Beyond this reason, Singapore is particularly significant because it is held up as a kind of political and economic model by many politicians and intellectuals in East Asia (with Lee Kuan Yew as the most prominent spokesman for the Singapore model), and China is significant as the world's most populous country and an emerging economic and political heavyweight.

For more detailed perspectives on human rights issues in other East Asian countries, the reader may want to consult Joanne R. Bauer and Daniel A. Bell, eds., *The East Asian Challenge for Human Rights*.

[22] Most recently, scores of Asian and Western leaders, journalists, and academics have sought Lee's views on the Asian economic crisis.

condition for persuading most Singaporeans of the merits of Western-style democracy.

This section is divided into two chapters. Chapter 3 examines Lee's criticisms against arguments commonly made by contemporary Western liberal democrats. Against the view that democracy can be defended by appealing to the value of individual autonomy, or the idea that citizens should have the right to make the decisions that affect their lives, Lee argues that this value may not resonate to the same extent in a culture where people are less concerned about enacting freely chosen life-plans and more reluctant to voice their interests in the political arena. Moreover, the most common consequentialist arguments for democracy also fail to resonate in a context where a paternalistic nondemocratic regime provides such goods as social peace, basic civil liberties, and sound economic management. In short, it seems that the most typical arguments for democracy made by contemporary Western liberal democrats may not be nearly as persuasive in the Singaporean context.

Chapter 4 turns to a more promising consequentialist justification for democracy in the Singaporean context. On this communitarian view, democratic rights can be justified on the grounds that they contribute to strengthening ties to such communities as the family and the nation.[23] This chapter begins with the argument that democracy can provide an important safeguard against politicians intent on destroying the family unit. The focus then shifts to the question of strengthening commitment to the national political community. The problem, Demo explains, is that authoritarian political practices have undermined communal solidarity in

[23] It is important to note that this argument is meant to stand or fall independently of other communitarian arguments, including those defended in my earlier book, *Communitarianism and Its Critics*. Nor do I wish to defend a grand dichotomy between liberals and communitarians; quite the opposite, in fact, since chapter 4 draws on John Stuart Mill's argument that democracy can contribute to public-spiritedness. Mill is of course one of the founding fathers of liberal theory, but for whatever reason this argument for democracy is more often advanced by communitarians today. So when I seem to be criticizing the arguments of Western liberal democrats in chapter 3, I have in mind the dominant justifications for democracy deployed by contemporary Anglo-American liberal democrats. But I do not wish to deny that there are many liberal communitarians around as well. I count myself as one!

Singapore. Next, Demo argues that there is a need to increase public-spiritedness for the following five reasons: (1) the need for the Singaporean government to live up to its communitarian rhetoric; (2) the link between civic virtue and long-term checks against political corruption; (3) the fact that communal solidarity can motivate fellow citizens to support a national welfare system that benefits the worst-off; (4) the fact that political alienation will cause some talented and creative individuals to leave the country; and (5) the link between patriotism and an effective and credible local defense force. These arguments are made by drawing upon particular features of the Singaporean context.

In short, strategic considerations of political relevance strongly speak in favor of communitarian justifications for democracy in Singapore, and perhaps in other East Asian societies as well. It is worth keeping in mind that communism in the Soviet Union collapsed swiftly due partly to the fact that its official defenders had lost faith in their own arguments, and it is not entirely implausible to believe that official defenders of "Asian communitarianism" (which is meant to suggest that Western-style democracy is not suitable for communitarian Asians) may also lose faith in their own arguments.[24] More realistically, perhaps, such communitarian arguments can aid critical intellectuals and prodemocracy opposition forces in East Asian societies (see the conclusion to chapter 4).

It is important to emphasize, however, that the debate over democracy in East Asia does not turn simply on the practical question of how best to persuade East Asians of the value of Western-style democracy (or drawing on East Asian cultural traditions only

---

[24] One might also note that apartheid collapsed so swiftly partly due to the fact that F. W. De Klerk lost faith in the arguments justifying institutionalized racism. Once De Klerk had been "converted," he says that "History did present me with an opportunity to move faster and take my constituency with me but we had to seize the opportunity" (quoted in *South China Morning Post*, 30 January 1999, 15). In the same vein, it could be that Pinochet decided to relinquish some power once he became persuaded that the costs of brutal dictatorship outweighed the benefits. One could make the same argument about Chiang Ching-kuo's decision to democratize Taiwan's political structure. The general point is that it may not be a waste of time to pursue a discussion on the pros and cons of democracy with relatively reflective autocrats who have the power to effect political change.

17

for the strategic purpose of finding different means to achieve the same end-goal). The more theoretically challenging question, perhaps, is whether one can identify aspects of East Asian cultural traditions relevant in the sense that they may provide a moral foundation for political practices and institutions different from Western-style liberal democracy.[25] This question is answered affirmatively in part III (chapter 5).

This section draws on the resources from Chinese political thought to develop a proposal for a political institution that is recognizably democratic but significantly different from Western models. It is assumed at the outset that the current political system in China is not stable for the long term, and that fairly radical alternatives for political reform may become relevant once the system opens up again.[26] This fictitious dialogue is set in Beijing, June 3, 2007, one day before a constitutional convention on political reform in China. In conversation with Demo, a professor of political philosophy at Beijing University named Wang presents and defends a political proposal for a democratic regime that combines elements of traditional Confucianism.[27] The chapter be-

---

[25] According to Chih-yu Shih, "nothing [in the current literature] about the Chinese democratic future seems to have a colour or configuration different from that of known democracies" (Shih, *Collective Democracy*, 324).

[26] It is worth recalling that radical political proposals were openly discussed (by independent intellectuals as well as "liberal" branches of the Communist party) in China prior to the June 4, 1989, massacre. At this time (mid-1999), it is possible to develop ideas for political change so long as reformers refrain from active efforts to challenge Communist rule.

[27] This proposal has been presented in Hong Kong, mainland China, Korea, and Japan. The audiences have been generally willing to engage with this idea, although one hostile and dismissive response was put forward, strangely enough, by a North American member of the audience who seemed to find it strange that a Westerner tries to defend a proposal meant to appeal to East Asian people's sensitivities and imagination. I replied that my aim is to provide food for thought, and of course it is up to the members of the audience to decide if they like the proposal. I then asked the "politically correct" questioner how he would react if an East Asian intellectual, relatively well versed in American culture and motivated by a certain degree of love for that same culture, proposed a political institution designed to appeal to the American imagination and to help deal with a contemporary political crisis in the United States. Would he listen with an open mind, leaving open the possibility that he might be persuaded by the proposal, or would he dismiss the proposal out of hand simply on account of the East Asian intellectual's racial and cultural background?

gins with an argument that modern democratic societies would benefit from the political input of a capable and public-spirited "Confucian" intellectual elite. The interlocutors then consider and reject alternative proposals for combining democracy with rule by an intellectual elite such as plural voting schemes and functional constituencies. Drawing upon the ideas of radical seventeenth-century Confucian political thinker Huang Zongxi, Professor Wang then sketches out his own proposal for a bicameral legislature with a democratically elected lower house and an upper house composed of representatives selected on the basis of competitive examinations. Demo is eventually persuaded by the proposal, though he presses the point that the "House of Scholars" should be constitutionally subordinate to the democratically elected house.

A NOTE ON THE NOTES

While this book can be read (and hopefully enjoyed) without consulting the notes, I have relied on footnotes to provide the reader with evidence for things said by the protagonists. The notes also include marginal commentary and qualifications of some of the arguments and empirical claims made in the main text.

PART I

THE EAST ASIAN CHALLENGE TO
HUMAN RIGHTS AND DEMOCRACY: REFLECTIONS
ON EAST-WEST DIALOGUES

*

Toward a Truly International
Human Rights Regime

SCENE: Hong Kong, December 29, 1997. Sam Demo, the East Asia program officer for the U.S.-based National Endowment for Human Rights and Democracy (NEHRD), enters the home of Joseph Lo. Lo heads the Hong Kong–based East Asian Institute for Economic and Political Risk Analysis, and he is also known locally as a well-connected human rights activist. Demo and Lo were acquainted with each other as fellow undergrads at Princeton over two decades ago.

DEMO: Thanks for receiving me. I always suspected we'd reestablish contact in this part of the world. Now I'm told you're the man to see on human rights in the region, so naturally I looked you up. But when I phoned, I wasn't expecting an invitation for dinner! (*handing a gift-wrapped package to Lo*) Let me contribute my share.

LO (*putting the package aside*): Thank you very much. There's no need for this, really.

DEMO: Aren't you going to open it?

LO: In this part of the world we don't normally open gifts in the presence of our benefactors.

DEMO: Really? Why is that?

LO: I'm not sure. As a gift recipient, I'm not supposed to act too enthusiastically, as though I expected a gift.

DEMO: Mmh, that's interesting. In the United States, we're expected to open gifts right away, and to "spontaneously" show some enthusiasm, regardless of how we actually feel about the gift. This can be a real burden for some people.[1]

---

[1] Immanuel Kant discusses the burden of gift acceptance for the autonomy-loving man. Kant writes, "A friend who bears my losses becomes my benefactor

Lo: It could be worse. The important thing is for each culture to have clear cut norms for dealing with such occasions. Imagine how difficult it would be if you had to think about the proper way to react every time you received a gift.

DEMO (*smiles*): You're right, that would be an even worse burden!

Lo (*pointing Demo to his seat*): Please, let's begin.

DEMO (*admiring the appetizers displayed on the dining room table*): My, that looks too good to be eaten! I hope you didn't have to spend too much time on this.

Lo: All I did was ask Remi—my Filipina domestic helper—to prepare something nice for dinner.

DEMO: Your domestic helper?

Lo: It's the politically correct word for "maid" in Hong Kong.

DEMO (*teasingly*): You have a helper now? It's quite a change from the time I knew you at Princeton. You were the most left-wing student on campus. I recall you once developed laryngitis after several hours of "Ho, Ho, Ho, Ho Chi Minh!" chants.

---

and puts me in his debt. I feel shy in his presence and cannot look him boldly in the face. The true relationship is canceled and friendship ceases." True friends should try to avoid giving gifts to each other, since "one cannot, by any repayment of a kindness received, *rid* oneself of the obligation for it, since the recipient can never win away from the benefactor his *priority* of merit, namely having been the first in benevolence." True benevolence, Kant argues, should not risk humiliating its beneficiary. It will disguise itself, and the virtuous benefactor will "show that he is himself put under obligation by the other's acceptance or honored by it" (quoted in Annette Baier, *Moral Prejudices*, 190, 191).

Baier comments that "This Kantian game of debt-avoidance and fake debt-acknowledgment by proud, mutually respectful persons is clearly an adolescent or an adult game—children are innocent of its ploys and counterploys. They do not naturally fear those bearing gifts, nor are they hesitant to appear to be making gifts. Belief in the possibility of making and taking free gifts is one of the blessings of childhood, and it seems a terrible condemnation of our society that this innocent blessing has to be withdrawn or circumscribed" (ibid.). One may add that this Kantian game is played primarily by adults in Western societies. Gift recipients in most East Asian societies do not typically feel humiliated when they accept gifts (obligations to reciprocate are accepted as a "natural" part of life, rather than being seen as burdens that autonomous individuals should try to avoid placing upon each other), nor do benefactors typically put on a show of feeling honored by the other's acceptance of it (there is no need to, since there is not the same reluctance to "impose" obligations on friends or family members).

Lo: I haven't really changed my ideals. It's just that I've become more realistic about the difficulty of implementing them. Besides, most professionals have helpers in Hong Kong. There's nothing to be embarrassed about. We generally pay them well— a government-set minimum wage of five hundred U.S. dollars per month, plus room and board. Some of us pay more than the minimum wage. . . . Perhaps you should speak to Remi before you jump to any conclusions.

DEMO: I didn't mean to pass any moral judgments. If she chooses to work as a helper, that's fine with me.

Lo: Actually, it's not a completely free choice: these kinds of arrangements depend more than anything else on the state of the national economy. In the 1950s Hong Kong sent helpers to the Philippines. Now, it's the other way around, and if I'm not mistaken, about 150,000 Filipina helpers currently work here. There's no better indicator of economic success than the number of migrant workers hired to do menial jobs locals shy away from.[2]

DEMO: Interesting. You said they're guaranteed a minimum wage. Are there other laws governing the treatment of helpers in Hong Kong?

Lo: Yes. They're also guaranteed one return flight back home every two years, time off on Sundays and public holidays, and

---

[2] Not surprisingly, a new Hong Kong government program to train local women as domestic helpers has become increasingly popular. With a sagging economy and a 5 percent unemployment rate, local women are increasingly attracted by the opportunity to earn U.S.$6.45 to U.S.$7.74 per hour (the market wage for non-live-in helpers). See Diane Brady, "Hong Kong Is Encouraging Locals to Get Down and Dirty, as Maids," *Asian Wall Street Journal*, 4–5 September 1998, 1.

It is also worth noting that the government has recently cut the minimum wage of foreign domestic helpers by 5 percent. The government apparently succumbed to pressure by politicians who argued that cutting the wages of Hong Kong's least well-paid group could help local families cope with the recent economic downturn. Provisional Urban Councillor Jennifer Chow Kit-bing went so far as to advocate a 20 percent pay cut and mandatory sixteen-hour work days (six days a week), explaining that "I have had complaints from several employers saying their domestic helpers started around 8 A.M. and are going into their rooms at 9 P.M. and will not do any more work" (quoted in the *South China Morning Post*, 19 December 1998).

so on. But most of the interaction with helpers takes place in the privacy of the home, and the informal codes of conduct with their employers can be just as important as the legal arrangements. Remi left her previous employer because she couldn't stand her boss's patronizing ways. Her employer issued a report card after dinner, with detailed grades for every dish. She scolded Remi whenever she didn't maintain a B average. But Remi's cooking improved, which made her more marketable, and she left when her contract expired. Luckily, I found her.

DEMO (*smiles*): That shows it's not just Western liberals who care about their rights. Human rights are universal, after all.

LO: I wouldn't be so sure. Not all rights that are valued in Western countries resonate to the same extent in Asia.

DEMO: You sound like a proponent of "Asian values"! In 1993 Asian leaders met in Bangkok to formulate an Asian stance on human rights. They questioned the universality of human rights on the grounds that these didn't accord with Asian values.[3] Surely you're skeptical of this, as a human rights activist.

LO: I'm skeptical of the motivation of Asian leaders, but they may be on to something when they criticize the way human rights have traditionally been understood in most Western countries. In my view, the debate about human rights in the West—and the United States in particular—has been somewhat parochial. Western values are cast in universalistic terms, with little room left for input by Asian viewpoints.[4]

DEMO: But does that mean human rights matter less in this part of the world? I'm sure you don't agree with government officials who justify repression in the name of defending Asian values.

LO: Of course not. But I think it's important to listen to what's actually being said, particularly if you want to have any impact

[3] Joanne R. Bauer, "Three Years after the Bangkok Declaration," 1.

[4] In a similar vein, Onuma Yasuaki points out that the human rights debate is often miscast within the framework of universality vs. particularity, as though Islam and Confucianism represent particularity whereas Christianity and "the European way" necessarily express universal values. There is little room left, Onuma notes, to think that something non-Western can be universally valid and that Western outlooks may be unique to particular societies (Onuma Yasuaki, "Toward an Intercivilizational Approach to Human Rights," 111–112).

in this part of the world. Some members of the "international" human rights community mistakenly assume that it alone has the best interests of the population at heart and that all leaders in the region act with the worst possible motives. This view is inaccurate: not all leaders despise their own citizens, and human rights failures by governments aren't always deliberate. It's also counterproductive, because it reminds locals of an earlier era of self-righteous missionaries sent by imperial powers to "enlighten" the natives. Instead of automatically condemning governments, human rights activists could play a more constructive role by understanding local viewpoints and working with officials to improve the human rights situation.[5]

DEMO: I don't think I'll ever understand why governments torture and murder their citizens.

LO: In fact, Asian governments don't try to make us understand their nastiest deeds. They won't admit to murdering political opponents, torturing members of ethnic groups, or forcing women and children into slavery.[6]

---

[5] Roger P. Winter, director of the U.S. Committee for Refugees, has made a similar criticism of the role of human rights activists in the African context (see Winter, "Advocates of Human Rights Could Get Better Results," *International Herald Tribune*, 24 February 1998, 8).

[6] It is interesting to note that even Pol Pot has denied being responsible for gross human rights abuses. In an interview with the journalist Nate Thayer (carried out shortly before Pol Pot died), he claimed that the Vietnamese were responsible for the mass starvation under his rule and that the infamous Tuol Sleng prison was a Vietnamese exhibition set up for propaganda purposes after Hanoi's troops invaded Cambodia in December 1978. (Independent scholars say that one million Cambodians died of mass starvation as a result of forced collectivization under the Khmer Rouge, and that 16,000 people were tortured and executed at the Tuol Sleng prison, often on direct orders of Pol Pot.) Thayer suggests that Pol Pot seems to be motivated by a mixture of misplaced idealism and self-delusion: " 'I came to carry out a struggle, not to kill people,' [Pol Pot] rasps, his voice almost a whisper. He pauses, fixing his interviewer with an almost pleading expression. 'Even now, and you can look at me, am I a savage person? My conscience is clear' " (Thayer, "Day of Reckoning," *Far Eastern Economic Review*, 30 October 1997, 14). This is not to deny that some dictators are unabashedly cynical. A BBC journalist reported that Nicaragua's Anastasio Somoza hosted a banquet on the roof of the Presidential palace in 1979 as the Sandinistas were preparing their final offensive on the capital (explosions were visible on the horizon). He seemed to be in a jolly mood, opening the dinner with a champagne toast:

DEMO: What about Burma? The military junta there doesn't exactly pride itself on its strict adherence to liberal values.

LO: But neither does it try to justify obvious human rights transgressions in public forums or discussions with outsiders.[7] I recall the observations of Yozo Yokota, the U.N. special rapporteur on Burma. He said that when he meets with members of SLORC, the ruling junta in Burma, everyone agrees on the need to protect basic human rights. The generals simply deny that torture occurs in their country.[8]

DEMO: But surely they're lying.

LO: Yes, but this has to be proven. So Dr. Yokota spends much of his time in Burma meeting opposition figures, visiting prisons, interviewing detainees, and so on, with the aim of uncovering evidence of torture. In a sense, he's like a prosecutor trying to prove that the defendant is lying. But there's no argument about the moral norms themselves.

DEMO: I don't quite understand. Is there, or isn't there, a cultural conflict over human rights?

LO: It depends which rights you're talking about. In public, nobody tries to justify genocide, murder, slavery, torture. No public official will deny that people have a right to food.[9] There's no

---

"I knew the party had to end sometime. Let's enjoy it until the last moment." The next day, Somoza left for Miami on his luxurious yacht.

[7] As Kenneth Roth, the executive director of Human Rights Watch, puts it: "Every government, even the worst outlaws, seek to portray an image of respect for human rights. For simple reasons of power, reputation is an important asset" (quoted in Steven Holmes, "Tidings of Abuse Fall on Deaf Ears," *New York Times*, 5 February 1995, E4). In response to a gathering of world leaders in New York to celebrate the fiftieth anniversary of the United Nations, the *New York Times* commented sardonically on various states' official rhetoric, juxtaposing statements by, inter alia, Iranian, Croatian, and U.S. officials with a brief analysis of those countries' policies. See Barbara Crossette, "Incredibility at the UN: Forget What I Do; Listen to What I Say," *New York Times*, 29 October 1995, E7.

[8] Dr. Yokota raised this point at the Foreign Correspondent's Club in Bangkok, Thailand, in March 1996. He has since resigned from his post on the grounds that he was not getting enough logistical support from the United Nations.

[9] In practice, however, some governments have deliberately created famines for political purposes: see David Keen, *The Benefits of Famine*.

point in arguing about the importance of these "minimal" rights.[10]

DEMO: Since the end of apartheid, there hasn't been any public controversy about the right not to be subject to systematic racial discrimination. And faced with new forms of inhumanity, this "minimal" list may well grow further.

LO: I hope so. But meanwhile, we also have to deal with the fact that some human rights are the subject of intense political controversy, both in practice and in theory. This gray area of debate includes social and economic rights, minority rights and the rights of indigenous peoples, the rights encompassed within family law and criminal law, the freedom of speech, and the participatory rights inherent in Western-style democratic practices. The problem is that Western human rights activists often try to promote these rights without understanding local ways. This often generates a lot of resentment in this part of the world. By the way, why don't you tell me something about your own human rights work?

DEMO: Well, that's a bit unclear. Normally I'd deal with the gray areas you mention. Now I'm actually on a scouting mission, talking to people and trying to find out about their human rights concerns. This will help us to set our priorities in the region. I've been appointed program officer for East Asia, though admittedly I don't have much experience dealing with this part of

---

[10] See Michael Walzer, *Interpretation and Social Criticism*, 24. The distinction between "minimal" rights and "thick" rights is developed in Walzer's book *Thick and Thin*. It is worth noting, however, that there is a problem when states interpret these "minimal" prohibitions in different ways. As Michael Posner, the executive director of the Lawyers Committee for Human Rights, points out, "Many states condemn torture, but then justify physical means of coercion, for example in extracting information from a detainee which affects national security interests. Who decides whether this is torture?" (letter on file with the author). Israel is the most obvious contemporary example of a state that tries to justify this form of "torture." Walzer's claim that there is a universal prohibition against deception is even more problematic. What counts as deception in the United States (for example, saying "yes" to an invitation when one really means to say "no") may be termed politeness in Thailand, Java, and Japan. More importantly (pace Immanuel Kant), one can think of circumstances when it may be justifiable to resort to deception, such as Schindler's recourse to lies for the purpose of protecting Jews from Nazis during World War II.

the world. Before that, as you know, I was a public-interest lawyer with the American Civil Liberties Union. I left because I opposed their stance on campaign-finance reform.[11] So I had to look for alternatives and East Asia came to mind. I'd been studying Chinese on and off the past few years,[12] and I always had an interest in the region. As you know, my wife is from Hong Kong, and she wanted to spend some time with her elderly parents. Naturally, I jumped at the chance to help set up a regional office here.

Lo: But what about your organization—the National Endowment for Human Rights and Democracy? I must confess I haven't heard much about it.

Demo: Like I said, we're new in Asia. And more generally, the NEHRD tries to keep a low profile. Groups such as Amnesty get more attention because they have the job of publicizing gross human rights abuses and putting international pressure on governments. We work on issues that don't get the headlines, like women's rights, the plight of migrant workers, human rights education, the rule of law, and building up civil society. Basically, our program officers award grants to individuals and groups that promote human rights and democracy in the long term. The ultimate aim is to support social and political reforms that will outlive our own involvement.

[11] The ACLU has lobbied furiously against campaign-finance reform, on the grounds that the right to free speech matters more than the nasty side-effects of massive campaign spending. This stance, however, has driven a deep split within the ranks of the ACLU, and roughly half the leadership is said to disagree with it (*Economist*, 4 April 1998, 38).

[12] In that sense, Demo is more qualified than a senior program officer working for an institute affiliated with the National Endowment for Democracy, the semi-official U.S. organization that aims to promote democracy abroad. David Samuels describes a meeting with an officer who had recently returned from a stint in Romania: " 'I knew very little about Romania. I didn't even speak the language,' [he] admitted over a plate of pad thai at a Washington restaurant. 'It was like going to Altoona or Arkansas, or one of those places, and trying to find common ground with the local people' " (David Samuels, "At Play in the Fields of Oppression: A Government-Funded Agency Pretends to Export Democracy," *Harper's Magazine* [May 1995], 53).

LO: Similar to the Ford Foundation?

DEMO: Yes. I've been talking to them about their programs. I was especially impressed by the work of Phyllis Chang, one of the Ford Foundation's program officers in China. Ms. Chang awards grants to Chinese organizations that do pioneering work in the fields of legal aid and public interest law. For example, she supports a legal services center for women in a rural county near Beijing. This center provides free legal counsel, representation in litigation to women, and nonlegal help such as pre-divorce counseling. It also organizes campaigns to encourage county women to run for office in elections for village committees. I was quite surprised to learn about this: it's not the sort of stuff one reads about in the *New York Times!*

LO: I'm not familiar with this particular project. Has it been successful?

DEMO: Apparently. Ms. Chang told me that the center has catalyzed new thinking about law among county women, and that it has heightened the government's response to women's issues. There are other indications of success, such as the fact that the number of women seeking legal advice and representation from the center's office has increased to the point that it needs to add more staff.

LO: I imagine this kind of project wouldn't work well without official support.

DEMO: That's correct. Ms. Chang said that local government and party leaders have enthusiastically supported the center's work. More generally, she noted that it's easier to be effective in the women's rights field (compared with other areas, such as workers' rights) because the Chinese government is already committed to strengthening protection of women's welfare and well-being. In this kind of long-term human rights work, the first step to success is to find areas of sincerely held common ground.[13] Ideally, there'd be a felt need for help on the ground as well as official support.

---

[13] I am grateful to Phyllis Chang for having provided this information.

Lo: Ah, ha. So we're back to the need to understand Asian viewpoints.

DEMO: Yes, of course. Like I said, that's why I'm here: to find out what locals think about human rights. But I'm still skeptical about the use of this term "Asian values." Apart from justifying repression, those using this concept seem to overlook the fact that Asia is a diverse mix of societies, cultures, and political viewpoints.[14]

Lo: The region of East Asia, at least, seems to have a certain institutional reality. Investment banks and multinational companies often have Asian divisions, covering primarily the developing countries of East Asia. The region's stock markets and currencies are intimately linked. I'm sure you're familiar with regional economic and political organizations such as APEC and ASEAN.[15]

DEMO: But is there a common Asian *culture?* East Asian societies have been shaped by a complex mixture of Confucianism, Islam, and Buddhism, not to mention the Western influences.

Lo: Of course. But the different religions and value systems may also have some things in common. One Japanese scholar named Yasuda Nobuyuki argues that East Asian culture has been shaped by its traditional mode of production. He points out that rice farming through paddy cultivation was the main form of agriculture in "monsoon Asia", and that it was essential for peasants to cooperate intensely in accordance with the rapidly changing weather. All steps of paddy cultivation, such as planting, water management, and cropping, required collective labor far beyond an individual's capacity. As a result, Yasuda argues that Asian religions developed rites of worship to common ancestors and "Gods of the Earth," which were divided by the stages of the monsoon season. These rites unified the community, and Asians became stamped with a communitarian outlook. Yasuda contrasts all this with traditional Europe, where

[14] See Tatsuo Inoue's devastating critique of "Asian Orientalism" in his essay, "Liberal Democracy and Asian Orientalism," esp. 37–42.
[15] The Asia Pacific Economic Cooperation Organization and the Association of Southeast Asian Nations.

individualistic hunters and gatherers sought food for themselves or their families.[16]

DEMO: Values in Asia, like anywhere else, have changed a lot over
time in response to various internal and external pressures. Do
the practices related to rice farming still affect people's outlook
in Hong Kong or Tokyo?

LO: It's hard to say. Some values get transmitted from generation
to generation, and they outlive their original material usefulness. For example, the practice of ancestor worship is still
very much part of our everyday lives. You must have noticed the
mini-altars all around you in Hong Kong: in people's shops,
their homes, even on the streets. Other East Asian cities, no
matter how modern, are similar. In that sense, you have an Asian
value that you don't find in the West.

DEMO (*short pause*): You may be right. What's puzzled me is the
phenomenon of *karaoke*, which seems to have spread from Japan
to most East Asian cities.[17] I can't understand why Asians seem
to enjoy singing to elevator music. Is this related to rice farming
as well?

LO (*smiles*): Not very likely. I'd look to early educational practices
for the explanation. From a very early age we're taught to sing
songs at school, and this continues until we enter university. My
two-year-old was recently issued a report card by his school, and
I was pleasantly surprised to learn that he was awarded an A for
"singing in front of the class."[18] He usually sings the songs he's
learned to himself just before he falls asleep at night. I suspect
he'll turn out to be a good *karaoke* performer.

DEMO: So that's it. I never did learn to sing at school.

LO: You see, I find that strange. It seems natural to me that singing
should be part of the educational curriculum.

---

[16] See Yasuda Nobuyuki, "Human Rights, Individual or Collective? The Southeast Asian Experience," 51.

[17] Even Macdonald's restaurants in Japan have *karaoke*. They are called "Mac-
Song" (see T.R. Reid, *Confucius Lives Next Door,* 37).

[18] My own son, Julien Song Bell, was given this grade for "public singing" on
his report card issued by a local Cantonese kindergarten in Hong Kong.

DEMO: Can we draw any political conclusions from this? Are you suggesting that learning to sing is an Asian value and that Asian states should try to promote this value in schools? Perhaps you're saying that Asians should have a human right to develop their vocal chords?

LO (*laughs*): I sometimes wish people had never used the term "Asian values." From a political point of view, it doesn't really matter if there's a common culture in East Asia that's supposed to underpin the same set of Asian political practices or human rights norms. What matters is that *some* traditional, relatively persistent values in *some* East Asian societies may diverge to some extent from human rights ideas and practices typically endorsed in particular Western countries. So let's talk about deeply rooted, politically relevant values in particular Asian societies.

DEMO: Fair enough. It's a good idea to be more concrete. But I'm still not too clear how we can distinguish between the sorts of values invoked by Asian government leaders for the purpose of buttressing authoritarian rule and "deeply rooted, politically relevant values" that may diverge from Western-style human rights norms. In other words, how can we distinguish between the substance and the rhetoric in the Asian values debate?

LO: That's a good question! I'd suggest looking at the arguments of East Asian intellectuals who don't have an obvious personal interest in justifying undemocratic rule. Unofficial voices in East Asia may not share the viewpoints of their governments, but that doesn't mean they automatically agree with traditional Western approaches to human rights.

DEMO: But how can you know? It's hard to find out about unofficial viewpoints in authoritarian societies. People are too afraid to speak out.

LO: I'm not afraid. Hong Kong isn't ruled by democratically elected leaders, but I'm perfectly willing to tell you my own views on human rights and democracy.

DEMO (*embarrassed*): Yes, of course. I was thinking of countries like Burma and North Korea.

LO: There are different kinds of nondemocratic states. The modernizing states of East and Southeast Asia haven't ruled by means of systematic terror, and most regimes have left some space left for critical intellectuals and NGOs. In fact, I've recently taken part in a multiyear dialogue on human rights and democracy involving prominent intellectuals from East Asia and North America.[19] It was quite fascinating. There was a lot of common ground, but East Asian intellectuals also came up with some persuasive criticisms of traditional Western approaches to human rights. Remember, the norms and institutions of human rights aren't settled visions. They're continually evolving, and East Asians may have something to contribute. If the aim is to formulate a truly universal human rights regime, I think it's important to understand East Asian perspectives as well.

DEMO: I'd like to hear more about this dialogue. What did the participants think about the Asian values rhetoric?

1. TRADE-OFFS

1.1. Rights vs. Development: A Zero-Sum Game?

LO: The first point to note is that much of the Asian values debate isn't actually a cultural clash over human rights norms. For example, when Singaporean elder statesman Lee Kuan Yew argues that Western-style civil and political liberties need to be sacri-

---

[19] In this chapter, Lo serves as the voice for my reflections on a series of dialogues between East Asian and North American intellectuals on the topic "The Growth of East Asia and Its Impact on Human Rights." The project was planned and administered by Joanne R. Bauer, director of studies at the Carnegie Council on Ethics and International Affairs, New York. Workshops were held in Japan, Thailand, and Korea, with a final wrap-up session at the Harvard Law School. My reflections on the first workshop appeared as the article "The East Asian Challenge to Human Rights," and my reflections on the first two workshops appeared as the article "Minority Rights." I have also coedited (with Joanne R. Bauer) a book that is the product of this multiyear project, *The East Asian Challenge for Human Rights*. This chapter draws on all three sources and some unpublished arguments made by participants at the workshops.

ficed in order to secure more basic material needs,[20] he's not articulating a new political ideal, nor is he saying that freedom is inappropriate in Asian societies. His point is simply that certain freedoms may need to be curtailed as a *short-term* measure in order to eliminate poverty and to provide the conditions for economic growth. If factional opposition threatens to slow down the government's efforts to promote economic development or to plunge the country into civil strife, then in Lee's view tough measures can and should be taken to ensure political stability. This is the message Lee delivers to receptive audiences in China, Japan, Vietnam, and the Philippines.

DEMO: But there's little social scientific evidence to vindicate the theory that political and civil rights hamper economic growth. Most cross-national studies don't support the claim that there's a correlation or a causal connection between authoritarianism and economic success. Quite the opposite, in fact. The eminent economist Amartya Sen has argued that civil and political rights help to safeguard economic security in the sense that such rights draw attention to major social disasters and induce an appropriate political response. Whether and how a government responds to needs and sufferings often depends on how much pressure is put on it, and the exercise of political rights such as voting and criticizing often makes a real difference. Sen has noted the remarkable fact that no substantial famine has ever occurred in any country with a democratic form of government and a relatively free press.[21]

LO: Well, the record is rather different with respect to eliminating severe malnutrition. Since Deng's economic reforms, authoritarian China has a better record in this respect than democratic India. Lee can also point to several examples of rapid economic growth under authoritarian governments: Meiji-era Japan; Korea, Taiwan, and Singapore in the post–World War II era; colonial Hong Kong; China since the early 1980s; and so on. But I don't mean to defend Lee's argument. No doubt he overstretches himself, drawing lessons from the Singapore experience and inappropriately applying them elsewhere, such as the

---

[20] See chap. 3, sec. 5.
[21] See Amartya Sen, "Human Rights and Economic Achievements," 92–93.

Philippines, which had a disastrous experience with authoritarian government under Marcos. When he sticks to the Singapore case he's on much firmer ground. Specific trade-off arguments are generally more persuasive, at least on the face of it.

1.2. The Need for Specificity

DEMO: What do you mean?

LO: I mean that "authoritarian" governments sometimes make a narrower claim for curbing rights that can't be refuted simply by invoking social-scientific evidence about general trends. I have in mind the claim that *particular* rights may need to be curbed in particular contexts, for particular economic or political purposes, as a short-term measure, in order to secure a more important right or to secure that same right in the long term. For example, Kevin Tan—who teaches law at the National University of Singapore—pointed out that the Singaporean government frequently reminds its local audience that Singapore was plagued by the threat of a Communist takeover and communalism that pitted Singapore's majority Chinese population against the minority Malays. Singapore made use of an Internal Security Act, originally established by British colonial rulers, to counter these threats when it was expelled from Malaysia in 1965. The Singapore government argues that without emergency powers, including the authority to detain without trial persons suspected of being subversives, it wouldn't have been able to prevent the country from plunging into civil strife.[22]

DEMO: But this sounds like another justification for authoritarian rule.

LO: Yes, but we can't dismiss these views. They're the sorts of situation-specific challenges to human rights that local audiences tend find more persuasive.[23]

---

[22] See Kevin Tan, "Economic Development, Legal Reform, and Rights in Singapore and Taiwan," 266–267.

[23] It is difficult to find empirical evidence to support this claim. Let it be noted that several participants at the East-West dialogue on human rights made this point (see also note 26), and that several of my own students and friends in

DEMO: Whatever the merits of such arguments, they don't present a fundamental challenge to the current international human rights regime. Article 4 of the United Nations International Covenant on Civil and Political Rights explicitly allows for short term curbs on rights "in time of public emergency which threatens the life of the nation." Not anything goes, however: the article states that such "emergency measures" can't involve discrimination solely on the ground of race, sex, language, religion, or social origin, and that derogation of rights against murder, torture, and slavery, among others, may not be made under this provision.[24]

LO: It's not surprising that an exception is made for such "minimal" rights. Like I said, governments don't try to justify the violation of these rights under any circumstances.

DEMO: I'd also like to point out that there's nothing distinctively Asian about situation specific trade-off arguments for the restriction of particular rights, as Western countries have also responded with "emergency measures" to combat crises. The British government not too long ago had the power to detain without trial suspected IRA activists in Northern Ireland. Magistrates in Italy have the power to imprison recalcitrant witnesses to aid the fight against the mafia.[25]

LO: There may be one difference, however. Whereas Western governments usually invoke situation specific trade-off arguments as a justification to maintain social order, governments in East

---

Singapore and Hong Kong tend to make such local, situation-specific arguments for rights trade-offs.

[24] International Covenant on Civil and Political Rights, adopted 16 December 1966, 999 UNTS 171 (entered into force 23 March 1976), G.A. Res. 2200 (XXI), 21 U.N. GAOR, Supp. (No.16) 52, U.N. Doc. A/6316 (1966). While it is possible to devise imaginary scenarios that justify violations of these rights, Michael J. Perry notes that even if one of those imaginable-but-extremely-unlikely conditions occurs, it is politically unrealistic "to believe that the fact that a human right is nonderogable under international law rights would keep political authorities from violating the right if they really did believe it necessary to do so in order to keep the heavens from falling. . . . Therefore, it makes very good sense, as a practical matter, that international law establishes some moral rights as unconditional (nonderogable) legal rights" (Perry, *The Idea of Human Rights*, 106).

[25] See Adrian Lyttleton, "The Crusade against the Cosa Nostra," *New York Review of Books*, 5 October 1995, 56.

Asia frequently appeal to the imperatives of economic development. For example, the Malaysian government asserts that de-
priving indigenous populations of access to forests and waters
is necessary for economic development in that country. In the
same vein, the Chinese government asserts that restrictions on
labor's right to protest is necessary to attract international investment.[26]

DEMO: But specific, short-term trade-off arguments in the West
also invoke factors beyond security concerns. Consider the case
for affirmative action in the United States. The argument is that
special opportunities for African Americans, and the consequent possibility of restrictions on the right to equal opportunity for some equally qualified white candidates who may not
be responsible for racist practices, is a necessary and effective
temporary measure to remedy years of discrimination against
African Americans in my country. The implication is that affirmative action is no longer justified once the effects of racism
are overcome.[27]

LO: Yes, you're right. In any case, distinctively Asian or not, as a
human rights activist I have to respond to these arguments in
an effective manner. Let's go back to the Singaporean government's justification for curbing freedoms in order to deal with
the threat of racial riots in Singapore. Liberal thinkers in the
West often counter this sort of argument by affirming the value
of civil and political liberties in general. But if all the Singaporean government meant to say is that rights had to be curtailed in response to the threat of ethnic riots, then it seems
beside the point to counter with the argument that rights are
absolute and can't be restricted under any circumstances. Singaporean government officials can concede that governments ideally ought to secure the full range of civil and political liberties,
adding that *in this case* some rights had to be sacrificed in order

[26] These examples were raised by participants at the workshop on "The Growth
of East Asia and Its Impact on Human Rights," held in Hakone, Japan, in June
1995. For other examples, see my article "The East Asian Challenge to Human
Rights," 646–648.

[27] See Amy Gutmann, "Responding to Racial Injustice," in *Color Conscious:
The Political Morality of Race*, ed. K. Anthony Appiah and Amy Gutmann, 119,
124–125.

to secure the more important right to life. In fact the so-called Asian side of the debate often concedes that human rights are important and that ideally governments ought to try to secure as many rights as possible. In other words, the East Asian challenge to Western liberal viewpoints on human rights isn't usually a dispute about the ideal of promoting human rights or about fundamentally incompatible cultural outlooks; it's more often than not a plea for recognition of the alleged fact that certain East Asian governments often find themselves in the unenviable position of having to curtail certain rights in order to secure other, more basic rights.

DEMO: So we're not dealing with a cultural clash over human rights.

LO: Well, actually, I need to qualify that claim. Cultural factors can affect the *prioritizing* of rights, and this matters when rights conflict and it must be decided which one to sacrifice. In other words, different societies may rank rights differently, and even if they face a similar set of disagreeable circumstances they may come to different conclusions about the right that needs to be curtailed. One example, perhaps, is that U.S. citizens may be more willing to sacrifice a social or economic right in cases of conflict with a civil or political right: if neither the constitution nor a majority of democratically elected representatives supports universal access to health care, then the right to health care regardless of income can be curtailed. In contrast, the Chinese may be more willing to sacrifice a civil or political liberty in cases of conflict with a social or economic right: there may be wide support for restrictions on the internal movement of farmers if these are necessary to guarantee the right to subsistence.[28] I'd want to emphasize, however, that differences over

---

[28] The recent decision by the Korean government to ban English-language tutoring during the regular school day is another example (see "Seoul's 'Language Cops': An Official Backlash Against English Tutors," *International Herald Tribune*, 16 April 1997, 1). Only rich families could afford to pay for expensive private English lessons, and government officials justified the ban in the name of equalizing educational opportunities (the government employed the carrot as well as the stick: backed by government funding, public television will bring the nation's best tutors into every home free of charge). It is difficult to imagine that the American government would curb the right to hire language tutors in the name of safeguarding the right to equal educational opportunities.

prioritization shouldn't be seen as conflicts over long-term, deeply ingrained cultural ideals. Even if values clash in the sense that different societies tend to rank rights differently, all sides can agree that the same set of rights must be secured once circumstances no longer force political authorities to make hard choices. This suggests a less intractable cultural conflict than the claim that different societies value different sets of rights as *end points*. I think it would help if governments and human rights activists recognize that they often share a common set of long-term moral and political aspirations.

DEMO: I'm reminded of John Maynard Keynes' line that in the long term we're all dead. People will go to war over short-term differences.

LO: Perhaps the more important point is that situation-specific, trade-off arguments for curtailing rights aren't usually justified with reference to cultural values. Most justifications for short-term restrictions of rights appeal solely to empirical considerations, such as the claim that emergency powers are necessary to deal with the threat of racial riots. Sometimes governments will actually try to justify attacks on traditional cultural values, as in the case of the Chinese government's claim that the one-child-per-family policy is necessary to curb the deleterious effects of a deeply held rural preference for siring male children.[29] So the critic doesn't always have to play things out in the normative arena, where tempers flare and positions harden.

DEMO: Mmh. What you're saying is that it's often sufficient to invoke empirical factors in order to refute short-term, situation-specific trade-off arguments.

LO: But it has to be the right kind of empirical factor. To repeat, it wouldn't be appropriate to respond with social scientific evidence based on generalizations. For example, the specific argument that in the Singaporean context emergency powers in the

---

[29] The aim was to curb the tendency to keep on having children until a male child was born, which (allegedly) contributed to the population explosion in China. As a result of the one-child-per-family policy, however, many traditional farmers resorted to infanticide if the first child was female. The Chinese government has recently "compromised" by making it quasi-official that farmers are allowed to have two children.

form of an Internal Security Act were the most effective way of dealing with racial riots isn't meant to be a general argument for repression. It's simply not relevant to point out that other countries don't face similar problems or that social peace can sometimes be secured without similar restrictions.

DEMO: So what do you recommend?

LO: Local knowledge. When countering plausible government justifications for rights violations of this sort, one can question either the premise that the society under question is actually facing a social crisis requiring immediate political action or the political implication that curbing a particular right is the best means of overcoming that crisis. But whatever the response, the social critic must be armed with detailed and historically informed knowledge of *that* society.

DEMO: I guess it's possible that the critic, after detailed study of the particular society under question, will conclude that the social crisis is real and that curbing a right is the most effective way of overcoming it. What does the human rights activist do at that point?

LO: Things are rarely clear-cut in the world of human affairs, as you know. Human rights activists and government officials rarely interpret "evidence" in the same way: the former tend to look harder for alternatives to rights curtailment as means of dealing with political crises. Besides, the human rights activist can point out that local justifications for the denial of rights are only of limited validity: they no longer apply once the crisis is overcome. A contemporary Singaporean, for example, can argue on the basis of local knowledge that the government should lift the Internal Security Act since Singapore no longer faces an imminent threat of a Communist coup or racial rioting.[30]

[30] In Taiwan, the "Temporary Provisions" restricting civil and political liberties were finally lifted after forty-three years in 1991. It should be said, however, that the "Communist threat" from the mainland is still present, which suggests that there were unstated motives for the "Temporary Provisions" (e.g., the ruling party's desire to stifle local opposition).

DEMO: What about foreign human rights activists? Locals tend to be more familiar with local situations, so where does that leave the human rights activist who also cares about suffering in foreign lands? Does that mean I can't criticize the Chinese government's human rights policies?

LO: Remember, I'm only talking about how to respond effectively to situation-specific, short-term trade-off arguments. The Chinese government also invokes more general justifications for abusing human rights, such as dubious appeals to "national sovereignty," and these can be refuted without detailed local knowledge.[31] But if the government is in fact presenting a situation-specific argument for rights curtailment, then yes, it's generally better to leave the fight to local critics.

DEMO: But what if local critics are weak because they lack education or information? And sometimes they may fear persecution.[32]

LO: Then foreign critics can help. But this must be done on the basis of local knowledge, which requires a great deal of investment in learning another society's culture, history, politics, and language. And not many human rights activists have the time or the inclination to do so. The problem is that there aren't any short cuts to sound and effective political judgments in the case of specific trade-off arguments. If human rights activists get one fact wrong—especially if they say something that's transparently false to locals—this can discredit the whole argument.[33] The Sin-

[31] Such arguments are persuasively criticized in Jack Donnelly, "Human Rights and Asian Values"; and Tatsuo Inoue, "Liberal Democracy and Asian Orientalism."

[32] It is presumably these kinds of considerations (along with the worry that "local sympathies" might bias one's judgment) that justify Amnesty's policy of preventing locals from investigating the rights conditions in their own countries. This policy is not without costs, however: a close Chinese friend of mine who joined Amnesty as an Oxford graduate student was disappointed when she was told she could not do research on China, and she eventually let her membership lapse since her main reason for joining Amnesty was her concern about the rights situation in her own country.

[33] For example, one foreign reporter begins a long article on Singapore with the claim that "People stand in interminable lines waiting for a taxi instead of

43

gaporean government, for example, frequently jumps on the missteps of foreign critics and parades these to the local audience, which effectively undermines the criticism.

DEMO: I suspect that the Singaporean government employs this tactic to divert attention from the substance of the criticism.

LO: Maybe so, but why make things too easy for them? Foreign critics need to be very careful about engaging with specific trade-off arguments for rights violations.

DEMO: Are you saying that I should endorse the government's line on specific arguments for rights violations in a society I don't know well?

LO: No. I'm suggesting that human rights activists should try to refrain from making firm moral and political judgments in disputes of this sort until they've acquired detailed knowledge of local political circumstances.

DEMO: I'll try.

LO: But it's easier said than done. Perhaps it's easier for me, because of my job. I've trained myself to prepare relatively descriptive reports on economic and political conditions in this or that East Asian country, and I leave it up to my clients to draw normative and policy implications. It could be that cultural differences also play a role. I find that Western liberals have the hardest time suppressing the instinct to judge, or perhaps I should say "prejudge," political decisions in foreign societies. I'm not sure

---

going out on the street to hail one, because this act is frowned upon by the authorities. Joggers routinely stop at 'DON'T WALK' signs—even on Sunday mornings, where there isn't a car in sight" (Stan Sesser, "A Nation of Contradictions," *New Yorker*, 13 January 1992, 39). Anyone who has lived in Singapore— and who has had to compete for taxis in chaotic situations outside housing estates—would know that Sesser has observed the exception rather than the norm. Besides undermining one's confidence in the rest of the article, Sesser's misinterpretation of Singaporean prevailing "shared understandings" leads him to miss out on one politically relevant feature of the Singaporean landscape: that the Singaporean government's authoritarian practices, far from causing ordinary Singaporeans to internalize "communitarian" norms, tends to have counterproductive "individualistic" effects (see chap. 4, sec. 3.2).

why that is. Perhaps it's a certain arrogant belief that the social experiences and political ideals of Western societies represent the "end of history," with a concomitant reluctance to study—and learn from—the ways of non-Western societies. It could be that a misplaced idealism prevents Western liberals from recognizing the need to deal with hard political realities.

DEMO: I can assure you that there are more sophisticated views out there.

LO: Yes, I know. Remember, I studied some political philosophy at Princeton. But even the greatest figures in the Western canon have contributed to the problem. Starting from Plato, most thinkers seem to rely on a universalistic ethic that leads them to found all political judgments on reasoning about human needs and interests rather than on the moral outlooks and pressing concerns of a society in this or that historically contingent condition.

DEMO: You're being unfair. Thinking about moral principles doesn't rule out appeal to local knowledge. Rather, the point is that there's a division of labor, and local knowledge may be relevant for the second stage. Most political thinkers divide their work into two tasks: first, thinking about morally desirable political principles, and second, persuading people to adopt them. No one denies that local knowledge can be helpful for the latter purpose of persuading people to do the right thing. But if one proceeds to tactics of persuasion too quickly, one may persuade someone to do something wrong.

LO (*raises voice*): Let me point out that "local knowledge" refers to more than a collection of facts that those concerned with effectiveness should try to understand. It also refers to values and norms. In my view, cross-cultural critics should try to leave open the possibility of revising their political ideals in response to an engagement with the local culture. In other words, they should try to understand—and learn from—the local culture *before* they move on to tactics of persuasion. There's something profoundly disrespectful about trying to persuade people to

45

adopt a "universal" ideal that was devised without any input whatsoever by the locals.

DEMO: Maybe you're right. The locals won't listen if they feel they're not treated with sufficient respect.

LO (*sighs*): There you go again, looking at this issue only in terms of what's the most effective strategy to make "them" come around to "our" viewpoint. My point is that the end itself shouldn't be fixed by Western perspectives. (*short pause*) But let me engage with your strategic concerns. Sometimes, the worry isn't just that "locals won't listen," that foreigners are wasting their time and money. Sometimes—and this is the really worrying part—human rights intervention that's uninformed by a sincere attempt to engage with the local culture is often counterproductive.[34] It achieves the opposite of what it's supposed to do.[35]

DEMO: Oh, come on, let's not exaggerate. Human rights criticism isn't always effective, but it doesn't make things worse!

---

[34] It is also worth noting that other kinds of culturally insensitive intervention can also have the unintended effect of worsening the human rights situation. Most notably of late, the International Monetary Fund (IMF) has received unprecedented criticism for its imposed solutions to the Asian financial crisis, which had the effect of exacerbating the crisis and undermining social and economic rights in the region. As Claude Smadja, managing director of the World Economic Forum at Davos, put it, "I am outraged by the errors of analysis which transformed a manageable crisis into a human disaster. . . . The fund wanted to imprint the U.S. model of financial capitalism on a global scale and this arrogance had consequences whose damage still has to be measured" ("IMF Accused of Fostering Asian 'Human Disaster,' " *Hong Kong Standard*, 28 January 1999, 12). The IMF itself admits to policy blunders in a recent assessment of its response to the Asian financial crisis, due partly to the fact that the IMF had been too remote from the situations in the three countries, detracting from the effectiveness of its decisions: "You can't force a package on a country from Washington and expect that country to forthrightly implement it. [Local] authorities have to buy into policy formulation" ("IMF Admits Bailout Blunders," *South China Morning Post*, 20 January 1999).

[35] This may seem like an obvious point, but the Singaporean scholar-diplomat Kishore Mahbubani notes that "The West cannot acknowledge that the pursuit of 'moral' human rights policies can have immoral consequences" (Mahbubani, *Can Asians Think?* 71). According to Mahbubani, this is one of ten "heresies" regarding human rights "that the West, including the United States, has either ignored, suppressed or pretended to be irrelevant or inconsequential in its discussions on these subjects" (ibid., 60).

LO (*losing patience*): Look at what the United States did in Vietnam: three million Vietnamese were killed in the Vietnam War, including two million civilians, and two million were affected by toxic chemicals, including 50,000 children born with deformities in the decade after the war.[36] This was all done in the name of human rights and democracy. All too often, practitioners turn to coercion when the real world won't bend to their principles.

DEMO: You can't blame human rights activists for the Vietnam War! They were against the war!

LO: Perhaps. But human rights intervention that's uninformed by local knowledge can worsen the situation in more subtle ways. In a recent case, the New York–based Lawyers Committee for Human Rights issued a report on Vietnamese refugee camps in Hong Kong.[37] Now this Lawyers Committee made some sensible suggestions, such as the need to improve living conditions in the camp, but they may also have undermined the cause of promoting refugees' rights by urging the Hong Kong people to integrate the Vietnamese refugees in the local community as a long-term goal.[38] Here in Hong Kong, already the most densely populated city in the world! You can imagine how this suggestion was viewed by the local audience. Why not try to get the refugees to the United States, was a typical response: you guys

---

[36] Graham Greene famously anticipated America's well-intentioned "descent into hell" in his novel *The Quiet American* (New York: The Viking Press, 1955). He portrays a well-intentioned American named Pyle who goes to Vietnam with the aim of implementing an American professor's idea for democracy in the East. Things do not go according to plan, and Pyle eventually sinks to (im)moral depths (he is responsible for over fifty deaths), all in the name of his ideal. Pyle himself is killed at the end. Greene seems to suggest that the problem lies partly with the attempt to intervene in Vietnam without sufficient local knowledge.

After the war Neil Sheehan, a former Vietnam correspondent for the *New York Times*, recounted the story of a well-intentioned U.S. soldier who would eventually justify (and commit) the worst kinds of atrocities in Vietnam in the name of capitalism and democracy. Sheehan suggests that the U.S. forces were led to disaster because that they seemed incapable of understanding (and sympathizing with) the Vietnamese tradition of nationalist struggles against foreign imperialists that motivated the Vietnamese side (Sheehan, *A Bright Shining Lie: John Paul Vann and America in Vietnam* [New York: Vintage Books, 1989]).

[37] *Inhumane Deterrence.*

[38] Ibid., 4.

bombed their country to smithereens, not us.[39] Eventually the colonial authorities in Hong Kong took an even harder line on the repatriation of refugees to Vietnam, with little need to worry about local opposition. (*short pause*) I'm not saying anyone is ill-intentioned here. But if the Lawyers Committee for Human Rights had really tried to understand local realities, or if they had issued a report with more local input, they would never have come up with a solution to a human rights problem that seeks to impose unreasonable burdens on the local community.

DEMO: The Lawyers Committee for Human Rights does try to obtain local input, but sometimes the locals won't talk. As part of a fact-finding mission on judicial independence in Malaysia, the Lawyers Committee met with social activists and NGOs. They wanted to meet with officials of the Malaysian government to get their point of view, but the government declined requests for meetings.[40] So I don't see how you can blame the Lawyers Committee for its lack of local input.

LO: In the case of the Vietnamese refugee crisis, they were given full access to Hong Kong government officials.

DEMO: Maybe the Lawyers Committee made a bad policy judgment. But is the problem that they lacked local knowledge? The Lawyers Committee is fully aware of the Vietnam War, and everyone knows that Hong Kong is a densely populated city.

LO: Perhaps I haven't clarified what I mean by local knowledge. It's not just a matter of knowing facts, or uncovering "hidden" information. It's knowing which "fact" has special resonance in this or that context, which "facts" to bring up in the course of moral argumentation and which ones to leave out. Those

---

[39] Some of the Vietnamese refugees were in fact former soldiers who fought on the American side, serving on dangerous reconnaissance missions and guarding U.S. advisers and military. Their story has a "happy" ending: following heavy lobbying by U.S. veterans, the U.S. State Department told the U.N. High Commission for Refugees that it would be willing to consider the case of former soldiers if they were declared refugees ("UN Accepts Former Viet Soldiers as Refugees," *South China Morning Post*, 3 June 1997, 3).

[40] *Malaysia: Assault on the Judiciary*, iii–iv. More recently, however, the Lawyers Committee for Human Rights did not attempt to meet with government officials as part of research for a report on the criminal justice system in mainland China (*Criminal Justice with Chinese Characteristics*).

without detailed knowledge of the context may not be able to do this. For example, I wouldn't even know how to begin arguing about the pros and cons of affirmative action in the United States. And I doubt I could come up with a sound policy judgment!

DEMO (*pause*): Fair enough. Personally, I'm not sure what to say about the Vietnamese refugee crisis in Hong Kong. I just don't know enough about the situation at the moment.

2. AN ASIAN VOICE ON HUMAN RIGHTS?

2.1. Human Rights: A Western Invention?

LO: Why don't we move on to a more direct "cultural" challenge to the way human rights are usually conceived in the Western liberal tradition. Actually, this wasn't an area of strong disagreement at the East-West dialogue I mentioned. But it does contain some valuable strategic lessons for human rights activists.

DEMO: Please elaborate.

LO: Well, some intellectuals in East Asia argue that the Western liberal tradition may not be the only moral foundation for realizing the values and practices similar to human rights regimes in the West. Put positively, the argument is that East Asian cultural traditions can provide the resources to justify and increase local commitment to values that in the West are typically realized through a human rights regime.

DEMO: This sort of argument wouldn't be out of place in contemporary, "politically correct" America. Everything good about Western civilization—great art, scientific and technological innovations, and now human rights norms—can also be found in non-Western traditions. But everything bad—imperialism, racism, hedonism, and so on—is uniquely Western.

LO (*smiles*): I know what you mean, but this particular argument about human rights may contain a grain of truth. And more important, appealing to local understandings can help generate support for human rights in East Asia.

DEMO: But can it be done? The theory of human rights—the idea that all human beings, simply because they're human, have certain inalienable political rights—was developed by English philosophers such as John Locke. I don't know of an Asian equivalent.[41]

LO: There may not be the exact equivalent of John Locke's theory[42], but values similar to aspects of Western conceptions of human rights can also be found in Asian cultural traditions.[43] The notion of *ren* in Confucianism, for example, expresses the value of impartial concern to relieve human suffering. In Mencius's famous example of a child on the verge of falling into a well, a man with *ren* would be moved by compassion to save the child, not because he had personal acquaintance with the child's parents, nor because he wanted to win the praise of his fellow villagers or friends, but simply because of his concern for the suffering of a human person.[44] The same sort of idea, presumably, animates concern for human rights in Western countries.

DEMO: Some values in non-Western traditions may be similar to the values underlying human rights regimes, but others aren't. It would be difficult to secure the rights of women by appealing to Islam, for example.

LO: Actually, some contemporary interpreters of Islamic teachings challenge the widely held belief that Islam justifies the subordinate position of women. They point out that the Qur'an's strictures on the family display a concern to ameliorate the status of women by abolishing pre-Islamic practices such as female infanticide, and by according women rights of divorce, property ownership, and inheritance.[45]

DEMO: But look at the reality of women's status in Islamic societies!

[41] See Donnelly, "Human Rights and Asian Values."

[42] See Locke's essay "Second Treatise on Government," in *Two Treatises of Government* (Cambridge: Cambridge University Press, 1963).

[43] See also Jefferson R. Plantilla and Sebasti L. Raj, S.J., eds., *Human Rights in Asian Cultures.*

[44] See Joseph Chan, "A Confucian Perspective of Human Rights," 218. See also Du Gangjian and Song Gang, "Relating Human Rights to Chinese Culture," 35.

[45] See Chandran Kukathas, "Explaining Moral Variety," 10.

Lo: I'm not familiar with the details, but I do know there's more than one Islamic reality. Women's status is far worse in Saudi Arabia than, say, in Malaysia. As you probably know, Southeast Asia's brand of Islam is relatively tolerant. It's simply not true that Saudi Arabia—with its restrictions on female drivers, and so on—necessarily represents "true" Islam.

DEMO: Why do you say that? Maybe it's the Southeast Asians who've distorted Islam's "true" message.

Lo: Perhaps. I guess it depends on the particular debate. I know a little bit about the debate on genital mutilation in Islamic societies, and I'm told that the "Islamic" defense of this practice rests on an inadequate understanding of the Islamic tradition. Apparently female genital mutilation predates the rise of Islam in northern African societies, and none of the major Islamic texts call directly for it.[46]

DEMO: I wonder about this strategy of picking and choosing values supportive of human rights from non-Western traditions. It seems kind of arbitrary—what do we do with the values that are inconsistent with human rights standards?

Lo: This problem isn't unique to non-Western traditions. The Western liberal tradition doesn't always provide intellectual support for contemporary human rights standards: John Locke denied that women were men's equals;[47] John Stuart Mill justified "civilizing missions" to uplift "barbarians" in India;[48] Thomas Jefferson kept slaves. Need I go on?

DEMO: This shows that leading liberal theorists occasionally betrayed the liberal principles of equality and freedom. It doesn't show there's a problem with liberalism's deepest principles.

---

[46] See Linda Burstyn, "Female Circumcision Comes to America," *Atlantic Monthly*, October 1995, 30. It is worth noting, however, that not all "progressive" interpreters of Islam agree with the argument that female circumcision should be abolished from Islamic societies. Some argue that it is better to maintain the symbol of female circumcision without the physical mutilation, for example, by means of a symbolic pinprick to the vagina (conversation with Abdullahi An-Na'im).

[47] See Susan Moller Okin, *Women in Western Political Thought*, 200.

[48] J. S. Mill, "Representative Government," in *Three Essays* (Oxford: Oxford University Press, 1975), 176.

LO: Exactly! That's what "progressive" interpreters of Confucianism and Islam say as well. They argue that their traditions' deepest principles support human rights norms. All traditions must answer the same question: whether or not it's possible to formulate persuasive interpretations of traditions supportive of contemporary human rights concerns while excising "contingent" aspects inimical to human rights. The way I see it, traditions are *ongoing* arguments, meaning that they maintain continuity with the past while also changing in response to contemporary concerns.[49] Western liberalism managed to do it while remaining an intellectually respectable creed with the capacity to motivate action in the contemporary era, so why can't other traditions?

DEMO: But your approach subordinates traditions to human rights standards. It fails to take traditions seriously, treating them as means toward the promotion of human rights. Sincere adherents to traditions—who won't take kindly to the thought that their cherished beliefs should be endorsed only on the strategic grounds that they help to promote another set of beliefs such as feminism or human rights—will oppose your approach.

LO: Naturally I come to this from the point of view of a human rights advocate. Other things being equal, I'd favor interpretations that better cohere with widely shared human rights standards. But there are other issues as well. You raise a deep and difficult question: what criteria should be employed to distinguish between desirable and undesirable aspects of traditions? I'm not sure what to say. I think I'd look for interpretations that don't rest on any obvious misconceptions, such as the belief that the Earth is flat. I'd also look for interpretations that aren't distorted by powerful interests: in the case of the Asian values debate, we're skeptical of arguments put forth by government officials because they often seem to be determined more by political requirements than by the desire to truly understand the tradition they're defending. It usually helps if interpretations are internally consistent, if they serve as a guide for practice in the contemporary world, and so on. No doubt some of these criteria will vary from one tradition to another. For example,

---

[49] For similar accounts of tradition, see Robert Bellah et al., *Habits of the Heart*, 27–28, 335–336, and Alasdair MacIntyre, *Whose Justice? Which Rationality?*.

some traditions place relatively more value upon the pronouncements contained in The Book.

DEMO (*pause*): Let me ask you something. You say that values *similar* to human rights can be found in non-Western traditions. Fair enough: only liberal dogmatists would argue otherwise.[50] But what about human rights *practices*? Can they be found in countries other than Western-style liberal democracies?

LO: Sometimes. Let's think about the aims of a rights regime. Western liberals typically say that the main purpose of human rights is to protect the individual from the exercise of arbitrary state power. If so, then the *functional equivalents* of human rights practices can sometimes be found in non-Western traditions. Consider the case of capital punishment in Qing dynasty China. Individuals guilty of offenses nominally calling for capital punishment were protected by lengthy, multilayered procedures, including the "right" to enter a personal plea before a Board of Punishments in Peking. Participating jurists at the Board of Punishments included prominent government officials and dignitaries, such as the tutors of the imperial heir apparent, and judicial proceedings were open to the public. A list of those found guilty was then submitted to the emperor, who made a circle on it with a brush dipped in vermilion—at random, it seems. The criminals whose names were traversed by the red line were then ordered for execution, and those who escaped the vermilion brush ten times achieved the status of "deferred execution."[51]

---

[50] There are, unfortunately, quite a few "liberal dogmatists" out there. John L. Esposito points out that "too often analysis and policymaking have been shaped by a liberal secularism that fails to recognize that it too represents a world view, not the paradigm for modern society, and can easily degenerate into a 'secularist fundamentalism' that treats alternative views as irrational, extremist, and deviant" (Esposito, "Political Islam," 24). The problem with "secular fundamentalism" is not just that it fails to treat nonliberal cultural traditions seriously, but that it plays into the hands of religious fundamentalists who seek to reject wholesale values and practices associated with the Western liberal tradition.

[51] See Derk Bodde and Clarence Morris, *Law in Imperial China*, 140–145. Pursuing a similar theme (i.e., the search for functional equivalents of human rights practices in East Asian cultural traditions), Stephen Young argues that "the theory of yin and yang was explicitly used by the Chinese to limit political power" (Young, "Human Rights Questions in Southeast Asian Culture," 190). In the

DEMO: That's what you call protection from arbitrary state power!

LO: You had multilayered, nationwide, highly rationalistic procedures, until the last stage—one might say it's a kind of due process. And in practice, less than 10 percent of those sentenced to death were actually marked off for execution.

DEMO: Well, I'll concede one thing: it's a better record on capital punishment than what you have in China today. (*short pause*) I still think, however, that there are some unique human rights practices in contemporary Western liberal democracies not replicated elsewhere. Liberal societies, for example, tend to be more tolerant and respectful of nonmainstream ways of life. I wouldn't want to be a Jew living in Iran.

LO: It's not well known that the Iranian Parliament guarantees five seats for religious minorities,[52] including one seat for a Jewish representative.[53]

DEMO (*raises voice*): Oh, come on! Are you saying that Jewish people in Iran have as many rights as Jews in the West?

LO: No, of course not. I only mean to point out that the functional equivalents of human rights can sometimes be found in non-Western countries. This matters because it means that the human rights activist can occasionally draw on local experience to justify the promotion of human rights. On the issue of protecting vulnerable minorities, for example, one need not always

---

same vein, Alan Wood argues that "the neo-Confucian legacy of the Northern Sung was clearly present in the modernization of both Japan and China and employed to advocate a limited, constitutional monarchy, not blind obedience to the ruler" (Wood, *Limits to Autocracy*, 170). Merle Goldman argues that the Confucian order "restrained political power by means of a vast array of rites, rituals, procedures, rules, and specific norms that the ruler and his officials were obliged to follow. If they did not, they risked provoking strong criticism from the literati" (Goldman, *Sowing the Seeds of Democracy in China*, 5–6). Michael Davis argues that according to Confucianism, "the government is not completely unencumbered by higher principles in the execution of power. In this light, Confucianism certainly does not appear to be hostile to human rights" (Davis, "Constitutionalism and Political Culture," 115).

[52] Article 13 of the 1980 Constitution of the Islamic Republic of Iran also guarantees Jews the right to practice their religious rites. Christians and Zoroastrians are guaranteed the same rights, but other religious minorities—including the Bahais, many of whom were murdered for their religious beliefs—are left out (see Jean-Jacques Gandini, ed., *Les Droits de l'Homme*, 144–145).

[53] See the *International Herald Tribune*, 13 March 1996.

draw on practices from Western liberal societies. It's useful to know, for example, that Chinese rule over Tibet in the mid-eighteenth century was primarily a matter of form, with the Tibetans in charge of their own affairs as long as they secured social peace and recognized a formal link with China. The Dalai Lama himself proposed the same thing in 1988, and he can defend his proposal in the name of continuity with Chinese tradition.

DEMO: But the current Chinese government, to say the least, doesn't seem to be particularly inspired by this historical precedent!

LO: Not yet. Someday, perhaps.

2.2. Increasing Commitment to Human Rights in East Asia: Strategic Considerations

DEMO (*pause*): I'm still not too clear. What exactly is the point of invoking local understandings for the promotion of human rights in Asia?

LO: If the ultimate aim of human rights diplomacy is to persuade others of the value of human rights, then in my view the struggle is more likely to be won if it is fought in ways that build on, rather than challenge, local cultural traditions. It helps to look at the relevant alternative: dependence on a foreign standard for promoting human rights, which is often counterproductive. For one thing, denying the very possibility that human rights have Asian roots unwittingly plays into the hands of ultraconservative forces in East Asia who seek to stigmatize human rights voices as "agents of foreign devils" and defamers of indigenous traditions.

2.2.1. ON THE PROSPECTS OF EXPORTING AMERICAN IDEALS TO EAST ASIA

DEMO: That's one risk, but hopefully people are sensible enough not to buy such arguments. And in fact "foreign" ideals have served to inspire struggles for human rights at home: take, for example, the Statue of Liberty clone at Tiananmen Square.[54]

---

[54] The "Goddess of Democracy" was not in fact a clone of the Statue of Liberty: Chinese students placed both hands on the torch, in order to illustrate the difficulty of achieving democracy in China.

LO: Unfortunately, such tactics also give governments an easy excuse to clamp down in the name of ridding the country of "foreign" influences. I'm thinking of the ruling junta in Burma, which gets a lot of propaganda mileage out of the fact that Aung San Suu Kyi is married to a British man.

DEMO: But no one can prevent repressive governments from twisting facts to their own advantage!

LO: Well, we can avoid making things too easy for them. For example, it doesn't help human rights activists in Asia when your president argues that "America's interests require the United States to lead an effort to build a world order shaped by U.S. values."[55] People in the region ask, "What about our values?" and governments get a lot of local support when they denounce American arrogance and interference.[56]

DEMO: I admit there are more sensitive ways of getting the point across. What Clinton meant, I think, is that it would actually benefit the United States if more foreign countries respected the kinds of rights enshrined in the Bill of Rights. He's responding to political "realists" who say that America's national interests may coincide with the interests of foreign dictators. That doesn't seem too problematic, does it?

LO: What's problematic is the assumption that only U.S.-style political institutions can secure human rights.[57] I recall the views Pro-

[55] See Christopher Layne and Benjamin Schwarz, "American Hegemony without an Enemy": 7. Some neoconservatives similarly argue that the United States has a duty to promote U.S.-style democracy and human rights abroad. See Joshua Muravchik, *The Imperative of American Leadership.*

[56] See also Wm. Theodore de Bary, *Asian Values and Human Rights,* 159.

[57] Stephen Young, former Assistant Dean of the Harvard Law School, notes that "Many Americans seem to believe that the constitutional pattern of governance in the United States today—as formalized in the Declaration of Independence, the Constitution, and the Bill of Rights—is a necessary prerequisite for protecting human rights. Thus, they evaluate the performance of other countries in the field of human rights by comparing their conduct with the standards of American politics" (Young, "Human Rights Questions in Southeast Asian Culture," 187). Young proceeds to criticize this standpoint: "Although the Anglo-American political and legal tradition has been a forceful expositor of human rights causes, it is not the only basis upon which to build a political system that respects human dignity" (ibid.). Nonetheless, Young falls into his own universal-

fessor Onuma Yasuaki, who teaches international law at the University of Tokyo. Professor Onuma is one of the leading proponents of human rights in Japan: he's been working to promote the rights of the Korean minority for over two decades, and he helped to draft the accord to compensate Asian "comfort women" forced to work as sexual slaves for the Japanese military during World War II.[58] I genuinely admire his human rights work. Yet Professor Onuma is also a harsh critic of the attempt to export the U.S.-style rights regime, which emphasizes civil and political liberties over social and economic rights.[59] He argues that this regime—with its excessive legalism and individualism—contributes to various social diseases, such as high rates of drug use, collapsing families, rampant crime, growing economic inequality, and alienation from the political process.[60]

DEMO: I think it's far-fetched to blame the U.S. Constitution for our domestic troubles. After all, the Constitution predates the ills you mention.

LO: But the view that a U.S.-style political system would lead to social breakdown is widely shared in Asia, and this undermines American moral authority in the region. The United States could afford to ignore such views back in the days when it was powerful enough to insist upon exporting its ways abroad. It's no longer the case, however, that the United States can dictate appropriate forms of government, as it did to Japan in the immediate post–World War II period. Today—given the relative economic and military strength of developing East Asian countries—the U.S. must rely primarily on moral authority to

---

istic trap when he fails to distinguish between democracy and human rights, apparently assuming that U.S.-style electoral mechanisms are necessary and sufficient to secure basic human rights (ibid., 187–188, 209). It is important to keep in mind that nondemocratic governments sometimes do fairly well at securing human rights, whereas democratic governments can sometimes have atrocious human rights records (see chap. 2, sec. 1.1).

[58] The Asian Women's Fund, which collects and distributes donations from the Japanese public as atonement money to the victims, is described by Yozo Yokota, "A Nation's Accountability and Responsibility," 14–16.

[59] See also Xiaorong Li, "A Question of Priorities," 7–12.

[60] See Onuma Yasuaki, "Toward an Intercivilizational Approach to Human Rights," 107.

promote human rights, and this makes things infinitely more difficult.

DEMO: I understand. Frankly speaking, I'm occasionally embarrassed by some of the self-righteous posturing of U.S. officials abroad. But still, recent developments in the international arena do seem to suggest that the American constitutional pattern of governance—the Declaration of Independence, the Constitution, and the Bill of Rights—has considerable *moral* appeal abroad. Several ex-Soviet bloc countries, as well as South Africa and Latin American countries, have recently adopted a U.S.-style constitution. We didn't "dictate" an appropriate form of government to those countries.

LO: In Asia, however, the German constitution—which secures a broad list of social and economic rights in addition to civil and political liberties, and which uses the language of duties as well as rights—has more frequently served as a model for constitutional reform. This may be related to fears that a U.S.-style constitution would exacerbate the atomizing tendencies of modernization.

DEMO: In my experience with the American Civil Liberties Union, I found that the problem lies mainly with the tendency to *violate* the U.S. Constitution. It's hard enough to stick to civil and political rights at home, never mind exporting them abroad!

LO: Good point! From my perspective, the main problem isn't so much *adherence* to U.S. political values. It's rather that these seem to go out the back door when other interests are at stake. This is what has really undermined U.S. moral authority in the region.

DEMO: Are you referring to the fact that the U.S. government has renewed most-favored nation status with China in response to pressure by American business, which seemed to subordinate human rights concerns to commercial interests?

LO: That's actually not a good example. I supported renewing MFN, as did just about everyone else in Hong Kong. You may know that former Governor Chris Patten also lobbied the U.S. Congress to renew MFN, on the grounds that the Hong Kong economy would have been decimated without it.[61] The debate over MFN was a strange case of some U.S. human rights activists opposing MFN renewal over and above the objections of most locals, including human rights activists. I don't want to rehearse my earlier point about the importance of local knowledge for making political judgments.[62] (*short pause*) In terms of undermining U.S. moral authority in the region, I was actually thinking of U.S. passive acquiescence in, if not active support for, gross human rights violations, as in the case of East Timor under Suharto. This sort of thing contributes to some cynicism in Asian circles as to the true motivation of U.S. policymakers— Prime Minister Mahathir of Malaysia, for example, is able to argue forcefully that the United States campaigns for workers' rights in Asia in order to undermine the competitiveness of Asian companies and to maintain U.S. economic dominance in the region.[63]

DEMO: I'm surprised to hear people respond to this sort of conspiracy theorizing.[64]

[61] See "Patten Warns New Leadership against Meddling with Economy," *The Asian Wall Street Journal*, 13–14 June 1997, 6.

[62] Some human rights activists may have been drawing inappropriate comparisons with the fact that widespread public support in Western countries for economic sanctions against South Africa turned the country into an international pariah state and helped to bring about the end of apartheid. In the case of South Africa, most local and well-informed views conformed with the views of the less well-informed Western public. In the case of China, however, most well-informed views (including those of locals and foreign experts) argue that it would be a disaster if uninformed Western citizens motivated by moral outrage against Chinese communism imposed a set of economic sanctions on the Chinese government: tens of millions of Chinese would be thrown out of work and the Chinese state would become even more xenophobic, not to mention the negative effects on the Hong Kong and U.S. economies. Fortunately, those armed with local knowledge have (so far) carried more political weight than ill-informed members of the general public.

[63] Mahathir bin Mohammad, "East Asia Will Find Its Own Roads to Democracy," *International Herald Tribune*, 17 May 1994, 3.

[64] This can only get worse in view of the Western response to the Asian financial crisis. The *People's Daily* claimed that the United States was using the authority of the IMF during the crisis to further its own strategic interests: "The United States is certainly not offering a New Marshall Plan to East Asia. By giving help, it is forcing East Asia into submission, promoting the U.S. economic and political model and easing East Asia's threat to the U.S. economy" (quoted in "America

Lo: But more well-documented cases of U.S. hypocrisy in the human rights field lend credence to such thinking. The decision in June 1995 to cooperate with the Burmese military junta in its fight against drug trafficking—in effect a decision that U.S. domestic drug problems can cause the U.S. government to overlook human rights concerns elsewhere—was well publicized in Asian countries at the time. And let me add that it's not just a problem with official U.S. policy, as nonstate actors can also send the wrong message by subordinating rights concerns when these conflict with commercial considerations. Malaysia's electronics industry is based on an explicit promise to American semiconductor companies that workers will be barred from unionizing. When the government considered lifting this ban, American companies threatened to move to China or Vietnam.[65] There's an even more blatant example of hypocrisy. The *New York Times* and the *Washington Post* tend to be unequivocal defenders of the right to freedom of the press at the level of rhetoric, but as co-owners of the *International Herald Tribune* they have recently accepted liability and paid a hefty fine for having "libeled"—i.e., criticized—members of the Singaporean government. My sources in Singapore tell me that the *International Herald Tribune* felt obliged to compromise its journalistic principles in order to maintain its market share and its regional headquarters in Singapore, but the probable effect was to discredit the ideal of freedom of the press in the eyes of the local audience.[66]

Demo: I guess that's not surprising. We shouldn't expect corporations to be at the forefront of battles for human rights.

Using IMF Bailout Rules to 'Crush Asia Rivals,' " *The South China Morning Post,* 7 January 1998). Mickey Kantor's statement that the United States should use the IMF as a "battering ram to open Asian markets to U.S. products" lends some credence to this speculation. Whatever the motives of Western decisionmakers, it is likely that the terms of the IMF bailouts—which effectively suppress the living standards of local populations "to protect foreign bankers from the foolishness of their loans" (Editorial, *Far Eastern Economic Review,* 9 April 1998)—are likely to fan resentment and cynicism regarding Western intervention in the East Asian region.

[65] See William Greider, "China Masks the Bigger Problem," *International Herald Tribune,* 6 March 1997.

[66] See William Glaberson, "Paper to Pay $214,285 in Singapore Libel Case," *New York Times,* 29 November 1995, A10.

Lo: I'm not arguing that businesses should always put human rights concerns at the top of their agenda. But when there's an exceptionally wide gap between the human rights rhetoric and the practice, this lends extra credibility to the view that *only* economic interests matter. More important, things can occasionally be improved: some corporations can be made to care about the human rights situation. As you know, my institute prepares reports on the political and economic conditions of East Asian countries for companies thinking of investing in the region. We look at many factors—taxation rates, infrastructure, levels of education, communications systems, corruption, and so on—but we also look at human rights. If the situation is really bad, we discourage investors, telling them that the country is too unstable. In China, for example, the government has broken contracts with major companies like McDonald's, and we warn our clients about the lack of the rule of law.

Demo: Come to think of it, we also work on similar issues: some of my colleagues have become involved in attempts to persuade U.S. corporations that being "good citizens" can also help the bottom line. For example, they try to show that corporations may find it in their own interest to improve human rights in the workplace.[67] Perhaps we can do the same sort of thing in Asia.

Lo: Not a bad idea, but that particular argument about workers' rights won't always be effective. In Hong Kong, for example, the government struck down a proposal for a law that would give unions the right to use collective bargaining to negotiate workers' salaries and fringe benefits. The Federation of Hong Kong Industries, not surprisingly, supported the government.[68] I doubt many employers could have been persuaded otherwise. In any case, there's a deeper problem if the concern is to improve American moral authority in the region. Even if the U.S. government and investors can be persuaded that it's in their own interest to care about human rights in Asia, it won't necessarily help. In most people's eyes, the only real test of moral

[67] See, e.g., Doug Cahn, "Human Rights, Soccer Balls, and Better Business Practices," 17–20.
[68] See my article, "Hong Kong's Transition to Capitalism," 19–20.

61

commitment is the willingness to sacrifice one's own interests for the sake of one's ideals.

DEMO: But it's not always easy to "prove" one's commitment to others.

LO: Well, sometimes it's quite obvious. Consider the fact that Vaclav Havel and Nelson Mandela were voted into power after being released from jail and allowed to run in free and fair elections. People voted for them because they admire and respect those who stick by their moral principles in the face of hardship. So if the United States really wants to improve its moral standing in this part of the world, it must show that it's willing to do more than pursue its own interests in the region. It must "put its money where its mouth is."

DEMO: For example?

LO: I'd suggest apologizing for the Vietnam War. When Asians look at what exporting "American ideals" meant in practice, they naturally remain a little skeptical about U.S. intentions.[69] The United States's refusal to make amends for the Vietnam War undermines its moral authority in Asia[70] in the same way that Japan's refusal to accept full responsibility for its war of aggression weakens its own moral authority in Asia.

DEMO: That's probably not feasible given the current political climate in the United States. Veterans' groups would be up in arms, the Republican right wing in Congress would never allow it . . .

LO (*interrupting*): What about President Clinton? I thought he opposed the war out of principle?

---

[69] Adding insult to injury, the U.S. government recently pressured the Vietnamese government to repay $145 million in debts incurred by the U.S.-backed government of the former South Vietnam, effectively putting "Hanoi in the position of retroactively footing part of the bill for a war against itself" (Clay Chandler, "Ghosts of War Haunt Rubin's Vietnam Trip," *International Herald Tribune*, 11 April 1997).

[70] Preparing for an attack on its human rights record by visiting U.S. Secretary of State Madelaine Albright, Hanoi officials made "it clear any rights criticism could fall on deaf ears given the impact of the Vietnam War and a continuing lack of development aid from Washington. 'Any criticism from the U.S. is simply not acceptable and is likely to create problems,' one senior official said privately"

DEMO (*laughs*): That's actually a political liability. The fact that he was seen as trying to evade the draft nearly caused him to lose the election in 1992—he was branded a coward, which didn't help in a competition against World War II war hero George Bush. Fortunately for Clinton, the economic downturn at the time mattered more, and he defeated the incumbent Bush.

LO: Well, there you have it. So long as the U.S. government won't apologize for the Vietnam War—and show willingness to put up with some domestic heat in the name of "doing the right thing"—the attempt to export "American ideals" abroad will lack credibility in Asia. And as a human rights activist in the region, I'd think twice about invoking the United States as a political model to justify my criticism of human rights abuses.

2.2.2. APPEALING TO THE UNIVERSAL DECLARATION OF HUMAN RIGHTS IN ASIA

DEMO (*pause*): I think we're overlooking something here. So far you present a stark choice between invoking local and foreign justifications for human rights norms. But there's another alternative: appealing to *international* accords as standards for promoting human rights. In fact, that's what some U.S.-based human rights groups do when they criticize the American government. Human Rights Watch, for example, recently excoriated the Clinton administration for its attempts to block international accords on the banning of antipersonnel land mines, the prohibition of use of child soldiers, and the establishment of an international criminal court.[71] Human Rights Watch argues that the U.S. government should embrace, rather than fear, the development of international human rights law. It

---

(Greg Torode, "Hanoi Prepares for Rights Attack by Visiting Albright," *South China Morning Post*, 22 June 1997).

[71] See Kenneth Roth, "Sidelined on Human Rights," 2–6. Roth is executive director of Human Rights Watch. It is also worth noting that Amnesty International—in its first campaign directed at any Western nation—recently published a harsh report on human rights violations in the United States, which helps to address the concern that "international" human rights organizations should seek balance by looking at industrialized as well as developing nations (Barbara Crossette, "Rights Group Gives U.S. a Harsh Verdict," *International Herald Tribune*, 6 October 1998, 7).

seems perfectly reasonable—and nonhypocritical—to direct the same sorts of criticisms against Asian governments that violate internationally recognized rights. It's no longer a question of appealing to a "foreign" standard.

Lo: That's one possibility. For example, Maria Serena Diokno, who teaches at the University of the Philippines, said that the Universal Declaration of Human Rights (UDHR) was employed as an effective tool by human rights campaigners in the Philippines during Marcos's rule. But this may be due to the particularities of the Marcos regime: she explained that this tactic was effective because Marcos depended to a great extent on U.S. economic and military support and was extremely conscious of his public image in the United States. This led him to employ legalistic justifications for his policies, which could then be challenged by his critics.[72] In the rest of East Asia, however, I'm not too optimistic about this approach. The main difficulty with the UDHR and other U.N. documents on human rights is that they don't reflect the result of worldwide consensus building,[73] and they tend to be biased toward Western liberal ideals. The UDHR, for example was formulated with minimal input from East Asia. Western Europe, the British Commonwealth, and the Americas dominated the initial definition and promotion of human rights, and the participation of authentically non-Western representatives was relatively meager.[74] As a result, the 1948

[72] Letter from Maria Serena Diokno, Convenor of the Program for Peace, Conflict Resolution, and Human Rights, University of the Philippines (on file with the author). The UDHR is sometimes invoked in Israeli courts, but this may not be good news for its defenders. When human rights activists invoke the International Bill of Human Rights (as the UDHR and subsequent documents are called), according to Joshua Schoffman (Israel's deputy attorney general), the government finds the same laws in local legislation or finds ways to override it, but when human rights activists ask for more than the International Bill of Human Rights, Israeli courts invoke the same document to justify not moving beyond it (discussion at "A Question of Human Rights" conference, University of Hong Kong, 17 December 1996).

[73] See Amitai Etzioni, *The New Golden Rule*, 236.

[74] But see Sumner B. Twiss, "Confucian Contributions to the Universal Declaration of Human Rights: A Historical and Philosophical Perspective," paper presented at Beijing University, June 1998. Twiss argues that the Chinese delegate P. C. Chang introduced a number of Confucian ideas, strategies, and arguments into the deliberative process leading up to the final formulation of the UDHR.

Declaration's conception of the human being is mainly a Western model: individualistic, secularizing, morally autonomous, acquisitive, and so on.[75] It's not always clear to Asians why the UDHR should constitute "our" human rights norms.

DEMO: But most East Asian states endorsed the UDHR, and this was reaffirmed at the Vienna Conference in 1993.

LO: I'd be careful about that reply. Human rights activists in East Asia often need to point out that their governments illegitimately present their own interpretations of human rights—often self-interested arguments for the denial of rights couched in the language of Asian values—as though it represents a society-wide consensus, but the kind of argument you're making undercuts our cause by implying that the government's voice should count as the normatively binding final interpretation of human rights issues in East Asia.

DEMO: But who else besides *governments* can endorse international human rights standards?

LO: Well, NGOs can participate in the decision-making process, as they did during the recent international conference on women's rights. What they come up with has at least as much normative force as a statement on human rights ironed out behind closed doors by a handful of international diplomats. When NGOs are involved, signatories at international conferences generally endorse the final document for the right reason, that is, because they genuinely agree on the outcome of an unforced dialogue. Things are less clear with respect to the UDHR. Most East Asian states endorsed it for pragmatic, political reasons and not because of a deeply held commitment to the human rights norms it contains. The UDHR thus doesn't have the normative force and political relevance of an international agreement or a national constitution that emerges from genuine dialogue between interested parties keen on finding a long-term solution to a shared political dilemma.

---

[75] Geoffrey Best, a senior associate at St. Antony's College, Oxford, makes a similar point in the *Times Literary Supplement*, 22 September 1995, 12. See also Henry Rosemont Jr., "Human Rights: A Bill of Worries."

DEMO: I still think that East Asians would be better off if their governments tried to implement the provisions of the UDHR.

LO: Is this a reasonable demand to place on a government? How influential is the UDHR in American society?

DEMO: There's less of a need to invoke the UDHR in the United States. We already have a Bill of Rights.

LO: Excuse me if I say this, but you're working with an American definition of human rights: human rights equals civil and political liberties. West Europeans, to repeat, generally have a more expansive definition of human rights that includes various social and economic rights, and it's worth noting that the UDHR also includes some typical "European" rights, such as workers' rights and rights to health care and free education.[76] So if you want to ask East Asian governments to enforce the UDHR, you'd have to place the same demand on your own government.[77] But

---

[76] See articles 23, 25, and 26 of the UDHR. The European emphasis on social and economic rights was vividly illustrated by a middle-aged railroad worker who joined a recent strike in France to protest Prime Minister Alain Juppe's proposal to slash welfare benefits. The worker "stared into the camera and declared that what drove him to revolt was that 'you can't go to the theatre anymore.' Numa Murard, a sociology professor, said, 'This worker's comment captured a wonderful moment in my opinion because it showed how, through decades of social engagement, we have created a sophisticated people to a point that a simple worker believes it is his right—indeed his human right—to go to the theatre and to eat at a decent restaurant on Sunday. In some other countries these are considered privileges deserved only by a few' " (Youssef Ibrahim, "For French, Solidarity Still Counts," *New York Times*, 20 December 1995, A14).

[77] The *New York Times* recently denounced several Asian countries for failing to observe the UDHR, but its editorial writers apparently failed to notice that the United States does a poor job of living up to the social and economic rights enshrined in the UDHR ("The New Attack on Human Rights," *New York Times*, 10 December 1995, 12). In the same vein, U.S. Secretary of State Madeleine Albright vowed that the United States would be "relentless" in opposing any review of the UDHR (in reaction to a suggestion by Malaysian Prime Minister Mahathir bin Mohamad that the UDHR might be in need of review to allow for more input from developing nations), apparently without realizing that (from an official U.S. perspective) the UDHR is both irrelevant (in the sense that it wouldn't have priority over domestic laws in U.S. courts) and imperfect (given that it affirms social and economic rights not affirmed in the U.S. Constitution). Moreover, Albright seems to assume that the particular human rights affirmed in the UDHR are enshrined in the structure of the moral universe: as Peter Van

while the United States insists on full compliance with the UDHR abroad, it typically affirms the supremacy of U.S. courts, laws, and regulations at home. Can you foresee the day when the UDHR would have ultimate authority in the American political system?

DEMO: No. But maybe it should. And you can't blame me just because my government fails to recognize the authority of international human rights accords.

LO: Of course not. But once we recognize that the UDHR is no more influential in the United States than it is in East Asia, we might be more sensitive to charges of hypocrisy. Plus, there are other problems with the UDHR. It lacks a proper enforcement mechanism: I don't expect the UDHR to gain greater legitimacy among states without an international U.N. force that's supposed to intervene in cases of human rights violations.[78] Another weakness is that some of its provisions are pitched at too high a level of abstraction to be of use for many actual social and political problems. For example, article 15 notes that "everyone has the right to a nationality," but this avoids the question as to which nationality is to count and thus can't help to resolve the conflicts over national identities that are the source of so many rights abuses in the contemporary world. Nor can U.N. documents provide much guidance when rights conflict: a developing country may well have to make some hard choices between funding education and health care, and the UDHR can't help the government to make the right choice.

DEMO (*pause*): Well, I must admit it's the first time I've heard a human rights activist deliver a scathing critique of the UDHR!

LO: It's because I'm concerned by the tendency of other rights activists to rely on human rights standards that resonate neither

---

Ness puts it, "Mahathir should instead [of being condemned for suggesting that the UDHR should be reviewed and possibly revised] have been encouraged to make a concrete proposal, because one of the basic requirements for achieving and sustaining consensus is to be prepared to reshape global standards whenever better principles are discovered" (Van Ness, ed. *Debating Human Rights*, 11).

[78] Canada has recently floated a plan for a U.N. force to help the United Nations respond to human rights crises. See Christopher Wren, "Canada Proposes Force to Help UN Respond Rapidly to Crises," *New York Times*, 29 September 1995, A7.

with governments in the region nor with the public at large. So-called "universal" justifications for human rights are not particularly promising from a tactical point of view in Asia, and to be effective human rights activists may need to pay more attention to local justifications for human rights.

2.2.3 LOCAL JUSTIFICATIONS FOR HUMAN RIGHTS

DEMO: Why do you think drawing on the resources of indigenous cultural traditions is any more likely to persuade East Asians— and their governments—of the value of human rights?

LO: It's easier to work with examples. Are you familiar with the case of the persecution of the Al-Arqam Islamic group in Malaysia?

DEMO: Vaguely. I don't know the details.

LO: This case was discussed by the Islamic legal scholar and human rights activist Abdullahi An-Na'im.[79] In August 1994 the Malaysian government launched a systematic campaign to suppress the Al-Arqam group, in accordance with a ruling from the National Fatwa Council and a decree by the Ministry of Home Affairs. Al-Arqam was declared "deviationist" and its leader, Ashaari Muhammad, was arrested and held without charge or trial. The group's written, audio, and visual presentations were banned, and Malaysian Muslims were prevented from joining Al-Arqam or participating in any of its activities.

DEMO: Sounds pretty bad. I wonder why this case didn't arouse much concern in the West.

LO: Perhaps because Al-Arqam favored a relatively "fundamentalist" interpretation of Islam. People tend to forget that human rights are supposed to protect unpopular individuals and vulnerable groups. In any case, the interesting part is that the persecution of the group can be condemned on *Islamic* grounds. An-Na'im argues that the Malaysian government misused Islam for the purpose of condemning Al-Arqam and violating its rights. He notes, for example, that deviationism is unknown to any orthodox formulation of Islamic Shari'a law, and that the

---

[79] See Abdullahi A. An-Na'im, "The Cultural Mediation of Human Rights."

government failed to conform to the demands of the principle of legality and rule of law under Shariʿa itself.[80] Of course I'm not an expert interpreter of Shariʿa, but I trust An-Naʾim's judgment in these matters.

DEMO: Personally, I'd worry about using religious arguments to promote human rights. You're opening up a whole can of worms by mixing politics and religion.[81]

LO: I'd worry more about what happens when you exclude religion from the political realm: the best way to nourish religious extremism is to stamp out the harmless expression of religious ideas. Besides, in this case, the can is already open. And once it's open, it's even more dangerous to abandon the cultural terrain to repressive governments. Human rights activists need to counter misuses of tradition with cultural arguments of their own.

DEMO: Is it really necessary to make such arguments? From what you say about this case, the Malaysian government's behavior can also be criticized by appealing to nonreligious political principles. The secular human rights activist, for example, can criticize the Malaysian government for denying a group of citizens their freedom of belief and for detaining them without charge or trial on the basis of a ruling from a council of religious scholars, hence violating the principle that religion not be used for political ends. Perhaps this secular activist could also invoke Article 27 of the United Nations International Covenant on Civil and Political Rights, which states that minorities shall not be denied the right to practice their own religion.

LO: But how persuasive are these secular justifications in a country dominated by a Muslim majority where rights are generally thought to have theocentric foundations and where Islamic legal codes already shape family and criminal law? In this context, arguments that appeal to widely shared religious values are

---

[80] Ibid., 163.

[81] Sydney Jones, executive director of the Asia Division of Human Rights Watch made a similar point when Professor An-Naʾim presented his paper at the Carnegie Council on Ethics and International Affairs in New York. Jones argued that it is dangerous to become involved in religious disputes and that human rights activists should stick to international human rights law.

far more likely to be effective than arguments founded on the principle that a human rights regime mandates a strict separation between religion and the state.

DEMO: You may be right. But was An-Na'im's Islamic argument for human rights really effective?

LO: It's hard to know. One of the difficulties with human rights work is that it's often hard to measure progress. The test of success is often that nothing happens—no one is arrested, tortured, murdered, and so on. Perhaps An-Na'im's argument will make the government of Malaysia think twice about invoking Islamic law to justify human rights abuses the next time around.

DEMO: Maybe. But that's not enough to persuade the skeptics. I need to justify the way that I spend the NEHRD's funds, and I can foresee some problems if I fund some religious groups that purportedly help to promote human rights. I'd need to show more concretely that the benefits of this approach outweigh the risks.

LO: Let me try to think of something else. (*short pause*) Actually, there's a relatively clear case of success in Malaysia. A Malaysian sociologist named Norani Othman discussed the example of a nongovernmental organization of Muslim women known as the Sisters of Islam, which tries to improve women's status in Malaysia. This group publishes and distributes booklets explaining how the Qur'anic conceptions of rights and duties of men and women in the family and in the economic and political spheres provide the basis for a more enlightened and egalitarian view of gender relations than the regressive ideas typically—and misleadingly—offered in the name of Islam itself. Sometimes the group intervenes directly with sympathetic officials in the Malaysian government to help formulate laws that improve women's status, and they've had some impact on legislation. In December 1993, for example, the group submitted a memorandum to the prime minister of Malaysia urging the federal parliament not to endorse the *hudud* law passed by the Kelantan state legislature. The *hudud* punishments included such troubling features as the inadmissibility of women as eyewitnesses and the implied endorsement of the view that compensation for death or injury to a woman should be half of that for a man. Sisters of

70

Islam argued against the endorsement of these punishments by rejecting the crude equation of *hudud* with Shari'a, and Shari'a with Islam, that helped to justify the Kelantan enactments. Apparently this was effective, because the federal parliament has stated that it will not pass the Kelantan *hudud* code. Othman argues that Sisters of Islam succeeded by creating awareness among some of the more powerful, modernist Muslim politicians that there is a valid Islamic argument to resist implementation of *hudud* laws in the contemporary context. If the group had limited its appeal to international human rights principles, it would almost certainly have lost the battle.[82]

DEMO: I wonder if politicians really respond to moral arguments for human rights grounded in traditional culture. Except for the Ayatollah Khomeinis of this world, they're generally motivated by much more immediate practical concerns. And I doubt that religious dogmatists would respond to these arguments.

LO: Admittedly, there's not much we can do with pure *realpolitik* types or with religious dogmatists who seem to rule out in advance the possibility that they may revise their initial viewpoints in response to dialogue with others. But not all politicians are like that. And even in such cases, there may be some hope. I recently came across an interesting argument that Khomeini could have been persuaded to exculpate Salman Rushdie within the terms of Islam.[83]

DEMO: You seem to be placing a lot of emphasis on persuading government officials to respect human rights. That will plug holes, but will it address the fundamental causes of injustice? Can it help those of us engaged in long-term human rights work?

[82] See Norani Othman, "Grounding Human Rights Arguments in Non-Western Culture," 185–189. (See also the example discussed in ibid., 186–189.)

[83] See Samuel Fleischacker, *The Ethics of Culture*, 153–159. It is worth noting, however, that some liberal Muslim clerics in Egypt did challenge Khomeini's position, but they were denounced as not true to the faith (though perhaps they did not use Fleischacker's particular argument about labeling Rushdie "insane" rather than blasphemous, which may have made a difference). Moreover, there is some evidence which suggests that Khomeini's motivation had a political component: he was slow to act against Rushdie, and appeared to do so only when his political position was weakening.

Lo: I didn't mean to imply that human rights work was just about pressuring government officials to redress human rights violations. Changes will be short-lived if the public at large isn't convinced of the value of new human rights. But for that to happen, it's best to ground new rights structures on those existing values and cultural reference points that have legitimacy for people on the ground. That's what the Sisters of Islam tries to do: its booklets on gender equality and Islam are meant to change attitudes toward women among members of the general public. The assumption is that building human rights practices on traditional cultural resources is more likely to lead to *long-term* commitment to human rights norms and practices.

Demo: Fair enough, but I wonder how much these arguments about culture will matter to "Joe Six-Pack". . . .

Lo (*interrupting*): "Joe Six-Pack"?

Demo: I'm sorry, that's an American expression. It refers to the ordinary guy who drinks beer, watches football on Sundays, and doesn't spend much time reflecting upon deeper issues.

Lo: It's perhaps not the best analogy if we're talking about the ordinary Muslim male. They're not supposed to drink alcohol.[84]

Demo: Fair enough! But my point is that these arguments about culture tend to appeal primarily to intellectuals, and I'm not sure to what extent intellectuals make a political difference. In the United States, not many of these arguments about cultural traditions affect life outside of the academy.

Lo: But things may be different in East Asia. In predominantly Islamic societies such as Malaysia, it's not just intellectuals who care about cultural disputes: Islam shapes the way people lead their lives, and new religious interpretations can make a social and political difference. Nor would I write off the potential contributions of intellectuals. In societies that have been shaped by Confucianism, intellectuals play an important public role: they

[84] In fact, this is an area of dispute within Islamic circles. Some "progressive" interpreters argue that the injunction against drinking alcohol refers only to certain types of liquor and the obligation not to be inebriated during prayer time, and not to a blanket ban on drinking alcohol (conversation with Addullahi An-Na'im).

72

are granted large amounts of respect and prestige, and what they say often has an impact on society at large. Professor Han Sangjin, who teaches at Seoul National University, pointed out that university students in Korea played an important role in galvanizing opposition to military rule and promoting human rights.[85] The more general point is that cultural traditions can shed light not only on the most effective arguments for human rights, but also on the groups most likely to bring about human rights reforms.

DEMO: Mmh. That's important for my organization, which must target funds to the groups most likely to bring about lasting human rights reforms.

LO: There's another point that is relevant for those concerned with the effective implementation of human rights in the region: the importance of not being too abrasive in pushing for human rights in the region. Blanket criticism of human rights practices is often seen in East Asia as high-minded and self-righteous, even by critical intellectuals. Professor Joseph Chan, who teaches at the University of Hong Kong, expressed his irritation at Western human rights advocates and lawyers who attend international conferences on Asian values and human rights and launch into lengthy denunciations of the appalling human rights records of some Asian countries, as though their listeners are unaware of the violations in question or would want to defend them.[86] What's the point of this grandstanding on human rights?

DEMO: I've been warned about that.

LO: Once again, cultural knowledge is useful: it can help to identify the right sort of attitude that should be displayed by the rights activist. Professor Onuma Yasuaki—I've already mentioned him—stressed the point that modesty is highly prized in the East Asian region.[87] Even if one believes in certain values,

[85] See Han Sangjin, "Political Liberalization, Stability, and Human Rights," paper presented at the workshop on The Growth of East Asia and Its Impact on Human Rights, Hakone, Japan, June 1995.

[86] See Joseph Chan, "Hong Kong, Singapore, and 'Asian Values' " 36.

[87] See Onuma Yasuaki, "In Quest of Intercivilizational Human Rights," and "Toward an Intercivilizational Approach to Human Rights," 106–108.

proselytizing for them is regarded as arrogant, uncivilized, and counterproductive.[88]

DEMO: Fair enough. Actually, I'm not one of those brash Americans. I'm normally on the quiet side. Besides, I'm not supposed to antagonize my audience: the NEHRD's mission is to develop productive, mutually respectful relationships with locals to promote human rights in the long term. Still, I'd find it hard to be polite to a dictator whose regime tortures political prisoners.

LO: Even if you're addressing the "bad guys," it's often more effective to present your point of view in a quiet and modest manner.

---

[88] This point is often made by East Asian intellectuals sympathetic to human rights, but somehow it has failed to sink in with members of the U.S. government. Speaking on the eve of the Asia-Pacific Economic Co-operation Forum summit in Kuala Lumpur, Malaysia, U.S. Vice President Al Gore said: "Among nations suffering economic crisis, we continue to hear calls for democracy, calls for reform in many languages—People Power, Doi Moi, Reformasi. We hear them today—right here, right now—among the brave people of Malaysia." Gore's aim was to encourage Malaysia's antigovernment movement, but its effect was the opposite. Following Gore's comment, Prime Minister Dr. Mahathir Mohamad regained some political credit and public support for the protests dwindled. Gore did not help his case by lumping together several unrelated phenomena. As the *Far Eastern Economic Review* noted, "Doi Moi was the attempt by Vietnam's communists to rejuvenate the party and stall demands for democracy. Even then, it has quietly faded. But of our more immediate concern, the reformasi movement begun by Anwar Ibrahim is about many things, but it isn't about democracy, *per se*. It's about due process and scrapping the Internal Security Act. It's about greater transparency in business; and it questions the business-government nexus, often dubbed 'cronyism.' Malaysians, however, have democracy" ("Speak Softly," *Far Eastern Economic Review*, 26 November 1998, 110). More counterproductive (in terms of the effect on Malaysia's reform movement), perhaps, was the way Gore delivered his message: directly insulting his host in a formal setting and then, "Adding visual insult to the verbal injury, Mr. Gore walked out at the conclusion of his speech surrounded by a phalanx of Secret Service heavies, like an emperor who had delivered an edict" (Ian Stewart, "Burdens of Autocracy Weigh on Mahathir," *South China Morning Post*, 22 November 1998, 7). Not surprisingly, the reaction in Malaysia was scathing, and even some critics of the political status quo sought to distance themselves from Gore's comments for fear of being labeled stooges of an imperial power. Surprisingly (or perhaps not?), the U.S. press was almost unanimous in praising Gore's intervention (see, e.g., the *New York Times* and the *Washington Post* editorials in the *International Herald Tribune*, 19 November 1998, and *The New Republic*'s "Notebook," 7 December 1998). Not one of these editorials pointed out Gore's errors of fact or the likely effect of his speech on Malaysia's reform movement. The assumption seems to be that the

For example, criticism of human rights practices can be prefaced by criticism of human rights practices at home and sincere praise for certain aspects of the society under question. I recall a story that was told by Jeffrey Garten at a memorial service in Beijing for the late United States Secretary of Commerce Ronald Brown.[89] Preparing for his first official trip to China two years ago, Secretary Brown had been warned that the merest mention of human rights to Chinese President Jiang Zemin would jeopardize the entire mission and scuttle negotiations over several big commercial deals. But Secretary Brown—as you know, an African American in the largely white U.S. power structure—vowed nonetheless to raise the issue. After launching into a sales pitch for one of the projects under discussion, Secretary Brown paused for breath and said, "Let me tell you something about myself." He went on to talk about his experience in the U.S. civil rights movement and continuing race discrimination in the United States. Neither he nor anyone else was in a position to preach, he said, "but it would really be to your advantage to do something about the abuses that occur here," he told President Jiang. "Don't do it for us. Do it for yourselves. Do it because you're a great country, because you're a great power." After a long pause, President Jiang said, "If you put it that way, I think we have something to talk about." Jiang eventually agreed to resume the human rights dialogue and told Secretary Brown that he could announce it that evening.

DEMO: Mmm, that's an interesting story. But Brown was notoriously smooth. I wonder if he was genuinely committed to human rights. These probusiness types tend to be motivated primarily by strategic concerns.

LO: In my experience, some businessmen really do care about human rights "deep in their hearts." Besides, it doesn't really matter, so long as the effect is to improve the human rights situation.

United States should stand up for its values in all times and places, regardless of the actual impact on prodemocracy movements.

[89] See Sara French, "Brown Much More Than a Superb Salesman," *Eastern Express* (Hong Kong), 13–14 April 1996, 28.

DEMO (*pause*): Maybe we're not that far apart. I can accept some of your arguments for appealing to local traditions to justify values and practices similar to a Western-style human rights regime. As you said, local justifications for human rights norms can be invoked to show that governments misuse cultural arguments for purposes of rights violations, as well as to promote long-term commitment to human rights norms in the community at large. Then you pointed out that awareness of cultural traditions can also shed light on the groups most likely to promote desirable political change and on the appropriate attitude to be employed by the rights activist. But these are all *strategic* arguments for persuading East Asians of the value of a human rights regime. That's very different from arguing there's a problem with the Western or international conception of human rights as an *ideal*, or that Asian values can provide a moral foundation for political practices and institutions different from the human rights regimes typically favored in Western liberal democracies.

LO: You're right. But that's the most controversial question, and I thought we should leave it for last. So let me just make one last strategic argument for invoking local traditions. This is the view that traditions can make one sensitive to the possibility of alternative, *nonlegalistic* mechanisms for the promotion of human rights.

DEMO: If people have a moral right to something, then the state has an obligation to enforce it by law. There's a necessary linkage between the concept of right and legal enforcement.

LO: But if the end result is the same—the protection of vital human interests from various kinds of threats, which presumably is the whole point of a human rights regime—it's unclear why one should place too much emphasis on this terminological issue. We can use a different word to refer to international norms best secured by nonjuridical means, although in my view the language of rights is too central to the international discourse to be entirely dispensed with. The important point is that legalistic thinking has been rather foreign to many East Asians, and resorting to juridical measures to enforce one's rights isn't always appreciated. Professor Onuma Yasuaki—himself a lawyer—said that one is often expected to reach the same goal by means of less forceful measures, such as patient negotiations, mediation, and other conciliatory measures.[90]

DEMO: But how is this possible?

LO: Well, let's look at Hong Kong. This is the most "legalistic" place in East Asia—largely a product of colonial rule by the British—but even here there's a widespread preference for nonlegalistic remedies. The Human Rights Equal Opportunities Commission, for example, initially emphasizes informal conciliation instead of court litigation as a response to complaints of discrimination.[91] There are plenty of other examples in the East Asian region. In Singapore, the "court" entrusted with the task of securing the obligations of filial piety—parents have a "right" to claim financial support from their children—also emphasizes mediation in the first instance.

DEMO: What if mediation doesn't work?

LO: Then legal means can be employed, but only as a last resort. Joseph Chan notes that from a Confucian standpoint we should first try to compromise in a way that is faithful to the ideal of mutual caring and love. One should only resort to rights if all else fails. To support his argument, he quotes the famous passage from the *Analects* of Confucius: "In hearing litigation, I am

[90] Discussion with Professor Onuma Yasuaki, Bangkok, Thailand, March 1996.

[91] See Michael Davis, "Chinese Perspectives on Human Rights," *Human Rights and Chinese Values*, ed. Davis (Hong Kong: Oxford University Press, 1995), 20–21, and Anna Wu Hungyuk, "Why Hong Kong Should Have Opportunities Legislation and a Human Rights Commission," 196–197. Another example that illustrates the aversion to legalism in Hong Kong concerns the recent proposal to introduce laws specifically outlawing racial discrimination. The government conducted a "consultation exercise," and of the 238 responses, 83 percent said that passing laws is not the best way to fight racism. Respondents were most worried by the possibility that outlawing discrimination would generate a plague of "vexatious litigation" that might actually create racial lines and disputes where none currently exist. The government eventually decided not to introduce such laws, a decision that was applauded by an editorial in the *Asian Wall Street Journal* ("Left out of the Race," *Asian Wall Street Journal*, 20–21 June 1997, 10). In summer 1998, however, this issue once again hit the headlines, after it was shown that some Hong Kong bars charge less for Caucasian than for Chinese and Indian customers, and it is possible that "the community" will change its mind on this issue.

no different from any man. But if you insist on a difference, it is, perhaps, that I try to get the parties not to resort to litigation in the first place."[92] This view is still widespread in East Asian societies. It's a different way of thinking about rights from, say, the United States, where suing often comes to mind first as a means for conflict resolution.

DEMO: First resort or last resort, you're still dealing with a legal question.

LO: But sometimes the judicial process may not be appropriate even as a last resort. There are many nonlegalistic ways of securing rights. It's hard to see this if you're working with an Anglo-American assumption that the point of a rights regime is simply to prevent the state from doing bad things to individuals.

DEMO: That's not my view. I'm fully aware that many threats to human well-being come from the nonstate sector: the International Monetary Fund, the World Bank, big corporations, and so on.

LO: Well, it's important to allow for nonjudicial remedies for human rights violations in such cases. The international lawyer Benedict Kingsbury—one of the participants at this East-West debate on human rights—pointed out that since 1991 the World Bank must prepare an indigenous peoples development plan in projects affecting indigenous peoples.[93] Though far from perfect, this kind of measure can sometimes do more to protect the rights of indigenous peoples than policies laid down by national governments. In many cases, the "rights" of workers are best protected by putting pressure on corporations, rather than governments, to change their ways.[94] In fact, many Asian NGOs argue that corporations should be held liable for the violation of rights.[95] And if the concern is to secure the "right" to

[92] Quoted in Chan, "A Confucian Perspective of Human Rights," 226.

[93] For an example showing that this clause has had practical effect, see Benedict Kingsbury, "The Applicability of the International Legal Concept of 'Indigenous Peoples' in Asia," 360.

[94] See, e.g., Debora L. Spar, "The Spotlight and the Bottom Line," 7–12.

[95] See Article 2.8 of the Asian Human Rights Charter, published on the occasion of the fiftieth anniversary of the UDHR. More than two hundred Asian NGOs took part in the drafting process of this document.

a clean environment, the key is often to empower local communities, or to give them stewardship over resources. Activists in Thailand say that deforestation can best be controlled by persuading members of local communities to play a role monitoring the activities of logging companies.[96] There are many ways to secure rights, and it seems counterproductive to rule out non-legalistic remedies.

DEMO: Mmh, yes, you're right, but there's nothing distinctively Asian about what you're saying. Everyone can agree about the need to consider nonjudicial ways of securing rights.

LO: The important point is that many rights activists in the West still seem steeped in the liberal legalistic tradition. They forget that the philosophy of the sovereign state either desisting from rights violations or enforcing rights by judicial means is only part of the story. East Asian traditions are useful because they open up the possibility of alternative means to secure international human rights norms.

DEMO: Fair enough, although I still think you're exaggerating the extent of the "civilizational" split on this issue. When I was working at the ACLU, we'd often get attacked by American communitarians for our supposedly excessive legalism and "rights talk." They argued that the tendency to resort to legal means, or to threaten to do so, as a first resort for the protection of rights had unintended consequences, such as justifying the neglect of social responsibilities and weakening all appeals to rights by devaluing the really important ones.[97] Of course, I often disagreed, but my point is that these critiques of excessive legalism also form part of the public discourse in the United States.

LO: I didn't mean to imply that these arguments are distinctly Asian. At this East-West workshop on human rights, the Canadian philosopher Charles Taylor also stressed the need to allow variations in modes of implementation of human rights in dif-

[96] Charles Taylor made this point at the Bangkok workshop on Cultural Sources of Human Rights in East Asia, March 1996.

[97] See Amitai Etzioni's criticisms of the ACLU in *The New Golden Rule*, 19–20, and *The Spirit of Community*, chap. 6. See also Mary Ann Glendon, *Rights Talk*.

ferent societies.[98] But—and please correct me if I'm wrong—my impression is that these sorts of arguments constitute a critique of the dominant outlook in the United States. In East Asia aversion to legalism *is* the dominant outlook. At the end of the day, however, it doesn't matter, so long as we agree that securing the conditions for the protection of vital human interests isn't just about the state leaving individuals alone or about relying on the judicial process to protect individual rights. What's important is to recognize the need for flexibility when thinking about how best to secure rights.

DEMO: Of course. I'm just arguing for the sake of it. In fact, the NEHRD does more than fund proposals for strengthening legal mechanisms for the protection of rights. We also fund human rights education in primary and secondary schools, on the assumption that this is an essential way of disseminating knowledge of rights and responsibilities, and thus of promoting human rights in the long term.

LO: A good idea, although I guess it depends what's taught. If you do this in Asia, I hope you'll say something about the way local cultural traditions can provide the resources for justifications of international human rights norms. It won't work if you simply push the old liberal story about the contributions of Locke, the French revolutionaries, Mill, and the American Founding Fathers to the theory of individual rights.

DEMO (*smiles*): We'll investigate the contributions of other traditions as well. At the end of the day, it seems that we don't really have any deep disagreements. The important thing is to promote the vital interests of individuals and to find the right means of doing it. Even if this means cooperation with the Communist Party—as in the Ford Foundation case mentioned earlier—then that's what we have to do.

LO: That's only part of the story. I don't think we should foreclose the possibility of norms and practices that justifiably differ from Western-style human rights regimes. With respect to the Ford Foundation example, it's not just a matter of securing party support for an end that's beyond question. It's perfectly plausible

[98] See Taylor, "Conditions of an Unforced Consensus on Human Rights," 129–133.

to imagine a scenario whereby it would be a mistake to improve the civil rights of rural women in China. For one thing, the attempt to improve rural women's access to legal services can displace effective nonlegalistic modes of conflict resolution, with the consequence that improving access to legal services would be counterproductive in terms of securing women's vital interests. It is potentially dangerous to assume *in advance*, prior to knowledge about local family patterns, religious practices, and community life, that improving access to legal services is a good thing.

DEMO: I don't disagree, but you're still making a practical argument about finding the best means to promote women's interests—and I presume this means a more equal relationship between Chinese men and women. If this end is best realized by means of reinforcing traditional modes of conflict resolution, then that's the way to go.[99] The Ford Foundation's mandate is to promote women's equality wherever they can do so in an effective way. There's no reason for them to dogmatically stick to the idea that access to legal services is the only appropriate means. But that's not the same as asking Ford Foundation program officers to consider the possibility that it may not be a good thing to try to promote women's equality in China!

LO: In my view, we should also allow for the possibility that local values can justifiably differ. I'm reminded of a film by China's most famous filmmaker, Zhang Yimou. Have you seen his film *The Story of Qiu Ju?*

DEMO: Yes. Isn't that the film about a rural Chinese heroine who persists in a difficult search for legal aid?

LO: That's correct. But this film ends with serious doubts about the benefits of recourse to legal remedies. Zhang Yimou seems to suggest that this "heroine" did profound damage to local ties and deeply rooted ways of life. I'm not sure if he would endorse your idea that liberal ideas about freedom and equality should be implemented in rural China.

---

[99] According to Phyllis Chang (conversation, April 1999), however, traditional modes of conflict resolution usually favored males over females. Chang argues that legal means are more likely to secure women's interests in the context of rural China.

DEMO: Strange, but I didn't get that message myself.

LO: There were other indications. The glamorous actress Gong Li was implausibly cast as a rebellious and "justice-seeking" farmer prone to histrionics. Her relatively silent, loyal sister, played by an "authentic" farmer, was a far more credible character. I suspect Gong Li was deliberately miscast to illustrate the dangers of trying to export big-city norms to the countryside.

DEMO (*laughs*): And I suspect you're reading far too much into this movie!

3. A Different Moral Standpoint?

[At this point, Remi enters the dining room with a dish of grilled meat in a brown sauce.]

LO (*serving Demo*): Remi made us her specialty. I'm really looking forward to the meal. Please, you begin.

DEMO (*tasting the food*): Mmh, it's very good. I'm not sure I've had this before. What is it?

LO: I believe they call it *afo* in the Philippines. In English it's known as "dog meat."

DEMO (*face turning white*): You're kidding?

LO (*laughs*): Yes. It's actually grilled suckling pig. It would be rude to serve dog meat to an unsuspecting American guest. But there's a serious point. Many Cantonese eat dog meat, although here in Hong Kong the colonial authorities banned the sale of dog meat for human consumption. And Remi tells me that dog meat is a real delicacy in the Philippines. Remi, how do you cook dogs?

REMI (*nervous laughter*): Oh no, not tonight, only special occasion! Wedding, birthday party. Very hot, with ginger and chili, like curry. The head is best part!

LO: Thank you. (*turns to Demo*) Now, let me ask you, do outsiders have compelling reasons to object to the cultural culinary practice of eating dog meat? The way I see it, there's no principled way of distinguishing between eating dogs and eating other domestic animals for human consumption.[100] They all have the capacity to suffer, and apparently the pig is the most intellectually gifted of the domestic animals. But Westerners—pardon me if I say this—often seem to think their ways are universal, and that everyone else should conform to the "Western way." In 1988, for example, the Korean government temporarily closed dog meat restaurants in Seoul so as not to offend American visitors to the Olympic games.

DEMO: Perhaps they were just being considerate to their guests.

LO: Fine, but do Western governments follow the same principle? Did restaurants in Baltimore—or was it Cleveland?—stop serving pork during last year's Olympic games so as not to offend Muslim visitors?

DEMO: Atlanta. The Olympic games took place in Atlanta.

LO: Whatever. Did restaurants in Atlanta stop serving beef in order not to offend Hindu visitors? Arguably there's a stronger case to respect this Hindu practice than to respect the seemingly groundless Western bias against dog meat. The cow, as you know, is considered to be a sacred animal in Hindu culture, more important in some ways than human beings. The Indian government actually subsidizes old-age homes for elderly cows.

DEMO (*laughs*): You're kidding?

LO: No. My point is that Westerners may need to do more to understand—and to respect—the cultural particularities of non-Western societies, especially those aspects considered to be sacred by contemporary adherents of particular traditions.

DEMO: Fair enough.

3.1. Cultural Respect vs. Liberal Neutrality

LO: But this may entail revising your political principles. It took me some time to understand why so many Western liberals—and let me be frank, I'm mainly talking about American liber-

---

[100] Yves Correc (my cousin in France), however, has suggested to me that most humans may have a special aversion to eating other carnivores (like dogs and cats) on the grounds that they are too similar to us.

als—seem insensitive not just to the cultural particularities of other societies, but also to the ways that that their own state gives political embodiment to cultural particularity, for example, by passing laws against selling dog meat for human consumption.[101] You mentioned communitarian critics of liberalism, and they may have identified the main problem. It seems that many Americans endorse the principle of state neutrality: the idea that the role of the state is to secure the rights that enable individuals to freely choose their own way of life, and hence that it should not promote any particular cultural or religious projects.[102] But if state and culture don't mix in principle, why should one respect other cultures that give political embodiment to cultural particularity? If the only just form of government is one that bars cultural particularities from the political realm, why even bother engaging in a dialogue with members of societies that favor the use of the state to promote certain kinds of cultural values? All parties in a dialogue among equals should leave open the possibility of learning something from the other interlocutors, including learning from alternative political values and practices, but the purpose of "dialogue" with members of "nonneutral" societies can't be more than the strategic aim of getting them to do otherwise.

DEMO: I wonder about that. Why should a commitment to neutrality make dialogue any more difficult than any other principled commitment? You're right that the aim of a dialogue with mem-

---

[101] In the same vein, a recent court case in Canada illustrates the particularistic character of a seemingly neutral law. Killing bears for sport is legal in Canada, and nothing stops the hunter from then using the head and skin for decorative purposes. Selling bear gall bladders is illegal, however, even though the bladders are used in Chinese medicine. A Canadian judge noticed this unfair cultural bias, and several people charged in an undercover sting operation in Vancouver's Chinatown were let off lightly ("Bear's Best Friend Takes on Hunters," *South China Morning Post*, 28 June 1997, 9).

[102] See, e.g., my *Communitarianism and Its Critics*, 3–4. Some contemporary Western liberal thinkers, however, offer persuasive critiques of the ideal of state neutrality from within the liberal tradition. See, e.g., Stephen Macedo's *Liberal Virtues* (Oxford: Clarendon Press, 1991). While it may be possible to formulate a defensible nonneutralist version of liberalism at the level of high philosophical theory, the fact remains that the value of neutrality still informs many of the actual political practices and legal judgments in the United States as well as popular thinking about life and ethics. See Michael Sandel, *Democracy's Discontent*.

bers of nonneutral societies would be to get them to see the light and adopt some version of neutrality. But aren't the nonneutralists also committed in principle to their position— so that all they would aim at is getting the neutralists to do otherwise?

LO: Perhaps. But what I have in mind is a dialogue between people who can put their conceptions of the good on the table, so to speak, with interlocutors leaving open the possibility of learning something and revising their initial standpoint in response to other people's conceptions of the good.

DEMO: I guess it depends whom you're talking to. For example, it may be inappropriate to invoke the principle of state neutrality during the course of dialogue with minority groups who seek some form of protection for traditional ways, such as restrictions on the use of land considered to be sacred by aboriginal peoples. In my view—and here I differed with most of my colleagues at the ACLU—there may be a good case to address the needs and aspirations of minority peoples and perhaps even to grant culturally based minority rights. Arguably, this can be done in the name of liberalism itself, as the only viable means of promoting liberal values in multicultural societies and in the world at large.[103] But I worry when majorities or powerful groups begin to talk about the need to respect their "culture." At that point, it may well be appropriate to invoke the principle of state neutrality. What motivates liberal neutrality, I think, is the worry that democratic *majorities* would unfairly vote themselves special rights and benefits. Far from being culturally insensitive, liberal neutralists fear that "moral majorities" would use the democratic system to push their ways on vulnerable minorities.

LO: But this sort of thinking is exactly what contributes to the excesses of legalism. Does it mean that the U.S. Supreme Court should strike down all nonneutral laws that benefit majorities?

---

[103] See, e.g., Will Kymlicka, *Multicultural Citizenship*, 195. Kymlicka, however, does not always distinguish between a strategic argument about the best way of selling liberal ideas to ethnic minority groups and a moral argument about the need to respect the aspirations of minorities and non-Western peoples. Given Kymlicka's "liberal" argument that cultural membership has value primarily because it provides the context for meaningful individual choice (82–93)—which

DEMO: No. The Supreme Court should stick to the Bill of Rights. But those who challenge the cultural preferences of majorities in the democratic arena can strengthen their argument by invoking the importance of state neutrality.

LO: It's worth pointing out that European states such as France, Norway, and the Netherlands don't worry so much about promoting the culture of the majority nation. They don't claim to be neutral with reference to the language, history, literature, calendar, or even the minor mores of the majority.[104] The French government, for example, recently issued guidelines to include material on culinary appreciation as part of the educational curriculum in state-run schools.[105] Gastronomical education begins in kindergarten, when five-year-old children are taught to distinguish between simple tastes, and things gradually become more complex in primary school. The program is justified in part by the need to combat the deleterious impact of U.S. fast-food chain restaurants on the eating habits of young persons in France, and ultimately by a desire to maintain the rich and distinctly French culinary tradition.

DEMO: I wonder how immigrants to France feel about this program to maintain French culinary traditions?

LO: Promoting the majority culture can be done in ways that tolerate and respect ethnic and religious differences. In this case, the French government tries to include the culinary practices of minority groups. The lunch menu is designed to promote an appreciation of French cuisine, although North African, Italian, and other "non-French" dishes are also served to promote the appreciation of the contributions of minority groups in France. Here in Hong Kong, the French International School, which follows guidelines issued by the Ministry of Education in France,

---

is not the way that most "national minorities" and non-Western peoples understand the importance of their culture—one suspects that the strategic argument does most of the work.

[104] See Michael Walzer, "Comment," 99, 100.

[105] See, e.g., Centre National de Documentation Pédagogique, *Programmes de l'Ecole Primaire* (Paris, 1995), 27–28.

also serves Chinese dishes on occasion.[106] I know this because I send my daughter to this school.

DEMO (*laughs*): I was wondering!

LO: It's also worth noting that every classroom in the French secular school system must display a copy of the 1789 French Declaration on the Rights of Man and Citizen. This document seems to have more emotional resonance in France than the Universal Declaration of Human Rights, just as ordinary Americans care more about the Bill of Rights in the U.S. Constitution. Needless to say, a proposal that the UDHR should have political priority over the French Declaration would be laughed out of existence in France. It's not just in Asia that the current "international" rights regime lacks credibility.

DEMO: Are *all* rights to be locally justified, in your opinion?

LO: Remember, I'm only talking about rights that are publicly contested in the international arena: social and economic rights, the rights encompassed within family and criminal law, the rights of indigenous peoples, the participatory rights inherent in Western-style democratic practices, and so on. These may well need to be renegotiated. There's a need for genuine dialogue— including more input from the non-Western world—over the shape of a truly international human rights regime.

3.2. Justifiable Constraints on Western-Style Rights

DEMO: Fair enough. However, it's worth pointing out that for dialogue and negotiation to be truly open, all participants in fact need a quite strong set of rights: the starving, those who fear arbitrary arrest, the uneducated, and victims of discrimination can't easily participate as equals in dialogues about rights. But let me just focus on one right that you seem to take for granted: the freedom of speech. This right can't be contested if you want to include the voices of minority viewpoints within traditions in the dialogue about rights. For example, you noted earlier that

[106] Interview with Josiane Volck, Responsable Pédagogique de l'Ecole Primaire, French International School, Hong Kong, 15 April 1996.

some contemporary interpreters of Islam argue that the Qur'an supports "modern" ideas about gender equality. But this is probably still a minority viewpoint within Islam, and for such a reinterpretation to become widely accepted it needs to be buttressed by a U.S.-style right to free speech so that majority viewpoints can be challenged and eventually replaced by values more supportive of women's rights.

LO: That reminds me of a point made by Abdullahi An-Na'im. He said that the right to free speech is essential to guarantee the widest possible multiplicity of voices and perspectives on the meaning and implications of cultural norms and institutions.[107] Without the freedom of speech, internal cultural discourse—and the same goes for cross-cultural dialogue—may be limited to the viewpoints of the most powerful sectors of the community.

DEMO: So we agree on the need to secure the freedom of speech, even if this right is publicly contested in the international arena. There's nothing to negotiate about the freedom of speech.

LO: I wouldn't go that far. At this East-West dialogue on human rights, everyone seemed to agree that the question of power—of who speaks for a tradition—is an important one, and that minority viewpoints must be given a say. No one questioned the need for a mechanism for change that allows for minority viewpoints to become dominant or, at least, politically relevant. But some participants questioned An-Na'im's position that this necessarily translates into an absolute right to free speech. They expressed the view that there may be some justifiable constraints on free speech.

DEMO (*raises voice*): What's that supposed to mean?

LO: Let's take an example. Dr. Sulak Sivaraksa—a Buddhist scholar, prodemocracy activist in Thailand, and nominee for the Nobel peace prize—raised an interesting challenge to the freedom of speech. In 1991 the leader of the Thai military government, General Suchinda, pressed charges against Dr. Sulak for *lèse majesté* and for defaming him in a speech given at Thammasat University. Fearing for his life, Sulak fled the country, but

[107] See An-Na'im, "The Cultural Mediation of Human Rights," esp. 151–159.

he returned in 1992, after the Suchinda government had fallen, to face the charges. In court, Sulak didn't deny that he had attacked the "dictator" Suchinda, but he did deny the charge of *lèse majesté*. He went out of his way to argue that he didn't stake his ground on an absolute right to free speech, and that he wouldn't affirm a right to insult the king and his royal family. Sulak also expressed his loyalty to the king and the royal family, referred to the many services he had performed for them, and argued that he had discussed the use of the charge of *lèse majesté* in current Thai political practice in order to highlight abuse and to point to the ways in which abuse might undermine the monarchy. In short, Dr. Sulak aimed to persuade fellow citizens that the dominant political system should be replaced with an alternative democratic political structure, but he made it explicit that he didn't want to challenge a mechanism for change that places a constraint on direct criticism of the Thai king.[108]

DEMO: Was Dr. Sulak *really* expressing his love of the monarchy, or was his defense merely strategic?

LO: Who knows? I'm not privy to Dr. Sulak's inner world. But let's assume that he, like many Thais, would feel deeply offended, if not personally harmed, by an attack on the Thai king. Is there anything wrong with a mechanism for changing a cultural tradition that has constraints like this one, endorsed by both defenders and critics of the prevailing views?

DEMO: I worry about this line of argument. It's difficult for me to go along with the suggestion that cultural traditions can provide a genuinely moral foundation for illiberal norms and political practices. This argument can be employed as an excuse to justify or "tolerate" the subjugation of members of cultural groups who've been denied the opportunity to reflect on and criticize norms of deference and humility to powerful leaders.

LO: Many East Asians think that humility is actually a virtue. Besides, I wouldn't agonize too much over this issue. There probably aren't too many other examples of illiberal constraints on

---

[108] See Sulak Sivaraksa, "Buddhism and Human Rights," paper presented at the Bangkok workshop on Cultural Sources of Human Rights in East Asia, March 1996. See also my article, "Minority Rights," 39–40.

challenges to prevailing cultural viewpoints endorsed by both political leaders and leading social critics.

DEMO: Still, your point is that a truly international rights regime shouldn't include a right to free speech.

LO: It's difficult to predict the outcome of a dialogue before it takes place. But were I to venture a guess, I'd say that most East Asians would prefer some constraints on free speech, perhaps in the form of libel laws to protect cultures from various forms of defamation and hate speech.

DEMO: It seems that my initial intuition may have been correct. Asian values in practice means curtailing Western-style liberal rights. It's all about justifying state repression.

LO: Now you're the one who's exaggerating the East-West split. Charles Taylor pointed out that relatively uncontroversial laws against hate speech also exist in Canada.[109] Expressions of anti-Semitism are against the law in Germany. These are still "liberal" countries, and there's enough free speech for minority viewpoints to become dominant.[110]

---

[109] Taylor made this point at the Bangkok workshop in March 1996. It can be argued, however, that there are different purposes behind the restrictions on speech, with implications for the justifiability of the constraint. A Western liberal might defend restrictions on hate speech on the grounds that they are necessary to prevent the alienation of some groups and to provide them with an environment in which they can function more effectively as equal citizens, whereas restrictions on criticisms of the Thai king might be more difficult to justify if they are designed to protect the authority of the monarch and tradition from critical scrutiny. It is worth noting, however, that the purpose of the latter kind of restriction may be to protect cultures from various forms of defamation and hate speech on the grounds that members of those cultures feel personally harmed by an attack on sacred aspects of their cultures (see also Bhikhu Parekh's discussion of communal libel, "The Rushdie Affair," 314–316). This is a particularly persuasive argument when both defenders and critics of the political status quo feel harmed by such an attack and thus defend the restriction on free speech, as seems to be the case in Thailand.

[110] It is perhaps even more important to separate the theory from the practice. Noam Chomsky argues that it is easier to put forward radical challenges to the status quo in Canada than in the United States, notwithstanding a formal commitment to absolute free speech in the latter country. He notes that the United

DEMO: But still, at the end of the day it comes down to the fact that proponents of Asian values favor restricting the set of rights typically enjoyed by members of liberal Western societies.

LO: That's true to a certain extent. Another example is the right to privacy, which is often defended in liberal societies regardless of the social costs. Most East Asians, I suspect, won't value this right to the same extent. Joseph Chan pointed out that in Singapore, the law empowers the police and immigration officers to perform a drug test on the urine of any person who behaves in a suspicious manner. If the result is positive, rehabilitation is compulsory. Now, Western liberals would probably see this policy as an unjustifiable invasion of privacy, but this is far less controversial in Asia. Many would consider such a restriction on freedom to be a legitimate trade-off for the value of public safety and health.[111]

DEMO: And I suspect many Americans would agree. The problem, however, is that it would probably violate the Fourth Amendment of the U.S. Constitution, which protects people against unreasonable search and seizure. And let me ask you, is that such a bad thing? A rights regime is supposed to protect unpopular individuals from the "rights-abusing" tendencies of majorities.

LO: But rights—if they're to be meaningful in practice—must have *some* grounding in the local culture. In Singapore, even opposition parties don't question the government's policy on drug searches. They do criticize other aspects of "authoritarianism"—in particular, curbs on political freedoms—but this kind of restriction on one's privacy is widely seen as necessary for promoting the common good, and oppositions figures probably know they can't get any political capital out of this issue.

States is "unusual among the industrial democracies in the rigidity of the system of ideological control exercised through the mass media" (Chomsky, *Language and Responsibility*, 8).

[111] See Joseph Chan, "The Asian Challenge to Universal Human Rights," 25, 36.

DEMO: But perhaps only a politically authoritarian regime could impose such curbs on civil freedoms.

LO: Not necessarily. In democratic South Korea, each household is required to attend monthly neighborhood meetings to receive government directives and discuss local affairs.[112]

DEMO: Really? Isn't there opposition to this policy?

LO: Not much, and that's my point. What may be viewed as a minor inconvenience in Korea would almost certainly outrage most U.S. citizens, and it's quite likely—correct me if I'm wrong—that the U.S. Supreme Court would strike down a governmental policy that forced citizens to associate for political purposes of this sort as a violation of the First Amendment.[113] Once again, most East Asians seem to be more willing to accept restraints on individual freedom in the name of serving the common good, perhaps as a legacy of the Confucian tradition.[114]

DEMO: I suspect that the women of East Asia wouldn't be so enthusiastic about preserving Confucian values. Hasn't Confucianism served to justify the worst abuses of patriarchal rule?

LO: Yes, but things aren't so clear-cut.[115] A Korean academic named Oh Byung-sun pointed out that adultery is proscribed in the Korean criminal code—guilty parties can choose between a prison term of up to two years or a fine—which he interprets as a reflection of the Confucian emphasis on preserving the integrity of family life. There's been some strong criticism of this article by criminal law specialists, but what's interesting is that many women's organizations in Korea have supported the continuance of this provision.[116]

[112] See Kim Dae Jung, "Is Culture Destiny?" 190.

[113] See Norman Redlich, Bernard Schwartz, and John Attanasio, *Understanding Constitutional Law,* 309–325.

[114] This leads to the important question of precisely how the values espoused in Confucian texts came to exert an influence on the culture of the people and how these values were transmitted from generation to generation. One can defer to the findings of sociologists and historians for this task—a recent book edited by Gilbert Rozman traces the spread of (some) Confucian values and behavior in China, Korea, and Japan (see Rozman, ed., *The East Asian Region*).

[115] See also de Bary, *Asian Values and Human Rights,* chap. 7.

[116] See Byung-Sun Oh, "Cultural Values and Human Rights," 233–234. See also Chongko Choi, "Confucianism and Law in Korea," 127–128.

DEMO (*laughs*): That's not necessarily for Confucian reasons: the law may be viewed as a weapon to keep their men in line.

LO (*smiles*): Maybe. But Korean culture has been shaped by Confucian values, and the large majority of Koreans—men and women—seem to want to keep it that way. One recent survey found that 88 percent of Koreans agreed with the statement that "It is necessary to maintain our ancestor worship tradition even in the waves of modernization," and 83 percent agreed that "Filial piety will even in the future be recognized as a virtue."[117] As you probably know, ancestor worship and filial piety are traditional Confucian virtues.

DEMO: You seem to believe that family values have been frozen in time since the days of Confucius.

LO: Don't be silly. Of course some family values—especially attitudes concerning women—have been undergoing massive change in East Asia. But other family values have been relatively stable, and this has implications for the applicability of Western-style rights in the region. People in cultures shaped by Confucianism—from state leaders to dissident activists—may well endorse some restrictions on rights that wouldn't be acceptable in Western liberal democracies.

DEMO: So it's really the influence of Confucianism.

LO: Not only. You'll find similar arguments in societies shaped by Islam. Professor An-Na'im discussed the example of corporal punishment. According to Islamic law, which is based on the Qur'an and which Muslims believe to be the literal and final word of God, and on the Sunna, or traditions of the Prophet Muhammad, theft is punishable by the amputation of the right hand and homicide by exact retribution or payment of monetary compensation.

DEMO: My God, there seems to be a serious problem with Islamic law!

LO: But that's not what adherents of Islam think. Islamic criminal law is endorsed in principle by the vast majority of Muslims

---

[117] See Geir Helgesen, *Democracy and Authority in Korea*, 128.

today. Even "liberal" critics within Islamic societies don't seek to challenge the legitimacy of Islamic criminal law.

DEMO: But corporal punishment of this sort is a gross violation of the human right not to be subjected to cruel, inhuman, or degrading treatment or punishment. I think there's a good case for outside intervention to challenge the Islamic view on corporal punishment.

LO: I'd favor a "hands-off" approach—pardon the pun. Outside intervention explicitly designed to change people's hearts and minds is almost inevitably counterproductive, and more often than not frustrated outsiders turn to coercion to try to achieve their aims (I don't want to say more about the U.S. experience in Vietnam). Besides, there may not be a need to step outside Islam to criticize the practice of corporal punishment. According to An-Na'im, Islamic law requires the state to fulfill its obligation to secure social and economic justice and to ensure decent standards of living for all its citizens *before* it can enforce those punishments. The law also provides for very narrow definitions of these offenses, makes an extensive range of defenses against the charge available to the accused person, and requires strict standards of proof. An-Na'im concludes that the prerequisite conditions for the enforcement of these punishments are extremely difficult to satisfy in practice and are unlikely to materialize in any Muslim country in the foreseeable future.[118]

DEMO: I hope that An-Na'im can persuade most Muslims to endorse his interpretation of Islamic law.

LO: It may not work. But other strategies for promoting human rights reforms are even less likely to work.

DEMO: I wonder if we're talking about a "human right" here? You say that Muslims generally endorse the *principle* of corporal punishment for theft, which means that they wouldn't want to call this a human rights issue. Internal critics could only point to the *practical* impediments to the legitimate implementation of corporal punishment under Islamic law, not to a human rights violation.

[118] See Abdullahi An-Na'im, "Toward a Cross-Cultural Approach to Defining International Standards of Human Rights," 34.

Lo: I'm not so sure. As I said, it's hard to know what would happen during the course of a truly international dialogue on human rights. It's entirely possible, for example, that Muslims and non-Muslims might agree to an international norm that human beings shouldn't be subjected to cruel and degrading punishment, though they may do so for different reasons. This reminds me of Charles Taylor's proposal for forging a global consensus on human rights. Communities that hold incompatible fundamental views on culture and worldviews can arrive at an unforced consensus on human rights if they allow for disagreement on the ultimate justifications of these norms as well as possible variations in the legal institutions and modes of enforcement.[119] I'm not saying that participants in a dialogue shouldn't try to reach consensus on basic justifications and modes of enforcement, by putting all their cards on the table at the beginning and allowing for the possibility of learning from each other. But if this doesn't work, if differences still remain, then I don't see any other alternatives to Taylor's proposal. In my view, it's the right way to create and expand a truly international rights regime.

3.3. New "Asian" Rights: Expanding the Set of Internationally Recognized Rights

DEMO (*short pause*): I'm probably beginning to sound repetitive, but I don't see how your approach to international rights discourse could *expand* the current set of international rights norms. At best, adherents of non-Western traditions will agree to human rights norms while agreeing to disagree on the liberal justification. Sometimes they'll disagree on the norm itself, as in the case of the liberal emphasis on privacy. But the end result will be to shorten the set of rights typically endorsed by Western liberals.

Lo: Not necessarily, and I'm sorry it has taken so long to get to your objection. Yes, it's true that the government-led debate on Asian values has centered on resistance to rights promoted by Westerners. East Asian intellectuals, however, add that the argu-

---

[119] See Taylor, "Conditions of an Unforced Consensus on Human Rights."

ment for respecting the norms and practices endorsed by many adherents of non-Western traditions can sometimes be employed to expand rather than restrict the set of rights typically enjoyed by members of liberal Western societies. They point out that Asian conceptions of human flourishing neglected in Western cultures could potentially be codified as rights. Consider the case of filial piety, the virtue of virtues in the Confucian tradition.[120] In East Asian societies influenced by Confucianism, there's a widespread view that children have a profound duty to care for elderly parents, a duty to be forsaken only in the most exceptional circumstances. In political practice this means that parents have a right to be cared for by their children and that it's incumbent on East Asian governments to provide the social and economic conditions that facilitate the realization of this right. Political debate tends to center on the question of whether the right to filial piety is best realized by means of a law that makes it mandatory for children to provide financial support for elderly parents—as in mainland China,[121] Japan,[122] and Singapore[123]—or whether the state should rely more on indirect methods such as tax breaks and housing benefits that simply make care for the elderly easier, as in Korea and Hong Kong.[124] But the argument that there's a pressing need to secure this right in East Asia isn't a matter of political controversy.[125]

[120] See Tu Wei-Ming, *Confucianism in a Historical Perspective*, 15.

[121] China also employs some indirect methods for promoting the obligations of filial piety: in Zhejiang province's Jinhua County, for example, villages put up public blackboards where elderly parents are supposed to jot down the sum of money given to them by their children every month (*China Daily*, 20 March 1997, 3).

[122] It is not simply a matter of political intervention to promote filial piety: "a number of architects in Japan are finding work designing multigeneration houses that enable two or three generations to live close enough that the miso soup won't get cold but far enough apart to maintain some autonomy for everybody" (Naomi Pollock, "Foundations for Japanese Life." *International Herald Tribune*, 7–8 November 1998, 8).

[123] The Singaporean judicial system does make exceptions if the parent had completely neglected his or her parental obligations.

[124] A recent survey in Hong Kong points to the importance of governmental support for home care: two-thirds of families thinking of putting elderly relatives in nursing homes said they would let them live at home if they had more governmental support (see Audrey Parwani, "Care at Home 'Best for Elderly,' " *South China Morning Post*, 17 July 1998).

[125] See Bell, "The East Asian Challenge to Human Rights," 665–666.

DEMO: Do East Asians use the language of rights when they argue about the political implications of filial piety?

LO: Not normally. But it doesn't matter if people have the same political practice in mind. Some will say that adults have a duty to care for their parents, others will say that parents have a right to be cared for by their children, but it's just two different ways of looking at the same issue.

DEMO: But I thought we were looking for an unforced consensus on human *rights*? So in terms of the international dialogue, different groups will need to frame their proposals in terms of rights.

LO: Must we stick to this terminology? As I said, I don't think it would be a good idea to try to entirely displace the language of rights, but not every single international norm governing human behavior needs to be expressed in terms of rights. Mencius said that "It is contrary to benevolence to kill one innocent man."[126] Is there really a strong case to translate this injunction against murder into a "right to life"? And there may be some positive reasons to avoid framing some international norms in the language of rights: we already discussed the widespread worry that excessive "rights talk" tends to promote the image, if not the reality, of a narrowly self-interested individual fighting for freedom from communal responsibilities.

DEMO: I worry about this line of thinking. You may know about the recent attempt by a group of former world leaders and politicians to persuade the United Nations to adopt a "Universal Declaration of Human Responsibilities." This declaration is supposed to complement the Universal Declaration of Human Rights, but its probable effect will be to dilute it. Most of this

---

[126] *Mencius*, trans. D. C. Lau (Harmondsworth: Penguin Books, 1970), VII, part A, 33. During the Qing (Ch'ing) period such injunctions against arbitrary killing did in practice function like the right to life. Geoffrey MacCormack notes that "it is obvious from the reasons sometimes given by the Board of Punishments in the Ch'ing period for its decisions in cases of homicide that the Board was concerned where an individual through no fault of his own was deprived of his life; such concern stemmed not from considerations of public order but from an expectation of the fact that an individual was normally entitled to expect that he would live for a reasonable span of years and that his life would not be cut short through the act of another" (MacCormack, *Traditional Chinese Penal Law*, 298).

new declaration consists of vacuous moralizing. Article 3, for example, affirms that "Everyone has the responsibility to promote good and to avoid evil in all things." My grandmother could have said that. Clearly there's no way to enforce this kind of aspiration, which tends to devalue the important rights that do need to be enforced.

LO: I'm not sure if it's much easier to enforce some of the declarations in the UDHR. Artitle 1 informs us that human beings "should act towards one another in a spirit of brotherhood." I wonder how a judge could enforce that one. Article 28 isn't much better: "Everyone is entitled to a social and international order in which the rights and freedoms set forth in this Declaration can be fully realized."

DEMO: Fair enough. But the more serious problem is that some sections of the Declaration of Responsibilities would be politically dangerous if they were taken seriously. Article 11, for example, begins with the statement that "All property and wealth must be used responsibly in accordance with justice and for the achievement of the human race." Does that mean people can't use their own personal possessions for their own pleasure, and that the state should force them to be more "responsible"? Or consider Article 14: "The freedom of the media is to inform the public and to criticize institutions of society and governmental actions, which is essential for a just society, must be used with responsibility and discretion. Freedom of the media carries a special responsibility for accurate and truthful reporting. Sensational reporting that degrades the human person or dignity must at all times be avoided." (*Raises voice, sounds upset.*) These are precisely the kinds of points made by dictators who want to curb the freedom of the press in their own country. I notice that the group of so-called former politicians includes Singapore's Senior Minister Lee Kuan Yew. In his quest for more "responsible" journalism, Lee has completely defanged the press corps in Singapore.[127] *The Straits Times*—once an admirably critical

---

[127] Singaporean diplomat Tommy Koh has written an opinion piece that argues for the Declaration of Human Responsibilities. He notes that "the right to free speech must be balanced by the responsibility not to defame others" ("But Consider Human Responsibilities, Too," *International Herald Tribune*, 10 December 1998). Perhaps Mr. Toh has inadvertently shed light on the Singaporean govern-

and well-respected newspaper—is now the official cheerleader for the government's policies,[128] no different than *The People's Daily.*[129] Is that what you want?

Lo: Of course not. Please, let's not forget we're basically on the same side here. I actually share your doubts about Universal Declaration of Human Responsibilities.[130] But that doesn't mean we should give up on the aspiration to expand the set of internationally recognized norms governing human behavior, not all of which need to be put in rights terms. In the case of filial piety, a Mongolian academic and political activist named Hashbat Hulan noted that the 1992 Mongolian constitution puts this norm in terms of a *duty* to care for elderly parents. Is there really a strong reason to oppose this formulation?[131]

Demo: Perhaps a deeper problem, if you want to make filial piety into an international norm, is that most people in Western societies don't seem to care all that much about filial piety. Few Westerners provide at-home care for their elderly parents anymore,[132] and I doubt that many would want to change the situa-

---

ment's underlying motivation, because Article 14 does not specifically use the term "defamation." Can it be a coincidence that the same government that uses laws against "defamation" to intimidate, sue, and bankrupt opposition politicians is now trying to elevate the responsibility not to "defame" others into an international norm?

[128] On the lack of freedom of the press in Singapore, see Francis Seow, *The Media Enthralled.*

[129] Demo is exaggerating here. The *Straits Times* does—unlike the *People's Daily*—occasionally present the views of local and foreign critics. More often than not, however, these views are heavily edited and rebutted within the same article. There are exceptions—on May 16, 1999, for example, the *Straits Times* published a relatively fair and balanced account of my interview with Asad Latif on the subject of universal human rights, which included criticisms of Singapore-style authoritarianism. Interestingly, on the previous page the *Straits Times* published an opinion piece by Mr. Latif that was critical of democracy.

[130] See also *Taking Duties Seriously.* This publication argues that current international human rights contain many references to individual duties and responsibilities, and that the risks of promulgating a new global agreement on individual duties outweigh the potential benefits.

[131] Hashbat Hulan made this point in a conversation with the author at the Bangkok workshop, March 1996.

[132] While 55 percent of Japanese aged sixty-five or older were living with their children in 1994, the comparable figures have dropped below 20 percent in West-

tion on the alleged grounds that filial piety is so important it should be elevated to the status of a state-enforced norm. And even if many people do endorse the norm of filial piety, it doesn't follow that the state should intervene to promote this norm. In my view, it's up to individuals to decide how they want to deal with their elderly parents; it shouldn't be a matter of official governmental policy.

Lo: I've already said, however, that Western liberals may need to revise their view that cultural particularities are strictly private matters. There's something disrespectful about entering cross-cultural dialogue with the assumption that any attempts by the government to promote the cultural value of filial piety should be ruled out of court.

Demo: Fine. But my point is that the value of filial piety may not resonate to the same extent in Western liberal societies. We agree that state-enforced moral obligations are supposed to protect "vital human interests," but it's not so obvious outside Confucian societies that elderly people have a vital interest in being cared for by their children. Democratic majorities in Western countries may prefer to spend state funds on nursing homes rather than contributing to at-home care for parents by family members. Even senior citizens probably won't like state-enforced filial piety. I know my mother would rather have her own money to buy a condo in Florida; she'd dread the thought of relying on me to provide help.

Lo: One of the advantages of cross-cultural dialogue is the possibility of learning from other cultural traditions. In an age when social security payments may no longer be economically sustainable at their current level, and when it's widely seen as morally acceptable in the West to commit relatively fit elderly parents to nursing homes, it may not be entirely implausible to promote the value of filial piety in liberal Western societies.

---

ern societies (see Sheldon Garon, "Japanese Are Used to the Long Arm of the State," *International Herald Tribune*, 4 June 1997, 8; also "Japanese, American Approaches Differ on Aging, Long-Term Care," *JEI Report*, no. 14A [10 April 1992]:13). More anecdotally, the prevailing American approach to dealing with elderly parents was aptly summed up by a bumper sticker I saw in New York: "Be Nice to Your Kids: They'll Choose Your Nursing Home." Americans of East Asian descent are less likely (compared to other groups in the United States) to send their parents to nursing homes.

DEMO: Maybe. But I still doubt that many Western liberals would want to include filial piety in an international document that includes rights against torture and murder. There's a risk of diluting the value of really important rights.

LO (*sighs*): What people think is important can vary from culture to culture. In any case, let's take a different example. It may be easier for a culture to learn from the moral claims it already shares with another culture, but which have somehow been neglected. The Malaysian academic and political activist Chandra Muzaffar discussed the example of the rights of the dead, as specified in the 1981 Universal Islamic Declaration of Human Rights. . . .[133]

DEMO (*interrupting*): The "rights of the dead"? What's that supposed to mean?

LO: This refers to the idea that dead persons should be treated with respect.

DEMO: That's not a distinctly Islamic idea. It would be outrageous not to allow a Christian, for example, to follow proper burial rites. Of course, the value of burying and grieving for the dead goes back further than Christianity in Western civilization. One thinks of Antigone defying Creon to give decent burial to her brothers, who lie in the dust because they defied the state.

LO: Exactly. In fact, anthropologists tell us that there's not a single culture where the fact of death is not ritualized in some way or other.[134] Strangely enough, however, none of the United Nations rights documents at the moment secures the rights of the dead. Perhaps the relevant parties will agree one day to enshrine the rights of the dead in a U.N. rights document.

DEMO: The problem is that rights typically protect the interests of real-life individuals. I worry about a slippery slope to protecting the rights of animals, trees, and rocks.

LO: I don't think Buddhists would be so casual about the rights of animals.[135] In any case, let's hope that most people will

[133] Chandra Muzaffar made this point at the Bangkok workshop, March 1996.

[134] Two anthropologists, A. L. Kroeber and Clyde Kluckhorn, note that "We know of no culture . . . where the fact of death is not ritualized" (quoted in Amitai Etzioni, "The End of Cross-Cultural Relativism," 181).

[135] The Buddhist perspective on the rights of animals is presented and defended in Jean-François Revel and Matthieu Ricard, *Le Moine et le Philosophe*, 270–

be able to distinguish between protecting significant interests and raising trivial issues to the status of an international human rights norm.

DEMO: But is there really a need to protect the rights of the dead? Human rights typically develop in response to pressing political problems—the torture of political prisoners, the massacre of minority groups, the exploitation of children in factories, and so on—but there isn't an actual crisis that would cause people to care about protecting the rights of the dead.

Lo (*grabbing a file marked with a skull and cross-bones on his bookshelf*): I'm not sure about that. Look at this issue of the *International Herald Tribune.* In the same day, two articles deal with political issues related to the rights of the dead. One article deals with the uproar caused by a Polish trading company that had planned to open a supermarket and a fast-food restaurant near Auschwitz. Jewish organizations and Israel both raised objections to the Polish government, and these plans were shelved. Another article deals with U.S. efforts to search for the remains of Korean War MIAs in North Korea.[136] In both cases, what animates the political controversy is the feeling that the dead are not being treated with sufficient respect.

DEMO: Fair enough. But even if people agree on the need to protect the rights of the dead, this may not mean much in practice. Different communities have entirely different ways of dealing with the dead. I recently saw a TV documentary about the Yamomani Indians in the Amazon Basin, who burn the dead in the village square. The dead person's relatives then eat the ashes in a banana stew. The Yamomani seemed to be profoundly disturbed when a member of a visiting camera crew informed them that Westerners prefer to bury their dead in the ground. What counts as respectful behavior toward the dead in one community may be a moral outrage in another.

---

273. The state of Bhutan has passed a national law against fishing and hunting, which is a "good example of what Buddhist ideals can accomplish at the level of a whole society" (according to the Buddhist monk Matthieu Ricard, in ibid., 221; my translation).

[136] See *International Herald Tribune*, 27 March 1996, 5, 7.

LO: But such feelings can change during the course of sustained cross-cultural dialogue as different communities come to understand and tolerate foreign ways of dealing with the dead. More important, it may not be too difficult to secure agreement on what counts as *disrespect* for the dead. Who can deny that defiling Jewish gravestones with Nazi insignia is an instance of violating the rights of the dead? Or recall the thugs who paraded that dead American soldier through the streets of Mogadishu. Perhaps enshrining the rights of the dead in an international document will make people think twice about doing this sort of thing, and if it does happen governments may have an extra incentive to bring the perpetrators to justice.

DEMO: I think I can go along with that.

LO: There you have it. International dialogue on human rights can have the effect of expanding the current Westcentric human rights regime. You need not fear that increasing participation by the non-Western world is a recipe for cutting back on rights.

DEMO (*suppressing an urge to take the last piece of grilled pork*): Well, thanks a lot. That was a wonderful meal. I hope I can remember all that we've talked about. I'll try to keep in mind some of the East Asian criticisms of traditional Western approaches to human rights.

SUMMARY

LO: Let me just clarify my position. I hope you don't think I'm anti-American or hostile to Western liberalism. My aim is simply to offer constructive suggestions for the effective promotion of human rights in the region and to suggest that there's a need for a more substantial East Asian contribution to the formulation of a truly universal rights regime.

DEMO: But not all claims emanating from the Asian values school are equally persuasive.

LO: Exactly. So I suggested that we look at the views of East Asian critical intellectuals, as opposed to relying exclusively on the views of government leaders who often seem motivated by the need to legitimize their authoritarian rule and resist foreign and local demand for human rights. We basically discussed three kinds of arguments that are important for human rights activists, beginning with trade-off arguments. You pointed out that Lee Kuan Yew–type general arguments for repression can be easily refuted on the basis of social scientific evidence. But I responded that situation-specific justifications for the temporary curtailment of particular human rights are more plausible, in the sense that they can only be countered following the acquisition of substantial local knowledge.

DEMO: But didn't you say that specific justifications for rights curtailment aren't usually put forward as cultural challenges to human rights, since both the governments in question and human rights proponents often share a common set of moral and political aspirations as an end goal?

DEMO: Yes, but cultural outlooks can affect the prioritization of rights, which matters in cases of genuine trade-offs. Then we moved on to two types of disputes that focus more directly on cultural values. First, we discussed local justifications for human rights. You suggested that human rights ideas and practices are distinctive products of the Western liberal tradition, but I noted that Asian cultural traditions can also provide the resources to justify and increase local commitment to ideas and practices similar to Western-style human rights regimes.

DEMO: This was essentially a tactical argument for the promotion of human rights in the region. You didn't challenge Western human rights principles.

LO: Yes. But then we moved on to the argument that cultural particularities in East Asia may justify a different moral standpoint vis-à-vis the human rights regime typically endorsed by Western governments, scholars, and human rights activists. There may be, in other words, morally desirable and politically viable deviations from Western positions on human rights. That's not the end of the story, however. Those involved in a cross-cultural dialogue on human rights can learn from each other; it's not just a matter of "tolerating" alternative viewpoints.

DEMO: Who can argue against that? I certainly wouldn't want to deny the possibility that East Asians, or anyone else, can make a substantial contribution to an international order based on universally accepted human rights. After all, human rights have been in constant evolution, and we should welcome the possibility of further positive contributions to this process.

LO (*smiles*): I'm glad we agree. In practice this means there's a need for more cross-cultural dialogue on human rights.

DEMO: Fine, but what do I do in the meantime, while I wait for the outcome of such a dialogue?

LO: As I said, there's already an international consensus that acts such as torture, slavery, genocide, institutionalized racism, and deprivation of food are unacceptable violations of fundamental human rights. They can never be justified, no matter what the circumstances. In such cases, there's nothing to do but to expose the gap between the rhetoric and the reality. But you seem to be dealing with the kinds of rights issues that are contested by public officials and critical intellectuals in the region, which makes things more complicated. One day, we may well achieve a genuine consensus on international norms governing these aspects of politically relevant human behavior. But meanwhile, I think it's best to refrain from firm moral and political judgments prior to detailed knowledge of local political circumstances and relevant cultural outlooks. I just don't see any other path to sound and effective political judgments. Perhaps it's late at night and I'm too tired to consider alternatives.

DEMO (*getting the message*): Well, I should be going. I hope we can pursue this dialogue in the future.

CHAPTER 2

Democratic Rights: On the Importance
of Local Knowledge

SCENE: Hong Kong, November 17, 1998. Demo has returned the previous evening from a trip to the NEHRD's Washington headquarters. He requested another meeting with Lo, and they decided to renew their discussion at Lo's office in the Bank of China building in central Hong Kong.

DEMO: Thanks for finding the time to see me again.

LO: No problem. I enjoyed our meeting last time. Besides, my business has dropped of late and I have more time to do human rights work.

DEMO: So this economic crisis does have a silver lining!

LO(*smiles*): I guess so. And for those who still have their jobs, it might allow them to spend more time with their families. People were so busy making money that they tended to neglect family obligations. (*short pause*) You said you've now settled on a program for the region?

DEMO: Yes. I did try to push for some of the issues we had discussed last time: social and economic rights, human rights education that draws on local traditions, support for elderly persons, and so on. But we have limited funds, and finally it was decided to use our resources to promote democracy in the region.

LO (*sighs*): Typical.

DEMO: Actually, it's not that typical. American efforts to promote democratic transitions have consisted mainly of support for elections. Typically, U.S. groups provided technical assistance to facilitate the administration of elections and deployed international observers to monitor them. After the elections, the Americans often packed up their bags and left. As you know, these "one-time events" rarely produced long-lasting results. So we hope to follow the example of European donors that typically place more emphasis on strengthening civil society in countries undergoing democratic transitions and consolidating democratic rule. In practice, this means providing support for local prodemocracy NGOs such as journalist associations and civic education groups. We may also back some opposition political parties if this isn't too sensitive. Basically, the aim is to keep a low profile and support local organizations that can help lay the foundations for stable democratic rule.[1]

Lo: But you don't question the end-goal itself.

DEMO: Of course not! Democracy is the ideal, isn't it?

Lo: That—and pardon me if I say this—is a Western viewpoint. I've yet to meet a Westerner who questions the need for democracy.

DEMO (*incredulous*): Don't you support democracy? I thought you were a human rights activist.

Lo: I am. But some democratic rights fall within the gray area of human rights in the sense that they're publicly contested and one needs to rely on local knowledge before making any firm political judgments.

DEMO: I must admit I'm getting a little suspicious of your brand of relativism.

Lo: I'm not sure if these labels are helpful. I'm also in favor of universal norms, but these have to emerge from a genuinely inclusive, unforced dialogue.[2] Only then could we say there's a universal consensus on human rights. And if certain rights are publicly contested, that's a sign the consensus has yet to emerge.

DEMO: But isn't there also a universal consensus in favor of democracy? Every government, no matter how authoritarian, calls itself "democratic."

---

[1] On the contrast between "American" and "European" approaches to promoting democracy, see Joel Barkan, "Can Established Democracies Nurture Democracies Abroad?" 377–381. Barkan notes, however, that the two approaches to democracy may be converging (382).

[2] See Charles Taylor, "Conditions of an Unforced Consensus on Human Rights."

LO: It depends what you mean by democracy. There are heated disputes over the meaning of the term.

DEMO: I'd begin with a minimally acceptable definition of democracy. At the very least, democracy means free and fair competitive elections under universal franchise for occupants of those posts where actual policy decisions are made, including the freedoms needed to enable opposition groups to compete effectively in these elections.[3] That's what most people mean by democracy, and it's the definition provided in international rights documents. Article 25 of the International Covenant on Civil and Political Rights, for example, includes "the right to vote and to be elected at genuine periodic elections." The elections must be universal and must be held by secret ballot in circumstances "guaranteeing the free expression of the will of the electors."[4] I don't think there's much controversy over this point.

LO: Such "international" documents—I think we talked about this last time—tend to be shaped primarily by the interests and aspirations of Western governments. Decision-makers in non-Western societies don't necessarily endorse this definition of democracy as free and fair competitive elections. In East Asia, only the governments of Japan, South Korea, Taiwan, Thailand, and the Philippines support the participatory rights inherent in Western-style democracy.[5] The rest argue that certain democratic practices, like the right to run for opposition without fear of retaliation, aren't suitable for their societies.[6] Of course, one might question the motivation of such governments. My instincts tell me that they're often making self-interested arguments to justify holding on to power, but I'm prepared to accept the possibility that they may have good reasons for opposing Western-style democracy. I just mean to say that we shouldn't pass firm judgments before we understand the local situation.

---

[3] See Andrew Nathan, "Chinese Democracy," 3. Joseph Schumpeter first formulated this "minimal" or "procedural" definition of democracy in his book *Capitalism, Socialism and Democracy* (excerpted in *Democracy*, ed. Philip Green, 88).

[4] United Nations International Covenant on Civil and Political Rights (1966), in *The Human Rights Reader*, ed. Walter Laqueur and Barry Rubin, 224. For an international law perspective, see James Crawford, *Democracy in International Law*.

[5] See Muthiah Alagappa, "Democratic Transition in Asia," 6.

[6] See, e.g., Bihahari Kausikan, "Governance That Works."

DEMO: I don't think I'll ever understand why governments jail political dissidents.

LO: Actually, most East Asian governments don't try to make us understand such ugly deeds. From the Chinese government's point of view, for example, Wei Jingsheng and Wang Dan are common criminals, not political dissidents.[7] It's the same story in Singapore: the government claims that opposition figures are guilty of such crimes as libel and tax evasion, but it won't accuse them of political crimes per se. In such cases, the task is to expose the gap between the rhetoric and the sad reality. But there are public disputes over some Western-style democratic rights, and Western human rights organizations tend to think that even the slightest deviation from the Western norm is a priori wrong, with no need to make informed judgments. In Hong Kong, political dissidents haven't (so far) been thrown in jail. But overseas human rights groups directed their fire at the Chinese government's decision to replace a partially elected legislature with a provisional legislature: in fact, this may well have been the most widely publicized human rights abuse in East Asia last year.

DEMO: Are you saying that you disagree with the conclusions of human rights groups?

LO: No. My point is that judgments that draw on fairly extensive local knowledge tend to be taken more seriously. Worse, uninformed judgments contribute to an impression of Western self-righteousness in the region, and the actions taken by Western groups are often perceived as aggressive among significant portions of the population.

DEMO: Now hold on a minute. My organization does recognize the importance of local knowledge. We take it for granted that strategies for democratization can differ from context to con-

---

[7] As President Jiang Zemin put it, Wei Jingsheng and Wang Dan "were brought to justice not because they are so-called political dissidents, but because they violated China's criminal law. Decisions on when prisoners in China's jails are released are matters for the judicial department to settle according to the law" (quoted in "Jiang Defends Rights Record," *South China Morning Post*, 20 October 1997, 7). The fact that both dissidents were (apparently) released following American pressure, however, does provide an obvious reason to question this claim.

text, and we draw on local knowledge to figure out the best way of promoting democracy in the region.[8] In one context, the main problem is ethnic conflict; in another, it's rampant corruption. We try to identify and support the groups most likely to help overcome the actual stumbling blocks to full democratization. We don't just give away funds without doing any research.

LO: But it still comes down to the purely practical issue of identifying the most effective strategies for promoting democracy. It's just a question of finding the best means of transferring Western democratic institutions to non-Western soil and making them work. You don't hold out the possibility of revising the end-goal itself.

DEMO (*raises voice*): That's correct! I don't think you can convince me that there's a superior alternative to democracy!

LO: I just mean to suggest that not all the participatory rights inherent in Western-style democratic practices are automatically accepted elsewhere and that some of this opposition may be justified. This isn't merely the viewpoint of self-interested authoritarian governments. In East Asia, critical intellectuals and even opposition groups sometimes criticize typical Western approaches to democracy. Basically, they make the same sorts of arguments for local knowledge that we discussed last time.[9]

DEMO (*skeptically*): Please refresh my memory.

1. TRADE-OFF ISSUES

1.1. On the Possibility of Decent Nondemocratic Regimes

LO: Well, the first point is that democratic rights can conflict with other goods, such as the rule of law, prosperity, and political stability. Sometimes these arguments are made in the name of

---

[8] For a useful survey of the different strategies and policy instruments for democracy promotion, see Larry Diamond, "Promoting Democracy in the 1990s."

[9] Note that this chapter draws on the same three arguments for local knowledge discussed in the previous chapter. These arguments emerged from a series of workshops between East Asian and North American intellectuals on human rights (see chap. 1, n. 19), but the workshops did not touch directly on the issue of democracy (with the exception of one paper by Xia Yong). Thus, I rely more

human rights: the claim is that pushing too hard for democracy in a particular context may have the effect of undermining other valued rights or the prospects for democracy in the long run. That's part of the rhetoric coming from the so-called pro-China camp in Hong Kong.[10] Once again, I'm not saying I agree, but there's no way to engage with such arguments without the help of detailed local knowledge.

DEMO: Rather than press this distinction between democracy and human rights, I'd argue that it's important to emphasize the interconnection between democracy and other rights. The fact of the matter is that democracy is a necessary precondition for human rights.

LO: That may be true as a general rule, but there may also be some exceptions. Looking at those exceptions, some people may think: if it worked for them, it may work for us.

DEMO: What exceptions? History is littered with the disastrous experiments of dictators. I can't think of a single good example of nondemocratic rule.

LO: I'm not sure about that. There seem to have been some pretty decent nondemocratic governments over the years.

DEMO (*raises voice*): Really? Like what? What do you have in mind?

LO: Never mind what I think, look at what great philosophers have come up with. Plato argued for a "Republic" ruled by meritocratically chosen philosopher kings and queens. He worried that democracy tends to degenerate into mob rule.[11] You'll find the same concern for meritocracy in Confucianism, which is the dominant political tradition in East Asia. Confucians argued for rule by a meritocratically chosen scholarly elite,[12] but unlike Greek thinkers they didn't even consider the possibility of giving ordinary people an equal say in the political process, so it wasn't necessary to argue against democracy. (*short pause*) My

---

on other conferences, conversations, and my own research to illustrate the arguments.

[10] This argument was pressed most forcefully by Percy Cradock (see the discussion in sec. 1.2).

[11] See Plato's argument against democracy in Book 8 of *The Republic*.

[12] See, e.g., Huang Zongxi's proposal discussed in chap. 5, sec. 2.3.

point is that philosophers from various traditions have advanced proposals for benevolent rule over the years, but that doesn't mean they were democrats.

DEMO: How did these proposals translate into practice? Plato didn't have much luck translating his political ideas into practice.

LO: Neither did Confucius. His followers, however, were more successful at shaping the values and practices of the Chinese imperial system.

DEMO: But that doesn't mean they were concerned with human rights. It's hard to think of an autocrat with a good human rights record.

LO: Once again, there are exceptions. Consider the example of Emperor Ashoka, who commanded a large Indian empire in the third century B.C. After being horrified by the carnage he saw at his own victorious battle against the king of Kalinga, Ashoka converted to Buddhism and turned his attention to public ethics and enlightened politics. He emphasized the value of tolerance for public policy, and he described the object of government as noninjury, restraint, impartiality, and mild behavior applied to all creatures.[13] Apparently he put some of these principles into practice, and Ashoka is still held up as an ideal Buddhist king today, even by political dissidents in Asia.[14]

DEMO: But his rule didn't last. No one denies that dictators can have "conversions" that make them into nice guys, but only democracy provides for stable, long-term, decent rule.

LO: There may be some counterexamples. The Tang dynasty, which lasted some three hundred years, was a period of peace, prosperity, cosmopolitan interchange of cultures, and relative freedom for women. The Tang system was the true start of the

[13] See Amartya Sen, "Human Rights and Asian Values," Morgenthau Memorial Lecture, presented at the Carnegie Council on Ethics and Public Affairs, 1 May 1997, 19–20.

[14] As Aung San Suu Kyi put it, "The Emperor Ashoka who ruled his realm in accordance with the principles of non-violence and compassion is always held up as an ideal Buddhist king" (Kyi, *Freedom from Fear and Other Writings*, 172).

civil service merit system, with national leaders being chosen by means of meritocratic examinations, and perhaps this was the key to stable rule. Men of intellectual ability became the strongest supporters of the system, and the lower classes also tended to support the established order, as there was always the possibility that a man of humble birth might pass the Confucian examinations to eventually became one of the emperor's chief ministers.[15] You also have examples of stable, long-term, "popular" nondemocratic rule in Western history. The Republic of Venice endured for about eight centuries. Like Chang'an, the capital of China during the Tang dynasty, the city was peaceful and prosperous, and it dazzled in its creativity in the arts and architecture. Democracy can't take the credit, unfortunately: the republic was ruled by aristocratic families, about 2 percent of the population, who were groomed almost from birth to participate in governing Venice. This might seem like a recipe for arbitrary rule, but the constitutional system was carefully constructed to ensure that the officials would act to secure the broader interests of the republic instead of personal or family aggrandizement. In fact, the regime suffered comparatively little from outbreaks of discontent and appears to have enjoyed widespread acceptance by the Venetian people.[16]

DEMO: That probably doesn't include the Jewish minority in Renaissance Venice. The city-state institutionalized the practice of discrimination against Jews.[17]

LO: I don't want to deny that these regimes had their faults. No doubt they would offend our modern sensibilities in some way or other.

DEMO: That's my point! None of these examples are relevant to today's world![18] In the modern world, democracy is the only

[15] See John Fairbank and Edwin Reischauer, *China: Tradition and Transformation*, 104.

[16] See Robert Dahl, *Democracy and Its Critics*, 64.

[17] See Richard Sennett, *Flesh and Stone*, chap. 7.

[18] "Demo" (Dahl's fictitious defender of democracy) makes a similar response to a defender of guardianship (who invokes the example of the Republic of Venice) in *Democracy and Its Critics*, 64. In Dahl's book, however, no attempt is made to rebut Demo's objection.

form of government that provides for the respect and protection of human rights.[19]

Lo: Well, there may be some contemporary examples of nondemocratic regimes with decent human rights records. Hong Kong was thoroughly undemocratic under the British colonial regime, but its government was relatively clean, and it provided the social conditions for the enrichment of its people. The regime had its faults, of course, but in the 1980s people's basic rights were generally secure—the government provided a broad range of civil freedoms as well as many social and economic rights—and it had a broad measure of popular support.

Demo: How do you know that? There's no way to measure support for a government that refuses to be tested at election time.

Lo: Political scientists can use survey data and poll results, just as they do in democracies. (*looking through one his drawers*) Here, look at this article by Professor Ming Sing, who teaches political science at the City University of Hong Kong. He provides plenty of empirical support for his conclusion that "a fairly stable and prosperous (city-) state, with sustained development, abundant (and perceived) prospects of upwards mobility, and a (relatively) corruption-free administration, can continue to enjoy a moderate degree of legitimacy and support—even in the absence of elections and democratic choice."[20]

Demo: Mmh. But Hong Kong in the 1980s may not be a good example of a decent nondemocracy. The Hong Kong government was democratic in the sense that colonial governors were answerable to the British Parliament. At the very least this element of democratic accountability prevented the colonial government from violating basic rights.

Lo: I'm not sure about that. British colonial rulers were often brutal elsewhere, and this didn't create much of a stir in the House of Commons. Even John Stuart Mill—one of the most famous

---

[19] The international human rights lawyer Christina Cerna also makes this argument in "Universal Democracy," 327. Cerna tests her principle against various cases, but none of her examples comes from the East Asian region.

[20] See Ming Sing, "Democratization and Economic Development," 355.

defenders of individual rights—closed his eyes to the abuses of colonial rulers in India. He really seems to have deluded himself into believing that the East India Company was exercising benevolent rule in India—training "barbarians" to "walk alone," and so on.[21]

DEMO: Fair enough. But things are different now. The media tends to put the spotlight on gross human rights abuses. The Hong Kong government, for example, couldn't have gotten away with systematic abuses of human rights in the 1980s: it would have created an uproar in Parliament. So I don't think Hong Kong is a good example of a nondemocratic regime that secures human rights.

LO: You may be right. In any case, we're talking about the past. The situation in Hong Kong changed drastically after the Chinese government's bloody crackdown on the 1989 Tiananmen movement. People began to worry about the human rights record of their future sovereign, and Hong Kong residents became more politicized. (*short pause*) Perhaps Singapore is a better example of a contemporary, decent, nondemocratic regime.[22] The Singapore government doesn't allow the full range of "Western-style" democratic rights, but it provides the conditions for political stability and economic prosperity. Simon Tay, a Nominated Member of Parliment who teaches law at the National University

[21] See J. S. Mill, "Representative Government," 176. On Mill's relationship with the East India Company, see Alan Ryan, *J. S. Mill* (London: Routledge, 1974), 193–200. More generally, the great Western critics in the humanities and social sciences—Kant, Marx, Mill, Nietzsche, and Freud—have almost nothing to say against European imperialism. The contemporary critic of imperialism needs to turn to critics of liberal rights such as Edmund Burke for inspiration: Burke argued against the East India Company's rule in India on the grounds that the company was motivated primarily by economic considerations and that it was destroying valued aspects of Indian civilization.

[22] Singapore is arguably the closest approximation of what John Rawls calls a "decent, well-ordered society" that liberal societies must tolerate if not respect and learn from. Such a society, he argues, need not be democratic, but it must be nonaggressive toward other communities, and internally it must have a "common good conception of justice," a "reasonable consultation hierarchy," and it must secure basic human rights (see Rawls, "The Law of Peoples," presented in three sessions at Princeton University's Center for Human Values, April 1995).

of Singapore, argues that Singapore's record does not show any gross human rights violations.[23]

DEMO: A "Nominated Member of Parliament"? Who nominates him?

LO: The ruling party. But he is supposed to be independent. In lieu of an opposition, Nominated Members of Parliament are meant to suggest alternatives to the ruling party's viewpoints.[24]

DEMO: (*laughs*): I have no further questions.

LO: Maybe you should ask further questions. It's best to keep an open mind about such matters.

DEMO: And what's your own view about Singapore's political system?

LO: I don't know the situation there well enough to make any firm judgments. Initially I'm not favorably predisposed, but I've met Singaporeans who like it, and some of my business clients rave about the place. So I'm prepared to accept the possibility that things may not be so bad there.

1.2. The Costs of Democratization

DEMO (*pause*): Look, I don't want to deny the possibility that there may be some nondemocratic regimes with decent human rights records. But given the choice between that kind of regime and a democracy with a good human rights record, most people would choose the latter. If you want to argue against democracy, you have to show that democratization would have a bad effect on other rights. You haven't done that.

LO: I don't want to argue against democracy. I'm worried primarily about inappropriate responses to arguments about trade-offs

[23] See Simon Tay, "Human Rights, Culture, and the Singapore Example." But if one's conception of human rights is expanded beyond basic rights against torture, political murder, and slavery to include the right to run for opposition without fear of retailiation and civil liberties such as the freedom of speech and the right to associate freely, the Singapore government's record is far more problematic (see chaps. 3 and 4).

[24] See the discussion in Garry Rodan, "State-Society Relations and Political Opposition in Singapore," 103–105.

between democratic and other rights. Western human rights groups seem to assume that democracies always promote human rights. But these arguments won't always work, given the theoretical and historical possibility of nondemocracies with decent human rights records. And if pushing for democracy in such contexts will worsen the human rights situation, this is a reason for caution.

DEMO (*frustrated*): But you haven't shown that "pushing for democracy" will undermine other rights! Where are the trade-offs you mention?

LO: Perhaps it's more obvious for those of us living in places that have been subjected to human rights abuses by democratic countries. Hong Kong was colonized by Britain as a result of the Opium War. This war was fought so that democratic Britain could continue to sell opium to the Chinese people.

DEMO: But how can you blame democracy for this war? For one thing, Britain wasn't really democratic at the time: women didn't have the vote, and there were still restrictions on the voting rights of non–property owners.

LO: Let me be more explicit about my motivation, which may clarify matters. I'm most worried about recent developments in Hong Kong, and I think that the recent push for democracy may be partly to blame. It's hard for me to say this, but Percy Cradock's critique of Patten's prodemocracy reforms may not have been completely off the mark.[25] Cradock, as you know, was the British official in charge of negotiations with China during the 1980s. He established the policy of cooperation with China, which he saw as the only way to go. Hong Kong's reversion to China in 1997 was unavoidable, and Cradock thought that it was better to have an agreed settlement with China. Confrontation, he argued, would simply leave China a free hand. So he negotiated the 1984 Joint Declaration between Britain and China on Hong Kong, as well as the 1990 agreement on directly elected seats to the Legislative Council, which provided for par-

---

[25] See Percy Cradock, "Losing the Plot in Hong Kong," *Prospect* (April 1997) 20–24. Cradock presents his case in more detail in his book *Experiences of China*, part 3.

tial democratization of Hong Kong. But when Chris Patten was appointed governor in 1992, the British abandoned this policy of cooperation, opting instead for the position that Britain should push for faster democratization in Hong Kong, with or without Chinese agreement. The rest is history. Patten proposed changes that would have had the effect of enfranchising almost the whole working population. China objected strongly to his plans, seeing them as a U-turn in British policy and a breach of previously agreed-upon constitutional and political settlements. The Chinese government was particularly incensed by the public nature of his proposals and the refusal of their request for private consultation before he went public. They made it explicit that Patten's reforms would be repealed if he went ahead with unilateral action, but Patten's reforms were pushed through the Legislative Council anyway. . . .

DEMO (*interrupting*): You say "pushed through" the legislature, almost implying that these reforms were imposed on a reluctant people. But I was under the impression that most Hong Kongers supported Patten's reforms.

LO: Actually, only about one-third of Hong Kong residents supported the political reforms.[26]

DEMO: Are you saying that most Hong Kongers don't support democracy?

LO: Yes and no. No doubt they support democracy in the abstract, if it's risk-free. Arguably, however, the only real test of commitment to democracy is whether or not people are prepared to sacrifice other valued goods in the interest of democracy. In that sense, there's far less support for democracy in Hong Kong.

[26] The Social Sciences Research Center at the University of Hong Kong summarized its poll findings at the time Governor Patten proposed his prodemocracy reforms: "The general level of support for Mr. Patten's reform proposals has stabilized at around 35% 'for,' 15% 'against,' and 50% neutral, and if people could be further sensitized (say, by a referendum) the 'for' and 'against' sides can go up by another 10%. We therefore conclude Mr. Patten can claim support, but not majority support" (Chung Ting Yiu, Robert, "Political Reforms? What the People Said; a Summary of Pop Poll Findings Up to 10 February 1993," *Social Sciences Research Center,* University of Hong Kong, 1993, 1). I thank Rowena Kwok for help in finding this and other information concerning recent Hong Kong politics.

Asked to choose between democracy on the one hand and economic prosperity and political stability on the other, one survey
found that 71.4 percent opted for the latter. Less than 20 percent chose democracy.[27]

DEMO: That's a silly question. It rarely comes down to such a radical choice between democracy and other values. In fact, democracy usually contributes to economic prosperity and political
stability.

LO: In the Hong Kong context, the choice was between increasing
the pace of democracy and a stable and peaceful handover.
Here too, large majorities favored the latter, with only 19
percent insisting on democratic demands.[28]

DEMO: But the dispute was over the pace of democratization, not
over the end itself. It was a practical, not a moral, argument
about the best way of introducing full democracy in Hong
Kong.[29]

LO: It depends what you mean by "full democracy." If this refers
to full-scale direct elections to the legislature, then you're right,
all sides agree on the end goal. The Basic Law, Hong Kong's
"mini-constitution," stipulates that a fully directly elected Legco
won't be considered until after 2007. Even the relatively conservative Chief Executive Tung Chee-hwa has endorsed the aim of

[27] See "Diaocha xianshi xuanze fanrong duo yo mingzhu" (Survey shows that
prosperity is favored over democracy), *Xing bao*, 19 October 1993. I tried to obtain more recent statistics on the willingness of Hong Kong residents to support
democracy in cases of trade-offs with other values, but one Hong Kong pollster
told me that he does not ask this question because he does not want his respondents to think that democracy can conflict with other goods.

[28] "Bacheng shimin bu man huitan wu jinzhan" (80 percent of residents unhappy with the stalemate of the negotiation), *Lianhe bao*, 18 October 1993.

[29] Arguably, the same claim can be made about mainland China. Consider the
views of Liu Ji, one of Jiang Zemin's top advisers on political reform: "Do we want
universal suffrage? Do we want direct elections? There is no question that these
certainly are our final goals. . . . We should have elections for all public positions,
including for top leaders. . . . But we can't do so immediately, because our education levels are not high enough. . . . By 2050, we will be a mid-ranking country
[in terms of GNP]. We will have basically eliminated illiteracy, and we will have
100 million or 200 million university graduates. Then we might have universal
suffrage, because education levels will be higher" (quoted in *Far Eastern Economic
Review*, 1 October 1998, 27, 28).

eventually having direct elections for all seats.[30] The Democratic Party and its allies, of course, favor a faster pace of democratization. But the question is whether or not Chris Patten's tactics helped to bring about this end, and the results are less than impressive. As you know, Beijing replied to Patten's proposals by disbanding Hong Kong's legislature after the July 1, 1997, handover and appointing a provisional legislature dominated by pro-China businessmen. Were it not for Patten's "prodemocracy" intervention, we might have been better off.

DEMO: Maybe it would have been even *worse* without Patten's proposals.

LO: That's Patten's own argument.[31] But others—including self-described liberals[32]—argue that it was a gross miscalculation on Patten's part to think that China wouldn't react badly to his refusal of their request for private consultation before he went public with his proposals.

DEMO: I must admit I haven't heard this argument before. Chris Patten is treated like a hero in the American press.

[30] See "Tung Defends 'Balanced' Pace of Democracy," *South China Morning Post*, 18 September 1997.

[31] Patten argues that Hong Kong would have been "ungovernable" if he had not taken as firm a line defending civil and political liberties in Hong Kong (Patten, "The Long View," *Far Eastern Economic Review*, Hong Kong: A New Beginning, Special 1997 Issue, 141). See also Christopher Patten, *East and West*, 69.

[32] For example, Frank Ching (senior editor of the *Far Eastern Economic Review*) writes "The new governor arrived in 1992 to implement a more assertive British policy, a departure from that of previous years. In this, he had the support of the colony's liberals, including myself. We wanted Britain to push China harder to see if more democracy could be given to Hong Kong to safeguard its autonomy. Four and a half years later, this policy has demonstrably failed. Patten pushed China extremely hard but failed to get any concessions. In a sense, this is a vindication of the previous British policy of quiet diplomacy. From the outset, Patten was handicapped by a lack of understanding of China" (Ching, "Patten: A Mixed Performance," *Far Eastern Economic Review*, 9 January 1997, 30). The relatively liberal *South China Morning Post* arrived at a similar conclusion in a critical editorial assessing Patten's legacy ("The Governor Who Tried to Get Away with It," *South China Morning Post*, 6 July 1997, 10).

Further evidence for this point of view comes from Macau: the outgoing Portuguese authorities managed to secure a portion of a directly elected legislature by means of a policy of cooperation with China ("Macau: Another End of Empire," *The Economist*, 6 January 1996, 26–27). For a detailed comparison of the democra-

LO: Well, outsiders can get it wrong if they aren't aware of the details. Perhaps it's this belief that "freedom fighters" should "stand up" for democracy, regardless of the costs. A fine principle in the abstract, but not if others are left to deal with the unpleasant consequences. Patten was gambling with the fate of the Hong Kong people—without detailed knowledge of China's ways—and leaving us to pick up the remains.

DEMO: I'll concede that it's important to have local knowledge if there's the possibility that pushing for democracy can be counterproductive in the long term, and that it seems reckless to take sides without such knowledge. But in this case I don't see the trade-off between democracy and human rights. It's just a question of whether too rapid a push for democracy can undermine the long-term prospects for democratization.

LO: It's more than that. Patten's reforms also had a bad effect on other rights. You must have heard about the Chinese government's threat to repeal civil rights legislation passed without its agreement by the Patten regime. This was widely publicized abroad.

DEMO: I've heard that the Bill of Rights is being watered down.[33]

LO: That's one issue. It must be said, however, that I never did like that Bill of Rights, which focuses exclusively on civil and political liberties. The government left out social and economic rights, claiming that they are not "justiciable"; worse, the Hong Kong Bank commissioned an opinion from the human rights lawyer Lord Lester to attack a proposal that private parties would also be bound by the Bill of Rights, and his opinion was sufficient to kill that proposal.[34] So we're left with a Bill of Rights that focuses exclusively on civil and political liberties and that implicitly reinforces the idea that the state is the only human rights violator to worry about.

DEMO: But that doesn't mean civil and political liberties aren't important!

---

tization process in Macau and Hong Kong, see Yash Ghai, "Hong Kong and Macau in Transition (I): Debating Democracy."

[33] See Margaret Ng, "Wrong Way on Rights," *South China Morning Post*, 23 January 1998.

[34] I thank Yash Ghai for this information.

Lo: Of course not, but I don't think they should be valued over social and economic rights. And it must be said that the handover hasn't—so far—had a devastating impact on civil and political liberties. The Chinese government seems to have actually relaxed its grip over Hong Kong.[35] Personally, I'm more worried about the steady erosion of social and economic rights since the change of sovereignty. This hasn't received much attention in the U.S. media, which seems almost exclusively preoccupied with reporting abuses of civil and political rights.

DEMO: Please elaborate.

Lo: The basic problem is that the new administration seems to have institutionalized rule by business tycoons. This was also a problem under the British, but it's become worse since the change of sovereignty. The chief executive, Tung Chee-hwa, is a billionaire shipping magnate. Most members of the Beijing-appointed executive council are successful businessmen: one of them, Leung Chun-ying, is a wealthy property surveyor who was put in charge of housing policy.

DEMO: A rather peculiar phenomenon! Most Americans think the Communists are taking over.

Lo: They are, in a sense. But the Chinese Communist Party has chosen to enter into a strategic alliance with Hong Kong's business class. The origins of this alliance can be traced to the early 1980s, when China first prepared for the Hong Kong handover. At that time, Chinese officials felt uncertain whether locals would support reversion—there was a general fear that Hong Kong's capitalist way of life was doomed, and everyone wanted to flee with their money. In response, China adopted the strategy of pumping money into the territory and aligning itself with local capitalists, which was seen as necessary to maintain the economic stability of Hong Kong. To earn the support of corporate bosses, the Chinese government organized timely interventions of Hong Kong companies—in one notorious example, the

[35] In his first posthandover visit, Chris Patten said that Beijing deserved some credit for "giving Hong Kong people breathing space for them to get on with their business" (quoted in "I Sympathise with Tung, Says Patten," *South China Morning Post*, 29 October 1998, 1).

Bank of China helped to save Tung Chee-hwa's Shipping Group and its public arm, Orient Overseas, from collapse. But the Chinese government consistently opposed the introduction of further social welfare programs in Hong Kong, presumably as a way of ingratiating itself with local capitalists. It seems to have worked, at least with most of my business clients—they view the so-called Communists as their allies.

DEMO: But surely local capitalists are having doubts about this alliance since the economic crisis. Isn't the crisis partly due to the change of sovereignty?[36]

LO: Not at all. The downturn would have been even worse without help from the Chinese government: interest rates were cut on the mainland last October so as to stimulate domestic demand and support the Hong Kong dollar, which was facing pressure from currency speculators.[37] Of course, this was done primarily to protect the interests of the business class in Hong Kong, and the new Beijing-appointed administration hasn't been so kind to the working class. One of the last acts of the outgoing legislature was to pass five laws significantly boosting workers' rights in Hong Kong, including one that gives unions the right to use collective bargaining to negotiate workers' salaries and another that protects workers against unfair dismissal for taking part in union activities. These laws were immediately condemned as dangerous by the chairman of the Federation of Hong Kong Industries, Henry Tang Ying-yen, who was appointed to Tung Chee-hwa's executive council. I tried to argue against this with my contacts in government, but to no avail. Following the hand-

[36] Senator Alfonse D'Amato (R-N.Y.), chairman of the powerful Senate Banking Committee, made a similar point: the dramatic fall of the Hong Kong stock market in October 1997, he said, was a "lesson for all freedom-loving people around the world" of the dangers "now that the Communist Chinese have taken over" (quoted in David Sanger, "The Real Culprit in the Asian Stock Collapse: A Bull Market in Hubris," *International Herald Tribune*, 28 October 1997, 10).

[37] This was only the second time in history that one of the world's great economic powers altered its macroeconomic policy with the aim of supporting a minor currency. (The other example is the U.S. Federal Reserve Bank's decision to cut interest rates on August 5, 1927, so that the British chancellor of the exchequer, Winston Churchill, could avoid the political ignominy of devaluating the pound against the U.S. currency after he took Britain back on to the gold standard at a cripplingly high rate.)

over, the Beijing-appointed Provisional Legislature voted to suspend those laws, with the exception of two relatively trivial ones that increased compensation for victims of occupational deafness and made May 1 into a legal holiday.[38] The new government's probusiness orientation is also being felt in other areas. The Hong Kong branch of Friends of the Earth has attacked the government's approach to the environment—our air pollution surpasses Mexico City levels on some days, but the government knocks back efforts to deal with the problem. Social welfare groups have been pressing the government to deal with Hong Kong's worsening income gap—one in seven Hong Kongers survives on less than U.S. $11 a day, and the proportion of people living below the poverty line has been increasing since 1971—but the government replies with the excuse that "Hong Kong is a free market."[39]

DEMO: But that may not be an entirely inappropriate response. Maybe there's not a lot the government can do to alleviate the plight of the worse off.

LO: That's true to a certain extent. Hong Kong's manufacturing sector has been almost entirely transferred to the mainland, with the consequence that Hong Kong's industrial workers now find it much harder to find decent jobs in Hong Kong. But it's worth keeping in mind that Hong Kong never was a pure free-market economy—in 1995–96, the government spent 47 percent of its public expenditure on social services, more than Singapore and Taiwan and only slightly less than Britain. More than half of the population lives in subsidized housing—in fact, the Hong Kong government is the world's biggest landlord.[40] Hong

[38] See my article, "Hong Kong's Transition to Capitalism," 17–21.
[39] See "Poor Left Behind as Income Gap Grows," *South China Morning Post*, 6 December 1997.
[40] The government froze land sales until March 31, 1999, in a measure to boost the economy, and in the process it admitted that Hong Kong is far from a free-market economy. Justifying the suspension of land sales, Financial Secretary Donald Tsang said, "We never try to dabble in the markets at all, but the property market is an exception. We have been intervening or messing around with that market since the 1950s, when we started to build public housing" (quoted in "$44b Rescue Bid for Economy," *South China Morning Post*, 23 June 1998, 1). Mr. Tsang neglected to mention that this "exception" accounts for most of the government's revenue (direct or indirect revenue from land transactions is also the

Kong also has most of the standard features of welfare states in Western Europe, such as a public health care system and an affordable public transport system.[41] In many ways, Hong Kong is a welfare state.

DEMO: I was referring to the recent economic crisis. It's almost inevitable that this will lead to rising unemployment and economic hardship, regardless of what the government does.

LO: I agree, but the government has ample reserves, and it can do more to alleviate the suffering of the poor. Look at this year's budget, which was designed to cope with the economic downturn. The government cut the corporate tax rate by half a percentage point to 16 percent, no doubt the lowest in the developed world. It also gave generous tax breaks to the middle class. But it has done virtually nothing for the unemployed and the poor.[42]

DEMO (*pause*): Now hold on a minute. I thought you were trying to make the point that Chris Patten's democratic reforms have had a negative impact on "nonpolitical" rights. You also said that you're most worried about the erosion of social and economic rights in Hong Kong. But now you seem to be putting most of the blame on Hong Kong's business class and the Chinese Communists! Weren't Patten's reforms partially designed to empower ordinary Hong Kongers and curb the political power of the business community? So you should be a supporter of Patten's reforms!

LO: It's the results that matter. Whatever the aim of the reforms, in practice they seem to have exacerbated the situation. For one thing, most of the political debate was centered on the appro-

---

main reason Hong Kong has such low rates of taxation), and that seven out of ten listed companies on the local stock market invest in property.

[41] See my article, "Hong Kong's Transition to Capitalism," 15–16.

[42] See "Tax Breaks 'Meaningless for Unemployed,' " *South China Morning Post*, 19 February 1998, IV. Later in the year—in the midst of Hong Kong's most serious economic downturn in thirty years—the government announced a sweeping welfare scheme that would slash welfare benefits for families of three and four by 10 percent and 20 percent, respectively, and force more than twenty thousand jobless people to do community work or lose their benefits ("20,000 Jobless to Be Put to Work," *South China Morning Post*, 10 December 1998, 1).

priate proportion of directly elected seats in the legislature, which diverted attention away from social and economic issues. And Patten's decision to confront the Chinese government had the effect of disrupting the "through train," which gave China a free hand to do exactly what it wanted. Remember, the Chinese government completely disbanded the legislature and replaced it with a group of hand-picked businessmen. The Provisional Legislature enthusiastically supported the administration's pro-business policies. I doubt things would have been as bad if Patten hadn't challenged the Chinese government. The Beijing-approved legislature in place when Patten took over—albeit less than ideal from a democratic point of view—at least could have challenged some of the administration's policies on social and economic issues.

DEMO: To be frank, I'm not sufficiently familiar with Hong Kong's history to argue with you. But that's the past. It doesn't mean people shouldn't try to pursue democracy *now*.

LO: I agree. The situation has changed. The Chinese Communists seem less defensive, and there seem to be more openings for political reform on the mainland. They may be less worried about political reform in Hong Kong, and pushing for democracy now probably won't lead to disastrous consequences. Perhaps this is the right time to demand more democracy in Hong Kong. We were pleasantly surprised by the large turnout—over 50 percent—at the recently held elections, and majority support went to the prodemocracy parties, which suggests there may be growing support for increasing the pace of democracy.[43] As you know, only one-third of the legislators were directly elected. The rest were chosen by various undemocratic means designed to stack the legislature with deputies favorable to the interests of the pro-Beijing business elite. I certainly hope that we can democratize the legislature before 2007, and I'll do my best to bring this about.

DEMO: I know I'm repeating myself, but all you're saying is that local knowledge is important for the purpose of finding effec-

---

[43] Voters may also have been motivated by more pragmatic considerations—they were promised collectible souvenir cards that also enabled them to obtain a 40 percent discount for clothes at Giordano's retail outlets on voting day.

tive arguments for democracy. Your argument against Patten is that he shouldn't have pushed so hard for democracy because his efforts had the unintentional effect of endangering civil liberties, social and economic rights, and the long-term prospects for democracy. But you're not challenging the ideal of democracy. The goal is democracy, and it's just a matter of finding the best way to get there. Whatever works is fine.

Lo (*sighs*): It's more complex that that. For one thing, there may be some constraints on what the democracy advocate can do in the name of democracy. Only yesterday I had lunch with two business clients from Singapore. They told me how much they dislike Western-style democracy, and it wasn't just a matter of timing—they genuinely seemed to prefer the nondemocratic status quo for now and the indefinite future. Their view was that a Singapore-type paternalistic regime does better at securing peace, prosperity, and the other benefits said to flow from democratic rule. Is their position so morally outrageous that I'd be justified in lying to them for the sake of promoting democracy?

DEMO: Perhaps not.

Lo: Would you support the use of an international armed force with the mission to promote democracy in Singapore?

DEMO: Of course not.

Lo: So then it's not a purely strategic matter. When we're dealing with "decent" nondemocrats, only dialogue is appropriate.

DEMO: But the end goal is still democracy. I'd try to persuade them to come around to my viewpoint, but I wouldn't change my end goal.

Lo (*raises voice*): Don't we share a conception of dialogue between equals? Don't you think we should treat our interlocutors with respect, which means trying to understand their viewpoints and allowing for the possibility that we might change our initial moral standpoints during the course of the dialogue?

DEMO (*raises voice*): Don't you think we stand up for our principles? I'm not that open-minded when it comes to questioning democratic ideals.

127

Lo: So you've decided, a priori, that there's nothing to learn from conversation with Singaporean defenders of a decent, nondemocratic regime? How can you be so sure that your initial moral standpoint is the absolute truth?

Demo (*pause*): In a way, you're more of a liberal than I am. Liberals from John Stuart Mill onward believe that the validity of beliefs can't be assured a priori, and that it's always important to keep open the possibility of changing decisions already made should better arguments come to light.[44]

Lo: That's not a distinctively liberal standpoint.[45] In any case, my point here is that we're not merely dealing with the strategic question of how best to promote democracy in a foreign land. There are constraints on the means that can be employed for promoting democracy, and if you agree with my idea of respectful dialogue between cultures we should also allow for the possibility of revising our initial prodemocracy moral standpoint during the course of dialogue with decent nondemocrats.

Demo: That sounds nice, but not all nondemocrats are decent. I'm not sure how far you'd get engaging in respectful dialogue with Adolf Hitler.

Lo: Of course I wouldn't limit myself to respectful dialogue with thugs and mass murderers. It really is a strategic matter when it comes to dealing with such people. Whatever works is fine.

Demo: Even force and fraud?

Lo: Yes. Consider the possibility that the failed assassination attempt against Hitler had been successful. Millions of lives may have been spared.

Demo: The CIA sometimes backs secret plots to assassinate perpetrators of human rights violations. This makes me feel a bit uncomfortable.

---

[44] See Charles Larmore, *The Morals of Modernity*, 184–185.

[45] The notorious critic of liberal theory, Alasdair MacIntyre, also defends the view that the "admission of fallibilism" is a condition for worthwhile cross-cultural

LO: What about employing international humanitarian armed forces in such places as Bosnia and Rwanda? It's pretty much the same idea—using force, with the possibility of bloodshed, in order to end gross violations of human rights.

DEMO: I guess that's OK, if the missions stand a good chance of success.

LO: There you have it. The use of fraud is even less controversial How many of us object to the fact that Schindler lied to the Nazis in order to save the lives of his Jewish employees?[46] If I found out that my clients said or did things that led to torture or political murder, I wouldn't think twice about lying to them to save their victims. And I definitely wouldn't keep them as my clients.

DEMO: What if your clients did things that led to the imprisonment of political critics? Would you lie to your clients in that case?

LO: Probably. Fortunately the Hong Kong government—so far—doesn't imprison its political critics. This hasn't happened in Singapore since the so-called Marxist conspiracy in 1987. But if the issue is simply arguing with Singaporeans about the merits of Western-style democratic rule in a Singaporean context, there are limits on what I could say or do to get my views across—I shouldn't resort to force or fraud. And when prodemocracy forces argue with decent nondemocrats, they should feel constrained by respect for competing ideals. So I hope by now it's clear that my defense of local knowledge isn't purely strategic.

DEMO: But what if I arrive at the conclusion that democracy isn't appropriate for a particular society at a particular time? Should I tell my boss in Washington to keep his money?

dialogue (see MacIntyre, "Incommensurability, Truth, and the Conversation between Confucians and Aristotelians about the Virtues," esp. 121).

[46] Immanuel Kant, however, argues that it is wrong to lie to a murderer, even if this assists the murderer to achieve his evil end (see also chap. 1, n. 10). The problem, according to Christine M. Korsgaard, is that Kant urges us to act in the actual world as if we were members of the ideal world (Korsgaard, "The Right to Lie."

Lo (*laughs*): I guess that would be the appropriate response. But you might find out that different justifications for democracy should be emphasized in different contexts, and you'd back groups that advance locally persuasive justifications. That would be a good way to use your money.

Demo: Please elaborate. This sounds more interesting.

2. Democratic Rights: Different Justifications

Lo: Well, as you know, we can argue for democracy in many different ways, and a persuasive justification for democracy in one context may not be as persuasive elsewhere. In other words, people may not always value democratic practices and institutions for the same reasons.

Demo: Surely most democrats care about the same things.[47]

Lo: Like what? You'll have to be more specific. Tell me why, for example, you value competitive elections.

2.1. Limiting the Power of the State

Demo (*shifting in chair*): Well, it seems so obvious. Perhaps I haven't given much thought to the matter. I guess it's about limiting power. People like to have power, but there's a problem—as Lord Acton famously put it, power corrupts, and absolute power corrupts absolutely. The main function of competitive elections is to limit political power, to prevent any one person or groups from having absolute power over the rest. Personally, I wouldn't trust any ruler who claims he should be given unlimited political power!

---

[47] The assumption that democrats are (or should be) ultimately motivated by the same considerations seems to be rather widespread in Western countries. For example, Fernando Teson writes, "People in hierarchical societies who believe in autonomy as the central moral value (for example, the democratic dissenters in China) can be validly frustrated by whatever collectivist idea is embodied in tradition (for example, the Chinese authoritarian worldview)" (Teson, "The Rawlsian Theory of International Law," 88). As will be argued below, most democratic dissenters in China justify democracy on the instrumental grounds that it

LO: Mmh, yes, I realize that's a widespread view in the United States. You guys worry most about limiting the power of the state.[48] It's perfectly understandable, given your historical experience. You fought a whole revolution just to get rid of one ruler who abused his power.

DEMO (*incredulous*): You don't think it's important to limit political power? Are Asian values any different?

LO: To a certain extent. Let's take the case of China. One of the most striking characteristics of Chinese civilization is the centrality and weight of the political order within that civilization. It's assumed that the political order has supreme jurisdiction over all domains of social and cultural life. The ruler has ultimate authority over social, religious, and family affairs.

DEMO (*raises voice*): So this is an Asian value? Totalitarian control over all parts of society?

LO: Of course I'm not talking about the whole of Asia. My impression of the religious order in India is that it's been quite independent of the political order. The Indian concept of the role of the political order as the policing agent of society seems relatively modest in its scope of application—perhaps closer to the dominant "Western" liberal model, which sharply demarcates between political and private realms. But in China—and in East Asian societies such as Japan and Korea that have been influenced by Chinese civilization—the political order presides in principle over every area of sociopolitical life.[49]

DEMO: I'm really surprised to hear you say this. How can you—a human rights activist—imply that East Asians don't mind living under rulers with absolute authority over them?

LO: We have to be careful here. I'm making a large generalization about a dominant and persistent cultural orientation. This orientation is most easily discerned when we contemplate the whole sweep of Chinese history, and it remains quite compatible

---

can contribute to nation-building. Far from believing in "autonomy as the central moral value," they turn to "collectivist" traditional ideas for inspiration.

[48] See J. H. Ely, *Democracy and Distrust*.

[49] See Benjamin Schwartz, *China and Other Matters*, chap. 9.

with vast and significant changes operative within its wide boundaries.

DEMO: But it still comes down to the point that rulers, generally speaking, are thought to have unlimited power over the whole of society. The Chinese are totalitarians at heart.

LO: It's important to separate the principle from the practice. The theoretically absolute power of the emperor was in practice subject to many constraints.[50] Moreover, this power rarely translated into an aggressive, positive interventionism in every area of life. In fact most ordinary people were left alone; the state didn't try to mobilize people in the service of collective goals. The state didn't intervene to prevent the diffusion of "deviant" religions such as Buddhism, nor did it prevent the emergence of a space for a market economy within a premodern economy.[51]

DEMO: How was the Great Wall built? That wasn't a strictly local effort, I suspect.

LO: It was started by the first emperor in Chinese history, Qin Shi Huang. Emperor Qin was inspired by the Legalist Han Fei Tzu, who argued for the widespread use of legal punishments. Han Fei did indeed argue for de facto control over all aspects of social life, to be accomplished by means of a strictly enforced

[50] As Albert Chen notes, "he was bound to observe the institutions established by the founder of the dynasty, immemorial constitutional customs, and the commands left by his ancestors. He would be conditioned by Confucian teachings (teachers were specially appointed to educate princes). He would also pay regard to how his actions would be assessed by future historians (the writing of history was an established state institution). And the institution of the counselors (*jianguan*) existed whose office expressly charged them with the solemn duty of scrutinizing the emperor's conduct and advising him where his faults lay" (Chen, "Confucian Legal Culture and Its Modern Fate," ms., 14).

The situation was not dissimilar in other East Asian countries influenced by Confucianism. According to Hyug Baeg Im, meritocratically chosen Confucian literati during the Chosun dynasty contributed to limited government by restraining the arbitrary use of power by the king and his appointed officials ("Confucianism and Democratic Civil Society in Korea," prepared for the conference on South Korea after the Democratic Transition: Political Economy and Civil Society, University of Southern California, 14–15 February 1997, 10–11). See also chap. 1, n. 51.

[51] See Schwartz, *China and Other Matters*, 133.

division of labor, with each sticking to their assigned role.[52] But Confucians generally stuck to de jure control. They believed that good government was light government, since intervention by the state—especially by legal means—was usually counterproductive.

DEMO: This may simply be a question of lacking the technological means to enforce control. Once the technology became available, there was no reason to stop. Mao—the Confucian turned Communist—took up this challenge.

LO: I don't think it's that simple.[53] The victory of the Communists can't be explained simply in terms of cultural continuity. For one thing, the Marxist-Leninist ideas themselves were of foreign origin. Perhaps the current situation in China—where significant de facto autonomy in social life is combined with the presumption of the ultimate authority of the political order—resonates more directly with traditional political culture than the aggressive totalitarian intervention under Mao's rule.[54] Of course, I'm not saying that traditional political culture shouldn't be upgraded for present-day realities. In my view, it's preferable to have even more de facto autonomy in China—which may or may not require more legal rights, depending on the local context.

DEMO: Still, don't you think it's important to challenge the traditional belief that the state should have formal authority over all social life? In my view this tradition is a recipe for disaster.

[52] Needless to say, this ruled out criticism of the government. More surprisingly, it also ruled out the opposite—as W. J. F. Jenner notes, "Qin went so far as to punish even those who praised the government" (Jenner, "China and Freedom," 74).

[53] For one thing, Jenner notes that "there was a growth between the tenth and the early twentieth centuries of de facto, unconceptualised freedoms as the state withdrew from trying to control all aspects of its subjects' lives while continuing to suppress any organisations that were not under its control" (ibid., 88). In other words, the Chinese state was *more* totalitarian in early, less technologically developed stages of Chinese history.

[54] Kuomintang rule in Taiwan under Chiang Kai-shek, which was harsh to dissidents but left the overwhelming majority alone, also seemed to resonate in deep ways with traditional Confucian ideas of political rule (see Steve Tsang, "The Confucian Tradition and Democratization," 36). See also Steve Tsang "Transforming a Party State into a Democracy," 7, 10.

Lo: Perhaps there's a cultural difference here. As I see it, there's no need to get all worked up over principles if they don't bear much on the reality. This reminds me of what a Japanese client once told me. He said he finds it strange that Americans tend to protest vehemently over minor, symbolic tributes to the "principle" of hierarchy in Japan—such as the practice of bowing at lower angles to one's "superiors"[55]—yet they don't nearly seem as perturbed by gross inequalities of income in the United States, the most unequal country in the industrialized world.[56] Americans seem to think Japan is a more hierarchical society simply because the Japanese pay more lip service to hierarchy, yet they ignore the relative equality "on the ground"![57]

DEMO: I'm not proud of income disparities in the United States, believe me. But I find it hard to believe that subordinates in Japan don't resent their inferior status. Surely they want to move up in the world, and to get the dominant status. That's why there's a need to curb the power of the dominant ones!

Lo: Power isn't always seen as a good thing. It can be a tremendous burden, filled with onerous responsibilities. That's what I see when I deal with my Japanese clients. The "inferiors" obey their "superiors"—I've yet to see a subordinate criticize a boss in front of me—but they're often rewarded by indulgence from the top.

[55] See Sandra Sugawara, "How Does Form Become Substance? Japan's Ritual Striving for Conformity and Harmony: Take a Bow!" *International Herald Tribune*, 11 June 1996, 1.

[56] According to Congressional Budget Office data, the rich are getting richer and the poor are getting poorer in the United States—between 1977 and 1994 the average after-tax income of the wealthiest 1 percent of the population rose 72 percent, after adjustment for inflation, the average after-tax income of the middle one-fifth of the population stagnated, and that of the poorest one-fifth of families shrank 16 percent (Clay Chandler, "Bull Market Bypasses Many Americans," *International Herald Tribune*, 8 April 1998). Moreover, the number of extreme poor increased from 13.9 million in 1995 to 14.6 million in 1997 (Peter Edelman, "Confronting Clinton with Facts on His Poverty Tour, *International Herald Tribune*, 9 July 1999).

[57] If Lo's diagnosis is correct, the Americans are committing what David Hall terms the "Good Principles Fallacy [which] suggests that ethical and humane principles in the absence of relevant action are of greater value than concrete and specific actions unaccompanied by high-sounding principles" ("The Irrelevance of Rights-Based Liberalism for Asian/Western Conversations," paper presented at the First International Conference on Liberal, Social and Confucian Democracy, 8–12 June 1998, Jirae and Kyongjiu, Korea, 16–17).

This seems to make life at the top as strenuous as the rituals of submissiveness on the bottom. More so, perhaps, because the responsibility for anything that may happen, even if it's entirely beyond his control, rests on the broad shoulders of the person at the top.[58] You're probably familiar with the phenomenon that Japanese company heads resign following the misdeeds of their subordinates.[59]

DEMO: Are you implying that Japanese "company men" prefer not to be promoted because they don't want to have too much power and the responsibility that goes with it?

LO: Perhaps they don't want to be promoted all the way to the top.[60]

DEMO: There's something fundamentally counterintuitive about what you're saying; it seems to go against human nature. Most rational people prefer to be offered more power—it's good for people who want it, and those afraid of the extra responsibility don't need to take it if they don't want to.[61]

---

[58] See Ian Buruma, *Behind the Mask*, 151. See also Tatsuo Inoue's argument that bosses are in a worse position relative to their employees in the sense that their heavier workload of responsibility further limits the time they can spend with their families or on personal pursuits (Inoue, "The Poverty of Rights-Blind Communality: Looking Through the Window of Japan," 537.)

[59] Consider as well the following examples of the rather demanding obligations (from a "Western" perspective) that superiors are expected to bear in the Japanese context: (1) many company bosses in Japan "see it as their duty to help their employees find a spouse" (Mary Jordan, "A Match Made by Hitachi: Finding Spouses for Workers," *International Herald Tribune*, 9 June 1997, 1); (2) a professor at Tokyo University told me that he is teaching an extra course at another university, motivated partly by the consideration that this will help one of his students find a teaching job at that university.

[60] Even some prime ministers seem to be reluctantly pushed to the top. Consider former Prime Minister Tomiichi Murayama's account of how he became chairman of the Socialist Party in 1993: "I said come what may, there's no way I can accept. . . . Then they come to me with tears in their eyes: 'Are you really going to let the party go to rot?' I gave in. There was nothing I could do. I was defeated by their tears." (quoted in Peter Landes, "Too Shy for the Big Time," *Far Eastern Economic Review*, 30 July 1998, 23). Six months later, Murayama was elected prime minister at the head of a coalition between the Socialists and the Liberal Democrats, a post he had rejected earlier.

[61] This argument parallels John Rawls's argument for the claim that a rational person always prefers to be offered more choices. Rawls's argument is criticized in my book *Communitarianism and Its Critics*, 140–141.

Lo: Prevailing ideas about rationality and human nature can vary from culture to culture. Japanese workers tend to be very dedicated to their companies, and it would be seen as disloyal or selfish to refuse a promotion simply because taking on extra responsibility might make them unhappy. So they usually take on more power, but not necessarily because they want to.

DEMO: I still wonder about this assumption that the Japanese aren't as power hungry as the rest of us. Are they really *that* different?

Lo: Perhaps it's a difference of degree.[62] But I'd have to look closer before I make any firm judgments.

DEMO: I knew you'd say that.

Lo: Do you really disagree? How can you make up your mind prior to in-depth engagement with the culture?

DEMO (*pause*): Actually, I don't want to deny the possibility that the quest for power may be more marked in some contexts than in others. Nor did I mean to imply that everyone seeks power above all else: parents may prefer to care for their children, artists may be devoted to the production of creative works, Don Juan types may use their free time to pursue their favorite activity,[63] and so on. But you can always find some who will fight for

---

[62] There is, however, one aspect of Japanese culture that seems to differ in kind from other cultures: it is the only culture that inhibits the eyeball flash recognition symbol (i.e., the slight lifting of the eyelid that is unself-consciously done when one sees a familiar face, emitted from a range of approximately ten meters in other cultures). This point was noted by Professor Dan Sperber in his lecture "A Naturalistic Approach to Culture," University of Hong Kong, 25 November 1997).

[63] There is evidence for this claim from the animal kingdom. American biologists who studied Rhesus monkeys, which tend to be ranked according to a fairly strict hierarchical system, were surprised to learn that dominant status isn't the ultimate goal of these monkeys and that the subordinate ones do not necessarily wish to move up in the world. The biologists noted that the monkeys on top were edgier, stress-prone, and seemed to burn out quickly (which lends support to Plato's argument in book nine of *The Republic* that the powerful tyrant is the unhappiest man), and the low-ranking ones seemed perfectly happy so long as they were getting mating opportunities. They also found that animals slightly lower on the social pyramid had more mating opportunities than their "superiors," apparently because the "subordinate" monkeys did not have to waste time

political power, and they're the ones to worry about. Even if it's only a minority, we still need democratic elections to keep them in check.

2.2. Democracy as a Means for Nation-Building

Lo: I'm not disputing that. My main point is that different justifications for democracy may be more persuasive in other contexts. Americans seem to worry most about curbing the power of their rulers, and democratic institutions tend to be justified on the grounds that they help to restrict and confine the powers of the state and hence to block tyranny. Your dominant political culture—correct me if I'm wrong—seems to have been shaped by your founding experience of rebellion against a monarch who abused his powers. Perhaps this outlook has been reinforced by a certain assumption that power is a good thing and that most people like to have as much as possible, with the implication that the most important political task is to limit the powers of political decision-makers. But things may be different elsewhere. As I said, the dominant tradition in China is that the political order presides in principle over all other social realms. Combine this with the experience of having been colonized and exploited by Western powers since the late nineteenth century, and you've set the terms for a very different kind of political debate. The main preoccupation this century has been with the weakness of the country vis-à-vis outside powers.[64] The question that's usually asked is how to increase power—national power in particular—not how to limit the power of rulers.

Demo: So you don't see any role for democrats.

---

defending their status, which allowed them to focus on sexual reproduction. Moreover, the "subordinates" seemed to purposely cultivate an image of inferiority to maintain their position (see Natalie Angier, "Dominant Status Isn't Everything, at Least for Monkeys," *New York Times*, 18 April 1995, C1, C6).

[64] See Andrew J. Nathan, "Sources of Chinese Rights Thinking," 161. See also Marina Svensson, "The Chinese Conception of Human Rights: The Debate on Human Rights in China, 1848–1949," Ph.D. thesis, Department of East Asian Languages, Lund University, 1996, 20. Given the presence of foreign aggression and the consequent threat to sovereignty and national survival, both Nathan and Svensson argue that human rights in the Chinese context were valued primarily as means to secure national strength.

LO: No, no, that's not what I mean. There are several ways of building up a country's power. Not surprisingly, Chinese democrats often try to show the connection between democracy and national strength. Democracy is justified on the grounds that it promotes the nation's economic and political power.

DEMO: Sounds peculiar. What's the connection here?

LO: Well, let's look at what some democrats have said over the years. (*reaching for his bookshelf*) Let me find something from a paper by Xia Yong, a legal theorist from mainland China. Here, he quotes from the early twentieth-century political reformer Wang Kang-nien. Wang said that "when people have no power, they do not realize that the nation belongs to all people, and they keep at a distance from the emperor. When the people have some power, then they will realize that the nation is their own concern, and they will be drawn close to the emperor. . . . When people's power is used to stand against the foreigners, then the force is strong."[65] The basic idea is that if people have more say in national affairs, they're more likely to do things on behalf of the nation, and the nation will be stronger in the long run.

DEMO: There seems to be a certain misunderstanding here. Democracies don't have emperors. The top political decision-makers are the people's elected representatives.

LO: But similar views were expressed after 1911, the beginning of the republican era. Let's look at the views of Sun Yat-sen, who's claimed as a "founding father" by both Taiwan and mainland China. As you know, Sun was a staunch opponent of the imperial system and the republic's first elected president. (*reaching for a book of Sun's writings on his bookshelf*) Let me try to find a good quote. Here, listen to a speech he gave in 1916, when he was no longer president. He said: "Now that our nation has become a democratic country, I will fulfill my obligations as one of its citizens. . . . Of course, all of us know, and it needs no

[65] Quoted in Xia Yong, "Political Participation: A Right or a Duty? A Historical and Cultural Perspective of China," paper presented at the workshop on New Rights Issues in Asia, Seoul National University, October 1996, 25.

repeating, that an autocratic state belongs to one man, while a republic belongs to all the people. The strength and prosperity of a nation cannot be created by the efforts of one man alone but must depend on the plans and efforts of all the people. Then only can we make China the most powerful and prosperous nation in the world. . . . Since we realize the nation belongs to all the people, every single person is fully responsible for whether the country is strong or weak."[66] Sun defended democracy on the grounds that it can help to energize the people and mobilize their force for the sake of building up the nation's economic and political power. This theme was picked up by student demonstrators in what become known as the May Fourth, 1919, movement. Their overriding objective was to "save the nation," and they strongly believed that democracy was the necessary and most economical way to achieve that end.[67]

DEMO: As you say, the main concern at the time was to "save the country" from imperialism. There was even a question of whether China could stay together as a united country. The situation today, however, is different. Outside powers no longer pose the same kind of threat to China's national pride and territorial integrity, so I suspect that these calls for "nation-building" won't motivate democrats to the same extent.

DEMO: I'm not too sure about that. The spring 1989 demonstrators in Beijing were directly inspired by their May Fourth predecessors, and they used the same kind of language. There wasn't the same preoccupation with "saving" China from foreign imperialism, but the aim was still to build up national power, and democracy was seen as the instrument. (*scanning his bookshelf for a work on the Tiananmen Square demonstrations*) Let's see what I can find. Luckily I have these materials handy—my clients often ask me to comment on political culture. (*short pause*) Here. Listen to a speech by Wuer Kaixi, one of the student leaders at Tiananmen Square. He said:

[66] Sun Yat-sen, *Selected Writings of Sun Yat-sen*, ed. J. L. Wei, R. H. Myers, and D. G. Gillin (Stanford: Hoover Institution Press, 1994), 130–131.

[67] See Tu Wei-ming, "Destructive Will and Ideological Holocaust: An Exploration of Maoism as a Source of Social Suffering in the People's Republic of China,"

At present, our country is plagued with problems such as a bloated government bureaucracy, serious corruption, the devaluation of intellectual work, and inflation, all of which severely impede us from intensifying the reforms and carrying out modernization. This illustrates that if the spirit of science and democracy, and their actual processes, do not exist, numerous and varied feudal elements and remnants of the old system, which are fundamentally antagonistic to large-scale socialist production, will reemerge in society, and modernization will be impossible. . . . [T]he spirit of May Fourth must be carried forward, and only then can our wish for a strong China be realized.

Fellow students, fellow countrymen, the future and fate of the Chinese nation are intimately linked to each of our hearts. This student movement has but one goal, that is, to facilitate the process of modernization by raising high the banners of democracy and science. . . . Our views are not in conflict with the government. We only have one goal: the modernization of China. . . . Fellow students, fellow countrymen, prosperity for our nation is the ultimate objective of our patriotic student movement."[68]

DEMO: I suspect that Wuer Kaixi was just being careful, that he didn't want to antagonize the government. He wasn't really speaking his mind.

LO: I don't think so. Remember, the students went on a hunger strike, and this was also justified in the name of nation-building. Look at this "Hunger Strike Statement of the Beijing University Students": "We do not want to die. We have a passionate desire to live on in the prime of our lives. We want to live and to learn. Our motherland is poor, and we do not want to leave her so. No, we are not seeking death, but if death could lead to improved conditions and prosperity for our country, then we ought not shun it."[69] The fact that they were willing to sacrifice themselves in the name of this ideal suggests that they meant what they said. It's also worth noting that the most outspoken dissidents

---

paper presented at the Seventh East-West Philosophers Conference, Honolulu, Hawaii, 14–15 January 1995.

[68] Wuer Kaixi, "New May Fourth Manifesto," 136–137.

[69] "Source Documents of the Democracy Movement," in *China, Marxism, and Democracy: Selections from October Review,* ed. Thomas Barrett, 165.

like Wei Jingsheng, Fang Lizhi, and Yan Jiaqi make the same point about democracy and nation-building.[70] Even in exile, when they no longer face any political constraints, they rarely change their views on this matter.

DEMO: So what you're saying is that both the Chinese government and its critics agree on the end goal—increasing China's national power—but they disagree about the way to get there. The critics favor democracy, and the government favors authoritarianism.[71]

LO: That's been the dominant approach this century, and there's no reason to expect that things will change in the foreseeable future.

DEMO: But that's a very flimsy defense of democracy, wouldn't you say? If other means are more appropriate for building a strong nation, then democracy loses its value. Don't you think democracy should be valued as an end in itself?[72]

---

[70] See Yan Jiaqi, *Toward a Democratic China*, chap. 17; Fang Lizhi, *Bringing Down the Great Wall*, 157–188; as well as the documents of democratic dissent under Chinese communism in *Wild Lily, Prairie Fire*, ed. George Benton and Alan Hunter. China's most famous dissident, Wei Jingsheng, "wrote his first articles on democracy precisely to show that the Chinese were not 'a bunch of spineless weaklings,' and that when individual citizens learned to straighten their spines China would stand tall in the world" (John Fitzgerald, "China and the Quest for Dignity," 47).

The fact that dissidents typically appeal to nation-building as an important justification for democracy is not meant to imply that Western-style liberal justifications are completely absent from the Chinese discourse on democracy: see He Baogang's discussion of the "liberal model of democracy" in his book *The Democratization of China*, chap. 3. Such justifications, however, have been, and continue to be, relatively marginal in Chinese democratic political discourse.

[71] Peter Zarrow writes, "[In the late 1980s,] The democratic elite, to a certain extent, shared a utilitarian approach with the government: how best to modernize China? This shared problematique perhaps explains why there has been a degree of mutual accommodation between the democratic elite, the government, and even the students" (Zarrow, "The Roots of Political Legitimacy in Modern Chinese Thought," paper presented at the Seventh East-West Philosophers' Conference, Honolulu, Hawaii, January 1995, 17).

[72] The editor of a recent collection of essays by some of the Western world's leading democratic theorists seems to take this view as a self-evident truth: "Few would seem to dispute today that democracy is the best form of government seen from the standpoint of principle, and that the political rights it embodies find

Lo: It doesn't matter what I think. If your concern is to promote democracy in China, you must take this into account. In a Chinese context, appeals to democracy for its own sake are far less likely to be successful than those that try to portray the instrumental value of democracy in the process of nation-building.[73] That's just the first step of the argument. The democrat should also try to show that alternative paths to nation-building are doomed to failure. This kind of argument, you won't be surprised to hear, needs to be quite detailed and historically specific. There's really no other way to get people on your side.

DEMO: There's a deep problem with your view. What if the Chinese government is right, and autocratic rule does work as a means for building up a strong nation. What should the democrat do at that point? Pack up his bags and leave?

Lo: Luckily that's not happening.

2.3. Identifying the Agents of Democratization

DEMO: But the Communist Party seems to have successfully promoted economic development the past couple of decades. Even some outsiders argue there's an authoritarian route to economic modernization in China.[74] Authoritarian development— if it works—does undermine the main plank of this instrumental justification for democracy.

Lo: Mmh, yes, you have a point there. I'm reminded about a report on the village democracy program in China. As you know, nearly one million villages directly elect committees to serve three-year terms and administer local affairs. In some villages, the system works remarkably well: elections are genuinely competitive, there's a high voter turnout, and the elected village

---

their justification above all in the worth they possess in themselves" ("Victory and Crisis: Introduction," in *Democracy's Victory and Crisis*, ed. Axel Hadenius, 7).

[73] More generally, William Alford argues that appeals to adopt human rights standards in a Chinese context are most likely to succeed if they endeavor to portray the instrumental value of rights in the process of building the state, and thereby securing the common good (see Alford, "Making a Goddess of Democracy from Loose Sand: Thoughts on Human Rights in the People's Republic of China," 75).

[74] See William M. Overholt, *China: The Next Economic Superpower.*

committees seem to play an active role in making decisions that affect the daily lives of villagers. In other places, however, the Communist Party exerts a great influence on the election, and "representatives" on the village committees enjoy little respect or autonomy. What's interesting is that most successful cases are actually to be found in the interior and poorer provinces. In Guangdong and other rich coastal areas, the interest and enthusiasm for elections seems to be relatively low. Overall, there seems to be an inverse correlation between wealth and commitment to village democracy.

DEMO: That's puzzling. What's the explanation?

LO: Well, it goes back to what we were saying. Most villagers seem to hold an instrumentalist conception of democracy. Village democracy is meant to improve the village's economic growth and development, and it loses its value if village development is already well under way. People think there's less of a need for democracy in rich areas.[75]

DEMO: That's really counterintuitive. Most political scientists think that economic development *increases* people's commitment to democracy. The standard view—known as modernization theory—is that economic growth creates a new liberalizing middle class that becomes too large and politically conscious to be willing any longer to defer to the judgments of the bureaucracy or to be excluded from the political process.[76] The more developed the country, the more important the political role of the middle class, and the greater the likelihood of a democratic transformation. But now you're saying that poor peasants are most likely to support democracy! Does that mean I should support peasants in China's poor interior provinces?

---

[75] See Allen Choate, "Local Governance in China." Choate concludes his study with the observation that "These features of village governance in China would not seem to support the opinions of those who consider the advent of village democracy as the first step in a bottom-up democratization process. Village democracy is not based on liberal, individual-rights protecting and capitalist economy-enhancing premises. Instead, it is founded on social and economic collective ideas, and is seen as a means to other ends" (16).

[76] This theory is applied to the East Asian context by Harold Crouch and James Morley in "The Dynamics of Political Change," 288.

LO: That's one possibility, if the aim is to support democracy at the local level. But villagers typically don't care much about national politics.

DEMO: So then it's the middle class.

LO: It depends on the context. In most Western countries, the prosperous middle classes may well have been the bearers of democratic ideals.[77] But in the Asia-Pacific region, they've tended to support the autocratic status quo. In fact, one might as well reverse "modernization theory": the more developed the country, the more important the political role of the middle class, and the greater the likelihood that authoritarian rule will be maintained.[78] We already talked about the conservative business elite in Hong Kong.[79] In China, the growing business class seems to be on the side of the nondemocratic status quo.[80] From the late 1980s to the mid-1990s, Malaysia and Indonesia seemed to grow more repressive as they attained new levels of prosperity, and the burgeoning middle classes seemed to actively support an increasingly authoritarian and interventionist state.[81]

DEMO: What about Korea and Taiwan? Surely the growth of a middle class favored the development of democratic rule.

LO: In Taiwan, most prodemocracy street demonstrators in the late 1980s came from the working classes. I'm told that taxi drivers were especially prominent.[82] In Korea, the urban middle classes only took to the streets in June 1987, when continued military rule threatened to bring on social chaos shortly before the 1988 Olympic Games. Moreover, it's unclear to what extent

[77] It is notoriously difficult to define the term "middle class." Usually, it seems to refer to entrepreneurs, managers, and well-to-do professionals.

[78] See David Brown and David Martin Jones, "Democratization and the Myth of the Liberalizing Middle Classes," in *Towards Illiberal Democracy in Pacific Asia*, Daniel Bell et al., and David Martin Jones, *Political Development in Pacific Asia*, esp. chap. 3.

[79] See chap. 2, sec. 1.2.

[80] See He Baogang, *The Democratic Implications of Civil Society in China*, 170; Wm. Theodore de Bary, *Asian Values and Human Rights*, 148; and Andrew Nathan, *China's Transition*, 12.

[81] See Brown and Jones, "Democratization and the Myth of the Liberalizing Middle Classes," 100–104.

[82] I thank Chris Fraser for this information.

these middle classes were liberalizing forces—the middle-class demonstrators spliced their demand for democracy with calls for "order, order."[83]

DEMO (*laughs*): Well, it's hard to make money in times of social chaos. I didn't mean to imply that the middle classes are necessarily motivated by the love of liberty. I suspect that they're generally quite selfish. But they usually find it's in their interest to push for democracy.

LO: It's different in East and Southeast Asia. Most countries in the region favored a state-led approach to economic development.[84] The middle classes were the main beneficiaries of state economic paternalism, which gave them a strong stake in the perpetuation of authoritarian rule.[85] The Malaysian middle class, for example, tends to be employed either in the state bureaucracy or in businesses with links to the ruling party.[86] In economic boom times, they benefited from the status quo, and they lacked an incentive to challenge the authorities.[87]

DEMO: But that's the past! Just about every country in the region is facing an economic crisis, and Asia's middle classes are sinking with the ship!

LO: Exactly. So now, perhaps, we should expect support for political change. The newly impoverished Asian middle classes have

[83] See Brown and Jones, "Democratization and the Myth of the Liberalizing Middle Classes," 87.

[84] On the overwhelming role of the state in the Korean case, see Seok-Choon Lew, "The Structure and Domination of Capital Accumulation in Contemporary Korea," prepared for the annual meeting of the American Sociological Association, 16–20 August 1996.

[85] See Kanishka Jayasuriya, "The Political Economy of Democratization," in *Towards Illiberal Democracy in Pacific Asia*, and Jones, *Political Development in Pacific Asia*, chaps. 1–3.

[86] See Brown and Jones, "Democratization and the Myth of the Liberalizing Middle Classes," 100.

[87] As Ming Sing puts it (with special reference to Hong Kong), "Instead of guaranteeing the growth of a pro-democracy civil society, economic development, especially of a sustained and spectacular nature, can frustrate the blossoming of pro-democracy opposition. It can raise the living standard for most people, foster satisfaction with the government and the political structure and, finally, discourage active popular participation in pro-democracy opposition" (Sing, "Economic Development, Civil Society, and Democratization in Hong

a fresh incentive to question the old authoritarian ways,[88] and they may be ready to finally adopt their "proper" role as the agents of democratic change.[89]

DEMO: Mmh. But how about China? It seems to have largely resisted the "Asian flu."

LO: So far. But in any case, there may be other prodemocracy groups besides the prosperous middle classes. Recall last time, I mentioned the importance of intellectuals in Confucian-influenced societies.[90] In China, patriotic intellectuals have long expressed the "conscience" of the nation.[91] When they're mobilized in support of democracy, they can be an incredibly powerful force.[92] Look at what happened at Tiananmen

---

Kong," 498). See also Jacques Bertrand, "Growth and Democracy in Southeast Asia," 356.

[88] As Michael Vatikiotis put it (with the Indonesian context in mind), "It boils down to this, perhaps: The middle class is intrinsically selfish and politically docile. But take away fear and threaten its comfort and it is capable of concerted action—which may become more apparent in times of economic stress" ("Caught in the Middle," *Far Eastern Economic Review*, 9 April 1998, 15). But for a more "pessimistic" view (regarding the democratic potential of the Asian middle classes in times of economic crisis), see Marie-Claire Bergère, *Le mandarin et le compradore*, 183–184.

Chandra Muzaffar notes that protest movement in Malaysia "wouldn't have happened if there hadn't been a decade of prosperity, then an economic meltdown. . . . Any abuse of power in the midst of an economic downturn generates strong feelings" (quoted in Murray Hiebert, "A Single Spark," *Far Eastern Economic Review*, 29 October 1998, 13).

[89] I argue elsewhere that this also depends on two additional factors—to what extent the authorities are held responsible for the economic crisis and whether there is a better alternative in sight (see my article, "After the Tsunami?" 22–25).

[90] See chap. 1, sec. 2.2.3.

[91] See Craig Calhoun, "Elites and Democracy," 289. See also Perry Link, *Evening Chats in Beijing*, esp. chap. 6.

[92] Yu Ying-shih discusses the important role of prodemocracy intellectuals at the turn of the century in China (see Yu, "The Idea of Democracy and the Twilight of the Elite Culture in Modern China," paper presented at the Seventh East-West Philosopher's Conference, Honolulu, Hawaii, January 1995). C. L. Chiou surveys the period between 1919 and 1990, and he notes that "in China between 4 May 1919 and 4 June 1989 and Taiwan from 28 February 1947 to 28 June 1990, most revolutionary actions, particularly the prodemocracy movements, were initiated and carried out mainly by the intellectual political elite, often in alliance with students, following almost exactly the 2,000-year Confucian scholar-official tradition" (Chiou, *Democratizing Oriental Despotism*, 3). Edward X. Gu discusses the role of Chinese intellectuals in promoting a concept of "elitist democracy"

Square—over one million ordinary Beijing citizens supported prodemocracy students and intellectuals from China's most prestigious universities.

DEMO: So perhaps the NEHRD should provide aid to prodemocracy intellectuals.

LO: But this is a sensitive area. As you know, the Chinese government keeps a watchful eye on intellectuals today. It's easy to get people in trouble, and you should be very careful before you make any final decisions.

DEMO (*pause*): I have to admit I still feel uncomfortable about this "democracy as a means for nation-building" argument. Surely there are reasons to value democracy besides the argument that it'll turn China into a xenophobic economic and military superpower. If the Chinese care most about building up national power, why should I—a foreigner—help them? If it's true that democracy will make China into a strong power—which seems to be a relative concept—I think that's something to worry about. They may want to exert more influence on the international scene, which can pose a problem for my own government. In fact, a powerful xenophobic democracy can do even more damage than a weak authoritarian government. I'm not too clear why I should be expected to promote Chinese nationalism.

LO: We're both worried by racist and strident assertions of nationalism, but there are kinder and gentler forms as well.[93] Surely there's nothing wrong with the aspiration to lift China out of poverty. And Chinese intellectuals can take pride in their language, their musical traditions, and their cultural achievements; the fact that China is a great civilization can also be seen as a

---

in the 1980s, and he argues that this proposal remains relevant to China's democratization in the future (Gu, "Elitist Democracy and China's Democratization: A Gradualist Approach Towards Democratic Transition by a Group of Chinese Intellectuals"). See also Mab Huang's account of how the efforts of four well-known academics in Taiwan in 1986, who acted as mediators between the Nationalist Party and opposition groups, helped to bring about a transition to multiparty politics in that country (Huang, "Political Ko'tung and the Rise of the Democratic Progressive Party in Taiwan: 1984–1986").

[93] See David Miller, *On Nationality*, and Yael Tamir, *Liberal Nationalism*. Both Miller and Tamir argue for the theoretical and historical possibility of relatively desirable liberal forms of nationalism.

form of national strength and celebration of Chinese rich cultural inheritance needn't take place at the cost of other cultures. Or perhaps national strength can be measured by such things as the ability to play a large role in solving the problems of the world.[94] If Chinese nationalism is here to stay, then perhaps you can support groups that are trying to develop less dangerous forms of nationalism.[95]

DEMO: I still find it strange to value democracy just on the grounds that it promotes nation-building, even if we're dealing with a "kinder and gentler" form of nationalism. What if China becomes rich and Chinese people become more cosmopolitan, in the sense that they lose their particular attachment to Chinese culture? Does that mean that they should stop caring about democracy? The kind of democracy you're talking about won't be stable.

DEMO: I really wouldn't get all worked up by hypothetical scenarios set in the indefinite future. Besides, democracy can also change people's initial outlooks. Initially, people may value democracy because they think it benefits the national community, but they may eventually come to appreciate it for other reasons as well. They may even come to value it for intrinsic reasons.[96] These additional justifications may well strengthen people's commitment to democracy and help to stabilize democracy in

[94] President Bill Clinton made similar points in his question-and-answer session with students at Beijing University ("Students Search for Answers," *South China Morning Post*, 30 June 1998, 12). Prior to this, Clinton had defended democracy in China on the instrumental grounds that it helps to promote prosperity and stability. It is quite likely that Clinton was briefed by Sinologists before he went to China, which helps to explain why the visit was perceived to be an unexpected success in both the United States and China. (I was at Beijing University at the time, and I can support this impression with my own personal experience: the main objection was to Clinton's translator, who botched several sentences.)

[95] According to Suisheng Zhao, however, nationalistic writing by Chinese intellectuals has increased in the 1990s, but few are pursuing the possibility of a relatively "modern," tolerant form of nationalism (Zhao, "Chinese Intellectuals' Quest for National Greatness and Nationalistic Writing in the 1990s," 744).

[96] Japan provides some evidence for this hypothesis: the historian Makoto Iokibe notes that initially democracy was viewed largely in instrumental terms, but that it later came to be viewed by the Japanese as a legitimate principle in itself (Iokibe, "Japan's Democratic Experience").

the long run.[97] Remember, it's only recently that democracy has come to be valued as an uncontested good in Western countries.

DEMO: That's interesting. You're suggesting that China will lose its distinctive political culture once it becomes democratic. Maybe they'll forget this romantic nonsense about "the nation"!

2.4. Nation-Building and Social Consensus in Confucian Democracies

LO: That's not what I mean. Additional justifications for democracy may become pertinent, but there's no reason to think that "the good of the nation" will lose its potency in political debate. It's instructive to look at Taiwan and Korea as a test case for what might happen in China. Both countries have been tremendously influenced by Chinese civilization—Confucianism in particular[98]—and yet they've recently adopted Western-style democratic rights. Let's find something from Taiwan. (*reaching for his bookshelf*) Here. It's the ex-Prime Minister Hau Pei-tsun. This was a speech to a graduating class in 1992. He said: "It is very important, I believe, for one to pursue success and to realize one's ideals, but it is even more important that individual successes are accumulated to make it the success of the nation as a whole, and the realization of individual ideals will result in the attainment of goals of the entire society. Only in a healthy society can the individual pursue self-improvement and be reasonably rewarded for worthy works done. What is a healthy society? It is a society that is truly free, democratic, and ruled by law. A healthy body is made up of healthy cells. Each cell is grown at a specific part of the body, absorbs a certain amount of nutrition, and performs a definite function. Individuals in the society

[97] Larry Diamond's comparative study of political cultures in newly democratizing countries shows that "democracy becomes truly stable only when people come to value it widely not solely for its economic and social performance but intrinsically for its political attributes" (quoted in Doh Chull Shin, "On the Third Wave of Democratization," 154).

[98] According to Kim Young Sam, the former president of the Republic of Korea, "conventional wisdom has it that Korea has a Confucian tradition more deeply implanted than in either China, the place of its birth, or Japan, where it has also contributed heavily to cultural patterns" (Kim, *Kim Young Sam and the New Korea*, 120).

are like cells in a body. If the body is to be healthy, each cell must grow likewise. The aim of education is to make every citizen a healthy cell in the body of our society. Ours is a free nation, in which the ethics for interpersonal relations as well as for the relationship between the individual and the group must be followed. Everyone should know precisely one's place in the society, establish one's proper relationship with the society, then set up one's personal goals and begin working for them."[99] Essentially, it's the same old story about sacrificing oneself for the good of the national community.

DEMO: But that's frightening!

LO: Well, that's the reality. The ideal of self-sacrifice for the sake of building up a strong country has deep roots in Chinese culture.[100] It's not entirely surprising that politicians in a democratic context should try to invoke this ideal in their speeches. That's one way to get votes.

DEMO: But why even bother with elections? If people are already willing to sacrifice themselves for the nation, why is there a need to give them a formal say in the political process? Democratic elections would be redundant in such a context. Unless, of course, elections serve the function of limiting the power of rulers, in which case there's no major difference between Western-style democracy and Asian democracy.

LO: It's important to look at this from the perspective of the people involved. (*shuffling through his drawer*) Here. Look at this paper, "Confucianism with a Liberal Face: The Meaning of

[99] Hau Pei-tsun, *Straight Talk*, 130. In the same vein, President Lee Teng-hui has recently invoked the German term *gemeinschaft* (a tightly knit group of people who share a common identity and purpose) to describe his vision of Taiwan's future: "Any thin and irresponsible passion can only weaken constructive forces and bring about social disorder. As long as everyone possesses a comprehension of *gemeinschaft*, many pointless struggles and conflicts would never happen" (Jason Blatt, "Taiwan Leader Urges End to Confrontation," *South China Morning Post*, 16 June 1997, 12).

[100] Even a majority of Hong Kongers—supposedly the most individualistic and liberal of East Asians—agreed with the statement that "Individual interests should sometimes be subordinated to national interests" (Timothy Ka-ying Wong, "The Ethnic and National Identities of the Hong Kong People," 118). Only 20.4 percent disagreed.

Democratic Politics in Postcolonial Taiwan." The two authors—Lily Ling and Chih-yu Shih—argue that for citizens of Taiwan, the purpose of democracy is not limited government. Rather, the Taiwanese typically support democracy as the most popular means of installing virtuous, benevolent elite rule. An electoral victory signifies the public's willingness to entrust power in a particular individual. Democratic elections, in other words, provide the ruler with an instrument for accruing moral legitimacy in the form of popular affirmation. It's a way of showing the public's trust in a ruler.[101]

DEMO: But is it really *that* different in Western countries? If people vote for particular politicians, it means that they trust them more than others. Or perhaps I should say that they *mistrust* them less than others.

LO: That's an important qualification. In Taiwan—perhaps as a residue of Confucian political culture—it's more a question of trust than of mistrust. When people vote for a ruler, they typically view him as a wise and virtuous leader, to be trusted and invested with power. More important, look at what happens *in between* elections. If democratic elections serve the function of limiting the power of rulers, one would expect checks on the ruler's power to be maintained between elections. But precisely the opposite happens in Taiwan. Recall the presidential elections last March. Lee Teng-hui won a big victory, and the former head of the KMT's Policy Institute cited this electoral landslide as evidence that confirms the public's wish that Lee wield supreme power. President Lee then proceeded to consolidate power in his own hands, stepping outside of institutional bounds and ruling with ad hoc committees. Lee justified all this by invoking the need to forge a moral consensus that would underpin social harmony and national strength. Far from being constrained by law, he pledged to *readjust* legal institutions to reflect this moral consensus: "From a position filled with a sense of mission and open-mindedness, each of you should jettison all stereotyped partisan or personal perspectives and faithfully act upon a sincere devotion to the country so as to concentrate

---

[101] See L.H.M. Ling and Chih-yu Shih, "Confucianism with a Liberal Face," 78–81.

on the issues through an overall and thorough discussion. . . . I would see to it that all your recommendations would later become realities through institutional and legal procedures."[102]

DEMO: I admit that's rather unusual rhetoric from a Western point of view. But how do you know the Taiwanese people support these attempts to consolidate power in the ruler's hands between elections?

LO: For one thing, the very fact that rulers such as President Lee resort to the rhetoric of social harmony and national strength suggests that this kind of language resonates with the people to a certain extent.

DEMO: Maybe. But fortunately, the Taiwanese can vote President Lee out of power the next time around if he loses their trust.

LO: That's one possibility. But elections can be used to reinforce the public's trust of the ruler. A fresh mandate can make it easier to mobilize the people in a more effective way. Perhaps that's what will happen in Taiwan, where the political culture seems to allow for top-down, state-initiated mobilizations.[103]

DEMO: I suspect that these traditional outlooks will disappear with time. The Taiwanese, after all, haven't had much experience with selecting national leaders—Lee Teng-hui is Taiwan's first democratically elected president. The South Koreans, in contrast, have experience with three direct presidential elections, with a very different kind of leader elected each time. And they seem to be adopting a more modern, liberal political culture.

LO: I think we have to be careful here. Professor Hahm Chaibong, who teaches political science at Yonsei University in Seoul, argues that liberal democracy has been the ideal for the majority of South Koreans in name only. He says that very few Koreans understand either the theoretical assumptions or the normative standards that undergird liberal democracy and its institutions, and that once they are explained to them few would espouse liberal democracy with as much ardor or enthusiasm. He draws on the example of President Kim Young Sam's anticorruption

[102] Quoted in ibid., 81.
[103] Ibid., 78.

reforms to show that Confucian values underpin political practices in Korea, notwithstanding liberal democratic rhetoric. In Confucian political discourse, the role of the ruler is to be the moral exemplar and to uphold the ethical order of the society. Kim could draw on this tradition to flex his moral muscles, root our corruption by extra-legal measures, "cleanse" the society, and reestablish the moral equilibrium and legitimacy that the society has lost for so long. To be sure, some critics were surprised and dismayed by President Kim's disregard of legal procedures, but Professor Hahm argues that most Koreans strongly supported Kim's actions. The president's moral stature was precisely the weapon that the illegitimate military regimes had lacked.[104]

DEMO: But Kim Young Sam's party was voted out of power in last December's elections! And Kim himself is now a reviled figure in Korea.

LO: According to Professor Hahm, President Kim fell out of favor after his son was convicted of corruption. A Confucian ruler is meant to supervise the activities of his close relatives, and he's held responsible if things go wrong. So Kim lost his moral stature and the trust of the Korean people.[105]

DEMO: In any case, it's clear that the Korean people have had enough of "Confucian" rulers. Last December, they voted for the former political dissident Kim Dae Jung, who is a strong supporter of liberal democracy.

LO: On the face of it, perhaps. In many ways President Kim Dae Jung is following in the footsteps of traditional Confucian rulers. One of his first acts was to pardon over 5.5 million Koreans who had been accused of various offenses ranging from traffic violations to clandestine visits to North Korea.

DEMO: Mmh, yes, I remember that. From a liberal perspective, this doesn't show a great deal of commitment to the rule of law!

LO: But it makes more sense from a Confucian perspective. In traditional China, emperors often issued general amnesties that

[104] See Hahm Chaibong, "The Confucian Political Discourse and the Politics of Reform in Korea," 73–74.
[105] Conversation with Professor Hahm Chaibong, March 1998.

freed criminals or reduced their sentences. On the average, the state flung open its judicial doors every two years—the docket was cleared, the jails were emptied, and the open cases were closed. This was a way for rulers to show their benevolence.[106] Of course, "the people" are also expected to reciprocate, especially in times of national emergency. There is clear evidence of this in Korea—recall that hundreds of thousands of Koreans gave their private holdings of gold to contribute to the national reserves, as a way of dealing with the economic crisis. Even some corporations agreed to pay an extra tax to help the government.

DEMO: I think that's quite admirable. But I don't see how this is supposed to show that Koreans dislike liberal democracy.

LO: What most Koreans dislike, apparently, is the absence of an official moral consensus, the sort of situation that's accepted as a fact of life in most Western liberal democracies. Korea, as you know, adopted a presidential system similar to that of France and the United States, which can lead to a situation where the executive and the legislative branches are controlled by different political parties. This is quite common in France and the United States, and competing political parties seem to work it out most of the time. But things are different in Korea—if a new president is elected and the National Assembly is dominated by opposition members, either the Assembly dissolves itself, with or without a legal basis, or members switch sides, joining the ruling party.[107]

---

[106] See Brian E. McKnight, *The Quality of Mercy*. McKnight argues, however, that general amnesties were driven more by bureaucratic imperatives (too few judges to handle too many criminals) than by imperial benevolence.

[107] The party system is weak in Korea, and politics tend to revolve around factional leaders and regions rather than policies or ideologies. The political scientist Byung-Kook Kim notes that since the democratization of the political system in 1987, "The political parties consciously avoided taking a position on socioeconomic issues and relied instead on the charisma of party bosses to mobilize mass support during elections. The consolidation of electoral democracy did not bring about a qualitative improvement in politics. The political parties remained shallow and weak as institutions, unable to offer distinctive programs and incapable of developing a complex network of organizational linkages to interest groups in the civil society. Elections were a mere popular contest of personalities, not a struggle over ideas" (Kim "The Crisis of a Success: Party Politics in Confucian Democracy of Korea," paper presented at the First International Conference

DEMO: Political opportunism is not unique to Korea!

LO: But joining the ruling party isn't necessarily seen as such. In Korea, the need to establish a moral consensus and to minimize political conflict is widely seen as something desirable, almost a moral obligation in times of crisis.[108]

DEMO: How do you know? You need to support your claims with empirical evidence.

LO (*searching though his bookshelf*): Here. Look at this book on Korean political culture. The author found that 92 percent of Koreans agreed with the statement that "The objective of democracy is harmonious social relations." Over three quarters of Koreans agreed with the statement that "The ideal society is like a family." Basically, the vast majority of Koreans seem to aspire to social and political harmony according to an ideal family relational model. Even politically interested and active students and intellectuals endorsed this outlook.[109] Naturally they expect harmony and consensus among their politicians as well!

DEMO: But I still think Kim Dae Jung himself is different. You may know about his famous article in *Foreign Affairs*, which was a response to Lee Kuan Yew's claim that Asian values differ from Western political values. Kim defends the values and institutions

---

on Liberal, Social and Confucian Democracy, 8–12 June 1998, Jirae and Kyongju, Korea, 9).

[108] President Kim has also sought to identify and blame his predecessors for the economic crisis by putting former cabinet officials on trial, perhaps as a way of "cleansing" the society of corruption. As Sheryl WuDunn notes, "It would be difficult to imagine cabinet officials in most other countries going on trial for policy failures, but South Korea has already sent two former presidents on jail for corruption and is reluctant to accept excuses for catastrophes" (WuDunn, "Goat or Scapegoat? Mr. Kang Wonders in an Angry Seoul," *International Herald Tribune*, 13 October 1998, 21).

Rather unusual practices (from the point of view of a Western liberal democrat) also occurred between January 5 and 8, 1999, when President Kim's ruling coalition (now a majority in the national assembly) "railroaded a record 130 bills and motions through the assembly. The bills were not debated or even put to a vote; they were simply declared 'passed' by Deputy Speaker Kim Bong Ho, standing in the centre of the chamber behind a phalanx of government legislators" (Shim Jae Hoon, "Push to Shove," *Far Eastern Economic Review*, 21 January 1999, 27).

[109] See Geir Helgesen, *Democracy and Authority in Korea*, 137, 122, 94, 123.

of Western liberal democracy and argues that this form of government is applicable in East Asia.

LO: But I wonder if he was really talking about the same thing. Let's look more closely at that article. (*scanning his bookshelf*) Here. Look at this passage, where Kim tries to argue that democratic ideas and institutions have roots in Asian culture. He praises the government of the Qin dynasty, founded by Qin Shi Huang, which "practiced the rule of law and saw to it that everyone, regardless of class, was treated fairly."[110] He developed this point in a keynote speech at the inaugural meeting of the Caucus of Asian Liberals and Democrats: "In China, modern systems had already been adopted 2,200 years ago. Qin Shi Huang of the Qin dynasty carried out many reforms. He abolished feudalism and replaced it with a system of counties and prefectures. The emperor enforced the rule of law, and abolished class discrimination, seeing to it that everyone was treated equally in accordance with the law. He regulated the standards for scales and measurements, thus protecting the rights and interests of the people. By organizing the letters into what we know today as Chinese characters, he greatly contributed to the development of culture and education. In light of this, I can say correctly that the fundamentally ideas of democracy existed both in Europe and Asia."[111]

DEMO: So what's the problem?

LO: I want to remind you that Kim is referring to the same emperor who built the Great Wall with slave labor. He also buried dissenting Confucians with their books. Kim likes Emperor Qin because he unified China, centralized the political system, and made the country into a great power, but that doesn't mean he was a liberal democrat. Unless you want to argue that Napolean was a great liberal democrat.

DEMO: Fair enough. But perhaps Kim Dae Jung didn't quite realize the implications of what he was saying. I'm quite sure he didn't want to defend gross abuses of human rights.

[110] See Kim Dae Jung, "Is Culture Destiny?"
[111] See Kim Dae Jung, "Democracy in Asia," in *Korea and Asia*, 211.

Lo: Yes, but my point is that his main concern seems to be increasing the country's strength and unity.[112] He'll favor whatever serves that end, whether it's democracy or Emperor Qin's strong arm measures.

DEMO: But surely Koreans value democracy for other reasons.

Lo: Yes, but I'm describing what appears to be the dominant outlook, one that's endorsed by political dissidents as well. Look again at Kim's article in *Foreign Affairs*—which was written, to remind you, while he was an opposition figure. He argues that "The invention of the electoral system is Europe's greatest accomplishment."[113] On the face of it, this is a rather startling claim—I've yet to hear a Western liberal democrat claim that the electoral system is Europe's "greatest accomplishment." Correct me if I'm wrong, but I suspect the reason is that most Western democrats value elections primarily on the grounds that they express or promote liberal values such as individual freedom and protection against arbitrary rule.[114] At the end of the day, liberal rights are more important than the electoral system per se. But most East Asians—including radical reformers like President Kim—care more about democracy than about liberalism. Put differently, they typically value democracy for nonliberal reasons.[115]

[112] Most Koreans, according to Professor Hahm Chaibong (private conversation), also defend the current, IMF-sponsored free-market reforms on the grounds that they can help to engineer national wealth and unity (as opposed, say, to valuing the free market on the grounds that it can promote a civil society composed of different groups with the capacity to check the state's power).

[113] See Kim Dae Jung, "Is Culture Destiny?" 244.

[114] As Charles Larmore puts it, "democracy is made subordinate to liberal principles precisely because the value of democratic institutions is held to lie chiefly, if not exclusively, in their being the best *means for guaranteeing* liberal freedoms" (Larmore, *The Morals of Modernity,* 182; Larmore's emphasis).

[115] For an interesting argument that prodemocracy social critics in Meiji Japan were not "philosophical liberals" (in the sense of endorsing a "philosophy of choice"), see Julia Adeney Thomas, "The Failure of Liberalism in Meiji Japan," paper delivered at Princeton University, May 1995. For an argument that "the East-Asian democratic experience shows that most countries in this region have adopted democratic institutions, but they have not followed liberal principles," see Ambrose King, "Confucianism, Modernity and Asian Democracy," paper presented at the Seventh East-West Philosophers' Conference, Honolulu, Hawaii, January 1995.

DEMO: This is getting more and more peculiar.

LO: What's peculiar—or maybe I should say "unique"—is the history of Western liberal democracy. In the modern age, liberalism preceded democracy and created a world to which the latter had to adjust. The entrenchment of liberalism prior to democratization gave Western liberal democracy its historically specific form, namely, a democracy shaped and structured within the limits set by liberal values and assumptions. But things are different in East Asia. Where there's been democratization, democratic practices have typically been grafted onto societies with different cultural backgrounds and different ways of organizing their economic life.[116] There's no reason to expect that democracy in Asia will be constrained by Western liberalism.

3. DEMOCRATIC RIGHTS: DIFFERENT CONSTRAINTS

3.1. Democracy vs. Civil Rights

DEMO: Democracy is *constrained* by liberalism? What's that supposed to mean?

LO: This shouldn't be controversial. Western liberal democracy isn't just about majority rule. The decisions of democratically elected politicians are *constrained* by respect for liberal rights. It's assumed that people will disagree about socioeconomic interests and moral outlooks, and that democratic majorities

[116] In terms of the latter point, the political economist Ronald Dore helpfully summarizes the differences between the individualistic practices of "Anglo-Saxon capitalism" and the more communitarian and elitist "East Asian capitalism" in his article "Elitism and Democracy," 67–68. Dore argues that "communitarian capitalism" is partly explained by a distinctive form of "East Asian democracy" where examination-selected officials have more power and social status than elected politicians. See also Lew Seok-Choon, "Confucian Capitalism." Lew argues that capitalism in Confucian societies was implemented from the top down by state bureaucrats, in contrast to Western capitalism, which had to break down the medieval feudal order before it could develop. As a result, "to search for models of arbitrators for the Confucian order from the Western notion of civil society that resisted feudal aristocrats, or from the labor unions that struggled against the capitalist state, is futile. The mediators of Confucian capitalism are intellectuals, not workers" (ibid., 92).

shouldn't try to push their ways onto minority viewpoints and dissenting individuals. In this sense, liberalism sets constraints on the decisions of democratically elected politicians in Western countries. Isn't that the case?

DEMO: If you mean that the state shouldn't force people to adopt a harmonious vision of the common good, then I agree. I don't know about the West as a whole, but in the United States we take it for granted that citizens disagree about things and that the political system should try to accommodate this fact.

LO: So it's not just a matter of choosing politicians who are free to do what they want.

DEMO: Of course not. In the United States, our founding fathers devised a common legal and constitutional system that secures individual rights held as trumps against "the tyranny of the majority." The decisions of democratically elected governments arc circumscribed by a constitutional bill of rights enforced by non-elected judges holding final powers of review. These rights secure the freedom to dissent from dominant views.[117]

LO: And I assume this concern for giving people the "right to differ" emerged for particular reasons. Why did this become a pressing political concern?

DEMO: Partly, to avoid religious warfare. In seventeenth-century England, Catholics and Protestants fought each other to impose their own conceptions of true faith on the other. Political thinkers such as John Locke learned the futility of this endeavor, drawing the lesson that a practicable political conception for a constitutional regime can't rest on a shared devotion to the Catholic or the Protestant faith.[118] This influenced our founding fathers, who sought to separate state and religion. The principle of religious tolerance was subsequently extended to other con-

---

[117] Akhil Reed Amar, however, argues that the original Bill of Rights was designed mostly to protect the workings of majoritarian government rather than individual liberty and unpopular minorities. The latter, more individualistic understanding of the bill, he argues, emerged in the Civil War era (Amar, *The Bill of Rights*).

[118] See John Rawls, "The Idea of an Overlapping Consensus," 13.

troversial questions. Basically the idea is that political authorities should tolerate, if not respect, competing conceptions of the good life. Didn't we talk about this last time?[119]

LO: Perhaps, but now I just want to make the obvious point that other places didn't undergo the same history. In China, for example, there wasn't the same need to devise a political system that makes the recognition of competing interests and moral ideals a primary political goal. Quite the opposite. The Chinese have historically placed great value on substantive moral consensus put forward by political authorities.[120]

DEMO: You mean there's been little tolerance for difference in China.

LO: In theory. But in practice, once again, the story's been different. Highly diverse and even conflicting modes of thought have coexisted, with little interference from the top. There's a long history of religious toleration in China—until the Taiping rebellion, when a "Christian" convert led a bloody movement for religious supremacy in the 1860s. The Taiping ruled their Nanjing-based Heavenly Kingdom for eleven years, and they implemented the most utopian, comprehensive, and authoritarian scheme for human organization ever seen in China up to that time.[121] Of course, things were even worse under the Communists, who attempted to push Marxist atheism down people's throats. Fortunately, the Communists are beginning to

[119] See chap. 1, sec. 3.1.

[120] According to Randall Peerenboom, this view is still widely shared by both state leaders and political dissidents (see Perenboom, "Confucian Harmony and Freedom of Thought," esp. 240–242). Frederic Schaffer notes that the hunger-striking students in Tiananmen Square stressed unity and elitism above majority rule, an interpretation of the Chinese word *minzhu* (misleadingly translated as "democracy") that also reflects official understandings of the term (Schaffer, *Democracy in Translation*, 143–144). It is also interesting to note that the Singaporean opposition politician Dr. Chee Soon Juan, who is critical of the way some Asian leaders use Asian values to limit human rights, proposes instead that Asian values should stand "for the ideals of wisdom and harmony" (Chee, *To Be Free*, 341).

[121] See Jonathan Spence, *The Search for Modern China*, 175. For a more detailed account of the Taiping rebellion, see Spence, *God's Chinese Son*.

retreat, and to revert to the more traditional practice of religious tolerance.

DEMO: What are you saying, exactly?

LO: My point is that there's been less of a need to institutionalize tolerance for competing viewpoints by means of individual rights in China. The history of China's defeat and humiliation at the hands of wealthier foreign powers has left more of a mark than civil strife and religious warfare. So other political concerns, such as modernization and nation-building, have been more paramount. I believe the story is similar in other parts of East Asia.

DEMO (*raises voice*): Are you saying that Asians don't care about individual rights? Is this what you're getting at?

LO: Remember, we're not talking about basic human rights. To repeat, these are not contested, at least publicly. And it could be that the Communists have done so much damage in China that it would be a mistake to rely solely, or even primarily, on traditional tolerance for religious freedom. Perhaps China needs something close to Western-style, legally enforced freedom of religion.[122] But I wouldn't expect most East Asian countries—democracy or no democracy—to place the same emphasis upon the need to secure a wide range of Western-style liberal rights. More precisely, different societies may draw the line in different places, as I tried to explain last time.[123] Asians may value the right to be cared for by adult children, whereas Westerners may place more emphasis on certain civil liberties, like the right to privacy.

DEMO: But aren't you now campaigning to maintain civil liberties in Hong Kong?

LO: Hong Kong is different. We've been colonized by Britain for so many years that our political culture has been shaped to a great extent by liberal values. Even here, however, there's a gen-

[122] See also chap. 2, sec. 2.1.
[123] See chap. 1, secs. 3.2–3.3.

eral acceptance of constraints that you wouldn't find in some Western countries. For example, all Hong Kongers are forced to carry an ID card with them at all times, and the police have the authority to stop people for random checks. This isn't particularly controversial in Hong Kong. Correct me if I'm wrong, but Americans wouldn't stand for this sort of thing.

DEMO: I know I wouldn't like it.

LO: There you have it—not everyone will accept the same constraints on democratic rights. In the United States, democratic rights—by which I mean the decision-making powers of governments elected by majority rule with universal suffrage— are constrained first and foremost by the need to protect the individual rights of vulnerable minorities and dissenting individuals. But democratic governments in Asia face somewhat different constraints.

DEMO (*skeptically*): You mean that they're not constrained by respect for civil rights?

LO: Not to the same extent. For example, you'll rarely hear about the decisions of democratic governments being overruled to protect the rights to privacy and private property—not to mention the right to buy a gun. Other concerns are typically more paramount.

3.2. Democracy vs. Social and Economic Rights

DEMO: Like what?

LO: Like economic development. As you know, post–World War II land reform in Japan, South Korea, and Taiwan was accomplished with the help of a U.S. occupying force. If instead there had been a democratic context in each country, the political process may have been captured by landed interests and it might have been more difficult to enact serious land reform. That seems to have happened in the Philippines under the democratic Aquino regime.[124]

DEMO (*surprised*): Are you suggesting the need for an occupying force to curtail the democratic process?

---

[124] See, e.g., Donald Kirk, *Looted.*

LO: Not necessarily. In Singapore, land acquisition and redistribution was done by locals. After independence, the PAP government deliberately left the right to property and to receive fair compensation out of the constitution. Instead, the government passed the Land Acquisition Act, which allowed it to acquire land for both industrial development and public housing.[125] This underpinned Singapore's spectacular economic growth, which benefited the large majority. I suspect it would have been difficult for the Singaporean government to curtail the rights to property and to fair compensation in a fully democratic context.

DEMO: Why not? If the majority benefits, they'd vote in a government that enacts such policies.

LO: You may not be working with a completely realistic picture of democracy. In a capitalist democracy, property owners tend to have greater say than their numbers warrant. You're familiar with the cynical description of American democracy: one dollar, one vote.

DEMO (*exasperated*): I really don't understand you. You're supposed to be a business consultant and a human rights activist, yet at times you sound like a raving Marxist! Are you defending the expropriation of the rich?

LO: I'm not defending anything. I'm sorry if I constantly have to repeat myself, but I'm not going to make any firm judgments before I know more about the particulars of the situation. It's like I was saying last time—we need local knowledge to decide if the government in fact faces a crisis and whether or not nonrepressive means are available for dealing with the crisis. Even then, repression would only be justified as a short-term measure.[126] Singapore is now a prosperous country, and the government can't use the same excuse to curtail rights.

DEMO: So there's nothing really to learn from the "Asian" way. I'd argue that liberal constraints on democracy are fully justified, not just in the short term but indefinitely, until we discover a better way of safeguarding people's fundamental interests. But

---

[125] See Kevin Tan, "Economic Development, Legal Reform, and Rights in Singapore and Taiwan," 268–269.

[126] See chap. 1, sec. 1.2.

Asian constraints—to be charitable—can be seen as repressive measures that governments are forced to adopt in response to a set of unlucky circumstances. More cynical people would say they're just excuses nasty dictators use to hold onto power.

Lo: I'd look more closely at the situation. Some Asian constraints on democracy may well be worth looking at, and learning from. Consider what was done to secure the relatively egalitarian distribution of wealth in modern East Asian countries.[127] In East Asia, as you know, economic policy has largely been the domain of government bureaucrats rather than elected politicians. In Korea and Singapore, the bureaucracy attracts the top talent, and it exerts a disproportionate share of political power. Basically, they followed the Japanese model, where the nearly autonomous ministries run the country on a day-to-day basis and usually exert more power than elected leaders. Budgets are prepared by the Ministry of Finance, and elected politicians make them into law. The "legislators" make laws, but they do what they're told by the bureaucrats, especially in the domain of economic policy.[128]

Demo: But politicians can criticize—and amend—their policy proposals in the legislature.

Lo: In Japan, questions in parliament are submitted a day in advance so bureaucrats can prepare answers for cabinet ministers to read out.

Demo: But surely this is a problem! How can you defend such an antidemocratic system?

Lo (*sighs*): I'm describing, not defending, and I'm trying to leave open the possibility that there may be something to learn. But it's worth noting that rule by a bureaucratic elite isn't necessarily antidemocratic. In Hong Kong, as you know, we have an exec-

---

[127] It is interesting to note that the most successful East Asian economies (prior to the 1997–98 economic crisis) were also the most egalitarian (contrary to the expectation that growth and economic equality do not mix). See Peter Passell, "Asia's Path to More Equality and More Money for All," *New York Times*, 25 August 1996, E5.

[128] See the discussion of "administrative guidance" in Shigeto Tsuru, *Japan's Capitalism: Creative Defeat and Beyond*, chap. 4.

utive-led government. In effect, what this means is that the Hong Kong government delegates much power to top civil servants known as policy secretaries. Under this system, policy secretaries devise policies, persuade the administration to support them, and then lobby the legislature to adopt them—all functions carried out by ministers in most democratic countries.

DEMO: So why do you imply the system is democratic?

LO: Because "the people" support it. Anson Chan, the chief secretary, is consistently chosen in public opinion surveys as Hong Kong's best-liked public figure, even in the midst of this economic downturn. She's far more popular than Martin Lee, the leader of the Democratic Party.[129]

DEMO: But most people vote for the democrats!

LO: Yes, but they're essentially voting for an opposition.[130] The legislature rarely initiates legislation. Even in its most democratic moments, it operates as a forum for criticizing and refining legislation proposed by the executive. Most residents of Hong Kong, including myself, would rather have the democrats perform this role, because the "pro-China" forces tend to treat the legislature as a rubber stamp. But it doesn't mean that we want the democrats to actually make the political decisions! Most people would rather stick with policy secretaries who are meritocratically selected according to rigorous criteria of excellence. For one thing, Hong Kong's welfare state developed under this system, which operated for nearly a quarter of a century.

---

[129] According to a poll taken in the midst of the economic turmoil, Anson Chan received a satisfaction rating of 86 percent and Martin Lee received a rating of 68 percent ("Tung Rating Slumps to Low of 71%," *South China Morning Post*, 18 May 1998, 1).

[130] In a recent poll, most people refused to support a government led by Lee's Democratic Party—"Only 23.8 percent in a survey on the eve of the handover in 1997 had confidence in an SAR government headed by the Democratic Party" (Lau Siu-kai, "Parties Weakened by Waning Public Trust," *South China Morning Post*, 5 January 1999, 13). This result suggests that the Democratic Party may not get most of the votes in truly open competitive elections for Hong Kong's top political decision-makers, and hence that conservative political forces in Hong Kong may actually benefit from further democratization of the legislature (contrary to their apparent fears).

DEMO: But I thought you said earlier that this "welfare state" is being eroded since the handover to China?[131]

LO: Yes, that's what's worrying me. The new administration looks set to transform the system. All incumbent secretaries, including Anson Chan, have been reappointed to their posts, but it appears that their "ministerial" functions are being curtailed by eleven executive council members, most of whom are conservative businessmen intent on dismantling Hong Kong's welfare state.[132] In terms of the actual exercise of power, this is far more significant than the composition of the legislature.

DEMO: You seem to be suggesting that the best way to secure welfare rights is to rely on rule by a bureaucratic elite. But why can't democratically elected politicians do the same thing? If most people want more welfare, why not just let the elected politicians follow the wishes of their constituents? (*reminds himself*) Oh yes, I forgot. You're a kind of Marxist who believes that democratic governments only serve the interests of a minority of capitalists.

LO: I didn't mean to sound so crude. Even if we grant the assumption that democratic governments serve the interests of the majority, this can lead to a situation where a voiceless minority is systematically excluded from benefits. Arguably, that's what Reaganomics was all about. The government enacted policies that benefited bare majorities, but an alienated and thoroughly marginalized underclass was left out of the boom. I'm not saying this was bad—if politicians want to stay in power, they have to look out for their constituents. Bureaucrats, however, can afford to enact policies that benefit more than narrow majorities. If they're dedicated and they do their job well, they can ensure that no one is left too far behind the rest. Perhaps that's what happened in East Asia.

DEMO: You seem to be comparing the *ideal* of rule by a bureaucratic elite with the *reality* of democracy. I suspect that "actually existing" bureaucrats aren't as virtuous as you seem to think.

[131] See chap. 2, sec. 1.3.

[132] See Bruce Gilley, "Movers and Shakers: Hong Kong's New Political Elite Is a Conservative, Businesslike Bunch," *Far Eastern Economic Review,* Special 1997 Issue, 32, and my article, "Hong Kong's Transition to Capitalism."

LO: I don't mean to idealize bureaucrats. But there's some evidence that equitable growth in East Asia can be partly explained by the fact that competent officials were put in charge of implementation and protected from continual political interference from legislatures and heads of government. (*scanning his bookshelf*) Mmh, I can't find the right book—my material on the East Asian "economic miracle" that combined relatively equitable distribution and fast economic growth used to be readily accessible, but my clients don't care about this stuff anymore. I'll send you the reference when I find it.[133] In any case, my point is that bureaucrats achieved remarkable results, and I doubt that democrats could have done much better. In Japan, for example, bureaucrats established an aggressive system of taxing the wealthy and subsidizing the poor—wealthy citizens must pay a 50 percent income tax, corporations pay a rate of 37.5 percent, and there's a 70 percent tax rate on inherited wealth. The result is a country where only 2 percent of households earn less than U.S. $16,000 a year, and only 2 percent have annual incomes over $160,000.[134]

DEMO: I'm still not convinced that democratic decision-makers couldn't have achieved the same results. In relatively homogenous countries such as Japan, there tends to be substantial support "on the ground" for economic distribution. And besides, what's worked in the past may not work as well in the future. We already have evidence of this in Japan—recall the government's decision to increase taxes and cut public works spending last year, at precisely the moment when the economy needed fiscal expansion. By all accounts this was a disastrous move, helping to create a deep recession in Japan and worsening the economic ills of other Asian countries.

LO: It was an unwise move at the time, but one can sympathize with the motivation behind the Japanese government's pursuit

---

[133] Lo may have been trying to locate the following book: Jose Edgardo Campost and Hilton L. Root, *The Key to the Asian Miracle: Making Shared Growth Credible* (Washington: Brookings, 1996).

[134] See Kevin Sullivan, "Has Japan Spent Too Much Sharing Wealth?" *International Herald Tribune*, 5 May 1997, 20. For some examples of how Japan's bureaucrats promoted policies that secured safety nets and avoided massive social disruption (at the cost of sacrificing some economic productivity), see Peter F. Drucker, "In Defense of Japanese Bureaucracy," 74–77.

of fiscal austerity—they're worried about the fact that the government's balance sheet will deteriorate as Japan's aging population collects its social security.

DEMO: Maybe so, but the government moved too rapidly and too far at the wrong time, and the pursuit of fiscal austerity can only hurt the future of the economy by delaying recovery.[135] Personally, I don't think the bureaucrats could have gotten away with such an unwise policy had they been challenged in a more democratic context.

LO: I don't disagree. There may well be a need to make bureaucrats more accountable and to introduce an element of transparency in the Japanese political system. There may also be a need to change the bureaucratic culture, so that decision-makers get rewarded for thinking in more innovative ways. This is particularly important in times of crisis. But that doesn't mean bureaucrats should be completely subject to control by democratically elected politicians. In Thailand, where the whole nasty thing got started, excessive "democracy" also contributed to the economic crisis—the central bank was too politicized and subject to the money politics of elected leaders.[136] Whatever emerges in the future, good governance will still require meritocratically chosen public servants who are insulated from the blandishments of special interests and the passions and whims of momentary majorities.[137]

DEMO: What you're saying, essentially, is that democracy needs to be constrained by bureaucrats who protect social and economic rights.

3.3. Democracy vs. Future Generations

LO: You can use the language of rights if you want to, but that's not typically how the locals put it. And sometimes it's difficult to understand the situation within the confines of "rights talk." For example, some East Asian governments seem to place constraints on democratic rights in order to secure the interests of

---

[135] See Edward J. Lincoln, "Japan's Financial Mess," 61.

[136] See Michael Vatikiotis, "Anatomy of a Crisis," *Far Eastern Economic Review*, 21 May 1998, 62.

[137] See Donald K. Emmerson, "Americanizing Asia?" 54.

future generations. Bureaucrats in Japan, for example, formulated policies that resulted in the accumulation of large financial reserves—Japan's foreign exchange reserves of U.S. $217 billion are far larger than those of the United States, Germany, and France combined.[138] This comes in handy, needless to say, during serious economic downturns. Contemporary Japanese can only be grateful for the frugality of their ancestors and the wise policies of their bureaucratic rulers.[139]

DEMO: But democratic rulers could have done the same thing!

LO: Perhaps. But we'd be entering the realm of counterfactual history, and people may not be willing to risk tampering with a system that works. Besides, there are good reasons for thinking that it's more difficult to encourage savings in relatively democratic contexts. Consider the justification behind a new political institution known as the "Elected Presidency" in Singapore.[140] Actually, this is a misnomer, because the president isn't elected by means of universal suffrage; rather, he's chosen by a group of establishment figures hand-picked by the ruling PAP. His main task is to protect Singapore's huge reserves against the "democratic" temptation to spend them for the sake of getting votes. Apparently, this institution is designed to compensate for a flaw in democratic countries—the fact that future generations don't have any say—and this is one way to safeguard their interests.

DEMO: You mean their rights.

LO: You can say that if you want. But I don't know of any Western constitutional system that enshrines the rights of future generations.

DEMO: Perhaps that's because it's a dubious concept. There's something strange about the attempt to restrict the rights of real people to protect the "rights" of hypothetical future generations.

---

[138] *International Herald Tribune*, 7 May 1997.

[139] Korea, of course, is different—the country seemed to be living beyond its means, which contributed to the economic crisis. According to Professor Hahm Chaibong, most Koreans regret this lapse from traditional Confucian frugality, and they view it as their moral duty to restore this value in the future.

[140] See Kevin Tan and Lam Peng Er, eds., *Managing Political Change in Singapore*.

LO: You do have debates over the rights of the unborn in the United States. In any case, things may seem less strange upon close examination. It seems strange to me that there's a debate in the United States over the constitutional "right" to buy a gun.

DEMO: The original idea was that ordinary citizens should have the means to overthrow an unjust government. This sort of argument makes less sense in the nuclear age, but it's important to place this argument in its historical context.

SUMMARY

LO: Exactly! And the same thing is true when we're talking about democracy in Asia! All I've been saying is that we can't make sound moral judgments concerning the desirability of Western-style democratic rights without taking into account the local context!

DEMO: But you seem to be drawing mainly on prudential, rather than moral, reasons. Your argument against Patten's democratic reforms was essentially that he picked the wrong time to promote democracy in Hong Kong. You didn't question the ideal itself.

LO (*sighs*): Not that again. Yes, I did say that local knowledge is important for determining the right time and place to promote democracy. But this debate isn't just about finding the right strategies to implement an end that's beyond question—I also said that prodemocracy forces should leave open the possibility of revising their initial moral standpoints when engaged in a dialogue with decent nondemocrats.

DEMO: Well, that worries me. I'm still disturbed by the implication that the context-sensitive observer might settle on the conclusion that "Western" democracy isn't appropriate in an Asian context.

LO: Why not look at the bright side? I argued that local knowledge can shed light on the most persuasive justifications for democracy in particular contexts. Surely that's a relevant issue for prodemocracy activists!

DEMO: You pointed out that Chinese democrats tend to favor democracy because it contributes to nation-building. I also feel uncomfortable with that argument, though I recognize there may be good strategic reasons to take it seriously.

LO: Once again, I think it's more than just a question of strategy. Perhaps if you really immerse yourself in the Chinese context, you'll come to sympathize with this sort of argument. I think it's important to go into this with an open mind, and to allow for the possibility that you might change your initial standpoint.

DEMO: What anthropologists call "going native."

LO: That's not what I mean. It's not a question of replacing one set of cultural values with a brand new set. But *aspects* of original belief systems may change, and we might find ourselves sincerely committed to this or that new idea.

DEMO: So I should "sincerely" appeal to the nation-building argument for democracy in China.

LO: If you're not really persuaded by your own argument, it will be difficult to persuade the intended audience.

DEMO: I think that's less of a problem in my case—I'm supposed to award grants to locals, not to join the political fray myself. If the grantee is sincere, that may be enough.

LO: Perhaps. In any case, it's not just a question of finding the right *justification* for Western-style democracy. It's also important to leave open the possibility that the decisions of democratically elected politicians may be *constrained* differently in different places. In other words, the political *practices* themselves may vary—the U.S. Supreme Court will check the power of elected politicians in the name of protecting civil and political rights, and bureaucrats may do the same in Japan in the name of promoting equality and the interests of future generations. I'm not defending any particular constraint on democracy, but I do think it's important to learn more about the local context before making any firm judgments.

DEMO (*pause*): My next stop is Singapore. As you point out, Singaporean representatives have been prominent in defending an Asian alternative to Western democracy. Several Asian coun-

171

tries—including China—look up to the "Singapore model" as a kind of formula for carrying out economic reform while maintaining political stability.[141] So I think it's important to understand what's going on there. I'm not going there with high hopes, but maybe you're right, I should try to figure out what's really going on I make up my mind.

Lo: Not a bad idea. Even if you don't change your mind about the universal applicability of Western-style democracy, you might come up with locally persuasive justifications for democracy. Let me know if you have any success!

Demo (*yawning*): I'll do that. But first I have to overcome one of the most troublesome impediments to sustained cross-cultural dialogue—jet lag. So if you don't mind, I'm going to have to wrap this up.

---

[141] See Meredith Woo-Cumings, "The 'New Authoritarianism' in East Asia," 413.

PART II

THE PROS AND CONS OF DEMOCRACY IN SINGAPORE:

A FICTITIOUS DIALOGUE WITH LEE KUAN YEW

*

CHAPTER 3

Is Liberal Democracy
Suitable for Singapore?

SCENE: Singapore, February 18. 1999. Demo meets Senior Minister Lee Kuan Yew to begin a prearranged discussion on the pros and cons of democracy in Singapore. Lee Kuan Yew, "the grand old man of Asia,"[1] has established himself as the leading spokesman for "Asian" guardianship as against "Western" democracy, with Singapore, the country Lee founded and ruled for over three decades as prime minister, held up as the ideal Asian regime. In this chapter, Demo presents several liberal justifications for democracy derived from the recent Western experience, which Lee tries to rebut on the basis of Singapore's particular history and special circumstances.

DEMO: First of all, I'd like to thank you for agreeing to the interview.

LEE: Not at all. I've heard good things about you. I make it a point of discussing political issues with influential visitors from Western countries.

DEMO: Is it just a matter of getting your viewpoint across to a Western audience?

LEE: It's more than that. Singaporeans may also have something to learn—that's why I asked Ezra Vogel, who teaches East Asian studies at Harvard, to give a tutorial to our entire cabinet when he came to Singapore. Of course, the visitor himself may change his perspective. I've met regularly with Samuel Huntington over the years, and he's come to change his view about the universality of Western values and democratic practices. Several years ago he predicted that Singapore's clean and efficient system of government was doomed to failure because it wasn't underpinned

---

[1] Nathan Gardels, "Interview with Lee Kuan Yew," 3.

by democratic values and institutions. But last time he came to see me, he said, "My book [*The Clash of Civilizations and the Remaking of the World Order*] is coming out," and I said, "I'm ready for it." He said, "No, you'd be surprised. I've got some good things to say of you." And he has. He lauds the Singapore government's initiative to define a Singaporean cultural identity that distinguishes Singapore from the West, and he's shown the courage to drop his previous assumption that Western civilization and values are universal. He accepts that America cannot remake the world in its own image.[2]

1. DEMOCRACY DEFINED AS FREE AND FAIR COMPETITIVE ELECTIONS

DEMO: Well, I disagree with Huntington. But I'm still fairly new in Singapore, and I'm leaving open the possibility of changing my mind. As you know, the NEHRD has entrusted me with the task of promoting democracy in East Asia. So the question I'd like to investigate is whether or not democracy is suitable for Singapore. Let's start with a definition of democracy. Perhaps we can avoid controversy by employing a "minimal" definition of democracy as free and fair competitive elections for the country's most important political decision-makers. Democracy thus understood is a procedure for the filling of political offices through periodic free and fair elections. But as Huntington himself notes, such elections are only possible if there's some measure of freedom of speech, assembly, and press, and if opposition candidates and parties are able to criticize incumbents without fear of retaliation.[3] Of course, my own view is that democracy involves much more—I'd like to see more forums for

---

[2] Lee's observations are quoted in "Huntington's U-turn," in Han Fook Kwang, Warren Fernandez, and Sumiko Tan, *Lee Kuan Yew: The Man and His Ideas*, 150. This is of course Lee's account, but it is not entirely implausible to believe that Huntington may have been won over to Lee's position during the course of their meetings. Asked by an interviewer what he thought about Lee, Huntington responded, "I think he is an extraordinarily impressive person. He may well have been the most successful head of government anywhere in the world over the past decades" (quoted in *Asiaweek*, 6 April 1994, 36).

[3] Samuel Huntington, "American Democracy in Relation to Asia," 28.

176

public deliberation,[4] more citizen influence on policy through such nonelectoral means as interest associations and social movements between elections,[5] and I'd also like to curb the power of "despots" and "guardians" in the family[6] and the workplace.[7] Nonetheless, I don't want to diminish the importance of genuinely competitive elections, and for our purposes it's sufficient to note that Singapore lacks even this necessary, minimal condition for democratic life.

LEE: Now hold on a minute. Our People's Action Party has been continuously elected since 1959 in fairly conducted and honestly counted regular elections, decided by the majority on the basis of universal suffrage. If you define democracy as competitive elections, then Singapore is democratic.[8]

DEMO: But a clean vote count on election day isn't the same as a free and fair electoral process. The absence of election-day fraud doesn't mean that elections were genuinely competitive. In Singapore, as you know, individual ballots are numbered (the government can check at least in principle who voted for what party, which could be a restraining influence on those who might otherwise vote for the opposition);[9] promising opposition candidates are publicly humiliated, bankrupted, and/or sacked from their jobs on dubious grounds;[10] elections are

---

[4] On the importance of democratic deliberation, see Amy Gutmann and Dennis Thompson, *Democracy and Disagreement.* But for some criticisms, see my review "Deliberation Is Not Enough," *Times Literary Supplement,* 17 January 1997, 25.

[5] See, e.g., Philippe Schmitter and Terry Lynn Karl, "What Democracy Is . . . and Is Not."

[6] See, e.g., Susan Moller Okin, *Justice, Gender, and the Family.*

[7] See, e.g., Robert Dahl, *Democracy and Its Critics,* 327.

[8] See Bilahari Kausikan, "Governance That works," 27.

[9] See Chee Soon Juan, "Backward in Singapore," *Asian Wall Street Journal,* 5 July 1999.

[10] See *Asia Watch* "Silencing All Critics" (1989), and Erik Paul, "Prospects for Liberalization in Singapore," 295. The PAP's bag of dirty tricks includes such tactics as interrogation by the Internal Security Department and harassment by taxation authorities, but its most common tactic is the politically motivated use of defamation suits against opposition members. For example, Workers' Party member Tang Liang Hong was forced to pay $8 million (Singapore dollars) to eleven PAP leaders who had sued him for defamation, with the largest amount, $2.3 million, going to Lee Kuan Yew (Ahmad Osman, "PAP Leaders Awarded $8 Million in Damages," *Straits Times* [weekly edition], 31 May 1997, 24). The PAP

called on very short notice,[11] apparently with the aim of catching the opposition by surprise and leaving them with insufficient time to organize; the government explicitly threatens to withdraw services from constituencies that support the opposition;[12] the progovernment media provide limited if any time and space for the opposition to present its views;[13] and the government banned political parties from making videos and buying television time after the opposition Singapore Democratic Party had sought a license for a party political video.[14] In view of this reality, one cannot conclude that the ruled have chosen the rulers. More specifically, the PAP may not have been elected in the context of genuinely competitive free elections.[15]

LEE: You're assuming that only Western-style democratic procedures allow one to know what constitutes the political will of the people. . . .

---

had labeled Tang—now living in exile—an "anti-English-educated, anti-Christian Chinese chauvinist" during the campaign for the January 2, 1997, election. Tang defended himself against these charges, but the Singaporean High Court ruled that they were justified. Singapore's Court of Appeals cut the amount of libel damages awarded to PAP leaders by more than half, but Tang was nonetheless declared bankrupt, which made him ineligible for the next election. The Prime Minister and ten other PAP leaders also filed defamation suits against Tang's running mate, J. B. Jeyaretnam, prompting one Singaporean friend to quip, "I've heard of sore losers, but never of sore winners." Not surprisingly, Jeyaretnam lost and was eventually forced to pay $100,000 plus court costs ("PM Wins Higher Award against JBJ on Appeal," *Straits Times* [weekly edition], 18 July 1998, 2).

[11] More precisely, fourteen days for the 1991 election campaign and nine days for the 1997 election campaign.

[12] See note 19.

[13] Moreover, the official media's reports on the opposition's views are almost inevitably followed by criticism, which is rarely the case in the media's reports on the government's views. In one typical example, an unsigned article that briefly reports on Jeyaretnam's criticism of the political system concluded with the following observation: "But if he was hoping to pack a wallop or put a sting, the effect was lost in the meandering way he made his points" ("A Bit of New, a Lot of Old from the Opposition," *Straits Times* [weekly edition], 28 March 1996, 14).

[14] See "BG Yeo Explains Ban on Party Political Films," *Straits Times* [weekly edition], 7 March 1998, 5.

[15] Hussin Mutalib, "Singapore's Elected Presidency and the Quest for Regime Dominance," Department of Political Science Working Paper, National University of Singapore, 1994, 31.

DEMO (*interrupting*): They're not distinctly Western. Taiwan and South Korea have recently adopted fair democratic procedures—their governments have stopped intimidating opposition candidates and ordinary voters, and there's no longer tight control over the freedom of association and political speech. That's the type of transition to democracy I have in mind for Singapore.

LEE: I understand. But my point is that there are other ways to determine what constitutes the will of the people besides what you call fair democratic procedures.[16] If—as you seem to imply—the majority of Singaporeans are against us, why is it that the opposition explicitly concedes that we enjoy the support of most Singaporeans? Instead of fielding a full slate of candidates as in previous elections, the main opposition parties deliberately adopted an electoral strategy in the 1991 general elections of contesting less than half the seats (forty out of eighty-one). The opposition hoped this would free voters to elect opposition candidates without challenging the position of the PAP. They told voters in contested districts that they could elect a few unproven opposition voices safe in the knowledge that the familiar PAP would still control our country. I recall the words of Chiam See Tong, the former leader of the Singapore Democratic Party: "There is no fear at all [that] there will be a freak election.

[16] Moreover, a vote does not imply anything about the depth of support for a political party or about the reasons that people vote as they do. Anthropological observation and in-depth interviewing can provide better (if not always representative) insights into such matters. Other methods—such as the analysis of a culture's heroic figures (see Ian Buruma, *Behind the Mask*) and specially designed polling techniques (for example, David Hitchcock's method of asking people in East Asian countries to select a list of values that they considered critically important to *others* in their society, which helps to get around the problem that people in authoritarian states often do not want to take responsibility and be publicly identified with certain opinions (see Donald Emmerson, "Singapore and the 'Asian Values' Debate")—can also provide insights into a society's dominant moral and political aspirations. More anecdotally, my own three-year experience teaching in Singapore and conversing with Singaporeans of various social backgrounds leads me to the conclusion that the PAP enjoys widespread and genuinely felt support among many, if not most, Singaporeans. The fact that the official perspective on democracy in Singapore resonated with many of my own students is what initially motivated me to take this perspective seriously.

There is absolutely no fear of any accident, of not putting the PAP back in power."[17] And to give the opposition some credit, this strategy of conceding that a mandate had already been given to the PAP worked to a certain extent, giving them 38 percent of the vote (from among the contested seats) and four out of eighty-one seats, or three more than in any election since independence in 1965.

DEMO: But how do you know that people voted for the opposition because they conceded defeat? It seems like a counterproductive tactic.

LEE: Tell that to the opposition—they seem to think it's a good idea to let people know in advance that they can vote for the opposition without worrying about a transfer of power. In the 1997 general election, they did the same thing. Chee Soon Juan, secretary general of the Singapore Democratic Party, explained that "Basically what we want to do is before the election itself, when nomination day arrives, to field less than half of [the maximum number of] candidates so that the PAP is returned to government and Singaporeans are free to vote for the opposition without fear of seeing the PAP being overthrown."[18] Of course, we eventually figured out ways of countering this tactic, and in 1997 we managed to capture 65 percent of the vote, losing only two seats to the opposition.[19]

[17] Quoted in Bilveer Singh, *Whither PAP's Dominence*, 57.

[18] Quoted in "Party Admits Defeat before Poll called," *Hong Kong Standard*, 14 February 1996.

[19] Shortly after the election, Prime Minister Goh claimed that voters had rejected "Western-style liberal democracy and freedoms" (quoted in Murray Hiebert, "Ring in the Old," *Far Eastern Economic Review*, 16 January 1997, 16), but opposition forces pointed out that voters were swayed by his threat to turn districts that elect opposition candidates into "slums" (85 percent of Singaporeans live in public housing estates). The more cynical interpretation was humorously endorsed by *The Economist*, which noted that "Mr. Goh's confident assertion that Singaporean voters have rejected 'western' liberal ideas may confuse a vote for property values with an endorsement of Asian values" (*The Economist*, 11 January 1997, 26). It also received unexpected support from Leslie Fong, editor of the progovernment *Straits Times*, who wrote that it was "self-interest at work that accounted largely for the nationwide swing towards the PAP. One rather gloomy reading is that, in future, fighting for a seat in Parliament would be reduced to a grubby contest in which votes would go to the highest bidder with the most inducements to offer" (quoted in Ian Stewart, "Dangers Seen in Goh's Poll Win,"

DEMO: I'm still not convinced that people vote for the PAP because they really want to. Besides, if you're so sure that a majority of Singaporeans prefer the PAP, why did your government recently create a new executive office, with the president having veto powers over the budget, Singapore's massive foreign reserves, and key public service appointments? If the country's elected parliamentarians aren't in fact the most powerful decision-makers, democratic elections don't serve the function of allowing the ruled to choose the rulers. In that sense Singapore is no different from Guatemala in the 1980s, where civilian control over the military barely existed, or Japan, where unelected bureaucrats tend to have de facto veto power over public policy issues. In a democracy, popularly elected officials must be able to exercise their powers without being subject to overriding opposition from unelected officials.[20]

LEE: But our President is *elected*. We call it an "Elected Presidency."

DEMO: I don't have to tell you that the rules and other criteria imposed upon prospective candidates are stringent. To be eligible, candidates for president have to be at least forty-five years old, with adequate financial expertise and of high conduct and reputation. One Singaporean academic noted that such stringent rules couldn't have been thought fortuitous since by the imposition of such rules only proestablishment personalities could hope to qualify.[21] Not surprisingly, your long-time nemesis, J. B. Jeyaretnam, twice elected to Parliament, was barred from participating in the first presidential elections on the grounds that he lacked the prerequisite "qualities" and "character" to qualify.[22]

South China Morning Post, 5 January 1997). One year later, Goh himself said that linking the upgrading program to electoral support was the "single most important" factor explaining the vote swing to the PAP in the last general election. He wholeheartedly endorsed this tactic: "It was decisive in tipping the floating voters in our favor. By linking the priority of upgrading to electoral support, we focus the minds of voters on the link between upgrading and the people whose policies make it possible. This has the desired result" ("Upgrading Link Swung Vote in GE," *Straits Times* [weekly edition], 17 January 1998).

[20] Schmitter and Karl, "What Democracy Is . . . and Is Not," 45.

[21] Mutalib, "Singapore's Elected Presidency," 34, 35.

[22] Ibid., 36.

LEE: To borrow the words of my successor: "Democracy is not about giving people the right to stand for election. It is about giving the electorate the right to choose good candidates."[23]

DEMO: For the purpose of this discussion, I'd like to work with a definition of democracy where it's the people deciding who counts as a good candidate. So please correct me if I'm wrong, but you just don't trust Singaporeans enough to grant them the right to freely vote for your country's most important decision-makers, and the Elected Presidency is the PAP's way of ensuring regime dominance in case it should lose its majority in Parliament.

LEE: Look, "the job of the Elected President is not to be popular, but to be strong. . . . [H]e would have to take a stand against the government which may be very unpopular with many of the government supporters, and he must be prepared to do that."[24] Think of the consequences: "if there is a freak election result and a coalition forms the government, all the reserves are available, the larder is wide open, you can raid it. Twenty-five years of work, savings, you can go on a spending spree for five years and then we are another broken-back country."[25] Only the Elected President could prevent unscrupulous people from raiding the country's financial reserves to win votes or from abusing their wide powers once elected.[26]

DEMO: Just admit that you're checking the power of the Singaporean people because you don't trust them. It's you versus the people.

[23] Prime Minister Goh Chok Tong, quoted in *Straits Times*, 4 June 1991.

[24] Quoted in Mutalib, "Singapore's Elected Presidency," 49.

[25] Quoted in ibid., 18.

[26] Prime Minister Goh Chok Tong made a similar point in the *Straits Times*, 30 December 1991. The "Elected Presidency" was also supported by development economist Tilak Doshi, who "commended the Government for 'acting so dramatically against the inherited tradition of Westminster' in choosing a mechanism to protect Singapore from populist demands for more public welfare. He says that democratic governments suffer from an inherent urge to run up budget deficits and pursue inflationary financing for the sake of votes" (quoted in Asad Latif, "The Pros and Cons of Singapore's Elected Presidency," *Straits Times* [weekly edition], 22 March 1997, 13). See also Doshi's, "Changing the Leviathan."

LEE: Look, if you condemn our presidential system because it conflicts with the democratic right to freely choose the community's most important decision-makers, then you should also be a principled opponent of judicial review in the 'democratic' country known as the United States. The same principle underlies both judicial supremacy in the U.S. and the "Elected Presidency" in Singapore—no one has a democratic right to an equal share of political power when other persons can be reliably identified and installed in power who are more competent to exercise political power and disposed to competent exercise.[27] In the American case, founding fathers worried about the tendency of political majorities to violate the rights of minorities, so they devised a system that allows competent and reliable unelected public officials, that is, Supreme Court justices, to restrain majority rule by striking down duly enacted legislation as unconstitutional. Our situation in Singapore is different—we have huge foreign reserves and savings, by far the largest per capita savings rate in the world—and my greatest worry is the unchecked power of legislators elected by majorities to take the majority's side in any serious argument about the "rights" of future generations against it. So we devised a system that empowers a competent public official to veto the decisions of elected politicians who promise economically unsustainable benefits such as massive food subsidies or free public transport. In neither case is it assumed that citizens have a right to elect a government with unlimited power to enact the preferences of existing majorities.

DEMO: But many Singaporeans see the Elected Presidency as yet another attempt at regime dominance. Nearly all American participants in the political arena, by contrast, accept the idea that Supreme Court justices can strike down legislative acts that violate constitutionally protected individual rights.[28] Whereas the

---

[27] See Richard Arneson, "Democratic Rights at National and Workplace Levels," 135.

[28] There are of course disputes about the extent of constitutional limits on majority rule, but Demo is correct that the large majority of American citizens seem to accept the principle that there are some constitutional limits on majority rule. See also chap. 5, sec. 1.1.

Elected Presidency breeds cynicism, the Supreme Court as an institution commands respect.

LEE: Give our president time to prove himself, and he'll gain respect. We don't have two hundred years of history to work with.

DEMO: There's a more fundamental difference. Supreme Court justices only rarely intervene to override the decisions made by elected officials, and their power to do so is carefully circumscribed by constitutional design. In fact, the whole point of intervention is often to maintain an open and fair democratic process. But you seem to have no faith whatsoever in the democracy—elections are not truly competitive, as I've already said, and you propose to strip away the last remnants of majority rule with this new scheme of yours.

LEE: Well, I guess I've changed over the years. In my younger days, as an opposition member, I naively asserted that "either we believe in democracy or we do not. If we do, then we must say categorically, without qualification, that no restraint from any democratic process, other than by ordinary law of the land, should be allowed. If you believe in democracy, you must believe in it unconditionally. If you believe that men should be free, then they should have the right of free association, of free speech, of free publication. Then no law should permit those democratic processes to be set at naught."[29]

DEMO: I'm reminded of Samuel Huntington's observation that political leaders have good reason to advocate democracy when they're out of power, but that the real test of their democratic commitment comes once they're in office.[30]

LEE: Sam has a point there. I realized things weren't so easy once I assumed political power and I had to be held responsible for what I said. As prime minister I learned about "the destabilizing tendencies of one-man-one-vote in a new society divided by race, language, religion."[31] "My first task was to lift my country out of the degradation that poverty, ignorance and disease had wrought. Since it was dire poverty that made for such a low pri-

[29] 1956 address to Parliament, quoted in Chee Soon Juan, *Dare to Change.*
[30] Samuel Huntington, "Democracy's Third Wave," 13.
[31] Quoted in Han et al., *Lee Kwan Yew,* 375.

ority given to human life, all other things became secondary."[32] Sometimes we had to apply harsh but necessary measures that weren't popular at the time. It may not have been possible to do this in a fully democratic context, but people today understand we did what we had to do.[33]

DEMO: Correct me if I'm wrong, but the people's actual preferences are totally irrelevant as far as you're concerned. You seem to have no principled commitment to democracy.

LEE: That's unfair. My view is that the people's preferences matter, but I don't define the people's preferences as merely the views of existing majorities. "The people," as I see it, includes future generations, and governments have a special responsibility to resist popular pressure for tax breaks and welfare measures that undermine the prospects of future generations. So perhaps we should define democracy as a government chosen by the people, including contemporary and future generations. A truly democratic government, that is, represents the interests of the people now and in the future.

DEMO: Look, do me a favor and stick to a definition of democracy as a political procedure in which existing majorities choose the rulers by means of competitive elections. On this basis, we can ask the question whether or not the people of Singapore have an interest in freely choosing their own rulers. This would be more fruitful, I think, than haggling over the meaning of democracy.

2. DEMOCRACY JUSTIFIED (ONLY) BY ITS CONSEQUENCES

LEE: For the sake of argument, I'll go along. Personally, I don't really care how political leaders get there, so long as they're competent. Good government is about results, not process.

DEMO: What do you mean?

LEE: I mean that democratic procedures have no intrinsic value. What matters is good government. "What is good govern-

---

[32] Quoted in Nathan Gardels, "Interview with Lee Kuan Yew."
[33] See sec. 5 for a more detailed evaluation of this claim.

ment? . . . As an Asian of Chinese cultural background, my values are for a government which is honest, effective and efficient in protecting its people, and allowing opportunities for all to advance themselves in a stable and orderly society, where they can live a good life and raise their children to do better than themselves. In other words:

a. People are well cared for, their food, housing, employment, health.
b. There is order and justice under the rule of law, and not the capricious, arbitrariness of individual rulers. There is no discrimination between peoples, regardless of race, language, religion. No great extremes of wealth.
c. As much personal freedom as possible but without infringing on the freedom of others.
d. Growth in the economy and progress in society.
e. Good and ever improving education.
f. High moral standards of rulers and of the people.
g. Good physical infrastructure, facilities for recreation, music, culture and the arts; spiritual and religious freedoms, and a full intellectual life."[34]

DEMO: That's a fine list, but where does democracy fit in?

LEE: Democracy is one way of getting the job done, but if nonelectoral procedures are more conducive to the attainment of valued ends, then I'm against democracy. Nothing is morally at stake in the choice of procedures.[35]

DEMO: But democratic procedures not only attain morally desirable outcomes; they also *express* intrinsically valuable values.[36] Most important, I think, is the idea that the electoral system expresses values by teaching valuable lessons about equality and participation that can be transferred out of public life and put into social and domestic and personal life. The electoral system may be reproduced, say, in some organization; or people in an organization or institution may demand not only representation but actual direct, democratic participation. Or think about

---

[34] Quoted in Han et al., *Lee Kuan Yew*, 380.
[35] See also Arneson, "Democratic Rights at National and Workplace Levels."
[36] See George Kateb, *The Inner Ocean*, chap. 2, esp. 61–62.

186

family life—relations between men and women may all be democratized or politicized, changed into something more citizenly or egalitarian.[37]

LEE: Democracy may, or it may not, teach such lessons—a "lesson" is just another word for a desirable consequence. Japan is probably more democratic in your sense than Singapore, yet family life is more egalitarian here. If you care about equality for women, the lesson to draw is that what you really need is a government committed to that principle.[38] Whether or not that government is democratic doesn't matter. More generally, the relationship between procedures and outcomes is an empirical question that can't be answered in the abstract—one's choice of procedures turns only on whether or not a certain set *in fact* produces desired outcomes. The procedures per se have no moral status; they're valuable only insofar as they increase the probability of good consequences.

DEMO: I'm worried about this line of argumentation. John Stuart Mill also took the view that political procedures are justified only insofar as they produce morally desirable outcomes, and this led him to favor granting extra votes to educated persons simply because this would have the consequence of minimizing the danger of class legislation![39]

LEE: That's not such a bad idea. After all, "what are we all seeking? A form of government that will be comfortable because it meets needs, is not oppressive and maximizes our opportunities. And whether you have one-man, one-vote or some-men, one-vote or other-men, two-votes, those are forms which should be worked

[37] Ibid., 63–64.

[38] Lee's government actively promoted women's equality and participation in the workplace in the 1960s (though perhaps for the "Platonic" reason of maximizing the use of human resources, as opposed to a feminist belief in the equality of women), making Singapore one of the least patriarchal societies in Asia. However, Lee has recently publicly expressed regrets that his government had given women equal rights on the grounds that equality has had the effect of limiting educated women's marriage prospects to Asian men who prefer marriage mates who learn the skills that make them "marvellous helpers of their husband's career" (quoted in *Straits Times*, 26 April 1994).

[39] See Mill's "*Considerations on Representative Government*," in *Three Essays* (Oxford: Oxford University Press, 1975), chap. 7.

out. I am not intellectually convinced that one-man, one-vote is the best. We practice it because that is what the British bequeathed us and we haven't really found a need to challenge that. But I am convinced, personally, that we'd have a better system if we gave every man over the age of 40 who has a family two votes because he is likely to be more careful, voting also for his children. He is more likely to vote in a serious way than a capricious young man under 30. But we haven't found it necessary yet. If it became necessary, we should do it."[40]

DEMO (*momentarily stunned into silence*): But isn't *fairness* or *equality* one of the ends of good government? Is it not the case that what we're all seeking is a government that treats its citizens with equal respect, and that anything less is unfair to some people? Yet you propose a voting system where some count for more than others!

LEE: Actually, this idea that all persons are equal by nature is a uniquely Western outlook, perhaps grounded in the Judeo-Christian idea that all are equal before the eyes of God,[41], but I won't go into that now. Besides, even if we agree that the government ought to treat its citizens with equal respect, that the interests of each member of the community matter, and matter equally, this belief cannot by itself justify a democratic procedure in the form of majority rule with universal suffrage[42]—it may well be that a voting procedure giving two votes to persons "between the ages of 35 and 60, married and with families"[43] will yield a government more likely to ensure the equal consideration of people's interests than a government elected by a one-person, one-vote procedure. The choice of voting procedures is an empirical question, not a matter of principle.

DEMO: Did you say between the ages of thirty-five and sixty? Just now you were saying between the ages of forty and sixty. And come to think of it, a couple months ago you were arguing along Confucian lines that the older one becomes, the wiser one becomes; yet now you want to deprive persons over sixty of an

[40] Quoted in *Straits Times*, 11 March 1994 (interview with *Foreign Affairs*).
[41] See Dahl, *Democracy and Its Critics*, 86.
[42] See ibid., 88
[43] Quoted in Han et al., *Lee Kuan Yew*, 385.

extra vote! You see, the whole thing seems arbitrary, and here lies the problem—even if it's true that not everyone is equally inclined to vote in a sensible manner, to vote for "good government," a plural voting scheme is at best a rough and unreliable procedure to distinguish the more competent from the less competent citizens. And since those denied an equal share of democratic rights are likely to perceive the denial as an official insult issued by public authority,[44] the bad consequences of implementing a plural voting scheme are likely to outweigh the benefits.

LEE: They may, and they may not. A plural voting scheme may be a rough procedure to distinguish the competent from the foolish, or the public-spirited from the selfish, but it may still lead to good government with greater probability than a one-person, one-vote procedure. And while the idea of equal and universal suffrage may be deeply rooted in Western societies, with the consequence that citizens denied extra votes may perceive the denial as an official insult, things may be different in East Asia. Our political culture is that of deference and dependence on one's betters.

DEMO: That may have been true in the past, but is it still true today?

LEE: Don't just take my word for it. These claims have been made by Lucian Pye and others, and they're backed up by empirical research.[45] I was about to say: given our political culture, it may be less problematic for those denied plural votes to accept the idea that the more competent should have an extra role in collective decision-making. In a Singaporean context, a good case can be made that the good consequences of a plural vote scheme will outweigh the bad.

DEMO (*frustrated*): But why do you think that giving extra votes to middle-aged family persons will have good consequences? You haven't produced an argument yet.

[44] Arneson makes this argument with reference to Mill's plural votes proposal in "Democratic Rights at National and Workplace Levels," 137.

[45] In an article dealing with research trends in political psychology in Asia, Lucian Pye found psychological dependency to be a general trait characterizing Asian people's leadership styles, in ties that produce political groupings, as well

LEE: Well, as I said, middle-aged people with children are more likely to vote in a responsible way that takes into account the interests of future generations than their younger counterparts, who are often bent on immediate gratification, regardless of the long-term costs. Surely having children is more likely to transform persons into responsible citizens than turning eighteen years old, yet many Western countries engage in the strange practice of granting the vote to eighteen-year-old "adults" and denying it to seventeen-year-old "children." In any case, my proposal is mainly tied to the aging of the population in Singapore. By 2020 "we will have a lot of old people—about 30 percent of the population. Then the interests of the old will be disproportionate in influencing policies [and] the system will malfunction. It is already a problem in America. President Reagan tried in 1982 to cut back on social security, because it was going to bankrupt the country. But the old people just solidly voted against him and so Reagan backed off.[46] There are not enough old people in Singapore yet. But I think in 20 years, there will be [and] they are going to vote for a government that promises them more."[47] "You get hold of all the senior citizens' corners, in no time you've got . . . free medical health, free this, free that. Productive people would then leave and there would be no one to push the economy forward and pay the taxes."[48]

DEMO: In which case, isn't it going to be even more difficult to change the system in twenty years' time? Old people can be expected to campaign fiercely against a new voting procedure that strips them of equal citizenship rights.

LEE: "Therefore the need for good timing by the Government, before the situation gets out of hand, to shift the center of grav-

---

as in the motivations behind individual political behavior (see the discussion in Geir Helgesen, *Democracy and Authority in Korea*, 112–113).

[46] For an argument that social security entitlements are economically unsustainable in the long term, see Peter G. Peterson, "Will America Grow Up Before It Grows Old," *Atlantic Monthly* (May 1996), 55–86.

[47] Quoted in *Straits Times*, 8 May 1994.

[48] Quoted in *Straits Times*, 30 July 1994. Similar fears seem to underlie the Singapore government's recent adoption of a Parents' Maintenance Bill, which compels middle-aged adults to provide for their elderly parents (besides concerns about maintaining the value of filial piety).

ity to the people who are at their most productive and carrying the responsibilities for the next generation. They have to bring up the next generation and protect their children's future interests. So it's logical to give one vote for themselves and one for their children. . . . But when you are old and your children have grown up . . . it's what they call 'empty nest syndrome'. . . . The eggs have hatched, the birds have flown, your views change. . . . You forget that you've got to worry about the next generation because your children are all grown up."[49]

But I don't mean to be too rigid about this. So long as you've got a good government that works without sacrificing the interests of future generations, I'm happy. It may require a competent president with veto power over the budget and use of the national reserves, and now I'm suggesting a voting scheme that gives more weight to those likely to consider the interests of future generations. There may be other means as well.[50] This is, let me repeat, an empirical matter, to be decided with expert advice from demographers and social scientists. All I'm saying is that we shouldn't get stuck on this notion that democratic rights are valuable apart from the outcomes they are supposed to reach.

DEMO (*pause*): Actually, I still think that democratic procedures are intrinsically valuable, and let me tell you why. Consider the purposes of "good government." Equality is one such purpose, although you argued that the value of equality standing alone can't justify democracy. Another end of good government, however, is the promotion of *autonomy*. Liberals believe that autono-

[49] Quoted in ibid.

[50] Amitai Etzioni suggests an intriguing "communitarian" solution to the problem of how to represent the interests of future generations in the context of disputes over the use of national parks in the United States: "Our solution is to represent future generations at public hearings, deliberations, and other occasions when issues of the tension between contemporary and future use of the park arise, by appointing one or more guardians for these generations. Just as children, the indigent, or those who are severely ill and have no family members may be protected by a guardian, we see merit in appointing public figures (not necessarily lawyers) to speak for the future. These advocates may use their reasons and legal recourse, if need be, to mobilize the public on behalf of generations not yet born and their right to enjoy a share of the park's goods" (Etzioni, "Introduction," xv).

mous individuals have an overriding interest in shaping a particular life plan or moral outlook, in making the decisions that affect them most closely and intimately, consistent with the equal right of others to do likewise. This means that governments should provide the conditions for individuals to be the directors of their own lives. And since matters of public policy importantly affect the way that we lead our lives,[51] everyone should have an equal right to choose the government that sets policy. Democracy, in other words, is a system of self-rule that *instantiates* autonomy, the only kind of regime justifiable to autonomous individuals. The equal right to participate in the collective decisions that affect our lives counts for something, more than any other political arrangement. Thus, democracy should be valued independently of any outcomes.[52]

LEE: That's the viewpoint of a Western liberal.

DEMO: What do you mean?

LEE: I mean that in the West you value individual autonomy, with democracy seen as a constituent part of autonomy. That conception of human flourishing, however, doesn't resonate to the same extent with the habits and traditions of East Asians. "Eastern societies believe that the individual exists in the context of his family. He is not pristine and separate. The family is part of the extended family, and then friends and the wider society."[53]

---

[51] This empirical claim can be criticized on the grounds that the decisions made in national political representative institutions may in fact not govern people's lives to nearly the same extent as decisions made in the international arena (say, concerning capital mobility or ecological issues) and in the workplace and family contexts (see Bell, "Democracy in Confucian Societies," in *Towards Illiberal in Pacific Asia*, Bell et al., 28–30). This line of argument (if correct) suggests that proautonomy democrats ought to consider shifting the main area of moral concern from the question "Is the state democratic?" to such issues as democratizing the workplace, the family, and international political institutions that deal with global issues.

[52] In response to Arneson's (pure) consequentialist argument for democracy, Robert Sugden similarly argues that being able to participate in the collective decisions that will affect one's life is an essential aspect of autonomy (see Sugden, "Justified to Whom?" 150). Perhaps Demo has read this book since his conversation with Lo in chapter 2, which helps to explain his relatively reflective views concerning the justifications for democratic rule.

[53] Quoted in *Straits Times*, 11 March 1994.

DEMO: With all due respect, Mr. Lee, it might help if you could back up your grand claims with some kind of evidence.

LEE (*impatiently*): Speak to psychologists, if you want more evidence.[54] In my experience, most East Asians don't think of themselves as individuals in the same way Westerners do. Westerners think of themselves first and foremost as autonomous individuals, whereas Asians think of themselves in terms of relationships with others, their family members in particular.[55] Of course, you can always disagree. So let me reverse the question: do *you* have any evidence to the contrary?

DEMO: Not off hand, but I'd like to point out that the "Western" outlook you describe doesn't rule out family ties and obligations. Individuals can mix with whomever they want to; it's up to them what kind of bonds they want to establish with what kind of people. The point about autonomy isn't that we must think of ourselves as unencumbered by social ties and commitments to the family. Nor is it that we must constantly subject our family ties to critical examination and decide on them anew.[56] As

[54] C. Fred Alford reports on differences between Koreans and Americans: "Almost every Korean spoken with, including psychologists and psychiatrists, said Koreans do not think of themselves in the same way Westerners do. Every contributor to *Psychology of the Korean People: Collectivism and Individualism*, published by the Korean Psychological Association, makes this claim, most on the basis of psychological tests administered to groups of Koreans and Westerners. Employing the method of Associative Group Analysis (AGA), Gene Yoon presented groups of Koreans and Americans a series of stimulus words such as 'self' and 'family.' Americans responded in terms of the person and his emotional state, Koreans in terms of their relationships to others. . . . For most Koreans, most of the time, people are defined in terms of their relationships" (Alford, "Koreans Do Not Believe in Evil—Should They?" 229–230). However, Koreans and Americans may be on the extreme ends of the collectivism-individualism spectrum, and it is possible that these differences may be less pronounced between other East Asian and Western countries.

[55] This kind of consideration seems to affect the practice of "abnormal" psychology in most East Asian countries—individuals are treated while being observed and counseled in the presence of family members, whereas in the West individuals are typically treated in the context of one-on-one interaction with a psychologist or psychiatrist.

[56] Some liberals, however, do make this argument. For example, Yael Tamir argues that spouses should reflect upon their choice to get married and decide upon it anew (Tamir, *Liberal Nationalism*, 21). It is not always possible to rationally

I see it, the liberal view requires only that we be able to critically evaluate, and to reject, this or that particular attachment if need be.[57] Liberal autonomy, in other words, is the right to say no. If I find that family bonds are stifling and oppressive, for example, then I should have the right to leave my family.

LEE: That's going too far. The East Asian view is that family ties are absolutely essential for the good life, that persons living apart from family members aren't leading the best kind of life. So if we have to choose between autonomously chosen life plans and family duties, the latter will more often than not have priority.

DEMO: Is that a choice we have to make? Caring for family members can count as a life plan, and if East Asians prefer to do that, that's fine with me.

LEE: Don't be so pedantic. My point is that some ties are beyond choice. For example, parents should care for a baby who falls ill. They shouldn't have the right to say no. In this case, there's something morally perverse about the very idea of putting into question family obligations.[58]

DEMO: I don't think anyone would disagree with that. In Western countries, parents don't have the right to abandon sick babies. But it's different when we're dealing with relations between adults—once they no longer want to stay together, adults should have the right to say no to each other. Unless, that is, you don't think people should have the right to get divorced.

LEE: Divorce shouldn't be automatic. In Western countries, you have "no-fault" divorce,[59] but here in Singapore people are pre-

---

justify love between people, however, and racking one's brains trying to find such grounds may well have the unintended result of undermining otherwise healthy relationships. Or to put it more colloquially: "If it ain't broke, don't fix it."

[57] See Will Kymlicka, *Liberalism, Community and Culture,* 52 Ronald Dworkin, "Liberal Community," 489; and Stephen Macedo, *Liberal Virtues,* 247.

[58] This is a recurring theme in Confucian ethical and political thought, the dominant tradition in East Asia. See Bell, "Democracy in Confucian Societies," 20–26.

[59] No-fault divorce is defended on the grounds that liberalism, as Stephen Macedo puts it, "creates a community in which it is possible to decide next week . . . [to] leave my wife and children" (Macedo, *Liberal Virtues,* 278). Most contem-

pared to accept waiting periods and other constraints that make it more difficult to get divorced. So I think there's a difference of emphasis. Western liberals think the right to say no matters most, whereas East Asians typically believe that obligations to the family should have priority.[60] In terms of political implications, it means that East Asians will prefer a Singapore-style paternalistic regime that first and foremost provides individuals with the conditions to lead fulfilling family lives,[61] even if this involves certain constraints on the right to say no.

DEMO: But at the end of the day, they can still say no. There's a big difference between placing constraints on the right to get divorced and forcing people to stay married forever. Correct me if I'm wrong, but divorce isn't illegal in Singapore, which means that you still recognize the importance of giving individuals the right to exit from relationships that turn sour. Marital ties aren't completely beyond choice.

LEE: In some cases, the state can justifiably intervene to promote family ties, even when the individuals involved choose otherwise. Consider what's done in Hong Kong to support the disabled. Part of an inheritance must go to support disabled members of the family, even if they've been explicitly left out of the deceased person's will.[62]

DEMO (*frustrated*): But how far do you want to go? There may be a case for rare paternalistic interventions, say, if they're necessary to support the weak members of society. But if you want to justify the kind of comprehensive paternalistic authority that's incompatible with democracy, you'd have to deny the fact that

---

porary liberals, however, do allow for the state to intervene in parental decisions about divorce if the interests of children are at stake, and a growing number of Western liberal states are placing constraints on no-fault divorce in the name of protecting children's interests.

[60] For some empirical evidence that in everyday life East Asians typically fulfill more duties and obligations for the sake of family members in comparison with Westerners, see my "Democracy in Confucian Societies," 24–25.

[61] In Singapore, this includes tax exemptions and housing benefits to those who care for elderly parents as well as government-subsidized "love boat" cruises for educated singles to have the opportunity of meeting marriage mates. See my *Communitarianism and Its Critics*, 230–231.

[62] I thank Lusina Ho for this information.

people are, generally speaking, the best judges of their own interests.[63] Is that your view? Do you think that people lack the ability to decide what's in their own best interests, hence that they should be subject to the authority of "benevolent" guardians who tell them how to lead their own lives?

LEE: I never said that. When it comes to family matters, work, and religion, people often know what's in their own interest. But that doesn't mean they can choose the best economic or foreign policy. When it comes to politics, ordinary people often lack the kind of knowledge that allows them to make the best judgments. "If I were in Singapore indefinitely, without having to ask those who are governed whether they like what is being done, then I have not the slightest doubt that I could govern more effectively in their own interests. That is a fact which the educated understand, but we are all caught up in this system which the British export all over the place hoping that somewhere it will take root."[64]

DEMO (*gasps*): I suspect that educated people are the *least* inclined to accept a paternalistic overlord deciding things in their own interest.

LEE: They understand that independent central banks composed of experts need to be insulated from political pressure. They understand that in a small, predominantly Chinese state surrounded by larger Islamic neighbors—"a Chinese island in a Malay sea"[65]—enlightened rulers need to clamp down on dangerous expressions of jingoism and racism from the masses below.

DEMO: Do you have any evidence to support these claims?

LEE: No. Do you have any evidence to the contrary?

---

[63] Robert Dahl justifies democracy (partly) by appealing to "The Presumption of Personal Autonomy: In the absence of a compelling [evidence] showing to the contrary everyone should be assumed to be the best judge of his or her own good or interests," in *Democracy and Its Critics*, 100–105. See also Carlos Santiago Nino, *The Ethics of Human Rights*, 247.

[64] Quoted in Alex Josey, *Lee Kuan Yew*, 70–71.

[65] Lee Kuan Yew, *The Singapore Story*, 23.

DEMO: Not off hand. But what really worries me about limited political discussion is that, no matter how enlightened the participants may be, the absence of those affected by the policies makes it probable that their interests will not be given due weight. People must be allowed to put forward their own interests so that everyone may know whether they've been taken into account in each proposal.[66]

LEE: A fine theory, but it won't be easy to implement in this part of the world. Even if it's true that people are the best judges of their own interests, it doesn't follow that they will want to put forward their interests in political debate. In East Asia, there's actually a strong cultural bias against voicing one's interests. People are reluctant to do so, for they fear this can undermine social harmony and destroy society as a whole. This belief has deep roots in Confucian political culture.[67]

DEMO (*raises voice*): Culture changes. I suspect that people are simply afraid of the consequences if they speak up too much. Give them the opportunity to voice their own interests, and you might be surprised.

LEE: I'm not sure about that. Look at how democratic politics works in Taiwan, which has also been influenced by Confucian political culture. Candidates in elections don't promote themselves as they might in the United States, for example. To do so would tar them as "selfish" or "self-centered." Nor do they take sides on policy issues whose advocates divide into distinctly opposite camps, such as prolife versus prochoice. Instead, candidates usually point to their public-mindedness and educational achievements to assure voters they're the "right" leader to make decisions on the public's behalf. Citizens, for their part, expect government officials to protect, rather than represent, their interests. They don't participate directly in liberal democratic politics, lest it expose their self-interest and deprive them of any moral legitimacy. Not surprisingly, democratic politics in Confucian societies doesn't coalesce around interest groups, espe-

[66] See Nino, *The Ethics of Human Rights*, 247–250.
[67] See Ling and Shih, "Confucianism with a Liberal Face: The Meaning of Democratic Politics in Postcolonial Taiwan," 78.

cially if they're economically based.[68] So even if we adopt demo-cratic procedures in Singapore, it doesn't follow that citizens will put forward their own interests. Put differently, you can't justify a transition to democracy by appealing to the ideal of autonomous individuals who put forward their own interests, since this ideal doesn't resonate to the same extent in this part of world.

DEMO: How about making their views known at election time? Peo-ple in "Confucian" societies don't seem to mind voting in com-petitive elections when they're given the opportunity. And if they use a secret ballot, there's no risk about being "exposed" as a self-interested citizen. (*short pause*) I still haven't heard an argument that Singaporeans don't want the freedom to say no to the government. Surely they care about autonomy, in the sense of having the right to change a government they don't like. And you seem to recognize this implicitly: why even bother going through elections—unfair though they may be—if Singa-poreans don't care about the right to say no to a government that loses their trust?

LEE: Once again, there's a difference of emphasis. Westerners will fight hard to preserve their autonomy, even in the face of un-pleasant consequences. This was expressed in graphic form on a license plate I once saw in New Hampshire: "Live Free or Die." But Singaporeans care less about autonomy, and they won't push as hard for this ideal in the face of competing values. Just as Singaporeans will endorse constraints on the right to get di-vorced if they're necessary to secure other goals, so they won't mind if other values have priority over democratic rights in cases of conflict.

DEMO: First of all, I don't think there are any "competing values" of greater worth than democracy. And even if there are, my view—as I said—is that democracy is *intrinsically* valuable. It's the only political system that instantiates the value of autonomy, and it should be valued regardless of its consequences.

LEE: So let's forget about consequences. Singapore should be-come a Western liberal democratic society, even if it means that

[68] See ibid., 77–78.

"we'd go down the drain; we'd have more poor people in the streets, sleeping in the open, we'd have more drugs, more crime, more single mothers, with delinquent children, a troubled society, and a poor economy."[69] But what do you care? You don't live here, and at least you can take intellectual satisfaction in the fact that our political system instantiates the value of autonomy.

DEMO: Your description of life in democratic society is, to say the least, one-sided. The problems you describe can't be blamed on democracy. In fact, they're often due to the lack of democracy. I can point you to dozens of studies which show that democracy has good consequences overall. In most countries, democracy contributes to such goods as economic development, political stability, and the other things we all care about.[70]

LEE: When I have to decide on policies, I'm concerned about the effects in Singapore, not what happens in "most countries." If democracy will lead to bad consequences here, that's what worries me. I don't care if Singapore is a statistical anomaly.

DEMO: I think democracy would have good consequences in Singapore as well.

LEE: I hope you're right. But I won't be persuaded to change until you can show me that those benefits *only* flow from democracy. There may be other ways of securing those same goods, and if that's what we do in Singapore, then it's OK with me. There's always a risk associated with changing from the status quo, and I'm not clear why we should change if the current political system has proven to be effective in the Singaporean context. Most Singaporeans—who are notoriously risk-averse—would probably agree.[71] Still, I'm prepared to consider the possibility that democracy can do some things better. So what I propose is the following. I don't mind pursing this discussion on the pros and cons of democracy in Singapore, but let's drop this nonsense about intrinsic justifications for democracy. Instead, let's focus

[69] Quoted in Melanie Chew, "Human Rights in Singapore," 935.

[70] See Amartya Sen, "Human Rights and Economic Achievements," 90–93.

[71] Singaporeans use the word "kiasu" to describe this cultural trait. See also chap. 4, note 34.

on the probable outcomes of democracy in the Singaporean context.

DEMO: I worry about that. It's dangerous to abandon the notion of autonomy as a justification for democracy, or the idea that democracy has intrinsic value. This, I fear, would open up a whole nasty can of worms. If arguments for democratic procedures turn solely on contingent claims about probable outcomes, think of what might happen: any two-bit dictator could point to bad outcomes to discredit democracy, and even Westerners may lose faith in the democratic project given enough social problems, as many Germans did toward the end of the Weimar Republic. The political implications are just too ominous to contemplate!

LEE: Well, I'm equally worried about the Western view of the family as a merely contingent means for human well-being. If people begin to think of family ties in purely instrumental terms, to be shed if the circumstances warrant, families will break up, the government will be forced "to provide for a person what the family best provides,"[72] you're on the road to economic ruin, and the whole society collapses.

DEMO: There you go again, making extreme claims without a shred of evidence.

LEE: I have the Singaporean context in mind. To repeat, let's talk about democracy and its likely consequences here. If you want to persuade me about the virtues of democracy, you're going to have to show that it's more likely to do better at securing desirable outcomes compared to the nondemocratic status quo.

DEMO: But if democracy doesn't deliver the goods, that's it for democracy! It's important to make an argument for democracy that's invulnerable to changes in empirical circumstances.

LEE (*impatiently*): Look, I made a concession earlier when I agreed to employ a definition of democracy as free and fair competitive elections, and now it's your turn to reciprocate. Perhaps the real problem is the lack of empirical evidence linking democratic procedures and desired outcomes, and you're afraid of losing an argument.

[72] Quoted in *Straits Times*, 11 March 1994.

3. Democracy and Security

Demo (*pause*): Fine, if that's what it takes to persuade you, I'll go along. I do in fact think that democracy produces more good consequences than alternative feasible arrangements. . . .

Lee (*interrupting*): In a Singaporean context?

Demo: I'll try to argue for that point as well. First, I guess, we have to agree on the ends of government, and then I'll try to convince you that democracy best serves the purpose of securing those ends. Let's begin in a Hobbesian vein, with the idea that individuals have an interest in security, in freedom from violence. On this point, I presume, we agree.

Lee: Of course. Personal safety is absolutely crucial whatever your conception of human flourishing, from which it follows that the state must secure the conditions for social peace. But why do you think that democratic procedures increase the chance of social peace?

Demo: Well, in ethnically plural societies like Singapore—77 percent Chinese, 14 percent Malay, and 7 percent Indian, correct me if I'm wrong—democracy can be defended on the grounds that it provides a mechanism for the peaceful resolution of conflicts. Without democracy, groups with conflicting beliefs, faiths, and cultural outlooks may resort to force to resolve their differences.

Lee: One can think of many counterexamples. Democracy's majoritarian principle can sometimes exacerbate conflict by causing minorities to feel systematically excluded from the political process. Consider the twentieth-century history of Northern Ireland, Burundi, and Sri Lanka—elected governments in those countries systematically persecuted minority groups.[73] That's

---

[73] Fareed Zakaria has used the term "illiberal democracy" to describe a system where the majority rules and decides democratically to oppress a minority (Zakaria, "The Rise of Illiberal Democracy.") This term has also been used somewhat differently in a book I co-authored with three former colleagues at the National University of Singapore. Our use of the term refers to a regime characterized by (1) a nonneutral understanding of the state; (2) the evolution of a rationalistic and legalistic technocracy that manages the state; and (3) the development of a managed rather than a critical public space and civil society (see the concluding chapter of *Towards Illiberal Democracy in Pacific Asia*).

not a particularly inspiring precedent for a multiethnic society like Singapore.

DEMO: Fair enough. In the absence of a deeply rooted culture of mutual respect and tolerance between groups, minorities need some sort of institutional protection against the tyranny of the majority, such as constitutionally enshrined individual rights enforced by unelected judges. Democracy can't be absolute in ethnically plural societies.

LEE: But in Singapore we rely on neither democracy nor individual rights to establish social peace and guarantee mutual respect between groups.[74] Plagued by a history of ethnic conflict and racial riots, we improvised a variety of mechanisms not part of the traditional liberal democratic repertoire that made our country one of the safest and most peaceful in the world.[75] These include various nation-building measures such as national service, public housing, and patriotic education,[76] the original aim being to construct a national identity that can override commitment to ethnic groups. We now recognize that ethnic ties won't readily disappear, so we implemented a system of formal representation of ethnic groups. We call this the Group

[74] For another historical example showing that pluralism can be accommodated and mutual respect between groups institutionalized without a commitment to individual rights, see Will Kymlicka, "Two Models of Pluralism and Tolerance." One implication is that some civil and political rights that liberals care about cannot be justified by an appeal to plurality per se (as, say, Charles Larmore tries to do in his book *Patterns of Moral Complexity*): mutual respect between groups requires neither democratic political participation (so long as a relatively benign despot allows groups to pursue their cultural activities in peace) nor the right to dissent and proselytize (as Kymlicka notes in *Liberalism, Community, and Culture*, 60).

[75] There may also be good reasons to question the usefulness of the "traditional liberal democratic repertoire" in some African states. Kwasi Wiredu notes that "in Africa, where minorities are usually ethnic groups, the struggles generated by majoritarian politics have led to radical disruptions that have devastated the prospects of economic development and other forms of progress" (Wiredu, *Cultural Universals and Particulars: An African Perspective*). Instead, Wiredu argues (drawing on traditional resources) for a "nonparty system," where the ideal of consensus is pursued not only in political decision-making but also in other spheres of group interaction (see ibid., part 4).

[76] See Jon Quah, "Government Policies and Nation-Building."

Representation Constituency: four seats are collapsed into a single voting bloc, with one seat reserved for a minority candidate.

DEMO: There's nothing wrong with such measures, if they're intended to secure social peace and mutual respect between groups.[77] The problem occurs when you restrict rights in the name of "social harmony."

LEE: Unfortunately, the carrot isn't always sufficient. We also need to employ various nonliberal measures designed to prevent the outbreak of violence between groups. You may know about the Religious Harmony Act, which makes it an offense to proselytize in a way that would cause disharmony among the religious groups. This law doesn't ban proselytizing altogether, but "if you want to convert, don't do it in an aggressive way. And don't convert a chap who already belongs to a religion that's fiercely against conversion. Avoid that. So far we have succeeded."[78]

DEMO: But why must you resort to authoritarian means to secure social peace? My point is that you can do the same with liberal democracy. Do you really need "sticks" to maintain intercommunal harmony in Singapore?

LEE: Don't forget that we're surrounded by larger, predominantly Muslim neighbors, and things easily could flare up if we antagonized our Muslim minority. The situation was under control until recently, "but when the Christians became very active and evangelical . . . wanting to convert the Muslims, and the Catholics decided to go in for social action, we were heading for trouble! . . . We've just got out of one trouble—communism and Chinese chauvinism and Malay chauvinism—and you want to head into another? Religious intolerance? It's just stupid. Stay out of politics. The Religious Harmony Act was passed: after

---

[77] Opposition groups, however, view the Group Representative Constituency (GRC) system as a transparent attempt at gerrymandering. This interpretation was lent some support when the ruling PAP increased the size of GRCs to six seats shortly before the January 2, 1997, election without increasing minority representation. The effect of this change was to cut the number of constituencies with a single candidate from twenty-one to nine, which made it more difficult for the fragmented opposition to get elected since they found it difficult to field so many team candidates.

[78] Quoted in Han et al., *Lee Kuan Yew,* 190.

that, it subsided. . . . But if you ask the human rights groups, that's a violation of human rights, we should allow everybody to do what they like. Free speech and free conversions, then you'll have an enlightened society. I do not accept that as the happy conclusion or outcome."[79]

The same sorts of considerations also serve to justify restrictions on certain sensitive racial and religious issues from being raised in the press. I'm aware of the fact that it's different in America. But "in Singapore's experience, because of our volatile racial and religious mix, the American concept of the 'marketplace of ideas,' instead of producing harmonious enlightenment, has time and again led to riots and bloodshed. . . . On July 21, 1964, a sustained campaign in a Malay language newspaper, falsely alleging the suppression of the rights of the Malay and Muslim minority by the Chinese majority, led to riots in which 36 people were killed and many more injured, during a Prophet Mohammed's birthday procession."[80]

DEMO: But that was 1964. Surely things have improved since then, with economic development, more education, and so on.

LEE: "I used to believe that . . . with higher standards of education, these problems will diminish. But watching Belfast, Brussels and Montreal, rioting over religion and language, I wonder whether such phenomena can ever disappear."[81]

DEMO: Actually, the authorities in Montreal didn't restrict the press or religious freedom in order to contain communal conflicts, and there hasn't been any communal violence since the early 1970s. It may in fact have been worse if the government had resorted to authoritarian means for the sake of maintaining social peace. Restrictions on rights are usually counterproductive. They may work initially, but conflicts are kept under cover, resentments build up, and the situation often explodes later.

---

[79] Quoted in ibid., 143.

[80] Quoted ibid., 213. On the PAP leadership's perception that democracy in the early 1960s "played into the hands of dangerous ideologues and rabble rousers, such as communists and communalists who were adept at exploiting the racial divisions and religious prejudices of the masses," see Chew, "Human Rights in Singapore," 939.

[81] Quoted in Han et al., *Lee Kuan Yew*, 213.

LEE: That's one possibility. But in Singapore, we can't afford to experiment with such nice theories. We need to clamp down right away on expressions of intolerance, because it doesn't take long for the situation to get out of hand here.

DEMO (*raises voice*): Even if you're right, why don't you try to persuade most Singaporeans of your viewpoint? You don't seem to trust anybody except a minority of "enlightened" PAP loyalists.

LEE: There are times when decisions can't simply be a reflection of the majority will. Consider the question of whether Singapore should adopt English or Mandarin as the primary language. In 1965 we chose English, but if we had left it to popular will, the Chinese, who formed the majority of the population, would have rooted for Mandarin. "Supposing we had chosen Chinese or tried to sponsor Chinese, how would we make a living? How would we fit ourselves into the region and into the world? We could not have made a living. But the Chinese then would have wanted it. And if we had taken the vote, we would have had to follow that policy. So when people say, 'Oh, ask the people!' it's childish rubbish. We are leaders. We know the consequences. . . . They say people can think for themselves? Do you honestly believe that the chap who can't pass primary six knows the consequences of his choice when he answers a question viscerally, on language, culture and religion? But we knew the consequences. We would starve, we would have race riots. We would disintegrate."[82]

---

[82] Quoted in ibid., 134. According to Will Kymlicka, Singapore is an exception among authoritarian Asian states because authoritarian states face the same nation-building pressures as democratic states, which often involves promoting (or creating) majority nationalism and discriminating against the economic/political/cultural interests of minority groups (Kymlicka, "The Future of the Nation-State," Fifth Kobe Lectures, December 1998, 13). Several other authoritarian states, however, have suppressed majority nationalism—Suharto's Indonesia and Mahathir's Malaysia, for example, suppressed political expressions of Islam. Sometimes, political elites in authoritarian states have co-opted members of minority groups to further their own interests—for example, Suharto's regime granted favorable economic terms to members of the Chinese minority, with the effect that Indonesian Chinese (3 percent of the population) controlled roughly 70 percent of the country's wealth—in ways that would have been impossible in more democratic contexts. The general point is that authoritarian states face less pressure to take into account actual or potential majority preferences, and there

DEMO: I find it hard to dispel the suspicion that some of these measures are also driven by the need to maintain political power.

LEE (*impatiently*): Look, don't just take my word for it. Sam Huntington also recognizes the need to rely on nonliberal democratic measures designed to prevent the outbreak of violence between groups in multiethnic societies. "He has spent several years thinking about it now, and he has concluded that in this multi-racial, multi-cultural society, when you remove the imperial power which kept the peace, you have inevitable racial, religious, cultural and language conflicts. So you have it all over the former Soviet Union. You have it in Yugoslavia, you have it in Africa because the Belgians have gone. You have it in Somalia, and so on. So we say this is a deep fault line."[83] You may disagree, but I have to be held responsible if things go wrong. There are serious risks associated with democratization in highly polarized, multiethnic societies, particularly for minority groups.[84]

---

is less reason (compared to democratic states) to expect a dynamic of economically/politically/culturally favored majority groups versus oppressed minorities. In authoritarian states, it is easier for political elites to suppress majority nationalism, and it might also be easier for minorities to strike bargains with political elites if it suits the interests of both parties.

[83] "SM Lee on Language, Stability, and the Future of Singapore," *Straits Times* (weekly edition), 7 January 1997, 13.

[84] For some empirical evidence, see Ted Gurr, "Communal Conflicts and Global Security." Gurr points out that "in the 1990s most [democratic] Soviet successor states have imposed discriminatory restrictions on non-titular nationalities, erasing most of the Soviet regime's socially engineered equality and status for national minorities" (213). With respect to the Southeast Asian context, a recent report on a Social Science Research Council workshop concludes that "in societies with intense levels of conflict, elections are probably meaningless, because the fundamental conflict will be over what the election is about or who it is for, not who will win a particular race. The current advocacy of elections as the *sine qua non* of democratic politics and good government needs to be examined in terms of who is expected to be the victors of these contexts and which contests will be recognized as genuine. . . . Elections are indeed Janus-faced, granting and constraining liberty depending upon the circumstances" (R. H. Taylor, "Delusion and Necessity," 85). But for an argument that democratization actually *reduces* the chances of bloodshed between groups, see Michael D. Ward and Kristian S. Gleditsch, "Democratizing for Peace." Of course, Lee can always reply that he is more interested in the likely consequences for Singapore rather than in general trends.

Personally, I'm not prepared to gamble with the safety of my people.

DEMO (*frustrated*): Well, I see you're not going to move on this one. But I think it's more difficult to refute the argument that democracy leads to social peace by facilitating smooth transitions of political power. The democratic system, as Friedrich Hayek put it, is the only method of peaceful change of government yet discovered.[85] Without a democratic system, competing political elites don't have a peaceful way of sorting out their differences.

LEE: Losing sides often reject the outcome of democratic elections, which can plunge countries into civil war—look at what happened a few years ago in Angola. Moreover, nondemocratic forms of government can also allow for peaceful transitions of political power. Think of hereditary monarchies: the Chinese dynastic system enjoyed long periods of stability, Japan experienced remarkable political stability during the Tokugawa Shogunate from 1603 to 1868, as did Korea during the Yi dynasty, 1391 to 1910.

DEMO: But that's the past! Today, only democratic rule provides for long-term stability and the peaceful transition of political power.

LEE: Is that really the case? Taiwan experienced a smooth nondemocratic transition of power after Chiang Kai-shek died in 1975, and later after the death of his eldest son, Chiang Ching-kuo in 1988. And, most relevant for our purposes, I myself resigned in November 1990 so that Premier Goh Chok Tong could take over. I know very well that political leaders are judged in part "by the grace with which they leave office and hand over to their successor."[86]

DEMO: But you were merely passing on the levers of political power to a favored heir. Lots of autocrats have done that. Only democracy, however, allows for the ouster and replacement of incumbents with a different, competing set of political elites. It may

---

[85] Friedrich Hayek, *Law, Liberty and Legislation*, vol. 3 (London: Routledge and Kegan Paul, 1979), 5.

[86] Quoted in *Straits Times*, 14 September 1988.

not always work, but no other method allows for the peaceful transfer of political power to a new and competing elite.

LEE: There are other ways of selecting rulers from competing political elites—by lot, say, or by examination. The latter is more in line with traditional Chinese practice, and that's what we do in Singapore. We select future rulers from among students competing for local scholarships and admission to top American universities. Singaporeans understand what you need to make it in politics: "an SAF [Singapore Air Force] scholarship, an overseas merit scholarship, preferably a first at a top university, and an MBA with distinction."[87] Of course, we care about other factors as well. "You've then got to assess him for his sense of reality, his imagination, his quality of leadership, his dynamism. But most of all, his character and his motivation, because the smarter a man is, the more harm he will do society."[88] That's the route for aspirants to ministerial office, and it has worked so far.

DEMO: With all due to respect, your system for selecting political decision-makers sounds pretty arbitrary.

LEE: It's not our own invention. We employ the same system as the Shell corporation. "I've spend 40 years trying to select men for big jobs—ministers, civil servants, statutory boards' chairmen. So I've gone through many systems, spoken to many CEOs, how did they select. Finally, I decided Shell had the best system of them all, and the government switched from forty attributes to three, which they called 'helicopter qualities', which they have implemented and they are able to judge executives worldwide and grade them for helicopter qualities. What are they? Powers of analysis; logical grasp of the facts; concentration on the basic points, extracting the principles. You score high marks in mathematics, but that's not enough. There are brilliant mathematicians but they make poor executives. They must have a sense of reality of what is possible. But if you are just realistic, you become pedestrian, plebeian, you will fail. Therefore you must be able to soar above the reality and say, 'This is also possible'—a sense of imagination."[89]

[87] "What If I Were a University Undergraduate Today?" speech delivered at the National University of Singapore, 30 July 1994.
[88] Quoted in Han et al., *Lee Kuan Yew*, 338.
[89] Quoted in ibid., 331.

DEMO: It still sounds pretty complicated. How can you test for those qualities?

LEE (*impatiently*): Ask the Shell corporation if you want more details.

DEMO: But why do you copy a multinational? Why not rely on the democratic process to select political decision-makers? For one thing, the politicians would have more legitimacy, and there'd be less of a need to rely on authoritarian controls to ensure social stability.

LEE: That system may work well in a larger country. "I do not want to be dogmatic. If we were thirty million and not three million, I think the system would work differently because the number of people available to form a Cabinet would multiply by 10, right? Or if we were 300 million people, then it will multiply by 100. . . . But when you're dealing with three million people and the talent pool is so small, I think really competent people to be in government, between the ages of 35 to 65, fit people I would entrust the government to, would not number more than 100. . . . We devised this system because we were confronted with a problem of succession. . . . Can you, in good conscience, hand over your authority, even for a few years or a few months, to people who do not have that helicopter quality?"[90] We simply couldn't afford to take any chances. Had we relied on a Western-style democratic process, we may have had a "government of duds,"[91] or worse, a charismatic maverick who gets elected by playing off Chinese chauvinism against the minorities,[92] more ethnic riots, and so on.

DEMO (*pause*): Well, I doubt we're going to agree. But for the sake of argument, let me concede the point that democracy won't always increase the likelihood of security and peace within an ethnically plural state governed by a competent technocratic elite. . . .

[90] Quoted in ibid., 98.

[91] "What If I Were a University Undergraduate Today?"

[92] As Melanie Chew puts it, "the 'maverick' can confound the delicate communal and political balances in the small state. The Singaporean leadership lives in fear of the 'maverick' " (Chew, "Human Rights in Singapore," 941).

LEE (*interrupting*): And let's not forget about nonpolitical violent crime. Singapore is a remarkably safe place. An American journalist working on a documentary told me that she had gone jogging in the streets around her hotel at Singapore's Marina Bay around two A.M. She said she "would have been mad" to do that in the United States. "Why was she able to do that? Because we have established a certain security and personal safety." Fortunately, we didn't copy "American ideas of how we should govern ourselves. . . . The American ideas are theories extracted from the American experience. They have not been successfully transplanted to a non-Anglo-Saxon society like the Philippines, although America ruled it for fifty years. And now in America itself, after thirty years of experimenting with the Great Society programs, there is widespread crime and violence, children kill each other with guns, neighborhoods are insecure."[93]

DEMO: First of all, violent crime has been declining in the United States. More importantly, you can't blame democracy for crime in the U.S. If anything, violent crime is due to the *lack* of democracy—some people feel marginalized and voiceless, and they don't have a stake in the system, which leads to all sorts of social pathologies. You're drawing completely the wrong lesson from the American experience—if the concern is to minimize violence, the answer is more, not less, democracy!

LEE: Look, I can't afford to experiment with such nice theories. Even if U.S.-style democracy doesn't cause crime, the fact of the matter is that it allows for the existence of violent society. In this respect, we're doing much better with less democracy. So what's the incentive to switch over?

DEMO: If you put it that way, it's hard to argue with you. In any case, I wasn't going to say anything about relationship between democracy and street violence. Maybe you're right, it's an open question whether or not democracy is helpful for this purpose. But let's move on to the question of war between states: this is where democracies have a particularly good track record. Democracies, quite simply, don't fight each other—citizens' inter-

---

[93] Quoted in Han et al., *Lee Kuan Yew*, 194, 206.

est in staying out of bloodshed and war, and the establishment
of democratic norms of peaceful resolution of conflict and of
other people's right to self-determination, among other factors,
introduce an element of restraint in the way democracies deal
with each other.[94] This argument was first developed by Immanuel Kant in his essay "Perpetual Peace," and it's one of the very
few philosophical insights that has been empirically confirmed
by political science research for the past two hundred years of
world history.[95]

LEE: That may be true as a general point, but it's the exceptions
I'm worried about.

DEMO: I can't think of any exceptions.

LEE: Really? Just look at your own country. The Spanish-American
War of 1898 seems to have been a direct product of democratic
decision-making. U.S. President McKinley apparently launched
this war in response to domestic public pressure. The U.S. public, it seems, was whipped up in a warmongering frenzy by the
American press, and the president couldn't resist the political
pressure.[96] Even worse, the United States has often subverted
the democratic regimes unfriendly to the interests of U.S.-based

---

[94] See Michael W. Doyle's two-part article on "Kant, Liberal Legacies, and Foreign Affairs."

[95] Michele Schmiegelow, "The Meaning of Democracy in Asia," paper presented at the conference on Democracy and Democratization in Asia, Université
Catholique de Louvain, May 1994, 1.

[96] See George Kennan, *American Diplomacy: 1900–1950*, chap. 1. Pakistan's decision to detonate a nuclear bomb (at least partly) in response to popular indig-
nation over India's nuclear tests is a more contemporary example of a democratic government facing pressure from the people to engage in warmongering
acts. India's own nuclear tests seem to have been approved by a large majority,
as indicated by the fact that all political parties (except the Communists) initially
endorsed the government's decision. Judging from news reports, it seems that
many Indian citizens derive self-esteem from the thought that "my" country can
now be officially recognized as a nuclear power by the outside world. More
optimistically, however, it can be argued that democratic forms of government at
least reduce the likelihood that the countries actually go to war, since the people
may not be willing to put their lives on the line without compelling reasons for
doing so.

multinationals, such as the CIA-backed coup in Guatemala in 1954 that plunged the country into three decades of nightmarish military rule.[97]

DEMO: Fair enough. But the situation has changed since then. The U.S. public is more attentive to human rights abuses now. There's a lot of public debate about the pros and cons of going to war, especially since the Vietnam War, and it's almost inconceivable that the public would back attempts to subvert democracies abroad.

LEE: It doesn't matter. Actually, we're not worried about the Americans. Quite the opposite: we welcome your stabilizing presence in the region, which is why we gave you guys access to our facilities after you were booted out of Subic Bay in the Philippines. Our main threats come from neighboring countries, and this theory about democracies not fighting each other won't help us, since most of our neighbors aren't democratic. The deepest problem in Southeast Asia is that most people's first allegiance lies with the ethnic group rather than the national community (notwithstanding our best efforts to instill a sense of nationhood), and democratization may well unleash ethnic hatreds better kept under wraps. I'm profoundly concerned about recent developments in Indonesia. Whatever we think about Suharto's domestic policies, the fact of the matter is that he presided over three decades of peaceful relations with neighboring countries.[98] Indonesia was far more dangerous to its neighbors in its democratic phase in the 1950s and early 1960s, and the new "democracy" may be less tolerant than Suharto's dictatorship. It may simply provide an outlet for the hatreds lurking among poor workers and peasants.[99] People are

[97] See Stephen C. Schlesinger and Stephen Kinzer, *Bitter Fruit*. For other examples of U.S. efforts to subvert democracies abroad, see Noam Chomsky, *Deterring Democracy*.

[98] Jusuf Wunandi, a harsh critic of Suharto's domestic policies, specifically praised Suharto's peaceful foreign policy when he was asked to evaluate the legacy of the Suharto regime (Asia Society talk, Hong Kong, May 1998).

[99] See Nicholas Kristof, "In Indonesia, Democracy's Dark Side," *International Herald Tribune*, 26 May 1998, 1.

already talking about expelling citizens of Chinese ancestry, which may lead to a wave of refugees washing up on our shores. I'm sorry to say this, but mutual hostility runs deeper among the people than among the more pragmatic political leaders, and more democracy may actually increase the probability of war.[100]

DEMO: But surely instability in the region is due primarily to the economic crisis? Ethnic passions will hopefully diminish in a few years time, once the economy gets back on track.

LEE: I'm less hopeful. Sometimes, ethnic passions can actually intensify in tandem with economic development. Consider the case of Quebec—the more modernization you have, the smaller the differences between Francophones and Anglophones, the worse the ethnic animosities.[101] In Singapore, it appears that blood ties will always run deeper than national sentiments, and we've recently recognized the fact by implementing ethnic-based welfare schemes, whereby Malays contribute to a fund for underprivileged Malays, Chinese to a fund for underprivileged Chinese, and Indians to a fund for underprivileged Indians. Economic growth doesn't help, I'm afraid—Singaporeans care little about the fate of the "worst off" in different ethnic groups.[102]

4. DEMOCRACY AND CIVIL LIBERTIES

DEMO (*sighs*): Well, I don't think I'm going to get very far pursuing this line of argument. So let's move beyond the right to life to consider other civil liberties, such as the rights to travel, marry, have children, speak freely, in short, the sorts of "negative" free-

---

[100] See also *The Economist*'s argument that it is dangerous to approach the future with the belief that democratic states do not go to war with each other ("Democracies and War," *The Economist*, 1 April 1995, 17–18) as well as Thomas Schwartz and Kiron Skinner, "The Myth of Democratic Pacifism," *Asian Wall Street Journal*, 11 January 1998, 8.

[101] See Kymlicka, *Multicultural Citizenship*, 87–88.

[102] See the discussion in chap. 4, sec. 3.3.

doms that protect people from unwelcome interference by the state. Even persons not prone to the critical reflection required of individual autonomy have an interest in being left alone by their government—Chinese peasants, for example, may not strive for Kantian autonomy or Millian individuality, but I'm quite sure that they don't want to be told how many children to have, how many crops to grow, where to live and to work, and what religion to practice. More generally, I can't imagine that anyone enjoys living in fear of their government.[103] So let me propose an excellent reason to support democracy: democracies safeguard civil liberties to a greater extent than other political regimes; they minimize if not entirely eliminate fear and governmental oppression.

LEE: There you go again making general claims. Those theories don't always apply in the East Asian context. Quite often, non-democratic governments in East Asia haven't oppressed individuals who stick to their own affairs. Perhaps we've been influenced by the legacy of traditional China—until the Communists came along, unelected political leaders interfered very little with the ordinary lives of the vast majority of Chinese people.[104]

DEMO: But that's the past! I'm talking about contemporary regimes.

LEE: Well, look around you. There are many "exceptions." The less-than-democratic government of Hong Kong extends to its citizens a whole panoply of civil liberties that would satisfy any Western liberal. Here in Singapore, law-abiding citizens who assiduously attend to their own affairs and otherwise live inoffensive lives have nothing to fear:[105] they can make money, leave

---

[103] For a similar defense of liberal rights—one that is also meant to appeal to those not inclined to favor individualistic modes of life—see Charles Larmore, *The Morals of Modernity*, esp. chaps. 6 and 7. But see the critique in my review essay, "The Limits of Liberal Justice," 568–573.

[104] Simon Leys argues that this hands-off approach to ruling helps to explain the stability of the dynastic system, in contrast to the Communists, who "betrayed a strange incapacity to understand their own people" (*New York Review of Books*, 11 October 1990, 10) by organizing recurrent waves of terror invasive of the lives of common people. See also chap. 2, sec. 2.1.

[105] Ralf Dahrendorf makes this point in his article "Can We Combine Economic Opportunity with Civil Society and Political Liberty?" 29–30.

the country, practice their own religion, get married, have children, and so on.

DEMO: But there have been many cases of flagrant abuses of civil liberties in Singapore![106]

LEE: Democratic regimes don't have a clean civil liberties record either—the internment of American and Canadians of Japanese descent should make Singaporeans émigrés nervous about what might happen to them in the event of a war with, say, China.

DEMO: It's not the same. Singapore, you must admit, curtails more civil liberties than any Western country. I can't buy chewing gum here, and even *Cosmopolitan* is banned!

LEE: We were faced with difficult choices, and we did what we had to do. "I am often accused of interfering in the private lives of citizens. Yet, if I did not, had I not done that, we wouldn't be here today. And I say without the slightest remorse, that we wouldn't be here, we would not have made economic progress, if we had not intervened on very personal matters—who your neighbor is, how you live, the noise you make, how you spit, or what language you use. We decide what is right. Never mind what the people think. That's another problem."[107]

---

[106] For example, an academic named Christopher Lingle (then teaching at the National University of Singapore) was interrogated by Singapore police for an article he wrote in the *International Herald Tribune* that included criticism of unnamed Asian "intolerant regimes . . . relying upon a compliant judiciary to bankrupt opposition politicians" (Lingle, "The Smoke over Parts of Asia Obscures Some Profound Concerns," *International Herald Tribune*, 7 October 1994). On this case, see the *New York Times* editorial entitled "Harassment in Singapore," 20 October 1994, and a subsequent article in the *New York Times*, 7 November 1994, A9. Lingle was subsequently charged with defamation, and he was forced to flee the country. The Singapore government went ahead with the trial in his absence, and the attorney general himself had to prove that Lingle must have been referring to Singapore, which entailed listing the opposition members that have been sued and bankrupted over the years. The joke in Singapore was that the government had to prove Lingle's case to prove their own case. The prosecution eventually "won," and Lingle had to forfeit U.S. $90,000 in savings that were impounded in Singapore. The whole sordid affair is described in Lingle's book, *Singapore's Authoritarian Capitalism*.

[107] Quoted in Christopher Tremewan, *The Political Economy of Social Control in Singapore*, 2. See also Francis Seow, *To Catch a Tartar*, 46.

DEMO: But why not try to convince the people that you're right? You just don't trust them enough.

LEE: It's not always easy to convince people that there are times when civil liberties should be curtailed, especially in a democratic context. Consider the drug problem, nearly as bad in the old Singapore as it is in America today. How did we deal with it? We passed "a law which says that any customs officer or policeman who sees anybody in Singapore behaving suspiciously, leading him to suspect the person is under the influence of drugs, can require that man to have his urine tested. If the sample is found to contain drugs, the man immediately goes for treatment. In America, if you did that, it would be an invasion of the individual's rights and you would be sued. . . . I would have thought this kind of approach would be quite an effective way to deal with the terrible drug problem you have. But the idea of the inviolability of the individual has been turned into dogma."[108]

DEMO: None of what you say is incompatible with democracy. If enough people become convinced that such measures are necessary to curb drug abuse, they'll elect politicians to pass laws allowing the state to test suspicious-looking people, just as policemen are currently empowered to carry out random checks for alcohol on drivers.[109]

LEE: You're right, in a sense. Most people do support our tough approach to crime—according to a 1986 survey, 97 percent of Singaporeans endorse caning for rape, and 79 percent endorse caning for drug trafficking.[110] But people aren't always so enlightened, particularly if their own short-term interests are at stake. Sometimes, justifiable curtailment of civil rights can be difficult if the vote is granted to a short-term-minded electorate. Consider, for example, the fact that nearly all Chinese intellectuals in the PRC accept the necessity of the one-child-per-family policy meant to curb China's staggering post-1949 population

[108] Quoted in *Straits Times*, 11 March 1994 (interview with *Foreign Affairs*).

[109] For a more nuanced version of a similar proposal, see Amitai Etzioni, *The Spirit of Community*, 173–174.

[110] See Han et al., *Lee Kuan Yew*, 205.

216

explosion.[111] This policy, however, is highly unpopular in the countryside, where the large majority of Chinese live, and it's quite likely that a democratic China would revoke this measure[112] even if this led to disastrous long-term consequences. And don't just take my word for this—Fang Lizhi and other democracy movement leaders in China have expressed only horror at a democratic formula that would give equal voting rights to peasants.[113]

DEMO: You criticize me for making irrelevant comparisons, but why should the "lessons" from China be useful for Singapore? There aren't any peasants in this city-state.

LEE: They're not peasants, but the bulk of our people are the children of immigrants from the lower rungs of society in Asia, and they have yet to cultivate the finer social graces that make state sanctions unnecessary. "Mine is a very matter-of-fact approach to the problem. If you can select a population and they're educated and they're properly brought up, then you don't have to use too much of the stick because they would already have been trained. It's like with dogs. You train it in a proper way from small. It will know that it's got to leave, go outside to pee and to defecate. Unfortunately, when I was in Britain in 1946, I compared Singapore to Britain, and found we were very ill-behaved, ill-trained. They were well-trained, they were polite, they were honest. . . . We did not have 300 years of cultivated living and training. . . . We had to train adult dogs who even today deliberately urinate in lifts. What do you do?"[114]

DEMO (*gasps*): "Adult dogs"? Is that how you refer to your people?

---

[111] See Link, *Evening Chats in Beijing*, 105–107.

[112] In the same vein, the policy of compulsory birth control that was initiated during the "emergency period" declared by Indira Gandhi in the 1970s was decisively rejected by the voters in the general election in which it was a major issue. Popular opposition to artificial contraceptives also explains why the democratic Philippines ranks behind other East Asian countries in family planning. According to the Asian Development Bank, unchecked population growth is the core long-term development problem in the Philippines (Thomas Crampton, "Philippine Family Planners Stymied by Powerful Opposition," *International Herald Tribune*, 3 June 1999).

[113] See Vivienne Shue, "China: Transition Postponed?" 163.

[114] Quoted in Han et al., *Lee Kuan Yew*, 195, 197.

LEE: It's just an analogy. My point is that it wouldn't "have happened in the Britain I knew in the '40s and '50s. It's a standard of behavior of people which springs from cultivated living over a long period and training of children in a certain way, so that they are considerate to other people. You tell me how long we take to reach that kind of a state. Maybe another hundred years of constant effort."[115]

DEMO: Let's hope it doesn't take that long. In fact, excessive reliance on punishment may delay your "civilizing mission," so your approach is probably counterproductive. If people refrain from behavior simply because they're afraid of the consequences, they won't internalize moral norms. Why not try to educate your people so that they do the right thing for the right reason?

LEE: That's the long-term aim. But meanwhile, we have to deal with the fact that "in areas like the public corridors in housing estates where nobody can see them, they just throw away the litter. But in the public places where they can be seen and fined, they've stopped. Now, there's no reason why they can't also stop for their own passageways, but they don't, right? We haven't reached that state yet. I would hope, one day, standards reach a point where, instead of punishing one in 100, you may have to punish one in 10,000. But I would not dare make such a prediction when this will be, because it depends upon how the policy evolves and whether it is pursued with vigor and subtlety, so that each generation is able to produce better results with children."[116]

DEMO: Interesting. You're not holding up Singapore as some kind of ideal that Western societies should emulate. Quite the opposite: you seem to be arguing for "the stick" as a short-term measure—well, not that short—until people improve to the point where there's no need to resort to punishment, like Britain in the 1950s.

LEE: That's correct. Our dispute—if there is one—is mainly over the appropriate means for achieving a commonly shared end.

[115] Quoted in ibid.
[116] Quoted in ibid., 209.

218

DEMO: But you also have a dispute with your own people— or perhaps I should say "adult dogs." You don't trust them enough to make a democratic decision about the need for harsh punishments.

LEE: Like I said, if I hadn't interfered in the private lives of citizens, "we wouldn't be here today." The educated people understand this.

DEMO: Do you have any evidence to support this claim?

LEE: Do you have any evidence to the contrary?

DEMO (*sighs*): It's going to be hard to persuade you if you're always shifting the burden of proof onto me.

LEE: Look, you're the foreigner here. You're the one who's supposed to persuade me to change my ways. You need to show me that there's something wrong with the status quo, and that democracy can do better at achieving desired ends. You haven't done that so far.

5. DEMOCRACY AND PROSPERITY

DEMO (*pause*): Well, let me try out another justification for democracy, perhaps the most common of all. This is the view that the practical power of modern democratic institutions today comes from their aptness to the economic world in which we now live. A prominent democratic theorist argues that the principal contribution of modern constitutional democracy has been to make both the modern state and the standard of democratic legitimacy compatible with the operating requirements of an international and domestic economic order founded on private ownership and market. In other words, democracy has managed to reconcile the needs of capitalist production with the practical and ideological requirements of effective rule in the modern world.[117]

LEE: A nice theory. But if the concern is material prosperity, I personally don't recommend democracy. "A country must first have economic development, then democracy may follow. With a few

[117] John Dunn, ed., *Democracy*, 251.

219

exceptions, democracy has not brought good government to new developing countries. Democracy has not led to development because the governments did not establish the stability and discipline necessary for development."[118]

DEMO: But you can't blame *democracy* for the lack of stability in Third World countries! In fact, democracy is more likely to help provide stability and discipline, because people have more faith in a democratic government and they're less likely to try to destabilize it.

LEE: Once again, a nice theory. But the reality is somewhat different. At the early stages of development, "there is an inherent defect in working that system [of one-man-one-vote]. . . . Where the majority of your population is semi-literate, it responds more to the stick than to the carrot,[119] and politicians at election time cannot use the stick. So . . . he who bids the highest wins. . . . At a time when you want people to work with less return and more capital investment, one-man-one-vote produces just the opposite.

Effective government . . . in an undeveloped situation means a government that must improve the investment rate, and that must demand more effort for less return over a sustained period—certainly more than five years. If you can make the demand for a period of two years, produce the results after the fourth, have the results by the fifth, then all is well. . . . Unfortunately, the process of economic growth is much slower and painful, and neither five nor ten years is an adequate enough period for the demands that you make on a population to be felt and enjoyed by the population. Therefore, the results would be— unless you had exceptional leadership and exceptional circumstances . . . to take the solution which is least painful . . . the least painful solution is not to make undue demands on your population . . . not to increase investment rate and not to jack up your society. . . .

Then you are competing against people who not only promise not to maintain the investment rate, but . . . to spend what

[118] Quoted in Han et al., *Lee Kuan Yew*, 139.
[119] Lee actually said "responds more to the carrot than to the stick," but he probably meant to say, "responds more to the stick than to the carrot."

there is [already saved] in the kitty . . . and if an electorate is sufficiently naïve to believe that these things can be done, you break the bank."[120]

DEMO (*raises voice*): To borrow you own words, "that's a nice theory"! It's particularly convenient for dictators who want to hold on to their power. The problem is that there's not a shred of evidence to support it. Many industrialized powers developed *with* democracy. Democrats didn't compete with each other to "break the bank" in order to satisfy an allegedly short-term minded electorate.

LEE: I don't deny that democracy can sometimes work. But in many "developing" countries, inflows of international aid were dissipated through incompetence and outflows of bribes, resources couldn't be harnessed as factional interests competed to undermine the polity,[121] and their countries were condemned to material deprivation.

DEMO: I fail to see the connection between democracy and these other problems. If you want to establish a causal link, you need to back up your claims with empirical support.

LEE: Look, I'm not a social scientist. But the fact of the matter is that democracy—even if it didn't directly cause these problems—allowed for things to go wrong, and that's worrying enough.

DEMO: But why are you so worried by worst-case scenarios? In some contexts, democracy allowed for economic development and the other things you care about. Why not be inspired by positive examples?

LEE: I agree that democracy can work both ways. My intention isn't to make any universal claims about the effects of democratic rule. There are constraints peculiar to Singapore, and that's really what worries me. Our country is a small island roughly the size of Brooklyn, we're almost completely deprived of natural resources, and we're overwhelmingly dependent on other econ-

---

[120] Quoted in Han et al., *Lee Kuan Yew*, 136, 135.

[121] See Tan Boon Teik (then Singapore's attorney general), "Human Rights and Economic Development," *The 7th Gordon Arthur Ransome Oration*, delivered in Singapore on 2 August 1984, 6.

omies. This means that we have to respond quickly by devising policy, modifying institutions, and constantly upgrading the talent of our people.[122] We have to survive the vicissitudes of the international marketplace, and we simply can't afford to give free reign to the sorts of interest groups and lobbies that paralyze the policy-making process in the U.S. Congress or to institutionalize "the checks and balances [that] interfere with governing in a developing country where executive action must be swift."[123] I'm not condemning your system. It may well be appropriate in a country with "an abundance of resources and immigrant energy, a generous flow of capital and technology from Europe, and two wide oceans that kept conflicts of the world away from American shores."[124] Unfortunately, we're not so lucky in Singapore, and you shouldn't expect us to copy your political system.

DEMO: No one is arguing that you should copy the complete set of American political institutions. I'd be the first to admit they're flawed. Our dispute is over the need to implement free and fair democratic elections in Singapore. And if the concern is to speed up policy-making, this can be done without sacrificing democracy. Policy-making in democratic Taiwan, for example, isn't paralyzed by competing interest groups. Why can't you learn from the Taiwanese experience?[125]

LEE: Taiwan only recently adopted democratic procedures. They needed to go through years of strong government. It's not easy to make people understand that they need to sacrifice their own interests to benefit future generations. Look at what we had to do. We adopted an economic strategy that relied on mainly U.S.-

---

[122] See ibid., 8. See also Garry Rodan's account of Singapore's industrialization in his book *The Political Economy of Singapore's Industrialization.*

[123] Quoted in Chew, "Human Rights in Singapore," 941.

[124] Quoted in Han et al., *Lee Kuan Yew,* 206.

[125] The Singaporean government does seem interested in learning from Taiwan's experience in promoting local business innovation—it is leading a group of small businesses to Taiwan to visit and learn from successful companies on the high-tech island (see "Ben Dolven, 'Taiwan's Trump,' " *Far Eastern Economic Review,* 6 August 1998, 12)—but presumably it thinks it can learn about promoting local entrepreneurship without adopting Taiwan's relatively democratic political institutions.

based multinational corporations to import capital and to provide employment, guaranteed home markets, and a sophisticated organization that would bring Singapore to an international standard of industrial technology and skills. Of course, multinational corporations require a healthy investment environment in order to make profits, and that was our task—we provided political stability, and we supplied a sound infrastructure funded with the forced savings of first-generation Singaporeans. We also provided them with a source of cheap labor. "Of course, the prevailing theory then was that multinationals were exploiters of cheap labor and cheap raw materials and would suck them dry. We had no raw material for them to exploit. All we had was labor. Nobody else wanted to exploit labor. So why not, if they want to exploit our labor? They're welcome to it. And we found out that whether or not they exploited us, we were learning how to do a job from them, which we would never have learnt."[126] Needless to say, this wasn't always popular. We had to deal with resistance from militant labor unions. "Their intention was not to get the economy cured and growing but to create more problems so there would be more unemployment, so the system would collapse. . . . Because if the economy got going, the system will prevail and communism will not take over. So . . . endless strikes, go-slows, sit-ins, all sorts of demonstrations to block the economy and slow it down. . . . Then after Malaysia, it began to clean up. If you call a political strike without taking a ballot, you get deregistered. Slowly, we enforced the law."[127] Basically, militant labor unions were curtailed and effectively barred from the political process,[128] measures that would have been difficult if not impossible to implement in a democratic context. And this strategy worked, if I can say so myself—"Singapore's economy prospered [because] private enterprises work within a stable and congenial framework of orderly and predictable government."[129]

[126] Quoted in Han et al., *Lee Kuan Yew*, 109.
[127] Quoted in ibid., 110.
[128] See Rodan, *The Political Economy of Singapore's Industrialization*, esp. chap. 3.
[129] Quoted in Mutalib, "Singapore's Elected Presidency," 11. More generally, see Rodan's account of the role of the state in Singapore's industrialization in *The Political Economy of Singapore's Industrialization*.

DEMO: But that's the past. Even if it's true that authoritarian rule can coexist with capitalist mechanisms and facilitate high growth rates in relatively undeveloped countries. . . .

LEE (*interrupting*): You must face the facts. Singapore, South Korea, and Taiwan developed rapidly under authoritarian leaders committed to economic development. And if you compare the experience of rapid growth in China since the early 1980s with the disastrous economic performance of postsocialist Russia, it's quite obvious that there's a serious risk of a sudden *volte face* to democracy in countries moving from a state-socialist system of directive planning into some form of a market economy.[130]

DEMO (*frustrated*): Fine, fine. But why is this relevant for a rich country like Singapore? I was going to say that once a country lifts itself out of poverty, economic growth requires more than political stability, cheap labor, a sound infrastructure, and copying other people's technology. Economically developed and technologically advanced countries like Singapore—with a per capita income greater than that of Italy and Great Britain—need to improve and innovate to maintain their competitive advantage relative to other rich countries, which can only be done in the context of a democratic environment allowing individuals to experiment, freely express themselves, and take risks as entrepreneurs.[131] It's not a coincidence that democracy is closely related to the economic systems of developed countries.[132]

LEE: A nice theory. But how can you explain the fact that we managed double-digit growth in the early 1990s, higher than in most developed countries? You may not be impressed, but others are. China frequently sends delegations to Singapore to learn

[130] See Gordon White, "Democratization and Economic Reform in China," 80. But for a different view, see Barrett L. McCormick, "Democracy or Dictatorship?: A Response to Gordon White."

[131] This argument is made by Chee, *Dare to Change*, 105; Chew, "Human Rights in Singapore," 947–948; Eric Jones, "Asia's Fate," 23; Michael Davis, "The Price of Rights," 305–306 and sec. 2; and Ben Dolven, "Let's All Be Creative," *Far Eastern Economic Review*, 24 December 1998, 10, 13.

[132] For the empirical evidence, see Larry Diamond, "Economic Development and Democracy Reconsidered," 487.

how we maintain a flourishing economy in a stable environment.[133] Deng Xiaoping himself described Singapore as a model for China.[134]

DEMO: I doubt that the Singaporean model can be replicated in China. What works in a tiny island city-state won't work in a country of 1.2 billion people.

LEE: Chinese leaders hope to replicate the Singaporean model in particular cities, not on a national scale.[135]

DEMO: I suspect that will change with the Asian economic crisis, which seems to have exposed the dark side of Asian values.[136]

---

[133] The Chinese government also sends delegations to study some less well-known features of the Singaporean system. One delegation was sent to learn from Singapore's approach to prostitution, which included interviews with "sex-workers" at "low-class" and "high-class" brothels. According to one source, however, the Chinese officials were shocked by the Singapore government's pragmatic approach to prostitution (prostitution is legal in Singapore, and "sex workers" pay taxes and undergo regular medical check-ups), while the Singaporeans in turn were dismayed that the Chinese seemed to prefer living with the growing problem of illegal prostitution (along with the related problems of crime and sexually transmitted diseases) rather than deal with the fact that prostitution is likely to be a permanent feature of the social landscape.

[134] See Murray Hiebert, "Almost Home," *Far Eastern Economic Review,* 25 April 1996, 61.

[135] Most obviously, Chinese and Singaporeans officials are developing an area in Suzhou township that is modeled upon Singapore's Jurong Industrial Township, an area that is literally cordoned off from surrounding cities. Singaporean public administrators train Chinese managers, with the Singapore government picking up the tab, and in return Singaporean public and private investors receive preferential treatment, such as lower taxes, and Singaporean business law applies in the special zone. The Suzhou Industrial Park even has its own customs officials. An obviously envious French diplomat based in Singapore compared this development to nineteenth-century concessions "granted" to Western imperialist powers, with the important difference that this time Chinese officials are willingly involved (private conversation). Recently, however, the Suzhou project has been experiencing unexpected economic difficulties, with the Singaporeans accusing the Suzhou municipal authorities of directing investors to their own wholly owned, nearby industrial and economic zone where land and service are cheaper. In response, Singapore is to cut its stake in Suzhou Industrial Park from 65 percent to 35 percent (Barry Porter, "Singapore Drops Control of Su-Zhou Park," *South China Morning Post,* 29 June 1999).

[136] See, e.g., "The Dark Side of 'Asian Values' Turns Miracle Into Mess," *International Herald Tribune,* 25 November 1997, 16.

Correct me if I'm wrong, but even Singapore went through a recession last year.

LEE: That's correct.[137] Fortunately, "we've got substantial reserves"[138]—the highest per capita in the world—which should help us to weather the storm. And let's not exaggerate the severity of the crisis in Singapore. The Swiss-based World Economic Forum has once again ranked Singapore as the world's most competitive economy. Another Swiss-based body, the International Institute for Management Development, has also rated Singapore first among forty-six countries surveyed for having a legal framework that supports a competitive economy.[139] And according to the latest report of yet another Swiss-based body—Business Environment Risk Intelligence—Singapore is still the world's second most profitable place to invest in.[140] Of course, we're not simply resting on our laurels. We're doing what we can to get out of this crisis: liberalizing our financial industry, retraining workers, streamlining companies, slashing costs, and so on. "Our strategy is simple: capitalize on our strength, stability, efficiency, low investment-risk ratings, to get high-value-added jobs which our neighbors will not be able to do until their workers are better trained."[141] And for the really long term, we're restructuring our educational system so that it does more to promote creativity, which should benefit the economy several years from now.[142]

[137] Singapore's economy shrank by 0.8 percent in the fourth quarter of 1998, the second consecutive quarter of negative growth (the technical definition of a recession), although the overall growth rate for 1998 was a stronger than expected 1.5 percent ("Economic Turnaround from June?" *Straits Times* [weekly edition], 27 February 1999, 4). In the first quarter of 1999, Singapore was technically out of recession, as the economy grew by 1.2 percent ("Recession Over, but It's Not Time to Rejoice," *Straits Times* [weekly edition], 22 May 1999, 3).

[138] Quoted in "Politically Incorrect," *Far Eastern Economic Review*, 24 September 1998, 12.

[139] See "Economy Feels Asian 'Flu' but Still Well-Rated," *Singapore*, July–August 1998, 7.

[140] "Singapore Still the Second-Most Profitable Venue," *Straits Times* (weekly edition), 15 August 1998, 24.

[141] Quoted in "Last Tiger Standing Sharpens Its Claws," *South China Morning Post*, 3 December 1998, 21.

[142] See "Education for Future Growth," *Straits Times* (weekly edition), editorial, 29 March 1997, 13; "Breaking the Mould," *Far Eastern Economic Review*, 23 July 1998, 47–49; and "Relax—A Little," *Far Eastern Economic Review*, 24 December 1998, 14.

DEMO: You seem to have forgotten about one thing: democracy. Clearly one lesson of this crisis is the need to promote open governments and the accountability of institutions. All the brilliant technocrats in the world can't save you without democracy. In the absence of independent and accountable decision makers, the economy will be plagued by dangerous, incestuous relationships between business and politics, and the forces protecting big business interests will override the broader needs of national economic policy-making.[143]

LEE: I realize that's a fashionable view. It's not completely false: it may help to explain why things went wrong in Indonesia. But democracy can also make things worse. In Korea, democratization brought paralysis and deadlock, particularly when the interests of powerful groups were threatened. In their effort to maximize their private interests, these groups played a game of attrition against their opponents instead of trying to find a negotiated settlement. This failure of dispute resolution has been the most salient feature of the Korean democratic experience and explains why Korea failed to reform its economic system, which precipitated the crisis.[144] Let's put it this way—it's not a particularly inspiring example for Singapore.

DEMO: You seem to select the countries that suit your antidemocratic biases. Democratic Taiwan seems to be doing quite well compared to its authoritarian Asian counterparts.

LEE: Look, I don't deny that democracy can work both ways. My point is that it's not essential for growth in developed societies. What you need is a "professional civil service, [an] effective central bank, and sound banks and companies."[145] We have that in

---

[143] See Mark Malloch Brown, "Why a Social Dimension to Foreign Policy Is Vital to U.S.–East Asia Relations," 5.

[144] See Jongryn Mo, "Political Culture, Democracy and the Economic Crisis of Korea," paper presented at conference on Confucianism and Democracy, Korea, June 1998, 4. Mo does not blame democracy per se, but rather the way it has been practiced in Korea (ibid., 10). In the same vein, Ha-Joon Chang notes that "Crony capitalism appeared in the last decade [in Korea], as government guidelines were gradually abandoned and a free-for-all of shady political exchanges ensued" ("Reform for the Long Term in Korea," *International Herald Tribune*, 13 February 1998, 10).

[145] Quoted in "Financial Crisis: SM asks EU to Be More Pro-Active," *Straits Times* (weekly edition), 21 February 1998, 3.

Singapore. What you need to avoid are "corruption, cronyism and nepotism."[146] We're free of those ills in Singapore. So why should we take the risk to switch to democracy in these uncertain times?

DEMO: What's the risk? Western investors will welcome democracy; they'll feel more confident about the system here. That can only help the economy.

LEE: It's more important to have "political continuity, to assure foreign investors that present and future governments will stay committed to reforms."[147] So far, they're happy: foreign investors and analysts have praised our government for its rational response to the regional economic crisis. For example, the Hong Kong–based Political and Economic Risk Consultancy, which provides reports to foreign investors, has ranked Singapore first among eleven Asian countries for its handling of the economic crisis.[148] What's the incentive to change our form of government?

DEMO: Foreign investors may be happy, but I'd also worry about the Singaporean people. The PAP derived most of its legitimacy from its ability to deliver the economic goods. But now, that's gone. People will turn against the government, and this will lead to trouble. In fact, Samuel Huntington himself pointed to this Achilles' heel in the Singaporean system. He predicted that in the absence of a Western-style democratic system allowing for the ouster and replacement of incumbents, an economic downturn could produce "revolutionary change."[149]

[146] Quoted in "Risky to Talk Down US$, Says SM," *Straits Times* (weekly edition), 20 June 1998, 2.

[147] Quoted in "East Asian Governments Have to Take Painful Reforms, Says SM Lee," *Straits Times* (weekly edition), 28 February 1998, 14.

[148] See "Look Beyond Present Crisis: PM," *Straits Times* (weekly edition), 16 May 1998, 24, and "Singapore's Response to Crisis Praised," *Straits Times* (weekly edition), 31 October 1998, 2. According to opposition politician Chee Soon Juan, however, the Singapore government has lost billions of dollars in overseas loans and secretive investments, but Singaporeans (and non-Singaporeans) "are seldom told of such debacles" by the state-controlled media (Chee, *To Be Free*, 316–319, 335).

[149] Huntington, "American Democracy in Relation to Asia," 42.

LEE: I wouldn't worry about that. There will only be trouble if Singaporeans blame us for the downturn. But even our critics acknowledge that most of our problems are external and beyond our control.[150] It's perfectly obvious that we're being lashed by economic waves from outside over which we have no control.

DEMO: I'm not sure how long that will last. There's only so much pain that people can take. If things don't improve soon, they'll begin to look for an alternative.

LEE: Well, that doesn't mean we should give it to them. In fact, constraints on democracy are easier to justify when the economy nosedives and tough measures are required to remedy the situation. As you know, our government has announced sweeping pay cuts for civil servants and private-sector workers as part of an effort to pull the country out of recession and sharpen our competitive edge against lower-cost neighbors. We're aiming for a 15 percent overall reduction in wage costs.[151] Needless to say, these measures are not popular. To be frank, they may be difficult, if not impossible, to implement in a more democratic context.[152] But we "are going to cut costs however painful, that's

---

[150] See my article, "After the Tsunami," 24–25.

[151] See "Singapore Aims to Cut Firms' Employment Costs," *International Herald Tribune*, 12 November 1998, 18; "Govt Decides on $10.5b Cost Cuts," *Straits Times* (weekly edition), 28 November 1998, 1; and "Singapore Trims Sails in Turmoil," *South China Morning Post*, 14 March 1999, 4.

[152] This point was actually made by Hong Kong's secretary for trade and industry, Chau Tak-hay. Mr. Chau noted that the Singapore government had "advantages" over Hong Kong's in implementing unpopular policies designed to tackle the economic downturn (such as wage cuts) because the PAP has nearly complete control over parliament, the media, trade unions, and the people. He added: "Of course we are different from Singapore. The opposition parties in Singapore do not raise opposition. If they do raise opposition, they might be arrested. . . . our legislative council has 60 opposition members" (Barry Porter, "Trade Secretary's Comments Anger Singapore," *South China Morning Post*, 4 March 1998, 10). The *Straits Times* replied with a bitter editorial that denounced Mr. Chau's "misinformed and inaccurate comments" ("Speak Not in Ignorance," *Straits Times* [weekly edition], 6 March 1999, 10), but the editorial failed to reply to the point that it would have been difficult, if not impossible, for the Hong Kong government to implement substantial wage cuts in a context where social critics are relatively free to express (and act on) dissenting views.

that."[153] People may not like it at first, but they'll eventually understand.

DEMO: How can you be so sure "they'll eventually understand"?

LEE: You may recall that Singapore was badly hit by the worldwide recession in 1985. We had negative growth, our worst economic performance in twenty years, a decline in exports, and a rise in unemployment to 6 percent.[154] So we took to harsh measures to deal with the recession, including wage restraints and a cut in employers' contributions to a forced saving scheme for workers. It worked—we were back to 8.5 percent growth and negligible unemployment in 1988, and most people were back to praising our economic performance.

DEMO: But what if it takes longer for things to improve this time? There's no guarantee that people will put up with authoritarian government indefinitely.

LEE: There will be trouble if the economy doesn't improve in the next few years. But you may not like the outcome. And I'm not just talking about Singapore. Look at what happened in some countries following a prolonged depression earlier this century. "In Italy in the 1920s the Depression led to the rise of Mussolini and the Fascist Party. In Germany Hitler and the Nazi Party came to power in 1932. In Japan the military took charge and led Japan first into Manchuria, in 1931, and next into China, in 1937. In 1941, General Tojo took charge openly as prime minister and led Japan into Southeast Asia in December 1941. In Spain, there was the dictatorship of General Franco, in Portugal that of Salazar. There is no guarantee that the present democracies will survive if there is a prolonged world depression."[155] I think it's in everyone's interest that the region, including Singapore, recovers sooner rather than later. And our government is best suited to lay the foundations for economic growth.

DEMO (*sighs*): Okay, let me concede that point, for the sake of argument. Another problem is that you seem to think economic growth per se is valuable. Authoritarian Brazil had high growth rates in the 1960s and 1970s, but only a minority benefited and

[153] Quoted in "Politically Incorrect," 12.
[154] R. S. Milne and D. K. Mauzy, *Singapore: The Legacy of Lee Kuan Yew*, 135.
[155] Quoted in Han et al., *Lee Kuan Yew*, 379.

the poor actually got poorer. For those who care about social justice, it's the distribution of wealth that matters, in particular, whether the worst off benefit from economic growth. If you agree with this, then you should also value democracy. In a democracy, the poor are allowed to put forward their own interests in political debate, which makes it probable that their interests will be given due weight. In effect, this means that democracies are also compassionate societies, compared with the feasible alternatives.

LEE: A fine theory. But when I look at "what happened to the British and the Australians," I'm not so certain. "They went in for compassionate welfare programs. They paid their unemployed almost as much as the employed when they lost their jobs. They had the right to refuse three or four jobs until the right one came along, commensurate with what they were getting the last time, to their liking. The result was layabouts. So finally the Australians gave up, and a Labour government in Australia has struck down unemployment benefits. If we do not learn from other people's errors, costly errors, we would be ruined, wouldn't we? We have got very little margin to spare."[156]

DEMO (*frustrated*): But what does this have to do with democracy? The fact—if it is one—that Australia embarked on counterproductive welfare policies isn't a reason to condemn *democracy*. The proper response is to learn from what other democracies are doing right in terms of social welfare.

LEE (*raises voice*): Let's look at the facts. On any account, the worst off in Singapore are better off than when we started.[157] In the 1950s there was no sanitation and no running water, hot or cold—for many not even electricity. Now, Singapore has virtually no poverty, no homelessness, no begging, and little crime. Unemployment is low. The air is clean. The prosperity of Singapore, where people lead lives that even many Japanese would envy, is shared widely.[158] I don't want to be so cruel as to compare

[156] Quoted in ibid., 391.

[157] But for a critical account of Singapore's contemporary social welfare policies, see Chee, *Dare to Change*, chap. 4.

[158] A reporter for *The New Yorker* made similar points: see Stan Sesser, "A Reporter at Large: A Nation of Contradictions," *The New Yorker*, 13 January 1992, 39–40.

the lives of the worst off in Singapore with the state of the underclass in American cities, but it will be immediately evident that American democrats are in no position to lecture us about social justice.

DEMO (*sighs*): I don't think we're going to get very far if we pursue this kind of debate. Why don't we . . .

SUMMARY

LEE (*interrupting*): It's not that your arguments are invalid, they just don't apply in a Singaporean context. You invoke arguments for democracy derived from the Western liberal experience that can't meet the aspirations, needs, and pressing concerns of Singaporeans. You appealed to the value of equal respect, but I replied that Western-style electoral procedures aren't ideal for selecting decision-makers that treat citizens with equal respect. Then you invoked the Western value of individual autonomy, or the idea that citizens should have the right to make the decisions that affect their lives, but I pointed out that this value doesn't resonate to the same extent in a family-oriented society like Singapore, where people are less concerned about enacting freely chosen life plans and more reluctant to voice their interests in the political arena. And I must admit that I wasn't persuaded by your consequentialist arguments for democracy. Our government secures the peace, we curtail civil liberties only when we have to, and we're doing a good job managing the economy. So why should we change?

DEMO: Let me try out one last consequentialist argument. Democracy also contributes to public-spiritedness and nation-building. . . .

LEE (*interrupting*): Sounds interesting, but I'm afraid we're going to have to wrap it up. I have a cabinet meeting in fifteen minutes.

DEMO: Can we meet again in two or three months time? I'll try to brush up on my local knowledge so that my arguments will be more specifically directed at the Singaporean context.

LEE: That's a good idea. See you then.

232

A Communitarian Critique of Authoritarianism: The Case of Singapore

SCENE: Singapore, May 25, 1999. Lee and Demo pursue their discussion on the pros and cons of democracy in Singapore. In this chapter, Demo turns to another consequentialist justification for democracy, namely, the view that democratic political practices can strengthen communal forms of life such as the family and the nation.[1] Demo—now well versed in Singaporean local knowledge—argues that this "communitarian"[2] justification is particularly appropriate for the Singaporean context.

1. COMMUNITY AND DEMOCRACY

DEMO: I enjoyed our discussion last time. In fact, I share many of your concerns regarding democracy. It's difficult to deny that ethnic warfare, poverty, and corruption pose serious obstacles to the successful establishment and consolidation of democratic political arrangements in developing countries. But your challenge to democracy—correct me if I'm wrong—amounts to more than that. You argue that Western democracy may not be appropriate even in modern East Asian societies. You pointed out that less-than-democratic governments in the region—Sin-

---

[1] An earlier version of this chapter was published (in dialogue form) in *Political Theory* 25, no. 1 (February 1997): 6–32. Reprinted by permission of Sage Publications.

[2] I do not intend to defend a grand dichotomy between liberal individualism and communitarianism in this chapter. In fact, I rely on the arguments of two nineteenth-century Western liberals—J. S. Mill and Alexis de Tocqueville—to support the communitarian claim that democracy can contribute to public spiritedness, which is part of the reason I label myself a "liberal communitarian" in the introduction to this book (the main reason is that I care about civil and political rights).

gapore in particular—can deliver social peace, economic success, basic civil rights, and political stability, and that moves to democratize may endanger these successes.

LEE: You took the words right out of my mouth.

DEMO: Well, I've been here for quite a while now, reading the paper, mixing with locals, and people seem to be talking about another argument against democracy. More than once, I've heard it said that modern, nondemocratic East Asian regimes can secure rich and fulfilling communal attachments instead of no-holds-barred individualism, rootlessness, alienation from the political process, and other phenomena allegedly related to the erosion of communal life in Western democracies. On the face of it, I must admit it's quite a powerful argument against democracy—perhaps the most tempting of all, since it might teach us something about how to deal with widespread social problems in Western societies.

LEE: This argument isn't meant to tempt Western liberals. It's a cultural argument, grounded in our communitarian traditions. Singaporeans have "little doubt that a society with communitarian values where the interests of society take precedence over that of the individual suits them better than the individualism of America."[3] We'll do what what's necessary to protect our communitarian traditions, including putting restrictions on people's democratic freedoms. But I'm not saying you should learn from us. Americans may prefer more democracy and less community, which is fine, but we prefer less democracy and more community.

DEMO: Actually, I don't want to question the premise that as a matter of moral aspiration Singaporeans are typically inclined to place special emphasis on the value of community. In my view, however, you tend to overstate the cultural differences. For example, the view that the protection of individual liberties is the final justification for political power may be dominant in the United States, but there's also a communitarian tradition

[3] Quoted in the *International Herald Tribune*, 9–10 November 1991.

234

buried beneath individualistic understandings.[4] So we're really comparing different dominant and persistent political outlooks. It's only a difference of degree. . . .

LEE (*interrupting*): It may be a matter of "difference of degree,"[5] but that doesn't mean it's not politically relevant. Communitarianism is the dominant social and political outlook in Singapore, and it looks like it's going to stay for the foreseeable future. Even if a small minority of Singaporeans endorse American-style individualism, it doesn't follow that we should adopt American political practices. There's still room for justifiable political differences between the two countries.

DEMO: Fair enough. To repeat, I'm prepared to grant the assumption that Singaporeans generally favor commitments to certain forms of community over the claims of individual freedom. What this means, I presume, is that citizens tend to support first and foremost a government that provides the social conditions that allow them to lead fulfilling communal lives.

LEE: That's correct. Singaporeans value community over democracy.

DEMO: But do the two goods really conflict? Is it in fact true that safeguarding democratic rights will undermine valued forms of communal life in Singapore? If more democracy need not lead to communal breakdown—or, even better, if political democratization can actually increase people's commitment to their communities—this should be a particularly compelling justification in a Singaporean context where political argument often takes the form of appeal to the value of community. It may well

---

[4] As the authors of *Habits of the Heart* put it, there is a "second language" of community buried beneath the dominant individualistic understandings in the United States (see Robert Bellah et al., *Habits of the Heart*).

[5] Notwithstanding the fact that the "Shared Values" document issued by the Singaporean government generally relies on a crude dichotomy between "communitarian Asia" and "the individualistic West," it does make the point that "The difference is not so stark as black and white, but one of degree" (presented to Parliament by the command of the president of the Republic of Singapore, 2 January 1991, paragraph 24).

be possible, in other words, to support democratic political practices from a *communitarian* standpoint.

LEE: That's abstractly conceivable. In Singapore, however, the reality is that democracy would threaten communitarian forms of life.

2. DEMOCRACY AND THE FAMILY

DEMO: I'm not so sure about that. As I see it, democracy is more likely to protect and promote communitarian forms of life. My argument begins with the observation that excessively interventionist political regimes, by seeking to control and dominate people's lives, actually undermine communal ties. At least in our century, nondemocratic regimes have posed the single greatest threat to communities. Such states cannot tolerate genuine communities within their boundaries because they would constitute competing sources of power and thus limit the individual's dependence upon and allegiance to the state. And it's a matter of historical record that antidemocratic forces have employed the most ruthless measures to undermine traditional communities such as the family and the church in the name of achieving an all-inclusive political community.[6]

LEE: That may be the historical record in the West, but East Asia is different. Consider the fate of the family in Chinese history. "History in China is of dynasties which have risen and fallen, of the waxing and waning of societies. And through all that turbulence, the family, the clan, has provided a kind of survival raft for the individual. Civilizations have collapsed, dynasties have been swept away by conquering hordes, but this life raft enables the civilization to carry on and get on its next phase. . . . The family and the way human relationships are structured do increase the survival chances of its members. That has been tested over thousands of years in many different situations."[7]

---

[6] See Allen Buchanan, "Assessing the Communitarian Critique of Liberalism," 858.

[7] Quoted in "A Conversation with Lee Kuan Yew," *Foreign Affairs* (March/April 1994): 115.

DEMO: But the Chinese Communist Party tried to change all that. Communist leaders were convinced that one of the weaknesses of the old system was its lack of control over the populace and the failure to utilize common people's energies by engaging them in the political system.[8] Family ties and obligations, which far outweighed other bonds, were undoubtedly the most threatening from the point of view of Communist leaders out to establish primary allegiance to the state, and consequently the party set out to transform families so as to mobilize their members to serve state interests. This didn't always translate into a conscious effort to destroy the family, but the new state-first policy did mean, at a minimum, that obligations to the state overrode obligations to the family in cases of conflict, as confirmed by the sorry history of family members betraying each other for political reasons during the Cultural Revolution.[9] The same thing happened after June 4, 1989, when some individuals were publicly rewarded for informing against family members.

LEE: You don't have to tell me about Communists. I saw how they worked in Singapore. "There was a certain ruthlessness about the way they manipulated people and got friends to fix other friends and control them. And if you break away from the organization, then they'll fix you and destroy you. There was a . . . lack of humanity about it."[10]

DEMO: If we agree about that, then we should also agree about the need for democracy. Modern-day governments ultimately dependent on support from citizens at election time won't risk incurring displeasure by employing ruthless measures to undermine traditional communities such as the family, and for family-oriented East Asians this is a good reason to favor democracy over despotic, unaccountable government.

LEE: But the choice isn't just between communism and democracy. In fact, the Singaporean government has a good track

[8] See Steven Goldstein, "Part 2: Politics (Introduction)," 171–172.

[9] The state-first principle in practice meant not only betraying family members but also neglecting basic family obligations. See, e.g., Jung Chang's vivid account of her father's insensitive behavior toward his pregnant wife in the heady days after the revolution in *Wild Swans*.

[10] Quoted in Han et al., *Lee Kuan Yew*, 42.

record in terms of protecting the family—much better than the Chinese Communists. One might say that we've taken seriously the need to be true to our pro-family East Asian cultural tradition. I know I've never deviated from my belief that the family is absolutely crucial for human flourishing, so the people have nothing to fear. Quite the opposite, I'd say. We actively promote the family unit, unlike the democratic West. It's quite peculiar to hear you lecturing me about the need to protect the family, because defenders of the family have far more to worry about in the United States. As Kishore Mahbubani, the top-ranking civil servant in Singapore's Ministry of Foreign Affairs, noted, "since 1960, the U.S. population has increased 41% while . . . divorce rates [have risen] by 300% [and] the percentage of children living in single parent households [is] up by 300%. This is massive social decay. Many a society shudders at the prospects of this happening on its shores. But instead of travelling overseas with humility, Americans confidently preach the virtues of unfettered individual freedom, blithely ignoring the visible social consequences."[11]

DEMO: It may be the case that "unfettered individual freedom" has contributed to the erosion of the family in Western societies, but you can't put the blame on the *democratic method*. In fact, democracy is most useful if your grim diagnosis of the state of the family in Western societies is accurate, because people can vote for politicians that favor policies designed to maintain and foster the family unit.[12]

LEE: But we don't have a problem in Singapore! Family life is flourishing here.

DEMO: What if things change in the future? The Singaporean people may still want the "insurance" of free and fair competitive elections.

LEE: Why should things change? I regard the family as a social institution whose flourishing is essential for individual well-being, not to mention political stability and a strong economy.

---

[11] Quoted in Chew, "Human Rights in Singapore," 936.

[12] Such policies, however, would be *illiberal* in the sense that the government that passes measures justified on the grounds that family life is an especially wor-

DEMO: What would you do if, say, a group of reliable social scientists presented you with a conclusive study showing that rearing children in communal barracks would have the effect of increasing the growth rate by 5 percent?

LEE (*laughs*): Ridiculous! Don't try to trap me with silly philosophers' tricks. I don't expect to be convinced that people would be better off materially in the absence of flourishing families. Tampering with the family, in fact, is likely to have disastrous economic consequences. "In the West, especially after World War II, the government came to be seen as so successful that it could fulfill all the obligations that in less modern societies are fulfilled by the family. This approach encouraged alternative families, single mothers for instance, believing that the government could provide the support to make up for the absent father. This is a bold, Huxleyan view of life, but one from which I as an East Asian shy away. I would be afraid to experiment with it. I am not sure what the consequences are, and I don't like the consequences that I see in the West. You will find this view widely shared in East Asia."[13]

3. DEMOCRACY AND THE NATION

3.1. Singapore: A Patriotic Nation?

DEMO: Well, let's hope that Singaporeans don't worry about the possibility that you'll change your mind about the need for pro-family policies. In any case, the family is one form of community, but familism won't suffice if the concern is nation-building, the forging of a sense of attachment to the overall national community. That was your task, of course, in 1965, when Singapore was expelled from the Malaysian Federation and hence reluctantly pushed into independence.[14]

---

thy form of life would be violating the political principle of state neutrality that bars appeals to "comprehensive conceptions of the good" (see Charles Larmore, *Patterns of Moral Complexity*, 44).

[13] Quoted in "A Conversation with Lee Kuan Yew," 113.

[14] For Lee's own account of this event, see Lee, *The Singapore Story*, chaps. 42–43. Lee's account was quite controversial in Malaysia, since he put all the blame for Singapore's expulsion from the Malaysian federation on hegemonic and cor-

LEE: Yes. "Remember, when we started, we were not even one society, never mind a nation. We were several different societies brought together under the British, an accident of history. Our loyalties and roots were in different parts of China, India and the Malay archipelago. . . . From these unpromising beginnings we have had to try to build one Singapore nation."[15] Basically, we had "to build a nation from scratch."[16] Our main task was to combat ethnic parochialism by fostering the growth of a new Singaporean identity that would underpin security and prosperity.[17] We knew it was going to be a difficult task—the ethnic groups were literally at war with each other in the late 1950s and early 1960s. Still, things were even more complicated than we suspected at the time, and "it was as well that we did not realize how daunting were the problems of building a nation out of peoples of totally different races, languages, religions and cultures. I would be appalled if I am asked to start off all over again on 21 November 1954 with the heavy knowledge of the almost irreconcilable divisions which were to open up."[18] By now we've just about given up on the aim of *replacing* ethnic identity with a new Singaporean identity on the political scene; instead, we seek to accommodate the fact of ethnic pluralism in various political ways, such as guaranteeing a seat for minority candidates in our multiseat constituencies.[19]

DEMO: But the failure of your nation-building project is more profound than you suggest. It's not just that Singaporeans by and large have failed to develop an *overriding* attachment to the nation, the problem is that most Singaporeans seem to lack *any* sense of patriotism, as measured by the degree to which one is prepared is to face harm on the nation's behalf.[20] The state is

---

rupt Malay politicians (see Michael Richardson, "Lee Kuan Yew's Controversial Memoirs," *International Herald Tribune*, 17 September 1998, 7).

[15] Quoted in Han et al., *Lee Kuan Yew*, 133, 440.

[16] Lee, *The Singapore Story*, 9.

[17] See also Jon Quah, "Government Policies and Nation Building," 45.

[18] Quoted in ibid., 83. In the same vein, Prime Minister Goh Chok Tong recently lamented the fact that Singapore, a country made up of disparate peoples, is "not a nation yet" (quoted in Zuraidah Ibrahim, "Singapore Not a Nation Yet," *Straits Time* [weekly edition], 8 May 1999, 1).

[19] See chap. 3, sec. 3.

[20] See Alasdair MacIntyre, *Whose Justice? Which Rationality?* 40.

regarded with cynicism,[21] and many "citizens" are deeply alienated from the political system.[22] The large majority have simply
withdrawn into the private realm, devoting their time and energy first and foremost to the accumulation of material goods,
or the "five C's," as Singaporeans put it—cash, credit card, car,
condo, and country club.[23] Singaporeans, in short, have become
apathetic, economically based "citizens," staying there because
the economic benefits are good, but feeling little attachment to
the country or its people. One of your protégés, Health Minister
and Minister for Information and the Arts George Yeo, recently
lamented the fact that Singapore is like a five-star hotel, where
residents might like to spend a vacation because the economic
benefits are good but never a lifetime.[24]

3.2. How Authoritarianism Undermines Patriotism

LEE: I wouldn't use the words "alienated," "apathetic," and so on.
Yes, Singaporeans are materialistic, but they are committed first
and foremost to the material well-being of *family* members, and
there are good historical reasons for that. Most of us are the
descendants of economic migrants from China, and, as I said
earlier, only the family has provided a survival raft for the individual in the midst of chaotic social and political change.
Perhaps this can help to explain the importance of the family
in Singaporean culture, along with the concomitant distrust of
nonfamily members, an indifference to public affairs, and a
reluctance to organize without government prompting and
support.[25]

---

[21] See Chew, "Human Rights in Singapore," 946.

[22] A recent survey by the Institute of Policy Studies "found that two-thirds of
Singaporeans think of themselves as having little or no political influence, although, interestingly, about the same proportion believe they should have at least
some say in the policy-making process. Such findings suggest that a large number
feel politically alienated" (see "Aware, But Not Interested," *Straits Times* [weekly
edition], 15 November 1997, 14). See also Chiew Seen Kong, "National Identity,
Ethnicity and National Issues," 71–73. On the lack of genuine patriotism in Singapore, see also Chee Soon Juan, *Singapore: My Home Too*, 14

[23] See Chiew, "National Identity, Ethnicity, and National Issues," 83.

[24] Quoted in Chew, "Human Rights in Singapore," 947.

[25] Lee's observation suggests that there may be a tension between part 2 (on
the need for commitment to the family) and part 3 (on the need for commitment

DEMO: But you can't put all the blame on history and culture. As you know, Singapore in the early 1960s was a vibrant, politically active society. A leading member of the opposition plausibly argues that it's the People's Action Party's decades of interference and control that has made Singaporean society the way it is today.[26] Another local intellectual draws on Tocqueville's description of "good despotism" to lament what has happened to Singapore. (*pulls out a magazine from his briefcase and proceeds to read from an essay*[27]) Under such a regime, Tocqueville wrote, citizens are ruled by "an immense and tutelary power, which takes upon itself alone their gratifications, and to watch over their fate. That power is absolute, minute, regular, provident, and mild. It would be like the authority of a parent, if, like that authority, its object was to prepare men for manhood; but it seeks on the contrary to keep them in perpetual childhood: it is well content that the people should rejoice, provided they think of nothing but rejoicing. For their happiness such a government willingly labors, but it chooses to be the sole agent and the only arbiter of that happiness: it provides for their security, foresees and supplies their necessities, facilitates their pleasures, manages their principal concerns, directs their industry, regulates the descent of property, and subdivides their inheritances—what remains but to spare them all the care of thinking and all the trouble of living?"[28]

---

to the national political community) of this chapter. There may an inevitable trade-off between extensive involvement in family life and public-spirited participation in public affairs—time constraints mean that in practice favoring one ideal is likely to erode the other, and it may be that commitment to one form of community transforms outlooks to the point that one cares less deeply about the other (e.g., parents caring for newborn children are often more interested in sharing their experiences with other parents than in following the news or attending a political assembly). An examination of the historical record lends some credence to these reflections—republican societies in the past (e.g., ancient Athens, or America in Tocqueville's day) relied on active, public-spirited, male citizens largely freed from family responsibilities, and conversely societies composed primarily of persons leading rich and fulfilling family lives (such as contemporary Singapore) tend to be ruled primarily by paternalistic despots who can rely on a compliant, politically apathetic populace.

[26] Chee Soon Juan, *Dare to Change*, 29.
[27] Kwok Kian Woon, "The Moral Condition of Democratic Society."
[28] Quoted in ibid., 23.

Not surprisingly, the consequences of "good despotism" are exactly as critics predicted.[29] Tocqueville is once more invoked by this local intellectual to make the point that subjects of such a regime would lack trust in their fellows, have no interest in public affairs, and certainly have no inclination to sacrifice their own private interests for the sake of the public good. Instead, "citizens" would turn their main attention to the material aspects of their private lives, once again to the benefit of the government itself: "everybody is feverishly intent on making money or, already rich, on keeping his wealth intact. Love of gain, a fondness for business careers, the desire to get rich at all costs, a craving for material comfort and easy living quickly become ruling passions under a despotic government. They affect all classes, even those who hitherto have seemed allergic to them, and tend to lower the moral standards of the nation as a whole if no effort is made to check their growth. It is in the nature of despotism that it should foster such desires and propagate their havoc. Lowering as they do the national morale, they are despotism's safeguard since they divert men's attention from public affairs."[30]

The author of this essay doesn't explicitly draw a comparison with contemporary Singapore,[31] but the reader cannot fail to get the message. . . .

LEE (*interrupting*): I am not a "despot." (*takes the magazine from Demo and writes down the reference*) The government isn't running the whole show. In fact, contrary to the dominant view in Western welfare states, my own belief is that the *family*, as opposed to the government, ought to be primarily responsible for an individual's welfare. The Western way is the road to economic ruin. In

---

[29] I have in mind Tocqueville, Kant (especially "What Is Enlightenment?"), and Mill (especially "On Liberty").

[30] Quoted in Kwok, "The Moral Condition of Democratic Society," 25.

[31] Those familiar with the plight of social critics in China and the ex-Soviet empire will understand the need to camouflage one's purposes in an authoritarian context that does not offer any protection to social critics. An issue of *Commentary: The Journal of the National University of Singapore Society* on "Cultural Freedom" was subjected to a cruder form of censorship—the alumni association that publishes the magazine canceled publication, and in response the four editors of *Commentary* resigned in protest (see the *New York Times*, 7 November 1994, A9).

Singapore, "the ruler or the government does not try to provide for a person what the family best provides."[32]

DEMO: Your government may not provide certain welfare services such as free health care and unemployment insurance, but that wasn't quite my point. I don't have to rehearse with you the familiar complaint about excessive governmental paternalism in Singapore, ranging from forced savings and public housing policies that cover 85 percent of the population to small-scale regulations governing aspects of people's everyday lives such as stiff fines for littering and a ban on the sale of chewing gum. Nor do I have to mention the many government-funded campaigns, such as the annual Courtesy Campaign to promote punctuality at wedding ceremonies and to warn people not to overstuff their plates at buffet tables. Perhaps these regulations and campaigns are meant to foster a sense of public responsibility and concern for the fate of others in the political community,[33] as opposed to Tocqueville's cynical suggestion that paternalistic guardians actually seek to keep their subjects in a state of perpetual childhood. But whatever the government's motivation, extensive social control has the effect of instilling in the people overwhelming dependence on, and conformity to, officially sanctioned directives and policies in civil, political, economic, and personal life, while justifying antisocial behavior where the official writ does not take effect. In my short time here, I can confirm one Singaporean's observation that in those few areas of human behavior not covered by rules in this society, Singaporeans' behavior is often found wanting: ruthlessly rushing to board buses, entering subway trains before passengers wishing to get out,

---

[32] Quoted in "A Conversation with Lee Kuan Yew," 113.

[33] It is worth noting, however, that the government tends to offer more self-interested reasons for doing good deeds. For example, Prime Minister Goh launched "Kindness Week" in late 1998 by quoting Confucius's saying that "He who wishes to secure the good of others has already secured his own," prompting a *Straits Times* editorial writer to note that such consequentialist justifications for kindness may not be persuasive since "good acts do not always have good consequences" (Geoffrey Pereira, "Be Good for Goodness' Sake," *Straits Times* [weekly edition], 28 November 1998, 13).

stampeding to obtain free tickets to a movie, becoming disorderly in a frenzy to buy shares, and so on.[34]

LEE: But things were even *worse* before our campaigns, regulations, and policies. Perhaps people haven't become as socially responsible and public-spirited as we'd hoped, but it's not the government's fault that many people are selfish toward nonfamily members. Look at Hong Kong, a society with few if any regulations instructing people how to lead their lives, and yet people are just as withdrawn from public affairs and focused on the material welfare of the family as they are in Singapore.[35]

DEMO: Actually, people are becoming more politicized in Hong Kong, especially since the introduction of direct elections in 1991. It's hard to blame people for being apathetic if they don't have a say in the political process.

LEE: You can believe that if it makes you feel better, but I think it has more to do with traditional Chinese culture than anything else. (*short pause*) Or it could be that most humans have finite amounts of love to give to others, and the Chinese give nearly all of it to the family.

---

[34] Chee, *Dare to Change*, 12–13. Singaporeans have a word for such behavior: *kiasuism*, a Chinese dialect word literally meaning "fear of losing," but referring to all kinds of petty, selfish, and overly self-protective behavior (see David Martin Jones, "Asian Values and the Constitutional Order of Contemporary Singapore," 293). The local branches of MacDonald's, presumably as part of the chain's interesting worldwide policy to adapt their food to local habits and culinary practices (see David Barboza, "New Luster for the Golden Arches," *International Herald Tribune*, 13–14 February 1999, 11), recently launched the "kiasuburger," a spicy chicken sandwich promoted with a humorous advertising campaign that pokes fun at *kiasu* behavior. Some Singaporeans subsequently criticized MacDonald's in the letters page of the *Straits Times*, arguing that the campaign may have the unintended effect of glorifying such undesirable behavior and projecting a bad image of Singapore abroad. Perhaps in response to such attacks, MacDonald's has since withdrawn the "kiasuburger." For an amusing account of the *kiasu* traveler overseas, see Rav Dhaliwal, *The Kiasu Traveler: True Stories of the Ugly Singaporean Overseas* (Singapore: Brit Aspen Publishing, 1994).

[35] For Lee Kuan Yew's views on Hong Kong–style individualism, see Lee, "China and Hong Kong Devoid of Liberal Democratic Tradition," in *Lee Kuan Yew on China and Hong Kong after Tiananmen*.

DEMO: Whatever the impact of culture on people's behavior, politics has a greater effect than you say. At the very least, paternalistic guardians serve to reinforce traditional cultural patterns and to prevent change that may otherwise occur. In Singapore, it's quite transparent that your government's political behavior fosters public apathy. Consider the vindictive way that your regime deals with political opponents: promising opposition candidates are publicly humiliated, bankrupted, imprisoned, sacked from their jobs on dubious grounds. . . .

LEE (*interrupting*): A government needs "big sticks" in order to govern. We "don't have to use it often. Use it once, twice, against big people. The rest will take notice."[36]

DEMO (*gasps*): That's precisely the problem. By such actions, you send an unpatriotic message to the community at large. I recall the words of the Singaporean journalist Cherian George—"in Singapore, better to mind your own business, make money, and leave politics to the politicians."[37] He was alluding to the fact that in most people's minds it's simply too dangerous to become involved in public affairs. One can predict that if there really were free and fair competitive elections, including the right to

---

[36] Quoted in *Straits Times*, 12 December 1992 (interview with Philippino television). Elsewhere, Lee explained more precisely how he would deal with his opponents: "I would isolate the leaders, the troublemakers, get them exposed, cut them down to size, ridicule them, so that everybody understands that it's not such a clever thing to do. Governing does not mean just being pleasant. If you want a pleasant result, just as with children, you cannot just be pleasant and nice" (quoted in Stephen Wrage, "Singapore Is a Dressed-Up Dictatorship," *Washington Post*, 11 February 1996). For one victim's story, see Francis Seow, *To Catch a Tartar*, and for a more general overview of the "big sticks" that have been used against opponents of the regime, see Christopher Tremewan, *The Political Economy of Social Control in Singapore*, chap. 6. The PAP also punishes "little people" on occasion, for example, by withdrawing governmental services from constituencies that vote for the opposition (as Lee stated in Parliament in 1985, "I make no apologies for it. As a PAP government we must look after PAP constituencies first because the majority of people supported us" [quoted in ibid., 63]).

[37] George argues that one could hardly blame people for ignoring their political obligations "when they hear so many cautionary tales: Of Singaporeans whose careers came to a premature end after they voiced dissent; of critics who found themselves under investigations; of individuals who were detained without trial or even though they seemed not to pose any real threat; of tapped phones and opened letters" (*Straits Times*, 11 July 1993).

run for the opposition without fear of retaliation, this would do more to promote a sense of attachment to the community at large than ineffectual "courtesy campaigns."[38]

LEE: If you're looking for a good electoral fight, you won't get it: "in the nature of Singapore a good opposition has not turned up because good men in Singapore do not go into politics."[39]

DEMO: How can you know that, if you haven't given the opposition a real chance? Besides, my point is that a free and fair electoral process contributes to patriotism; it's not my role to favor a particular electoral style or outcome.

LEE: I'm not convinced that elections per se would make that much difference. Only a tiny minority of professional politicians will run for Parliament even in the best of times. The large majority will stick to their own affairs, just as they do in the democratic West: 50 percent or so of American citizens don't even bother to cast their vote during presidential elections.[40]

DEMO: But democracy also contributes to patriotism in a more indirect way, by providing the conditions for a vibrant associational life, the real secret of patriotism.[41] Even the most minimal

---

[38] It would be interesting to find out whether patriotism has increased in Taiwan, South Korea, and South Africa, countries that have recently adopted some of the procedures of "minimal democracy."

[39] Quoted in *Straits Times*, 8 June 1996.

[40] There may be more technical explanations for these low voting figures (compared to West European standards): Americans move more and vote more (in elections at different levels of government), and some fail to register.

[41] It is less well known that Hegel also argued in a Tocquevillean vein that participation in intermediary groups can lead to a broader notion of public-spiritedness, hence that "the secret of patriotism [lies in recognizing that] the proper strength of the state lies in its associations" (Hegel, quoted in A. Buchwalter, "Hegel's Theory of Virtue," *Political Theory* 21 [1992]: 572). Mill also favored voluntary associations and local political institutions (and trial by jury) on the grounds that they take people "out of the narrow circle of personal and family selfishness, and accustoming them to the comprehension of joint interests, the management of joint concerns—habituating them to act from public or semi-public motives, and guide their conduct by aims which unite instead of isolating them from one another" (Mill, "On Liberty," *Three Essays* [Oxford: Oxford University Press, 1975], 134).

Note, however, one possible ambiguity. Hegel's concern seems to be the strength of the state, whereas Mill seems primarily concerned with increasing

definition of democracy as free and fair competitive elections includes the right to freely associate as groups and participate in public affairs, whether this be political parties competing in elections or interest groups and neighborhood clubs airing their opinions on political matters in various ways.[42] The point here is that intermediary associations between the family and the state, which emerge as a by-product of the freedom of association, are absolutely essential for patriotism, because they break down social isolation and allow people to cooperate and to discover common interests that may otherwise have gone unnoticed. As Tocqueville put it, they are "large free schools," where citizens "take a look at something other than themselves,"[43] political interests stimulated and organizational skills enhanced. Such associations counter the disposition to give precedence to personal ends over the public interest and lead to a broader sense of public spiritedness.

LEE: A nice theory. But when I look at intermediary associations in the United States, I see interest groups such as gun lobbies and insurance companies fighting tooth and nail to block change that's obviously in the public interest, I see ethnic groups and cultural associations preaching the virtues of separation and disengagement from mainstream American life, I see suburban not-in-my-backyard campaigns fighting hard to protect property values,[44] I see the Ku Klux Klan and the Michigan militia. . . .

DEMO (*interrupting*): So what do we conclude? The way I see it, not all groups foster wider forms of cooperation and encourage their members (directly or indirectly) to give precedence to public over personal ends,[45] and it may be an important (but

---

people's commitment to the national political community (not necessarily to the current ruling party or this or that political institution). Demo is trying to develop an argument for a Millean version of patriotism and nation-building.

[42] Demo could also have discussed the freedom of speech, another important precondition for free and fair competitive elections (see section 4).

[43] Tocqueville, *Democracy in America* (New York: Doubleday, 1992), 510.

[44] See my article "Civil Society vs. Civic Virtue."

[45] Two recent articles helpfully distinguish between different kinds of intermediary associations and their varying effects on character: Stephen Macedo, "Community, Diversity, and Civic Education: Toward a Liberal Political Science of

neglected) task for the government to identify groups more likely to do so and to promote them by such means as tax exemptions and matching grants. In other words, the freedom of association may not be *sufficient* to foster the kind of intermediary association most likely to stimulate concern with public affairs and train members in the use of their energies for the sake of common enterprises, but this freedom is nonetheless *necessary.*[46]

Coming back to Singapore, it's most worrisome that even greater constraints have been placed on civil associations since the 1980s.[47] Concerned citizens who attempt to organize discussion groups on public issues are subjected to intimidating visits and interrogation by the widely feared Internal Security Department;[48] public gatherings of more than five people must apply for a government permit; legislation was passed in the late 1980s to erode the power and status of the Law Society after it had

---

Group Life," paper presented at Princeton University's Center for Human Values, September 1994, and Nancy Rosenblum, "Civil Societies: Liberalism and the Moral Uses of Pluralism."

Tocqueville preferred "American" associations that allow for and encourage independent behavior, as opposed to "French" associations that are tyrannical within themselves, thus producing passive and servile behavior instead of training members in the use of their energies for the sake of common enterprises (*Democracy in America*, 198). In other words, patriotism requires intermediary associations with established norms and practices of individual independence, a form of association that may not be readily transferable to a Singaporean context that downplays the significance of personal autonomy (in part because family and work obligations leave little time for any personal projects).

[46] Why is it necessary (or, more precisely, why is it tremendously helpful)? If people join associations because the government tells them to do so, as opposed to being self-motivated, they are likely to do only what is required of them, with personal (or family) interests dominant the rest of the time. Thus, by combining an argument from the previous note we get the following claim: an association is more likely to produce citizens motivated to forsake personal for public ends if (1) people join it voluntarily (or unreflectively slip into it) and (2) it allows for and encourages independent behavior.

[47] See Beng-Huat Chua, *Communitarian Ideology and Democracy in Singapore*, 38, and Michael Hill and Lian Kwen Fee, *The Politics of Nation Building and Citizenship in Singapore*, 245.

[48] A founder of a small group known as the Socratic Circle, which meets to discuss domestic politics in Singapore, was paid a late-night visit by a member of the Internal Security Department and subjected to hostile interrogation. He was understandably quite shaken after the experience.

engaged in public criticism of the government's policies regarding control of the media; the Maintenance of Religious Harmony Act was passed in 1990 to prohibit religious groups from engaging in political activity such as providing legal aid and shelter to foreign domestics facing problems with their employers or the Labor Ministry; and even political parties are prevented in various ways from debating and criticizing domestic politics in Singapore. In fact, just about all the independent forces in civil society have been co-opted into official organizations or expunged from the political scene, with the possible exception of the relatively autonomous women's group AWARE and the Nature Society of Singapore.[49]

LEE: A few years ago, I said, "It is my job as Prime Minister in charge of the Government to put a stop to politicking in professional bodies. . . . You want to politick, you form your own party or you join Mr. Jeyaretnam."[50] I still hold these views.

DEMO: But how can you expect people who aren't professional politicians to develop a sense of belonging and concern for the national political community when they're not supposed to have anything to do with public affairs, when they're barred from "taking a look at something other than themselves"?

LEE (*sighs*): Yes, that's what the new generation seems to think. Information and Arts Minister George Yeo has argued that in-

---

[49] Garry Rodan, "The Growth of Singapore's Middle Class and Its Political Significance," 65. Rodan attributes the success of these two nongovernmental organizations to their strategy of deliberately avoiding public debate and open contestation of government policy.

The Socratic Circle and The Roundtable, two groups composed primarily of professionals that discuss matters concerning the public interest, have been allowed to register (see N. Ganesan, "Democracy in Singapore," 70). Even members of these discussion groups, however, do not necessarily believe that civic organizations are truly independent: as The Roundtable's Raymond Lim put it, "In Singapore, the state is extremely powerful. The Government calls the shots here. Civic organizations only test rather than determine the limits of the growth of civil society" (quoted in Zuraidah Ibrahim, "What Grows beneath the Banyan Tree?" *Straits Times* [weekly edition], 18 April 1998, 14).

[50] Quoted in Tremewan, *The Political Economy of Social Control in Singapore*, 197 (Jeyaretnam is the head of the opposition Workers' Party in Singapore, and he has been the unfortunate recipient of several "big sticks" meted out by Mr. Lee; see ibid., 164–166). See also Hill and Lian, *The Politics of Nation Building and Citizenship in Singapore*, chap. 9.

termediary organizations give individuals their sense of place and involvement in the larger community, and that the Singaporean government should try to make more room for civil society in Singapore.[51] So now we have Neighborhood Committees in Housing Board Estates and Community Development Councils. These groups are supposed to give people more opportunity to contribute to life outside their backyards and to help others.[52]

DEMO: But they're not independent civic groups! They don't challenge government policy or express dissenting views; rather, they work in tandem with government objectives, allowing for more efficient implementation of the government's policies.[53] These groups will serve the function of extending the political reach of the state,[54] but if the aim is to foster genuine attachment to the national community, it won't work—only independent civic groups can stimulate a broader form of public-spiritedness. So long as people worry about challenging the government, they'll stick to private affairs.[55]

[51] See Hill and Lian, *The Politics of Nation Building and Citizenship in Singapore*, 225–226. This theme was recently echoed by Prime Minister Goh, who said, "People should not leave it to a few leaders when it comes to national issues, but take part actively, building bonds to the country in the process. The government must be prepared to take a step back and perhaps even a back seat, especially on local community issues, and allow some free play to develop" (quoted in "People First—PM's Vision for Singapore in 21st Century," *Straits Times* [weekly edition], 7 June 1997, 1).

[52] Koh Buck Song, "Make Space for Civil Society," *Straits Times* (weekly edition), 18 April 1998, 13.

[53] Even the *Straits Times* acknowledges that the government's idea of civil society is to tolerate groups whose objectives are nonpolitical and nonthreatening that work in tandem with the government's objectives (see Koh Buck Song, "Singapore behind Schedule, but Still Top," *Straits Times* [weekly edition], 16 May 1998, 15). Needless to say, the Community Development Councils exclude opposition politicians as members (Leong Ching, "Have CDCs Succeeded in Bonding Singaporeans?" *Straits Times* [weekly edition], 29 August 1998, 14; this article answers negatively, noting that only 14.7 percent of Singaporeans want to participate in neighborhood activities).

[54] See Garry Rodan, "Expect Asia's Values to Turn Out Much Like Everyone Else's," *International Herald Tribune*, 4 August 1997, 8.

[55] As one of my former students put it in July 1998, "They are now talking of producing a civil society in Singapore (ohh please!). How can you have that when those with dissenting views are intimidated and threatened—the best being Cath-

LEE: A nice theory, but the real world doesn't necessarily work like that. There are many ways to foster patriotism besides a lively associational life. Consider the Japanese in World War II, a most patriotic people (as I found out to my detriment when the Japanese occupied Singapore from 1942 to 1945[56]), more than willing to sacrifice their personal interests for the sake of the nation, yet they didn't get that way by being schooled in independent intermediary associations.

DEMO: It's difficult to judge the extent of genuine patriotism in authoritarian contexts (how much patriotism stems from fear?). More importantly, even if the Japanese were genuine patriots, the particular social and historical factors that made them so aren't reproducible in modern conditions—the whole country was closed off to outsiders for two and a half centuries during the Tokugawa Shogunate, and people were made to believe that they were one people united by the figure of a divine emperor at the top.[57] How feasible is this strategy in contemporary Singapore, a small city-state intimately tied to the worldwide capitalist system? As I see it, only the right to join freely organized intermediary associations, combined with the right to run for the opposition without fear of retaliation, can possibly make Singaporeans more concerned with and committed to public affairs.

LEE: Well, even if you're right that democracy is the best means to increase public-spiritedness now, things may change in the future. Look at what happened in China after the May Fourth Movement in 1919, the first student-led uprising for democracy in Chinese history. Chinese intellectuals were convinced that democracy was necessary to save the nation from extinction,[58] but most of them changed their minds in the 1930s and 1940s when they became persuaded that a Stalinist brand of Marxism

---

erine Lim's case?" (Catherine Lim is one of Singapore's most famous writers. She was criticized in 1994 for an article about Goh's style of government, and she says that the episode has taught her that it has become practically impossible to write any political commentary. As things stand now, "the media and the people can do little because of fear"; quoted in Koh Buck Song, "What Plants Will Grow under the Tembusu tree?" *Straits Times* [weekly edition], 16 May 1998, 14).

[56] See Han et al., *Lee Kuan Yew,* 21–22, 27, 29.

[57] See, e.g., Harumi Befu, ed., *Cultural Nationalism in East Asia.*

[58] See Su Shaozhi, "Problems of Democratic Reform in China," 222.

was an even better means for building a stronger nation and promoting widespread commitment to the political community.

DEMO: As you know, Soviet-style Marxism is thoroughly discredited by now, and I don't expect you to be convinced by any argument in favor of Marxism. I stick to my point that democracy is the best means for promoting patriotism in a Singaporean context, now and in the foreseeable future. (*short pause*) I'm glad, however, that you bring up the example of the May Fourth Movement. The demand for democracy as a means for nation-building is a recurring theme in twentieth-century Chinese history; perhaps it's a way of thinking that resonates well with Chinese cultural traditions.[59] We have yet another reason for you to consider my argument.

LEE: I'm not sure why I should be inspired by the example of student protesters for democracy in twentieth-century Chinese history, even if the protesters aimed to increase commitment to the public good. In such cases demands for democracy came from the bottom, not from the top. Remember whom you're talking to. I'm pretty pleased as things are now, so why should I care about democratizing in order to make my people more patriotic?

DEMO: You wouldn't have to do much to achieve this goal. All you need to do is loosen up a bit on the paternalism[60] and allow people to associate freely in civil society and to run for the opposition without fear of retaliation. Patriotism will then emerge as a happy by-product of political reform.

3.3. On the Need for Patriotism in Singapore

LEE: You're not answering my question. I'm still not persuaded that Singapore has a problem that we need to address. I understand your argument thus far. You assert that few Singaporeans are genuinely patriotic in the sense that they're willing to sacrifice their own personal interests for the sake of the political

---

[59] Demo seems to have learned from the discussion with Lo in chap. 2.2.2.

[60] This is not meant to be a general argument against paternalism: the concern here is only "excessive" paternalism that has the effect of undermining patriotism.

community. This phenomenon, you say, can be explained by excessive governmental paternalism that fosters a sense of dependence on the state and implicitly condones a free-for-all when rules do not apply, by stern measures against opposition candidates that make people reluctant to involve themselves in public affairs, and by the absence of independent groups in civil society where Singaporeans could learn to cooperate, develop a taste for collective benefits, and forge a sense of common purpose in the wider political community. You then pointed out that twentieth-century Chinese social critics have often appealed to the idea that democracy is a means for nation-building, an argument that seems to resonate well with traditional political argumentation in East Asia.

But now I'm saying that I can agree with your description of the status quo—a notable absence of public-spiritedness in Singapore—and yet not regard the situation as a particularly desperate state of affairs in need of political remedy. It may well be true, as I said earlier, that we haven't succeeded in our nation-building project to the extent we had hoped when we started off, but from my current perspective I think that we've done enough. At least we've created the semblance of a nation, and we haven't had any racial rioting in a quarter of a century, so why do we need more patriotism now, why should Singaporeans manifest a greater willingness to set aside their personal interests for the sake of the nation?

DEMO (*pause*): Well, it may seem peculiar to have a foreigner urging another country's political ruler to adopt measures that would lead to greater patriotism,[61] but . . .

LEE (*interrupting*): No need to feel embarrassed. There's a long tradition in Chinese history of intellectuals roaming from state to state offering advice to foreign rulers, and some were pushing similar ideas. Confucius left his native state of Lu hoping to find a ruler more receptive to his social and political teachings, but he failed elsewhere as well. Also toward the end of the Warring

[61] Jean-Jacques Rousseau's advice to the Poles in his commissioned work *The Government of Poland* was even more peculiar: he urged the Poles to become more patriotic in the xenophobic sense, i.e., more hostile to foreigners like himself. Demo, in contrast, recognizes that Singapore is necessarily bound up with the worldwide capitalist economy and does not advocate an insular and xenophobic type of patriotism for Singapore.

States period, which lasted from 403 to 221 B.C., the legalist Han Fei Tzu left his own political community when he failed to influence its incompetent ruler, and fortunately he did have more luck outside—he managed to gain access to the young ruler of Qin, the ruthless Qin Shi Huang who drew on Han Fei's ideas to found the first Chinese empire.[62]

DEMO: Yes, I know Han Fei. Perhaps he was more successful because he taught the First Emperor about the need for harsh punishments and bureaucratic organization as necessary means to enhance state power, as opposed to the Confucian stress on rituals and nonlegalistic political practices designed to serve the common good. I suspect most rulers prefer to hear the kind of advice Han Fei had to offer.

LEE: I'm pragmatic. I'll take whatever works for Singapore.

DEMO: That's my approach too. I offer my advice after prolonged study of Singaporean society and a sincere desire to benefit your country. I try to offer practical advice, although I'm not motivated solely by strategic concerns.

LEE (*looking at this watch*): Perhaps we can move on to what you have to say.

DEMO: Fine. My understanding of the situation has led me to the conclusion that Singapore would be better off with more patriotism, and I do hope that you'll be persuaded by at least some of my reasons. Let me begin with the point that governments ought to try to live up to the standards that they honor.[63] It's relevant to remind you that on January 9, 1989, four core values were identified in the presidential address to Parliament, one of which was communitarianism, defined as "placing society above self." These values are meant to capture the essence of what it means to be a Singaporean, and your government's view is that they should be taught in schools, workplaces, and homes.[64]

---

[62] Han Fei, however, was eventually executed by Qin Shi Huang. Benjamin Schwartz notes that Han Fei may have paid the ultimate price because "his advice to the First Emperor concerning the treatment of his own native state of Han led the latter to suspect that his view reflected partiality for his native land rather than an unreserved loyalty to the interests of the Emperor himself" (Schwartz, *The World of Thought in Ancient China*, 345).

[63] See Walzer, *Thick and Thin*, 41–42.

[64] See "Shared Values." For discussion, see Quah, ed., *In Search of Singapore's National Values*, 1–2, and Hill and Lian, *The Politics of Nation-Building and Citizen-*

LEE: That's right. To repeat, Singaporeans have "little doubt that a society with communitarian values where the interests of society take precedence over that of the individual suits them better than the individualism of America."[65]

DEMO: But the practice is a long way from the ideal. You know very well that a genuine sense of caring for the community is rare in Singapore, even compared with supposedly individualistic Americans. Why is it that 40 percent of the population in the United States is involved in volunteer work[66] compared with only 6 percent in Singapore?[67] If you want to close the gap between the individualistic reality and the communitarian rhetoric, then you should consider my suggestion that democratic change in the form of competitive elections, including the freedom of association allowing groups to organize and to participate in public affairs, is the most feasible means of making people really believe in and act on the "society over self" principle. Either that, or you change the rhetoric.

LEE: Well, I don't think that the need for a government to live up to its professed standards on this particular matter outweighs the defects of democracy. Besides, I may have been exaggerating a little. To my mind, what matters most is to have a talented and public-spirited political elite; I'm less worried about the psychological characteristics of the masses. As you know, "Singapore is a society based on effort and merit, not wealth and privilege depending on birth." Our tiny country simply can't afford to squander human capital. So we aim to identify the most intelligent members of society who can provide "the direction, planning and control of [state] power in the people's interest. . . . It is on this group that we must expend our limited and slender resources in order that they will provide the yeast, that ferment,

---

ship in Singapore, 212. The government's agenda was buttressed by visiting Western academics such as Harvard Business School's Professor George Lodge, who was invited to Singapore as a Lee Kuan Yew Distinguished Visitor to deliver a laudatory lecture on Singapore-style communitarianism that was subsequently reprinted in the *Straits Times* (27 January 1991).

[65] Quoted in the *International Herald Tribune*, 9–10 November 1991.

[66] The extent of civil involvement in the US is declining, however: see Robert Putnam, "Bowling Alone: America's Declining Social Capital."

[67] M. Ramesh, "Social Security in Singapore," 1105.

that catalyst in our society which alone will ensure that Singapore shall maintain. . . . the social organization which enables us, with almost no natural resources, to provide the second highest standard of living in Asia." We do this by means of an educational system "in which Singapore's brightest students [are] groomed for future command. . . . The ideal product is the student, the university graduate who is strong, robust, rugged, with tremendous qualities of stamina, endurance and at the same time with great intellectual discipline and most important of all, humility and love of community."[68] Not many people satisfy these criteria, unfortunately. "The main burden of present planning and implementation rests on the shoulders of some 300 key persons. . . . These people come from poor and middle-class homes. They come from different language schools. Singapore is a meritocracy. And these men have risen to the top by their own merit, hard work and high performance. Together they are a closely knit and coordinated hard core. If all the 300 were to crash in one Jumbo jet, then Singapore will disintegrate. That shows how small the base is for our leadership in politics, economics and security. . . . It is strange, but true, that the fate of millions often turns around the quality, strength and foresight of the key digits in a country. They decide whether a country gains cohesion and strength in orderly progress, or disintegrates and degenerates into chaos."[69]

DEMO: But surely it matters what ordinary citizens think as well. Even if you successfully identify "the best and brightest" in society for purposes of political rule, most people must still buy into the system, so to speak—they must be willing to forsake their own interests on occasion for the sake of the common good (as

---

[68] Quoted in Tremewan, *The Political Economy of Social Control in Singapore*, 100–102. The value of rule by an educated elite is often accepted by members of the opposition in Singapore as well. A recent speech by opposition leader Dr. Chee Soon Juan at the National University of Singapore was explicit about the need to attract "credible" candidates from the professional class to his party. Given the risks of opposition politics in Singapore, however, few professionals actually join opposition parties (see also Seow's account of the difficulties recruiting a "cohesive group of professionals" in *To Catch a Tartar*, 168, 170).

[69] Quoted in Han et al., *Lee Kuan Yew*, 315. For more on the selection of leaders in Singapore, see chap. 3, sec. 3.

defined by the elite). Otherwise the social system won't be stable. That, in any case, was Plato's view—he suggested that a "Golden Lie" be disseminated to help secure legitimacy for rule by philosopher-kings in his ideal Republic.

LEE: No need to lie. We're open about our meritocratic system in Singapore. But you're right, we do have to get the masses on our side as well, though I'm not very hopeful. "Our community lacks in-built reflexes—loyalty, patriotism, history or tradition. . . . [o]ur society and its education system was never designed to produce a people capable of cohesive action, identifying their collective interests and then acting in furtherance of them. . . . The reflexes of group thinking must be built to ensure the survival of the community, not the survival of the individual, this means a reorientation of emphasis and a reshuffling of values. . . . We must have qualities of leadership at the top, and qualities of cohesion on the ground."[70]

DEMO: So you agree that ordinary citizens should be patriotic as well, at least to the extent of being willing on occasion to go along with the decisions of the political elite, which may entail a certain degree of self-sacrifice.

LEE: Yes. "It is the duty of leaders to instil confidence in the people so that they will stand up to be counted, otherwise all is lost. . . . When together they fight against all odds and win, a bond will be forged between people and leaders, like the deep unshakable feeling of trust between an army and its generals who have been in battle." This is particularly important in a crisis situation, such as the one we're facing today. "All opinion formulators" should understand what's at stake and help mobilize the people. "High morale is crucial in a crisis. Faint-heartedness in the face of danger must mean disaster."[71]

---

[70] Quoted in Tremewan, *The Political Economy of Social Control in Singapore*, 100.

[71] Quoted in Koh Buck Song, "Testing Times for Singapore and Leaders," *Straits Times* (weekly edition), 22 August 1998, 24. This theme was recently echoed by Deputy Prime Minister Lee Hsien Loong (Lee Kuan Yew's son), who said that Singaporeans should participate actively in the life of the nation, "not only to discuss and argue, but also to take part and do something." (Irene Ng, "'New Govt Agenda for 2000," *Straits Times* [weekly edition], 19 June 1999, 1).

DEMO: Fine, we're on the same side here. If you want "high morale" and "cohesion," ordinary people need to be prepared to sacrifice themselves for Singapore. So let's return to the question of why Singapore would benefit from more patriotism. I try to offer highly specific reasons, remaining sensitive to the realities of the Singaporean context. Given the great pride you take in clean government, you may be persuaded by the republican point about the connection between civic virtue and corruption. Republicans thinkers prescribe civic virtue as the requisite antidote to corruption. That is, in contrast to traditional liberals, republicans believe that institutional protections against the abuse of power by public and private authorities won't suffice—the best long-term bulwark against corruption is widespread civic virtue, for only individuals with the character that disposes them to support the common good above their own interests will be sufficiently motivated to resist corruption when it occurs.[72] In the absence of citizens habituated to act from public or semipublic motives, a polity will eventually succumb to corruption.

LEE: You say you want to remain sensitive to the realities of the Singaporean context, but the facts in Singapore tell a different story. Colonial Singapore, especially after World War II, was infected by corruption from top to bottom, but since then we've made Singapore into one of the least corrupt countries in the world.[73] Our administration "is absolutely corruption-free. . . . Every member knows that there is no easy money on the take. That's the way we are. Nobody believes that we spent money to get into this House. . . . How do [we] ensure that a fortuitous, purely accidental group of men who came in power in 1959 and after 26 years of office . . . have remained stainless?" Luckily, we don't have to depend on transforming the character of our citizens. Our anticorruption strategy includes stiff penalties for

[72] See Shelley Burtt, "Children and the Claims of Community," paper delivered at the annual meeting of the American Political Science Association, New York, September 1994.

[73] According to the 1998 Corruptions Perception Index, published by the Berlin-based Transparency International, Singapore is the seventh least corrupt country in the world (Susan Sim, "Singapore—Asia's 'Cleanest' in Graft Index," *Straits Times* [weekly edition], 26 September 1998, 24).

corrupt behavior, and we reduce the incentive for corruption among civil servants [and ministers] by constantly improving their salaries and working conditions. Several years ago I said, "I'm one of the best paid and probably one of the poorest of the Third World prime ministers."[74] I've always held to the belief that public servants need to be paid well, or they will succumb to corruption. The World Bank seems to agree. "Let me read what they said: 'Not surprisingly, Singapore, which is widely perceived to have the region's most competent and upright bureaucracy, pays its bureaucrats best.' "[75]

DEMO: But will that strategy work indefinitely? Who can guarantee that political leaders one or two generations from now won't be an especially greedy bunch clever enough not to get caught? And who will enforce the anticorruption laws if political leaders decide to plunder the country's wealth? The only *long-term* check against corruption, let me repeat, is the presence of a large number of public-spirited citizens willing to take some personal risks for the sake of exposing and challenging corrupt rulers. And this is a problem, if I can quote the concluding sentences of Mill's *On Liberty*, in a "State which dwarfs its men, in order that they may be more docile instruments in its hands even for beneficial purposes. . . . the perfection of machinery to which it has sacrificed everything will in the end avail it nothing, for want of the vital power which, in order that the machine might work more smoothly, it has preferred to banish."[76]

---

[74] Quoted in Quah, ed., *In Search of Singapore's National Values*, 100, 99. Demo could have questioned the definition of corruption as taking bribes for political or business favors, pointing out that the Singapore government would not fare so well on a worldwide corruption index if the definition of corruption were expanded to include government officials using their power to vote themselves the world's highest salaries (nearly U.S. $1.3 million for Lee last year, and nearly $1 million for his son Deputy Prime Minister Lee Hsien Loong) in an authoritarian context without the freedom of the press, the freedom of association, and the democratic right to run for the opposition without fear of retaliation. There is also the "sensitive issue of what would happen in the case of Lee's own indiscreet violation of the law" (Ronald Keith, *China's Struggle for the Rule of Law*, 222). Had Demo raised these points, however, he may well have been thrown out of Lee's office.

[75] Quoted in Han et al., *Lee Kuan Yew*, 335.

[76] Mill, "On Liberty," 141.

LEE: Such dramatic language! Back in the real world, I think that it's much more feasible to work on the political leadership than to transform the whole population into a virtuous community of public-spirited citizens. As you know the Singaporean government has recently adopted my proposal for an "Elected President" who serves as a check against a future government intent on plundering Singapore's reserves.[77] As a condition of eligibility the "Elected President" must prove himself a man worthy of character, and who knows, it may not always be easy to find the right person, but it's certainly easier than trying to change the motivation of the general public. I'm still not convinced of the need for patriotism in the community at large.

DEMO: Well, let me turn to what I see as an even more compelling reason for patriotism. If you care about the interests of the worst-off in society . . .

LEE (*interrupting*): Of course I care, and I think that the better-off should care as well. "If we are to remain a socially mobile society, with no class distinctions or class hatreds, those who have risen up through meritocracy must take an active interest in the welfare and well-being of the less fortunate. Not to do so is to risk a gradual stratification of Singapore society. Then, the less successful will begin to resent those who are successful."[78]

DEMO: But if Singaporeans lack a strong sense of patriotism, if they're unwilling at least on occasion to put the interests of fellow citizens before their own, how can you expect to implement a national welfare system that benefits the worst-off? Any effective scheme of distributive justice presupposes a bounded world of people deeply committed to each other's fate, for most people won't agree to enshrine generous actions in law, and to live by those laws, if they can't identify in some way with the recipients of those generous actions.[79]

LEE (*sighs*): Yes, that's true. Singaporeans care more about their own ethnic community than about the nation as a whole. Until

[77] See Kevin Tan and Lam Peng Er, eds. *Managing Political Change in Singapore.* See also chap. 3, sec.1.

[78] Quoted in *Straits Times*, 26 June 1993.

[79] See, e.g., David Miller, "The Ethical Significance of Nationality," and Yael Tamir, *Liberalism Nationalism*, 117–121.

such a time when history has made Singapore a nation of one people, no amount of rational analysis can defeat the biological instinct to care, when pressed to prioritize, for one's own ethnic group first.[80] "That is an instinct of all human tribes or societies. In every culture, there is a desire to preserve your distinctiveness. And I think if you go against that, you will create unnecessary problems, whether it is with the Indians and their caste or with the Chinese and their clans. That is why, in the end, we discovered we had to recognize facts. And so I encouraged Mendaki to be formed because you could not get Chinese officers to enthuse Malay parents to do something for their children. But Malay leaders can. They share a certain common destiny. . . . So once I recognized that as a fact, I then built government policies around those facts."[81] In 1992 we reluctantly scrapped the idea of a national organization for the underachievers of all ethnic groups in favor of an ethnic-based welfare scheme. Chinese contribute to a fund for poor Chinese, Malays care for underprivileged Malays, and Indians look after poor Indians.

DEMO: But a good number of Singaporeans are profoundly worried by this development. Many fear that this scheme will rekindle latent ethnic tensions, and some argue that the scheme is unfair because it may favor the disproportionately well-off Chinese group.[82] So if you can avoid these drawbacks by means of a *national* system of distributive justice, and if more patriotism will serve to provide the psychological underpinnings for such a system, that's a good reason to consider the need for more patriotism.

LEE: I still don't think you can do away with ethnicity so easily. "You know there are innate prejudices. And I don't pretend that I don't share those prejudices. I do. If one of my sons had come back and said, 'I've got this American lady whom I met in America,' my first question is, what color is she?"[83]

DEMO: I'd say prejudices are social constructions and I don't have to inform you that ethnicity is often manipulated by political

[80] See the *Straits Times* editorial, 23 September 1992.

[81] Quoted in Han et al., *Lee Kuan Yew,* 165.

[82] See, e.g., Lily Zubaidah Rahim Ishak, "The Paradox of Ethnic-Based Self-Help Groups."

[83] Quoted in Tremewan, *The Political Economy of Social Control in Singapore,* 131.

forces for dubious purposes. This isn't the place, however, to try to understand why your government has recently moved toward explicit recognition and accommodation of ethnicity.[84] Let me turn to yet another argument for patriotism in Singapore. As you know, Singapore suffers from a high level of emigration, and things seem to be getting worse—2,000 families left in 1980 and 4,707 families emigrated in 1988 alone,[85] a high attrition rate for a tiny country. More worrisome, the most skilled and educated sections of the population show the greatest propensity to leave[86]—more than 10,000 skilled workers left the country between 1988 and 1990, mostly to Australia, Canada, the United States, and New Zealand. A survey by a government think-tank found that "the young, singles, the better educated, those with high incomes, those educated in the English stream and the politically alienated,"[87] amounting to 15 percent of the respondents, have considered leaving Singapore for good. Worse, this number is growing rapidly: according to a poll taken in 1997—before the Asian financial crisis had hit Singapore—40 percent of young people said that they were prepared to consider leaving the country for greener pastures.[88]

LEE: Yes, that's a problem: "Singaporeans must have conviction that this is their country and their life. . . . [An emigrant is] a washout."[89] But meanwhile we have to deal with the facts, so we've been replacing emigrants with wealthy and skilled migrants from Hong Kong, mainland China, India, and elsewhere.[90] We also offer attractive packages for skilled expatriates to live and work in Singapore.

DEMO: But I wonder how many will want to come in the next few years? It won't be so easy to attract talented migrants anymore.

[84] See ibid., 138–144.

[85] Chee, *Dare to Change*, 31.

[86] Garry Rodan, "The Growth of Singapore's Middle Class and Its Political Significance," 59.

[87] Quoted in Chiew Seen Kong, "National Identity, Ethnicity and National Issues," 73,74.

[88] See "Most Young People Prefer to Stay Here, Poll Shows: But 40% of 208 Surveyed Would Consider Settling Elsewhere," *Straits Times* (weekly edition), 4 October 1997, 5.

[89] Quoted in Tremewan, *The Political Economy of Social Control in Singapore*, 123.

[90] See Cheah Hock Beng, "Responding to Global Challenges: The Changing Nature of Singapore's Incorporation into the International Economy," 111.

A strategy that may have worked in economic boom times won't work in relatively difficult times.[91] The only other solution is to give people a greater say in political affairs so that they'll be more motivated to stick with their fellow citizens in the less-than-happy days ahead.[92]

LEE: Wishful thinking. Don't worry, we'll find people. Our neighboring countries are worse off than we are, and they can provide a source of talented economic migrants in the future.

DEMO: Well, good luck.[93] In any case, there's another problem for you to consider. Many talented local artists have left because of the undemocratic and overregulated political system that provides few opportunities for creative and innovative endeavors,[94] and they can't be replaced by economic migrants who are attracted by the economic benefits. Why is that a problem? As you know, Singapore is often referred to as a "cultural desert," and part of the explanation has to do with the fact that many talented artists have left for more inspiring places. Had these people stayed, they may have created artistic and cultural products of value.

LEE: The cultural scene will improve in the future. "You're going to see world-class concerts and plays in Singapore because we're going to put up the facilities for it, and we're on the main trunk route. And whether you're Pavarotti or Placido Domingo or

---

[91] According to the *Asian Wall Street Journal*, Singapore is already beginning to suffer from an exodus of expatriates: "There are a lot more people leaving than coming," says Jamie Dale, Singapore-based partner with Hewitt Associates, a big U.S.-based human resource consulting firm. "I've heard that for every expat coming, five to 10 are going" (Peter Waldman, "Singapore Business Climate Is Facing a Hazy Future," *Asian Wall Street Journal*, 2 March 1998, 1). This article notes that expatriates are also worried by the pollution from Indonesia's fires that envelops Singapore every year or so.

[92] See my article, "After the Tsunami," 25.

[93] Many Singaporean workers resent the policy of importing foreign talent—they feel that foreigners are getting preferential treatment such as access to subsidized flats while avoiding obligations such as National Service—and the economic crisis has aggravated their frustration since "some were asking why foreigners were brought in at a time when job security was low and some Singaporeans had even been retrenched" ("Many Uneasy over Foreign Talent Policy," *Straits Times* [weekly edition], 21 March 1998, 6).

[94] See Chee, *Dare to Change*, 31.

whoever, they have to travel, because Europe has heard enough of them and everybody's watched them on television. So we are no longer isolated."[95]

DEMO: But what about *local* culture? It's a depressing local cultural scene, not expected to improve in the foreseeable future,[96] and as I said, part of the explanation is that many talented people have left.[97]

LEE: I wonder about this assumption that émigré Singaporeans are a particularly talented lot. Remember, we're working with a tiny talent pool here. (*pause*) It's hard to think of Singaporeans who have achieved great artistic success abroad.

DEMO: First of all, many cultural products are often recognized as such only by fellow members of one's native land—they may not make any sense to outsiders unfamiliar with the smells, sights, and sounds that give meaning to the product. Secondly, and more seriously, deracinated persons often lack the inspiration necessary for them to exercise their talents. . . .

LEE (*interrupting*): Oh, come on, there are plenty of wonderful writers-in-exile! Joyce, Becket, Rushdie—need I go on?

[95] Quoted in the *Straits Times*, 30 July 1994. On the plan to make Singapore into a center for the arts partly with the aim of curbing emigration, see also Hill and Lian, *The Politics of Nation-Building and Citizenship in Singapore*, 236–241.

[96] Demo may be too pessimistic. For example, the Singaporean film "12 Stories" (directed by Eric Khoo), which won acclaim at the 1997 Cannes Film Festival, portrays the dark side of Singaporean life in graphic detail and yet did not draw an official response, "a sign that Singapore's heavy-handed censors may be lightening their touch just a bit" (Darren McDermott and Fara Warner, "Singapore Film Signals a New Openness," *Asian Wall Street Journal*, 25 June 1997, 1).

[97] The problem may be not the lack of democracy per se, since some nondemocratic regimes have actively patronized the arts (e.g., the court of Queen Elizabeth or Louis XIV) and provided the conditions for creative work (I thank Michael Walzer for this point). The main problem in Singapore is that the government clamps down hard on artistic and public expression that deviates from the official conception of morality (e.g., a prize-winning artist was recently fined and publicly humiliated for "molesting" a policeman; "molesting," in this case, seems to mean that the artist fell victim to the government's policy of sending out decoys to entrap gay persons in public parks; see "Prize-Winning Artist Fined for Molesting Cop," *Straits Times* [weekly edition], 29 November 1997, 5). But if it is the case (as I suspect) that nondemocratic regimes in the modern world find it easier to enforce a strict puritanical code laid down by the political rulers, then one can say that the lack of democracy is to blame.

DEMO: Who knows, they may have done even better if they had stayed at home. In any case, we're talking about Singaporean artists, and at least some of them could have led more fulfilling creative lives if they had not left their country. You can never really tell how many budding artists you may have killed off by means of a stifling social and political system that so alienated them they had to go abroad, but I think it's something to be concerned about.

LEE: That's pure speculation, not the sort of argument that I find compelling. And I still don't see why it's so important to have more local culture if we succeed in our aim to turn Singapore in an international center for the arts.

DEMO: Well, consider the fact that a sense of community as well as achievement can often be gained even by mere spectators of those activities that bring glory to their participants.[98] It seems irrational, but that's how it works: the French bask in their World Cup–winning soccer team, Americans take pride in the writings of Mark Twain, and so on. Only *local* participants, it's important to emphasize, contribute to those activities that lead to a sense of communal pride (people don't normally take pride in the achievements of foreigners), so that's a good reason to foster the sort of environment that would allow the creative members of the community to develop their talents. Singapore, as a member of the opposition put it, lacks a cultural element "that forges an identity with the people living in it . . . which makes the members feel that they are one people, one nation,"[99] and reducing emigration by the "creative few" most likely to create products of communal pride would thus have the effect of forging a nation, of increasing people's commitment to Singapore.

LEE: So what you're saying, if I understand you correctly, is that the government should promote local culture, which can be accomplished by adopting democratic practices and hence

[98] See Quentin Skinner, "The Italian City-Republics," 65. For a Singaporean view on how a lively local culture can contribute to "a genuine sense of national community," see Philip Jeyaretnam, "What Sort of Culture Should Singapore Have?" 92–94.

[99] Chee, *Dare to Change*, 9.

making people sufficiently patriotic to want to stay in Singapore, because creative Singaporeans may produce goods that will further increase patriotism in Singapore. But I thought you were supposed to be offering reasons for why I should care about patriotism in Singapore—your reasoning is circular, because now you're saying that I should care about patriotism because doing this or that will have the ultimate effect of promoting patriotism! This argument doesn't tell me why I should care about patriotism in the first place.

DEMO: I'd say that it's a virtuous circle, but in any case let's move on to my last reason for patriotism. This argument begins with the premise that some countries can get by with professional, quasi-mercenary armies, but that Singapore, a small country surrounded by large, potentially hostile neighbors, may require much more for purposes of common defense, namely, a policy of military conscription for all adult males, a need recognized even by some of the most radical opponents of the regime (though some argue for a shorter period of national service and the inclusion of women). Needless to say, any community that relies on its own citizens to provide for common defense must be concerned with the issue of instilling a strong sense of patriotism, as measured by the degree to which one is prepared to face harm and danger on the nation's behalf. A good, citizen-based fighting force, in short, *requires* patriotism.[100]

But here we encounter a problem. Many Singaporeans, I'm told, would flee to Australia given the opportunity rather than risk their lives in combat, and some say they'd stay but on account of their family (living in Singapore), not "for the sake of the nation."[101] Even the *Straits Times* seems to acknowledge this problem. (*searches for a newspaper article in his briefcase*) Here, let

---

[100] An atomic bomb may also help if the aim is deterrence, but Singapore does not appear to have the capability to build a nuclear bomb at the moment. Even if Singapore had nuclear weapons, however, it may still need to depend on patriotic citizens for purposes of common defense—nuclear capability does not seem to be sufficient deterrence in the case of Israel, a country that similarly sees itself surrounded by a "sea of potentially hostile neighbors."

[101] Here I am relying on a source from within the military establishment as well as on anecdotal evidence from university students in Singapore (in response to the question "Would you willingly fight for your country in the event of a war?").

me quote the words of the *Straits Times* columnist, Koh Buck Song: he wonders whether "Singaporeans will prove patriotic enough when it comes to the crunch. . . . There is, quite clearly, still some cynicism about the whole business of defending a country. . . . The way some people react when others talk about National Service duty shows that military service is not something they look up to and appreciate readily. . . . anyone who speaks well of National Service is sometimes accused of mouthing official propaganda. Anyone who comes across as patriotic risks being tagged pro-government. . . . I have seen some, from bosses to observers without vested interests, not only being dismissive of the sacrifice involved in National Service, but also apparently devoid of any patriotic feeling."[102]

LEE: Yes, that's a problem. When we first implemented national service, we thought naively that nothing creates loyalty and national consciousness more speedily and more thoroughly than participation from all strata of society in defense and membership of the armed forces. It turns out not to be so simple.[103]

DEMO: So it appears that we can agree at least on this issue—there's an urgent need to increase patriotism if Singapore is to survive as a political entity in the event that, God forbid, your country is attacked by hostile neighbors.

LEE: Yes, but we're building up our defenses in other ways—under the Civil Defense Shelter Act passed by Parliament on October 7, 1997, all new homes in the future will have to be equipped with bomb shelters.[104] And of course, we see the strategic value

[102] See *Straits Times*, 11 July 1994. Several years later, Koh returned to similar worries over "an apparent lack of nationalism" and national servicemen who might not fight for the country "when it comes to the crunch" ("Keep Nationalism to the Defensive Kind," *Straits Times* [weekly edition], 1 August 1998, 12).

[103] This view was articulated by Minister of Defense Goh Keng Swee in 1967 (see *In Search of Singapore's National Values*, ed. Jon Quah, 52). Dr. Goh, by the way, is a brilliant economist commonly referred to in Singapore as "the architect of Singapore's economic miracle." If and when Singaporeans begin to write honest accounts of local history (i.e., when they can write without fear of retaliation), I predict that Goh's star will rise just as fast as Lee's will fall.

[104] See Chang Ai-Lien, "500 Flats in Hougang Are First with Own Bomb Shelters," *Straits Times*, 15 October 1997, 51.

of an American military presence in the region. That's why we gave you guys access to our facilities after you were booted out of Subic Bay in the Philippines.

DEMO: But that won't be enough! In the event of an invasion, you'll also need some soldiers prepared to sacrifice their lives for Singapore![105]

LEE: Of course. At the end of the day, we have to depend on ourselves. Unlike, say, oil-rich Kuwait, Singapore can't count on international support in the event of a war. So we have to put up a credible local defense force, at least to let the enemy know that an invasion would be very costly. "We intend to fight for our stake in this part of the world, and [to] anybody who thinks they can push us around, I say: over my dead body. . . . We opted for the Israeli fashion, for in our situation we think it might be necessary not only to train every boy but also every girl to be a disciplined and effective digit in defense of their own country."[106] But, like I said, we now recognize that national service isn't sufficient to build up patriotism. So we're relying on other means as well, such as patriotic messages in the media[107] and citizenship education in schools designed to promote identification with Singapore and foster the willingness to defend it if called upon.[108]

DEMO: But is that really going to produce loyal and patriotic soldiers? You're forgetting about one vital ingredient: democracy.

---

[105] There may also be some less dramatic incidents that require the involvement of patriotic citizens prepared to sacrifice their self-interest for the sake of the country: in 1998, the government feared an influx of refugees and illegal workers fleeing Indonesia's economic crisis and anti-Chinese pogroms, and the *Straits Times* noted that "citizen volunteers may have to help guard the nation's shores. Singaporeans should be prepared for that" (*Straits Times* [weekly edition], editorial, 21 March 1998, 12).

[106] Quoted in Tremewan, *The Political Economy of Social Control in Singapore*, 107–108.

[107] Koh's response to what he sees as the lack of patriotism in Singapore is to call for more governmental propaganda (see note 102).

[108] See Tan Hsueh Yun, "Minister of Education Spells Out How to Nurture Whole Person," *Straits Times* (weekly edition), 24 January 1998, 1.

And since you invoke Israel, how can you not notice the link between democracy and patriotism? Israel simply can't afford the political alienation that normally accompanies authoritarian practices. The same goes for Switzerland, another small country that's both democratic and intensely patriotic. So if democracy, including the right to run for the opposition without fear of retaliation and the right of self-generated groups to participate in public affairs, is the most feasible way of increasing patriotism in Singapore, then maybe it's time to think seriously about democratizing.

LEE (*pause*): Well, thank you for your advice. Perhaps we can begin one step at a time, say, by increasing the possibilities of free association in civil society and feedback to the government. I'm less convinced about the need to provide the right to run for the opposition without fear of retaliation, however.

DEMO: It would be most imprudent to provide for the freedom of association without allowing the opposition to freely compete for political power. Consider what happened in Taiwan's burgeoning civil society in the ten years prior to the lifting of martial law in late 1986. Long before the political process had opened up for opposition forces, people organized into social movements and developed a taste for public affairs.[109] But since they were all but excluded from the political process, they formed their own conceptions of national identity (a patriotic attachment to Taiwan) instead of the conception of national identity as stipulated by the KMT rulers (Taiwan including mainland China). Thus, I don't recommend beginning with the freedom of association alone, as the final result may be competing conceptions of national identity and state boundaries,[110] and

[109] See Hsin-Huang Michael Hsiao, "Political Liberalization and the Farmer's Movement in Taiwan," 208.

[110] One can think of other cases where people had the right to associate freely and form groups in civil society while being almost completely marginalized from the political process, with the consequence that they formed their own conceptions of national identity (or reinforced preexisting communal ties that conflict with those to the national political community): Yugoslavia had independent (relative to other East bloc states) intermediary associations in an undemocratic context, and many developed an attachment to their ethnic group as opposed to the "Yugoslav" community; many Catholics in Northern Ireland developed an

a lot of bloodshed may be shed in the process of determining the issue of who counts as "we the people." (*pause*) In the Singaporean context, the freedom of association alone may strengthen ethnic ties and decrease people's attachment to Singapore. If the aim is to increase people's patriotic attachments to *Singapore*, then the right to associate freely and the right to run for the opposition without fear of retaliation must come together.

SUMMARY

LEE (*glancing at his watch*): Well, I guess our time is nearly up. Let me just conclude with the point that I do agree with your observation that genuine patriotism is uncommon in Singapore, and I also think that you may be on to something when you suggest that more democracy may be a cure for the lack of public-spiritedness in Singapore. But do we really need more patriotism in Singapore? To be sure, our government may not live up to its communitarian rhetoric, but few governments meet all their promises. You say that public-spiritedness in the community at large is the best bulwark against corruption, but our anticorruption measures seem to be working quite well. And what's wrong with successful ethnic-based welfare schemes? It's no less arbitrary to favor one's own ethnic group than to favor co-nationals against the interests of foreigners who may live only a few kilometers away in Malaysia or Indonesia. You raised a point about emigration, but if the "creative few" want to leave, let them go, they can be easily replaced by productive immigrants less likely to create trouble. (*pause*) I am, I admit, slightly more troubled by your last point that more patriotism may be necessary for purposes of common defense. There's nothing I care more about than the survival of Singapore,[111] and I'll think about your advice.

---

attachment to Ireland as opposed to the U.K.; and many Tamils developed a commitment to their own group as opposed to Sri Lanka.

[111] Note, however, that Lee recently took Singaporeans by surprise by floating the idea of reunification with Malaysia if the latter country becomes "meritocratic" (see *Straits Times*, 8 June 1996). Several days later an alarmed letter writer to the *Straits Times* commented "I'd rather die a Singaporean than a semi-Malay-

DEMO (*flattered*): Well, thank you for this wonderful opportunity to share my ideas—it's not often that political leaders welcome free-flowing discussions on local politics with outsiders.

LEE: You're different from most of them. There's nothing that tires me more than self-righteous Westerners preaching the virtues of democracy in places they neither understand nor respect. But your arguments are factually detailed and historically specific, grounded in a good understanding of Singaporean society and a sincere respect for our moral aspirations.[112] So thank you for this discussion, and have a safe trip home.

DEMO: I'm sticking around for a little bit longer. You see, culturally sensitive arguments for political reform need not only be addressed to rulers—they can also have political effect if they're suggested to local critics of the ruling regimes, who may need more ammunition in their fight for democracy. In Singapore, for example, opposition forces brave enough to withstand "big

---

sian. . . . The last thing I want to see, and I believe most Singaporeans would agree, is for Singapore to become part of Malaysia, and cease existing as a sovereign state. . . . Does that mean I will stop calling myself a Singaporean, we will have to stop celebrating National Day and pledge our unswerving loyalty to Malaysia?" (13 June 1996). But as it turns out, Lee's offer was spurned by Malaysian Prime Minister Mahathir, who said, "We do practice meritocracy, but one which is based on race" (quoted in the *Hong Kong Standard*, 16 June 1996).

[112] In the same vein, Bilahari Kausikan (Singapore's permanent representative to the United Nations) urges Western democrats to refrain from judging Singapore's political system prior to detailed understanding of local complexities ("Governance That Works"). Lee himself, however, does not always respect the principle of refraining from political judgments prior to a detailed understanding of local complexities: he delivers the same antidemocratic message to audiences in China, Japan, Vietnam, and the Philippines, regardless of differences in history and stages of economic development (see also Chee, *To Be Free*, 315–316). In 1996 he told foreign reporters in Singapore that only the army could rule Burma and that Aung San Suu Kyi should stay "behind a fence, and be a symbol" (quoted in *Hong Kong Standard*, 9 June 1996), and more recently he urged the new chief executive in Hong Kong to scrap Chris Patten's democratic and civil rights reforms ("Ditch Patten Reforms, Lee Kuan Yew Urges," *South China Morning Post*, 13 May 1997, 6). The Hong Kong people, he added, should not "waste time talking about democracy" ("Lee Kuan Yew Blast against Democracy," *South China Morning Post*, 12 June 1997, 6).

sticks" can use whatever limited space they have to advance the kinds of arguments I've been suggesting. I've been talking with opposition leader Dr. Chee Soon Juan. Dr. Chee, you may know, opens his political manifesto *Dare to Change: An Alternative Vision for Singapore* with a chapter exposing the gap between the official rhetoric of communitarianism and the more individualistic reality in Singapore, arguing for measures that would lead to greater national cohesion. The solution he proposes boils down to one word—democracy!

LEE: Well, it didn't work for him. "He has lost, and lost badly in an open, free election, one to one against one of our candidates."[113]

DEMO: We already went over this! Elections are not truly open and competitive in Singapore! They're completely rigged against the opposition! Dr. Chee himself was the target of a relentless campaign of ugly personal attacks. . . .

LEE (*interrupting*): "He is a liar. . . . he's had exposure on television, which was disastrous for him because he was caught out lying and fibbing and fabricating evidence on a health care paper which he presented."[114]

DEMO: I believe you're referring to the fact that he misstated a statistic on health care. Nobody who's looked at the evidence—other than PAP hacks—believes this was a deliberate lie, and yet he was fined $51,000 for an honest mistake. And let's not mention all the other "big sticks" that have been administered to Dr. Chee—he was sacked from his teaching job at the National University of Singapore, sued for "defamation" by his former head of department—a PAP member of Parliament—and

[113] Quoted in William Safire, "Interview with Singapore's Senior Minister Lee Kuan Yew," February 1999 (circulated on the Internet), 7. Lee is referring to the 2 January 1997, general election, which Dr. Chee lost, following a press campaign filled with vitriolic personal attacks (not to mention other factors, such as Prime Minister Goh's threat to turn districts that elect opposition candidates into "slums"; see chapter 3, note 19).

[114] "Interview with Singapore's Senior Minister Lee Kuan Yew," 8, 7.

forced to pay hundreds of thousands of dollars in "damages,"[115] and now he's been thrown in jail for giving a political speech without a police permit![116]

LEE: "He's been away for two years, in Australia, licking his wounds, so he wants to find a way to get a splash back, so he tries to—so he gets a big splash in the Western press—because they want to beat me up. It's all right; it doesn't bother me."[117]

DEMO: Of course it doesn't bother you—you're not the one who was sent to jail. I must confess, however, I was a bit surprised myself that he came back. Why did he do it, when he knew the consequences he'd have to face? I don't think it was to get a "big splash in the Western press"[118]—no sane person goes to jail just to get into foreign newspapers. Dr. Chee gave a more plausible reason—"Singapore is my home. I want to contribute to my home and have a say in its future."[119] Personally, I'm moved by his patriotism. Here's someone who's willing to forgo his personal interests—lose out financially and go to jail—all

---

[115] Dr. Chee was dismissed from his post as lecturer in neuropsychology at the National University of Singapore two months after he ran (unsuccessfully) for the opposition Social Democratic Party in a December 1992 by-election, allegedly for misusing 226 Singapore dollars (U.S. $137) of a $27,000 research grant and for trying to mislead his department head, Dr. S. Vasoo, member of Parliament for the ruling People's Action Party (Dr. Vasoo dismissed allegations of conflict of interest with the declaration that "I separate my duties as head of department from my role as PAP MP"). Dr. Chee then embarked on a hunger strike to demand that the university retract its accusation of dishonesty, called off ten days later following a debate in Parliament on "the Dr. Chee Soon Juan affair." Several weeks later Dr. Chee was slapped with a defamation suit by Dr. Vasoo and two other university officials. A Singapore judge found Dr. Chee guilty; damages and court costs amounted to about U.S. $156,000. Dr. Chee sold his house to pay off his debt and avoid bankruptcy, which would have disqualified him from running in the next general election.

[116] Dr. Chee was sent to jail twice in 1999 after he refused to pay fines for giving unlicensed speeches in a deliberate move to test the limits of public discussion in Singapore.

[117] "Interview with Singapore's Senior Minister Lee Kuan Yew," 7–8.

[118] As a matter of fact, Dr. Chee's recent trials and tribulations have been reported far more extensively in the Asian press—in Hong Kong, Malaysia, and Taiwan in particular—than in the Western press.

[119] Quoted in Alison Nadel, "Singapore's Voice of Reason," *South China Morning Post*, 8 March 1997, 2). See also Dr. Chee's second book, *Singapore: My Home Too*.

for the sake of his country. He wants, as he puts in chapter 1 of *Dare to Change*, "to forge an identity which makes [Singaporeans] feel that they are one people, one nation," and he's driven by the conviction that democracy is the only way to increase public-spiritedness and commitment to the Singaporean nation.[120] And he's not the only one: many Singaporeans are worried about what authoritarianism is doing to the Singaporean nation, and some of them are explicitly advancing communitarian arguments for democracy.[121] They don't want to be living in a five-star hotel—or perhaps I should say a four-star hotel, the way the economy's looking now—and they think they can't have a real home without democracy. I hope to talk about this with local intellectuals and members of the opposition during my stay in Singapore.

LEE (*face turning red*): Well, I wish you good luck. I'm sorry, but our time is up. I must get ready for my next meeting.

(*Demo exits Lee's office; Lee then calls in Internal Security Department officers for his weekly briefing.*)

LEE: Do me a favor and let me know what that guy is up to.

---

[120] Ian Buruma overlooks this possible account of Dr. Chee's motivation (see Buruma's review of *Dare to Change* in the *New York Review of Books*, 19 October 1995). Describing his own reaction to a meeting with Dr. Chee, Buruma writes: "I wondered what possessed him to go against his own interests, against the wishes of his family, against all the advantages of conformity." Not satisfied with Dr. Chee's "vague answer," Buruma offers his own cynical explanation: "To be an opposition leader in a system which does not recognize loyal opposition takes a steeliness, a fearlessness, a ruthlessness that very few people possess. Lee Kuan Yew had it . . . Dr. Chee appears to have it."

[121] For example, Chua Beng-Huat argues that a more open political process is necessary to establish "communitarian democracy" in Singapore (see Chua, *Communitarian Ideology and Democracy in Singapore*, esp. chap. 9). Chua's book, however, is carefully crafted to avoid direct criticism of PAP leaders, perhaps because Chua believes that the current set of PAP leaders will be sufficiently persuaded by communitarian arguments for democracy to undertake political reform. A more serious theoretical concern is that Chua defines communitarianism as "consensus" rather than as public-spiritedness, and he advances the empirically dubious argument that freedom of the press and the right to interest-group formation will likely produce a true consensus regarding national interests (though Chua seems to take it all back in a peculiar footnote on p. 202). My own view is that democratic rights may increase commitment to the common good in Singapore, not that Singaporeans are more likely to converge on the same interpretation of the common good.

PART III

DEMOCRACY WITH CHINESE CHARACTERISTICS

*

A Political Proposal for the
Post-Communist Era

SCENE: June 3, 2007. Beijing University in Beijing, China.[1] Sam Demo, now based in Beijing, steps into Professor Wang's[2] office to begin a prearranged interview. Professor Wang, a respected political philosopher at Beijing University in his mid-forties, has been selected to participate in a constitutional convention due to begin the following day in Beijing.

DEMO (*out of breath*): Thank you for receiving me today. I realize it must be a very busy time now. (*pause*) I'm sorry I'm late. I was stuck in traffic for over two hours.

WANG: I guess that's the price a society pays for economic development. One reads in the textbooks that modernization is supposed to increase the pace of living, but the opposite may well be the case.

DEMO (*laughs*): It could be worse—in the mid-1990s, the average commuter in Bangkok had to bring a potty in his car. But the traffic situation improved after the economic crash. (*short pause*) Well, I still find it hard to believe that we're here to discuss the prospects for democratic political reform in China, and no need to worry about the secret police. Think about it. Five or six years ago, who would have been able to anticipate the possibility of a national convention designed to formulate a democratic constitution appropriate for China?[3] And on June 4, no less!

[1] An earlier version of this chapter was published (in dialogue form) in *Philosophy East and West* 49, no.4 (October 1999). Reprinted by permission.

[2] Wang is a common Chinese surname. It means "king" or "emperor."

[3] While most of the contributors to a symposium addressing the question "Will China democratize?" "find themselves unable to identify any groups that are sufficiently powerful, motivated, and aligned to produce the democratic changes that supposedly are inevitable," Andrew Nathan notes that "several contributors

279

WANG: In retrospect, it may not seem that remarkable. Remember we had a fairly open debate about political reform in the late 1980s, prior to the Tiananmen massacre. People tend to forget that the Communist Party itself set up a Political Reform Office, which sometimes evaluated radical proposals for political change. And Deng's death seemed to open up some possibilities. New signs of tolerance emerged at the Communist Party's Fifteenth Congress in October 1997, and intellectuals began to speak out for political reform once again.[4] Besides, the party couldn't postpone the day of reckoning forever, marking the days prior to the June 4 anniversary with detentions, tighter surveillance of leading dissidents, controlling access to Tiananmen Square, and so on. Once again, it's easy to say this in retrospect, but in my view it was inevitable that the party would apologize for the Tiananmen massacre, just as the KMT apologized for February 28, 1947, massacre in Taiwan (though it took over four decades) and the Korean government indicted those responsible for the 1980 Kwangju massacre more than ten years after the fact. Of course, we know what happened to Li Peng. After that, it was no longer possible to hold back demands for political reform.

DEMO: Well, stranger things have happened. How many of us managed to predict the sudden collapse of the Soviet empire,[5] or

---

acknowledge China's history of surprising political eruptions and breakthroughs, and point to the ever-present possibility of surprises" (Nathan, "Even Our Caution Must Be Hedged," 62, 63–64).

[4] See, e.g., "Beijing Spring," *Far Eastern Economic Review*, 2 April 1998, 20–22. Two periodicals—*Reform Magazine* and *ResPublica*—publish articles calling for democratic reform. *ResPublica*, which is partly funded by the Ford Foundation, published an abridged, Chinese-language version of this proposal for a bicameral legislature with an upper House of Scholars ("A Confucian Democracy for the 21st Century," *ResPublica* 4 [1997]: 378–392; the English-language version was published in *Archiv fuer Rechts-und Sozialphilosophie*, ed. Morigiwa Yasutomo, Beiheft 72 [1998]: 37–49).

[5] Some observers did in fact predict this event. In 1986 Emmanuel Todd of the Paris National Institute for Demographic Research predicted "with clinical precision that the Soviet Union would soon disintegrate" (see Erazim Kohak, "The Search for Europe", *Dissent*, Spring 1996, 15). Peter Frank of the University of Essex also predicted some of the events in the early 1990s along with their causes. But the more important point is that most political thinkers were still working within the "realist" paradigm of how to deal with communist-type institutions at the time the Soviet empire collapsed instead of thinking in concrete

the swift and peaceful dismantling of apartheid in South Africa? (*short pause*) I'm still not too clear, however, about your proposal for tomorrow's constitutional convention. I've heard it said that you favor a democratic political system "with Chinese characteristics." What does this phrase mean? I'm well aware that Chinese reformers typically argue for democracy as a means for strengthening national power[6]—in contrast, say, to American theorists who tend to justify democracy with reference to the value of individual freedom[7]—but this is a dispute over the *justification* for a democratic political system. I've yet to hear an argument, I must admit, that a unique *kind* of democratic system is appropriate for this part of the world, one that differs to a significant extent from Western-style democratic institutions. In other words, both Asians and Westerners seem to agree on the political ideal, though they may typically do so for different reasons.

WANG: Let me try to explain my scheme. I do in fact have a proposal for a different kind of democracy, a democratic political system that's particularly appropriate for the Chinese context. And tomorrow I'll try to persuade fellow Chinese, although I think foreigners can also come to appreciate my reasons for defending this scheme.

DEMO: Please elaborate.

1. CONSTRAINING DEMOCRATIC POPULISM

1.1. On the Need for Capable and Far-Sighted Rulers in Modern Societies

WANG: Well, we agree that a democratic system at minimum must include regular elections based on universal franchise. The aim is to give ordinary citizens a say, no matter how distant, in politi-

---

terms about what should come after communism, with the consequence that the options were narrowed to a choice between Western-style democracy and a "return to communism" (see sec. 3.5).

[6] See, e.g., Yan Jiaqi, *Toward a Democratic China*, chap. 17; Andrew Nathan, *Chinese Democracy*, 127; Orville Schell, *Discos and Democracy*, 198; and the discussion in chap. 2, sec. 2.2.

[7] Even some American communitarians tend to argue along these lines (i.e., community is seen as a means for liberty): see, e.g., Benjamin Barber, "A Mandate for Liberty," 194.

cal decision-making, and to hold political rulers accountable at the end of the day. But it's also the case that many relevant issues and policies in the political systems of modern societies have become so complex that most ordinary citizens can't even begin to make sound judgments. Does the man on the street really know the probable impact of increasing interest rates[8] or reforming administrative law? The sheer complexity of public affairs in the modern era means that a substantial amount of decision-making power must be placed in the hands of an intellectually agile and well-qualified elite, almost as a functional requirement of modern political societies. More than ever before, there's a need for brains in government.

DEMO: Fair enough. But on the other hand, many modern societies seem to function quite well with a democratic system.

WANG: That's true. But those same societies also place substantial constraints on democratic majorities, presumably on the grounds that some things are better left to more capable hands. I spent six years as a graduate student in the United States, and I must say I was consistently shocked at the gap between the rhetoric of popular sovereignty and the reality of rule by an intellectual elite. One antidemocratic device, of course, is the constitutional Bill of Rights enforced by nonelected judges holding final powers of review. The U.S. Supreme Court, as you know,

[8] Hong Kong's monetary chief Joseph Yam (the highest-paid civil servant in Hong Kong) provides an example of the difficulty of monetary issues: "Monetary issues are unfortunately very technical and elusive, but they affect everybody. Money is dear to the heart of everyone. So, quite naturally to us, the price and value of money are things we should be concerned about. Here, already to a lay person or to the average politician, we are being esoteric. What is the price of money? What is the value of money? And what are the differences between the two? Why should we be concerned about them? These are legitimate questions. And they are not easy concepts to put across. So, imagine trying to explain, and obtain support for, the following proposal: 'To dampen interest rate volatility and lessen the interest rate pain by redefining the monetary base to include debt paper discountable at the HKMA through overnight repurchase agreements and fully backed by foreign reserves without departing from the monetary rule of currency board arrangements which requires the monetary base to change only with a corresponding change in foreign reserves.' This really is a mouthful. And to some, I must have been speaking Greek. But I can assure you that the wording of the proposal is precise and technically 100 percent correct." (Yam, "The Management of Our Money," *South China Morning Post*, 22 October 1998, 19).

has the power to override the decisions of elected politicians said to violate the U.S. Constitution.

DEMO: Mmh, yes. Perhaps you can also support your argument with the less well-known example of central banks in Western societies. In the United States, for example, the Federal Reserve Board has the power to make monetary policy, which can have important economic effects such as influencing people's decisions to buy consumer durables.[9] This secretive institution is explicitly insulated against interference by elected politicians, on the grounds that it must have the power to take tough economic decisions that benefit the country in the long run. So, for example, the Fed sometimes increases interest rates so as to ward off inflation, even if this means increasing unemployment. A more responsive central bank may not be able to act against the wishes of politicians who might find it in their interest to combat unemployment, whatever the long-term economic consequences. There seems to be an implicit understanding that secrecy and insulation from political pressure are essential to the successful conduct of monetary policy, and that most elected politicians have neither the competence nor the political will to make sound economic decisions.[10]

[9] The Federal Reserve Board also has direct influence on countries that peg their currencies to the U.S. dollar. As the Hong Kong Monetary Authority chief Joseph Yam put it, "The cost of operating a fixed exchange rate system is that you have conceded your sovereign right over monetary policy to the central bank of the currency to which you are linked. In our case it is Alan Greenspan [U.S. Federal Reserve chairman] who determines monetary policy for us" (Peter Seidlitz and David Murphy, "Yam Calls for Asian Facility to End Crisis," *South China Morning Post*, 14 June 1998, Money section, 4). It is also worth noting that the new British Labour government has empowered the British Central Bank to set interest rates, on the grounds that, as the chancellor of the Exchequer explained, "politicians for too often [had been] setting policy to suit their needs, with the result that the British economy had been plagued by damaging cycles" (Erik Ibsen, "Labour Empowers U.K. Central Bank to Set Interest Rate," *International Herald Tribune*, 7 May 1997, 10).

[10] See, e.g., John Cassidy, "Fleeing the Fed," *The New Yorker*, 19 February 1996, 45–46. The title of this article refers to Alan Blinder, who is supposed to have "fled the Fed" due to differences over the lack of transparency and accountability at the central bank, but it is interesting to note that Blinder has nonetheless written an article extolling the virtues of the Fed and arguing for the need to extend such "apolitical" decision-making bodies to other domains (Blinder, "Is Government Too Political?").

WANG: Yes, that's a good example.

DEMO: But keep in mind that the people still have the ultimate power. Super-majorities have the power to amend the U.S. Constitution,[11] though admittedly it's a time-consuming and difficult process. And Federal Reserve Board governors are appointed by the president and have to be confirmed by the Senate.

WANG: I wonder if this "ultimate power" means much in practice.[12] And when we look at democratic political systems in East Asia, it seems that intellectual elites have an even greater say relative to elected officials. In Japan, meritocratically chosen bureaucrats continue to wield power and authority that would make even their semifictitious colleagues in *Yes Minister* envious. The political system empowers them to make most of the nation's policy, and they effectively answer to no one, including the nation's elected politicians.[13]

---

[11] Ronald Dworkin argues that the "antimajoritarian" Supreme Court *is* democratic (as opposed to acting as a constraint on the decisions of elected politicians), not simply because ultimately the people could override a court decision by amending the Constitution, but also because people realize that the majority needs to be restrained in certain circumstances and so support the Supreme Court and its role as constitutional watchdog (Dworkin, *Freedom's Law*, 16). Dworkin can make this move because he defines democracy not as decision-making by elected politicians but rather as decision-making that treats "all members of the community, as individuals, with equal concern and respect," but he provides no reason for the argument that this "alternate account of the aim of democracy . . . demands much the same structure of government as the majoritarian premise does" (17). If less-than-democratic institutions composed of unelected decision-makers such as the House of Scholars can feasibly do a better job at treating people with equal concern and respect compared to political institutions composed of elected politicians then Dworkin should endorse the former. In my view, Dworkin should "come clean" and admit that he is really talking about justice, not democracy, and that (like Wang) he would favor more constraints on the powers of democratically elected politicians if this can achieve the end of securing more justice.

[12] Consider the following reflections by Robert Reich, the U.S. secretary of labor from 1992 to 1996: "only he [Alan Greenspan, head of the U.S. Federal Reserve Bank] has the power to raise or lower short-term interest rates. Like Paul Volcker, the Fed chief before him, Greenspan can put the economy in a tailspin simply by tightening his grip. Volcker did it in 1979, and Jimmy Carter was fired. Bill Clinton knows that. Greenspan has the most important grip in town: Bill's balls, in the palm of his hand" (Reich, "Locked in the Cabinet," *The New Yorker*, 21 April 1997, 44–45).

[13] See, e.g., Karel Van Wolferen, *The Enigma of Japanese Power.*

DEMO: But do you endorse this kind of system? Isn't there a need for more openness and accountability in the Japanese political system? There's no need to remind you of the Ministry of Finance's role in prolonging, if not causing, Japan's crippling economic crisis in the 1990s.[14] And let's not mention that incident involving bureaucrats at the Health Ministry, who resisted allowing imports of sterilized blood until 1985, well after they had been told of the risks of HIV contamination. As a result, several hundred Japanese hemophiliacs died from AIDS.[15]

WANG: Of course intellectual elites make tragic mistakes, but so do elected politicians. I worry about political systems that empower "feel-good" politicians who manage to get elected by promising the moon to their constituents—"we'll cut taxes and increase spending," or "full steam ahead with economic development," the story goes, and never mind the long-term consequences. Let future generations worry about massive deficits and ecological disasters.

DEMO: Fair enough. But you may be overestimating the intelligence of some elected politicians. Not all of them consciously subordinate the long-term good for short-term gain. Ronald Reagan, for example, seemed too intellectually feeble to even grasp the long-term implications of what he proposed.

WANG (*smiles*): For better or for worse. He was playing with fire, but he did fuel an arms race that contributed to the economic collapse of the Soviet bloc. In any case, from my perspective the ideal is a political system that guarantees bright and far-sighted rulers and yet holds them somewhat accountable for what they do. The problem with the Japanese system is that "bureaucrats"—in effect the nation's top political decision-makers—decide things in secret and then can't be held responsible when things go wrong.

DEMO: We seem to have come a long way from democracy. A democratic system simply can't ensure that a country's top decision-

[14] See, e.g., Benjamin Fulford, "Japan's Reluctant Reformers Basking in the Status Quo," *South China Morning Post*, 7 July 1998, Business section, 5. For a book-length indictment of the Ministry of Finance's failures from the late 1980s to the late 1990s, see Peter Hartcher, *The Ministry*. But for a more favorable account of Japanese bureaucracy, see the references in chap. 2, note 134.

[15] See Sheryl WuDunn, "Japan's Bureaucrats Fumble Away the Traditional Center of Power," *International Herald Tribune*, 7 May 1996, 4.

makers will be "bright and far-sighted." The rulers are whoever the people say they are, and it must be assumed that ordinary citizens can generally be trusted to choose the right sorts of leaders.

1.2. A Confucian Tradition of Respect for a Ruling Intellectual Elite

WANG: You see, this is where cultural differences may be relevant. In East Asia, to put it a bit crudely, the tradition has been to place trust in competent and virtuous bureaucrats. As you may know, East Asian political culture has been shaped by the Confucian idea that public service is the way to achieve complete self-realization. There's a saying in the Confucian *Analects*. (*short pause*) Let me try to translate: "Tzu-lu asked about the qualities of a true gentleman. The Master said, He cultivates in himself the capacity to be diligent in his tasks. Tzu-Lu said, can he not go further than that? The Master said, He cultivates in himself the capacity to ease the lot of other people. Tzu-lu said, Can he not go further than that? The Master said, He cultivates in himself the capacity to ease the lot of the whole populace. If he can do that, could even Yao or Shun find cause to criticize him?" (14.45)[16] Promoting the common good, in this view, is life's highest achievement, and this sort of idea may have inspired the "best and brightest" in East Asia to compete for civil service appointments.[17] Not surprisingly, occupants of bureaucratic posts have typically been held in high regard by the population at large, in the same way that self-made entrepreneurs in the United States tend to be granted large amounts of respect.

DEMO: Correct me if I am wrong, but Plato also proposed a political system of "rule by the wise." The value of political elitism is not foreign to the West, I can assure you.

[16] Unless otherwise indicated, I rely on Arthur Waley's translation of *The Analects of Confucius* (London: Allen & Unwin, 1938).

[17] According to Bruce Brooks, however, the person we refer to as "Confucius" was probably directly responsible only for the ideas expressed in chapter 4 of the Analects, and an interest in the well-being of the populace does not appear until Book 12, which may date to more than 150 years after the death of Confucius (Brooks, *The Original Analects*; I thank Chris Fraser for bringing this reference to my attention). Whatever the truth of this argument, the fact remains that the

WANG: But there's a difference. Plato's philosopher-king is *bur-dened* with the task of public duty—true self-realization lies "outside the cave," in the realm of the ideal forms. The same goes for Aristotle, for whom intellectual contemplation is the highest pleasure. And when we turn to Christianity, the bias against secular public service is even more deeply felt—one lives, and suffers, in "the city of man" in order to find happiness in "the city of God." (*short pause*) Now, I don't mean to deny that some Chinese philosophical systems also devalue the political—Daoism comes to mind[18]—but certainly the dominant philosophical tradition in East Asia values public service over and above other activities. And all the world is promised to those who succeed.

DEMO: I think you may be overestimating the sociological importance of philosophical texts.

WANG: Perhaps. But recall that Confucian societies *institutionalized* a stable mechanism capable of producing at least on occasion what was widely seen as a "government of the best men"—China's famous two-thousand-year-old meritocratic civil service examination system. Entry to the civil service through competitive examination was open to all males with a few exceptions, and those who eventually succeeded at passing, often having to undertake half a lifetime of study to do so, were thought to be in sole possession of the moral and intellectual qualities necessary for public service. (*short pause*) Think about it. In the West, defenders of rule by an intellectual elite could do nothing more than *argue* in favor of their superior abilities in political theory texts, universities, churches, and so on, whereas Confucians could actually prove themselves by succeeding in a fair and open examination process. I think this helps to explain why scholar-bureaucrats were granted uncommon (by Western standards) amounts of legitimacy, respect—and power.

DEMO: But look at what happened in China—the Communists uprooted the traditional value of rule by an intellectual elite and

---

dominant interpretation of Confucianism transmitted over the past two thousand years has valued public service as life's highest achievement.

[18] However, many aspiring scholar-officials opted for Daoism only after they failed the civil service examinations, which suggests that public service would have been their first choice.

its institutional manifestations. There's no need to remind you of the Cultural Revolution.

WANG: You're right, but ideology began to take a back seat to considerations of talent and expertise with the advent of economic reform. In the Deng reform era, intellectuals were again held in high esteem and regarded among the leaders of the country.[19] And when we look at the May/June 1989 prodemocracy demonstrations—recall that over one million ordinary Beijing citizens participated in a movement led by students and intellectuals from China's most prestigious universities—it becomes clear that the value of respect for the leadership role of an intellectual elite was not killed off by the Cultural Revolution.[20] Of course, it's much easier to trace philosophical and institutional continuity in other East Asian countries fortunate enough not to have experienced a full-scale Cultural Revolution.[21] In Japan, the top candidates of the nationwide pre-university examination system enter the law faculty at Tokyo University, and upon graduation they obtain posts with the most prestigious government ministries. In Singapore, the top graduates from the National University compete not for prime jobs in the private sector but rather for the best jobs in government. And those who scored highest on their A levels are given government scholarships to study abroad at Princeton, Harvard, and such, and when they return to Singapore they're almost immediately given responsible positions in the public sector. Moreover, as a condition of having accepted the scholarship, they're under a legal obligation to work for the government for a minimum of eight years. How's that for a productive use of talent!

[19] See Merle Goldman, "Politically-Engaged Intellectuals in the Deng-Jiang Era," 38.

[20] When we think about the (un)likelihood of the "American" equivalent—a few dozen students from Harvard and MIT leading a massive movement for social change with the enthusiastic support and participation of a million working-class Bostonians—it becomes clear just how distinctive the Chinese value of respect for rule by an intellectual elite really seems to be. See chap. 2, sec. 2.2.

[21] As Tu Wei-ming puts it, "the Confucian scholar-official mentality still functions in the psychocultural construct of East Asian societies" (in Tu, ed., *Confucian Traditions in East Asian Modernity*, 15). See also Ronald Dore, "Elitism and Democracy," 70, and Ezra Vogel, *The Four Little Dragons*, 101.

DEMO: Are you suggesting that China should revive the Confucian practice of rule by meritocratically chosen government bureaucrats?

WANG: Not exactly. As I said, I favor some accountability for political decision-making, which was lacking in traditional Confucian societies and still seems to be lacking in Japan and Singapore. And I think the political talent selection procedures should be made more transparent than they currently are in East Asia. But I also want to preserve the Confucian political value of conferring respect and power to an intellectual elite, on the grounds that modern societies generally fare better if they're ruled by bright and far-sighted public servants. So the challenge is how to implement dual commitments to democracy and rule by a public-spirited intellectual elite in a contemporary Chinese context.

DEMO (*intrigued, yet slightly skeptical*): And what's the answer?

2. ALTERNATIVE PROPOSALS

WANG: Well, I racked my brains for many years trying to resolve this question. I considered various alternatives, but none seemed to offer a persuasive way out. (*short pause*) The solution, strangely enough, came to me one day as I was having lunch at the Kentucky Fried Chicken outlet at Tiananmen Square.

DEMO (*laughs*): Why not? In the old days, philosophers like Jean-Jacques Rousseau had sudden revelations under oak trees,[22] but it seems to be getting more and more difficult to find greenery in Beijing.

WANG: Of course I'm not comparing myself to Rousseau, although I won't deny that it was a moment of tremendous excitement when I thought of this political arrangement.

DEMO (*getting more curious*): Well, let's have it.

[22] See Jean-Jacques Rousseau, *The Confessions*, trans. J. M. Cohen (Harmondsworth, England: Penguin, 1953), 327–328.

WANG: The tricky part was how to institutionalize rule by an intellectual elite in an overall democratic context. I never had any difficulty with the question of institutionalizing the democratic component of the equation—any workable and legitimate political system in the modern era must, I think, include free and fair competitive elections. But how to ensure a "government of the best"?

DEMO: What about letting the people decide?

WANG: I'm not too sure about that. Sometimes politicians can only get elected by pandering to the short-term interests of the populace. In developing countries it's often easier to get elected by promising the conditions for rapid economic development, regardless of the ecological costs for future generations. In developed countries, voters prefer politicians who favor policies that benefit the middle class and the rich, regardless of the impact on the poor. Or sometimes they promise to maintain economically unsustainable welfare benefits.

DEMO: Democracy isn't perfect. But if the solution is to give more power to an intellectual elite, then democratic elections may do the trick in East Asia. As you suggest, ordinary people have imbibed the ethic of respect for Confucian "gentlemen," so one should expect citizens to vote for such persons.

WANG: That's possible. In Korea and Taiwan, for example, candidates for national office often flaunt their educational qualifications, apparently with the hope that people are more inclined to vote for a ruler with a Ph.D. from a prestigious university. But overall the situation is not encouraging. In Japan, voters appear to be swayed primarily by short-term material benefits, and still now most political talent finds its way to the bureaucracy rather than the legislature. And even supposing that voters try to identify "Confucian" political rulers, they may not always be able to identify persons of character and ability. The Singapore government controls for this possibility by administering a battery of tests to PAP candidates, including an IQ test and other psychological tests to eliminate candidates who are self-interested.[23]

---

[23] See Hill and Lian, *The Politics of Nation Building and Citizenship in Singapore,* 192. See also chap. 3, sec. 3, and chap. 4, sec. 3.3.

DEMO: But you don't have truly competitive elections in Singapore. The Singapore government also controls for the possibility of "bad" rulers by numbering ballots, humiliating and bankrupting opposition candidates, and instilling an atmosphere of fear in the population at large. That's not what you want for China, is it?

WANG: No, of course not. But neither do I want to leave it all up to the people. It's simply too risky in China. Most people are still uneducated peasants, and . . .

DEMO (*interrupting*): Now hold on a second. Peasants—or perhaps "farmers" is a more politically correct word—already vote in China. Surely you're familiar with the village democracy program, with farmers choosing among candidates competing for posts on village committees. Even the Communist Party endorsed this program in the mid-1990s, on the grounds that local leaders needed to be made more accountable.[24] You're not against that, are you?

WANG: No, no, don't be silly. Of course "farmers" should choose the leaders of village committees. They should have the power to remove corrupt local leaders from office. But do you think "farmers" are qualified to choose *national* political rulers who are deciding such complex matters as macroeconomic management and foreign policy? I'd be nervous about granting too much power to relatively uneducated people, and I know many "democrats" also worry about the possibility of a farmer-dominated legislature.[25] In China, the problems we face are so se-

[24] See "Village Committees: The Link between Economic and Political Reform," *China Development Briefing* 4 (January 1997): 18–20. The Sichuan township of Buyan has recently extended the practice of electing leaders to the township level ("Democracy for Chinese" [editorial], *International Herald Tribune*, 2 February 1999, 8).

[25] According to Vivienne Shue, democracy movement leaders such as Fang Lizhi "have expressed only horror at a democratic formula that would give equal voting rights to peasants" (Shue, "China: Transition Postponed?" 163). In a recent survey of proposals for political reform in China, Andrew Nathan notes that he is "not aware of any proposal to move to one-man-one-vote." The possibility of a farmer-dominated legislature has led some reformers to endorse the current system of malapportionment, which favors urban over rural voters (Nathan, "China's Constitutionalist Option," 48). See also chap. 2, sec. 2.3.

vere—overpopulation, pollution, increasing economic inequality, a risk of civil war—that's it's just too much of a gamble to invest all our hopes in the capricious likes and dislikes of a largely rural population in a free-for-all political fest held every four or five years.

DEMO: But what are the alternatives?

WANG: Exactly. Remember, I don't have a quarrel with democracy per se. My aim is simply to temper the democratic process with a concern for the selection of talented decision-makers. And to repeat, even Western societies like the United States do in practice place constraints on the decision-making powers of elected politicians. But your solutions may not be readily transferable to our country, and the question is how to combine democracy with a stable, legitimate, and effective system of rule by an intellectual elite in a Chinese context.

2.1. Plural Voting Schemes

DEMO: This reminds me of Lee Kuan Yew's proposal for a plural voting scheme. Lee, as may you know, isn't convinced that the one-man, one-vote system is the best way to select a government of the "best men." So he floated the idea of giving middle-aged family men two votes on the grounds that they're supposedly more likely to be careful, voting also for their children. Lee said that young men bent on immediate gratification are more likely to vote in a capricious way, not taking into account the interests of others, and that elderly people are also focused on the short-term, supporting policies like free health care that may harm the economic prospects of the future generations.[26] Is this what you have in mind?

WANG: No. I considered Lee's idea, as well as John Stuart Mill's proposal for granting extra votes to educated people on the grounds that they're less likely to vote in accordance with material interests.[27] But I rejected these schemes, as well as other proposals for giving extra votes to certain groups of citizens.

[26] See "A Conversation with Lee Kuan Yew." See also chap. 3, sec. 2.
[27] See John Stuart Mill, "Considerations on Representative Government," in *Three Essays* (Oxford: Oxford University Press, 1975), chap. 8.

DEMO: Why is that?

WANG: I concluded that plural voting schemes are simply too arbitrary. I accept the premise that not everyone is equally inclined to vote in a sensible manner, but selecting target groups of "rational" voters is a rough and unreliable procedure. And those denied an equal share of democratic rights are likely to perceive the denial as an official insult issued by public authority.[28] People would object to being treated as unequals at the very start of the political process. (*short pause*) It boils down to the fact that I could never get past the question of "who decides?" If the government decides who gets the extra votes, people may think that the government is motivated by a desire to select the groups most likely to perpetuate the dominance of the ruling party. Recall what happened last year in Singapore—Lee tried to implement his proposal, but it was blocked after the opposition Singapore Democratic Party embarrassed the government with a study from a National University of Singapore sociologist— the poor fellow paid with his job—which showed that middle-aged family men are twice as likely to vote for Lee's party relative to any other segment of the population. Of course, Singapore-style clampdown on dissenting views makes this proposal particularly problematic.

DEMO: But giving people extra votes would also be problematic in a more democratic context. Political parties would promise special favors to groups with extra votes,[29] and elected officials might try to award extra votes to their own constituencies, regardless of merit. It would be a mistake to let politicians decide these matters.

WANG: I agree. And there aren't any obvious alternatives to letting politicians decide in these matters. Who would trust an "independent" body of social science experts to identify the groups most likely to vote for competent and public-spirited rulers? Even if it were feasible, who would appoint this body?

DEMO: You won't get any objections from me. Things could get even more complicated. The target group of sensible voters may

---

[28] See Richard Arneson, "Democratic Rights at National and Workplace Levels," 137.

[29] I thank Joe Lau for this point.

change over time, so I imagine this body of social science experts would have to revise the "extra-voting" rules at every election.

WANG: Yes. No one could be trusted with this sort of power, in a Chinese context or anywhere else. So I dropped the idea of extra-voting proposals.

2.2. A Corporatist Assembly

DEMO: O.K., let's move on to your own proposal.

WANG: We'll get there eventually. For a while, I was also tempted by Hegel's account of the ideal state in the *Philosophy of Right.*

DEMO: You mean his argument for investing power in disinterested civil servants, chosen on the basis of competitive examinations (§291)?[30] I can see why you'd be tempted by Hegel's political views.

WANG: Actually, from a Chinese perspective, there's nothing particularly original about Hegel's argument for an impartial civil service. I was most interested by Hegel's attempt to reconcile political rule by expert bureaucrats with a concern for representing the voices of different segments of society. He argued for a bicameral legislature, an upper house of the landed propertied class and a lower house of corporations and professional guilds. The legislature would serve the function of helping the civil servants to make rational decisions by providing detailed information on the urgent and specialized needs of particular constituencies (§301). As well, he argued that the legislature should hold its deliberations in public, hence developing the political virtues and abilities of the legislators and educating "the mass" about the various ways political bodies help to promote the common good of the polity (§315). Hegel recognized that individuals are now interested in the conduct of the state's affairs and want a voice in determining its policies, and he concluded that only an open and transparent assembly could instill respect for political institutions.

---

[30] See G.W.F. Hegel, *Elements of the Philosophy of Right,* ed. Allen Wood, trans. H. B. Nisbet (Cambridge: Cambridge University Press, 1991).

DEMO: But he opposed direct suffrage!

WANG: That's correct. Hegel worried that individuals not tied to any groups or organizations would be, in his words, "elemental, irrational, barbarous, and terrifying" (§303; see also §308). Anticipating Tocqueville's argument on the importance of civil society for promoting civic virtue, Hegel argued that individuals come to take an interest in common enterprises and to develop a certain degree of political competence only by joining and participating in voluntary associations and community groups (§253). That's why Hegel favored a lower house composed of corporations and professional guilds—whereas individuals are likely to vote with their pocket books, representatives of corporate bodies in all probability would display a certain amount of organizational ability and concern for the common good (§308).

DEMO: It's worth keeping in mind that Hegel's scheme was implemented by Mussolini and his National Union of Fascists, who held that corporatism was a way of eliminating social conflict by integrating the people through their work groups into the state.[31]

WANG: I think that's unfair. Hegel may not have been a democrat in the sense of favoring universal suffrage, but he was still a kind of liberal, concerned with articulating the social framework within which freedom can be realized.[32] It's just that he thought the modern aspiration for freedom could best be sustained in a nondemocratic political context.

DEMO: Fortunately history has proved him wrong.

WANG: I'm not so sure. Consider the Legislative Council of Hong Kong in the 1980s and '90s, perhaps the closest approximation anywhere to Hegel's corporate assembly.[33] De facto power in

---

[31] See Steven Smith, *Hegel's Critique of Liberalism*, 142.

[32] On Hegel's conception of freedom, see Charles Taylor, *Hegel and Modern Society*.

[33] According to Steven Smith, however, Hegel's form of liberal corporatism is "probably closest to the contemporary experiences of Scandinavia, France, and Britain, with their highly structured relations between interest organizations and administrative bodies" (Smith, *Hegel's Critique of Liberalism*, 145). But West Euro-

Hong Kong, it seems, was more often than not exercised by a group of relatively able and honest "Hegelian"—or should I say "Confucian"?—bureaucrats in the colonial administration.[34] But the composition of the Legislative Council is more relevant for our purposes. From 1844 right up to 1985, all members of the council were directly appointed by the governor. In order to represent more authoritatively the views of Hong Kong people, however, the government decided to institute elections for a number of the seats. But it disparaged the idea of introducing direct elections by universal suffrage on the grounds that this might lead to instability at a crucial time. So the government decided that a large number of seats should be allocated to functional constituencies based on various interest groups, a system that was kept in place following the handover to China.[35] Doctors and dentists had one seat, as did teachers, lawyers, engineers, and accountants. The largest chunk of functional constituency seats went to business interests, such as the Chinese Manufacturer's Association, the Chinese Gold and Silver Exchange, and the Hong Kong Tourist Association. Altogether twenty-one out of sixty seats were allocated to functional constituencies, a number that increased to thirty in the 1995 and 1998 elections.

---

pean–style corporatism still includes a house of government composed of representatives elected by individuals rather than groups.

[34] See chap. 2, sec. 3.

[35] The post-handover authorities slashed the number of eligible voters for functional constituencies by 2.5 million (the last British governor of Hong Kong, Chris Patten, had broadened the groupings of most constituencies to include ordinary employees), but it is interesting to note that the "Democrats" did not always favor widening the electorate for the functional constituencies—when the "pro-China" DAB proposed amending the social welfare functional constituency to include *kaifong* associations and other nonprofit providers of social services, they were opposed by the Democrats, apparently because these new groups were less inclined to vote for them. More generally, "political parties were acting out of naked self-interest by introducing amendments [altering the composition of the functional constituencies] to boost their power" ("Poll Change Approved," *South China Morning Post*, 28 September 1997, 1), which suggests that it is difficult, if not impossible, to determine the composition of eligible voters for functional constituencies (and to draw the line between functional constituencies) in a way that avoids political controversy and avoids undermining the moral credibility of a corporatist legislature. To be fair to the Democrats, however, they also favor scrapping the whole functional constituency system in favor of a one-person-one-vote legislature.

As far as I know, this was a truly unique "Hegelian" legislative assembly—in no other country at the time was the largest block of seats in a house of government assigned to business groups and professional organizations.[36]

DEMO: But this wasn't a stable and legitimate political arrangement. The Hong Kong people wanted the right to vote!

WANG: That's not immediately obvious. When they were given the opportunity to exercise the right to vote for a limited number of seats in 1991 and 1995, only 30 percent or so bothered turning out for the elections.

DEMO: But in 1998 that number increased to over 50 percent. And voter turnout would have been even higher if people were actually voting for their community's most important decision-makers. Remember, in Hong Kong, the unelected members of the executive made policy, and elected members of the legislature functioned more as opposition critics than as legislators.[37]

WANG: I actually agree with you. I was playing the role of—how do you say it?—"devil's advocate."

DEMO: Yes. This term comes from an established practice of the Catholic Church. At the canonization of a saint, the Church appoints and listens carefully to a "devil's advocate." The idea is that the holiest of men can't be admitted to posthumous honors until all that the devil could say against him is known, weighed, and refuted.

WANG: I remember reading about that in John Stuart Mill's work.[38] The Confucian equivalent is the "censor," who was obligated to protest against bad officials and harmful policies. It was a risky job, and some high-minded Confucian officials paid with their lives.[39] (short pause) In any case, my point is that the right to vote, for whatever reason, seems to have emerged as an ineliminable symbol of political recognition for citizens in the modern world.

[36] See Norman Miners, *The Government and Politics of Hong Kong*, 111–117.

[37] Demo seems to have learned from his conversation with Lo in chap. 2, sec. 3.3.

[38] See Mill, "On Liberty," 28.

[39] See, e.g., "A Censor Accuses a Eunuch," in *Chinese Civilization: A Sourcebook*, ed. Patricia Buckley Ebrey, 263–266.

No polity that denies the right to vote, I think, can ever hope to achieve a stable and legitimate political system. In that sense, Hegel was quite mistaken when he predicted that given the opportunity to participate in mass elections, with individual votes having little effect, citizens would inevitably become indifferent and fail to make use of the vote (§311).

DEMO: Let me support that with the observation that political apathy tends to be even higher in political regimes like Singapore that place substantial constraints on the electoral process.[40] (*short pause*) But I'm a little confused. It seems that you do not, after all, endorse Hegel's proposal for a corporatist legislative assembly.

WANG: No, definitely not. Hong Kong tried to make do without a fully elected assembly, but it never did achieve much legitimacy among ordinary citizens who placed more value on universal suffrage. Denying most people the right to vote, in other words, just didn't work. The second problem with Hegel's proposal can also be vividly illustrated with the Hong Kong case. The small size of most functional constituencies meant that it was possible for the voters to keep a close watch on what their representative was doing, and to instruct him on what he should say and how he should vote. In one case, the chairman of the Hong Kong General Chamber of Commerce publicly rebuked its representative—I believe McGregor was his name—for voicing liberal views in the Legislative Council that didn't have the Chamber's support.[41] It was the same old story after the handover—more often than not, professionals asked their representatives to protect their own interests in making a living rather than serving the community as a whole.[42] In short, most functional constitu-

---

[40] See chap. 4, sec. 3.1.

[41] Miners, *The Government and Politics of Hong Kong,* 117–118.

[42] "Lone Voice in a Tame Wilderness," *South China Morning Post,* 17 May 1998, 11. Later in 1998, Human Rights Monitor denounced the "extremely unfair" functional constituency system that allows tycoons to control multiple votes through their companies and constituencies. It cited the case of property tycoon Robert Ng Chee Siong, "who controlled an estimated 41 votes in total" ("Rights Group Attacks Electoral System," *South China Morning Post,* 14 December 1998, 14).

ency representatives were serving the narrow concerns of the richest and most privileged sectors of the community. You can imagine the effect this had on the legitimacy of the functional constituency system in the polity at large.

DEMO: Mmh. Just as Hegel may have underestimated the importance of the right to vote for ordinary citizens in modern societies, so he seems to have overestimated the capacity of "corporate" representatives to function as more than servants of powerful interest groups.

2.3. A Parliament of Scholar-Officials

WANG: Exactly. So I had to consider other options for tempering democracy with a concern for institutionalizing rule by an intellectual elite in China. I was most inspired by Huang Zongxi's proposals for political reform. Huang was a radical seventeenth-century Confucian critic of the Chinese dynastic system. . . .

DEMO (*interrupting*): Did you say Confucian *critic* of the Chinese dynastic system? I was under the impression that Confucian mandarins were loyal supporters of imperial power. Isn't there something in *The Analects* about learning the virtue of obedience in the family in order to instill habits of obedience to the ruler?

WANG: I think you're referring to the following passage: "Master Yu said, Those who in private life behave well towards their parents and elder brothers, in public life seldom show a disposition to resist the authority of their superiors. And as for such men starting a revolution, no instance of it has ever occurred. It is upon the trunk that a gentleman works. When that is firmly set up, the Way grows. And surely proper behavior towards parents and elder brothers is the trunk of Goodness?" (1.2). The point here is to stress that the family is the main educative institution for learning morality. Morality, however, doesn't mean blind obedience even in the context of the family—later in *The Analects*, Confucius says, "In serving your father and mother you ought to dissuade them from doing wrong in the gentlest way"

(4.18).[43] So the family may be an important institution for instilling the virtue of respect for legitimate authority, but even filial sons have an obligation to persuade parents to refrain from wrongdoing.[44]

DEMO: I must say I'm quite impressed. You seem to have memorized the whole of *The Analects*.

WANG: Well, there's been somewhat of a resurgence of tradition lately, and you'd be surprised just how many educated Chinese can recite passages from "sacred" texts. Besides, *The Analects* is only one hundred pages or so—it's not like the *Bible*.

DEMO (*smiles*): Is pithiness a Confucian virtue?

WANG: Yes, actually. There's a strong bias in Confucianism against eloquence and clever argumentation not matched by the required actions. As Confucius put it, "A gentleman covets the reputation of being slow in word but prompt in deed" (4.24; see also 14.29). (*short pause*) In any case, I was hoping to return to the doubts you expressed about the critical potential of Confucianism. Remember that Mencius—Confucius's most famous follower—went so far as to justify the assassination of rulers who fail to serve the people's interests.[45]

DEMO: But you seem to be drawing only on the "liberal" parts of the Confucian tradition, leaving out the rest. Unfortunately, actually existing Confucianism tended to draw more on the part that supported the authoritarian, hierarchical status quo.[46]

[43] See D. C. Lau's translation of *The Analects* (London: Penguin, 1979), 74.

[44] See Joseph Chan, "A Confucian Perspective on Human Rights," esp. 222–226.

[45] Mencius, "On Government," in *Chinese Civilization: A Sourcebook*, ed. Ebrey, 23. However, it is also possible to interpret this passage to mean that "the fellow Zhou" deserved to have his head cut off not because he didn't serve the people but because he was a bad person in a way that mattered to Mencius. "The people," in other words, may not have been the source of legitimacy in Mencius, only its beneficiary and perhaps an operational indicator of its presence or absence (I thank Andrew Nathan for this point).

[46] For an account of the "dark side" of Confucianism, see Ci Jiwei, "The Right, the Good, and Rights," paper presented at a conference on Confucianism and Human Rights, Beijing University, June 1998.

Lo: It's not that simple. The critical potential of Confucianism also influenced the practice. In fact, Confucianism was challenged by its rivals precisely on the grounds that Confucian morality fails to instill political obedience. Han Fei Tzu, for example, repeatedly attacked Confucian "wandering scholars" (sec. 49)[47] for sowing a critical attitude vis-à-vis the laws of the land.

Demo: Say that again?

Wang: I was referring to Han Fei Tzu, the major synthesizer of Legalist thought. Han Fei was a profoundly cynical proponent of *realpolitik*—Machiavelli was a naive idealist in comparison. He wrote a political handbook for rulers, arguing that state power can be strengthened by means of harsh laws and punishments. His aim was nothing less than total state control, and he stressed that moral considerations should not get in the way. Not surprisingly, rulers were quite receptive to this sort of advice, starting with the ruthless King of Qin who ascended to the throne in 246 B.C. and drew on Han Fei's advice to conquer and rule all of China under the title of First Emperor of the Qin dynasty. (*short pause*) In any case, Han Fei had nothing but contempt for Confucian morality. He was understandably horrified, for example, by the famous Confucian argument that the requirements of filial piety justify breaking the law.

Demo: Did Confucius really say that?

Wang: Yes. Let me quote *The Analects* once again: "The 'Duke' of She addressed Confucius saying, In my country there was a man called Upright Kung. His father appropriated a sheep, and Kung bore witness against him. Confucius said, In my country the upright men are of quite another sort. A father will screen his son, and a son his father—which incidentally does involve a sort of uprightness" (13.18). Han Fei recounted this episode, and his view was of course quite unfavorable. He added another story—probably a fabrication—about Confucius rewarding a man for running away from battle in order to care for an aged father, with the result that the people thought nothing of surrendering or deserting (sec. 49). The "family over state" princi-

[47] See *Basic Writings of Han Fei Tzu*, trans. by Burton Watson (New York: Columbia University Press, 1967), 108.

ple, in Han Fei's view, is incompatible with successful warfare, and more generally Han Fei urged governments not to promote Confucian values.

DEMO: I suspect that Han Fei may have been agonizing over a nonissue. No government would promote a moral system that justifies breaking the law!

WANG: You'd be surprised. Filial piety as a preeminent value was in fact enshrined by law in Imperial China. Already in Han times people were permitted to conceal the crimes of close relatives without legal penalty, and they weren't compelled to testify in court against family members.[48] In the Qing dynasty, a son who brought an accusation of parental wrongdoing before the authorities was subject to strangulation if the accusation was false, and even if it was true the son was punished with three years of penal servitude plus one hundred blows of the heavy bamboo.[49] Scolding one's parent or grandparent was punishable by death.[50]

DEMO (*stunned*): Really!

WANG: Yes. So remember, my point is to stress that *realpolitik* types in imperial China criticized Confucianism for encouraging disobedience and fostering a critical perspective vis-à-vis the state. Far from justifying blind adherence to the political status quo,

---

[48] Similar provisions exist in contemporary Korea. For example, article 155 of the Criminal Law "guarantees exemption from punishment for the crimes of suppression of evidence, concealment and forgery or alteration of the evidence in criminal cases if such acts were committed by a relative, head of the house, or a family member living with the said person, for the benefit of the criminal." While such laws "may be explained as a means of securing a fair trial, they could also be explained as remnants of Confucian family ethics which protect the intimacy of family relations" (Oh Byung-Sun, "Cultural Values and Human Rights," 235).

[49] See Derk Bodde and Clarence Morris, *Law in Imperial China*, 40.

[50] See Albert Chen, "Confucian Legal Culture and Its Modern Fate," ms., 17. It is worth noting that the state in imperial China did more than punish those who failed to live up to Confucian virtues: the Ministry of Ritual also *rewarded* the virtuous by, for example, putting a banner at their doors so that they could serve as exemplars and models to their communities (see Mark Elvin, *Another History*, chap. 10).

Confucian values often provided the intellectual resources for social critics.[51]

DEMO: My perception of Confucianism must have been influenced by Lee Kuan Yew, who appeals to Confucianism to buttress authoritarian rule.

WANG: It's a sad fact of the real political world that rulers often distort ideas to suit their own narrow political agendas. No doubt Marx would also have been horrified by what people did in his name.[52] (*short pause*) In any case, perhaps I should return to that seventeenth-century Confucian scholar Huang Zongxi. Huang's book, *Waiting for the Dawn: A Plan for the Prince*, is a powerful Confucian critique of despotism. Let me try to remember a relevant passage. (*short pause*) Well, in the very first chapter Huang says: "In ancient times all-under-Heaven were considered the master, and the prince was the tenant. The prince spent his whole life working for all-under-Heaven. Now the prince is the master, and all-under-Heaven are tenants. That no one can find peace and happiness anywhere is all on account of the prince" ["On the Prince"].[53]

This was written around the time of the collapse of the Ming dynasty. Huang was resisting the conquest of China by the Manchus, who went on to found the Qing dynasty.

---

[51] This is not to suggest that each Confucian value, taken by itself, can encourage disobedience and foster a critical spirit—for example, an ethic of filial piety will not breed a critical spirit so long as the ruler does not require a person to act wrongly toward his or her parents (I thank Michael Walzer for this point). But taken together with other values, such as Mencius's idea that the use of force is justified to overthrow an emperor who has violated the Heavenly Mandate (see David L. Hall and Roger T. Ames, *Democracy of the Dead*, 171), the ruler's obligation to provide for the welfare of the people above all else, the idea that conformity to norms and rituals must come "from inside" (see Philip J. Ivanhoe, *Confucian Moral Self-Cultivation*, 12–13), and the preference for persuasion and transformative education over coercion as means to achieve social and political order (see David L. Hall and Roger T. Ames, *Thinking Through Confucius*, 169–170), Confucianism did provide a philosophy which always (or nearly always) coexisted uneasily with the political status quo.

[52] See my article, "From Mao to Jiang," 63.

[53] See Huang Zongxi, *Waiting for the Dawn: A Plan for the Prince*, trans. Wm. Theodore de Bary (New York: Columbia University Press, 1993).

DEMO: And how did the new Manchu emperor react to this point of view?

WANG: Huang wasn't so foolish as to publicize his ideas. Judging by his scornful characterization of existing dynastic rule, it's unlikely that Huang was actually addressing the emperor of his day.[54] Huang's hope, it seems, was that a future ruler inclined toward benevolence would seize his ideas to build what we might term a just political order.

DEMO: So how did the book get transmitted to future generations?

WANG: Well, initially it was distributed to a few colleagues and students. His book was then circulated "*samizdat*"—pardon the anachronistic language—for two and a half centuries, finally seeing the light of day in the latter part of the Qing period, with the dynasty in disarray. Huang came to be acclaimed by late nineteenth- and early twentieth-century reformers as an early champion of native Chinese "democratic" ideas.[55] For example, Liang Qichao—China's most famous writer in the early twentieth century—reprinted Huang's book to provide more ammunition for political reform.[56]

DEMO: Did Huang provide any concrete alternative to dynastic power, or was he merely criticizing the status quo?

WANG: That's what's interesting. Unlike most Confucians, he went beyond merely affirming the need for a virtuous ruler of exemplary character, arguing for specific laws and institutions designed to curb imperial power. Huang favored establishing a strong prime minister, so as to balance the power of the emperor ["Establishing a Prime Minister"]. If the aim is serving the people, according to Huang, then the role of ministers should be strengthened, and the emperor should welcome criticism from ministers who point to the plight of the people ["On Ministership"]. And I want you to pay special attention to his proposal for strengthening the political role of the schools for the

[54] See de Bary, "Introduction," 7.
[55] See ibid., xi—xii.
[56] See Nathan, *Chinese Democracy*, 68.

304

training of Confucian scholar-officials. Schools of all levels, in Huang's view, should serve as fora for open public discussion. He noted that during the Eastern Han, A.D. 25–220, scholars at the Imperial College—the top school for the training of scholar-officials—engaged in outspoken discussion of important issues without fear of those in power, and the highest officials were anxious to avoid their censure. Moreover, Huang proposed that the rector of the Imperial College, to be chosen from among the great scholars of the day, should be equal in importance to the prime minister, and that once a month the emperor should visit the Imperial College, along with the prime minister and some ministers. The emperor was to sit among the ranks of the students while the rector questioned him on the administration of the country ["Schools"].

DEMO: It sounds like question-time in Parliament!

WANG (*excited*): Exactly! He wanted rulers to be held accountable to a "Parliament of Scholars"![57]

DEMO (*pause*): Now hold on a second. Is that what you're proposing for China? A Parliament of Scholars? How would you choose the scholars?

WANG: The standard Confucian practice is to select scholar-officials on the basis of fair and open competitive examinations.

DEMO: Are Confucian examinations really appropriate for modern China? Correct me if I'm wrong, but examinations in Imperial China tested the memorization of the Confucian classics, and I doubt that's a sound basis for selecting a political ruling class in the contemporary era.

WANG: Once again, Huang Zongxi's proposals for reform are relevant. Huang condemned the examinations of his day for rewarding superficiality and plagiarism, and thus failing to identify men of "real talent." He didn't oppose testing knowledge of the classics and subsequent commentaries, but he emphasized that candidates must also offer their own interpretation of a

[57] This is de Bary's term in "Introduction," 83.

question. To use Huang's own words—I think I can get this right—"After listing one by one what is said by the various Han and Sung scholars, the candidate should conclude with his own opinion, there being no necessity for blind acceptance of one authority's word." ["The Selection of Scholar-Officials, Part I"] The examinations should test for both the capacity to store information and the capacity for independent thought.

DEMO: Interesting. But let me ask you a question—what happened to democracy? If rulers are selected on the basis of competitive examinations rather than elections, how do the people fit in? How can ordinary people express their political will in your scheme, and how can they have control over the conduct of government?

WANG: That's precisely the problem with Huang Zongxi,[58] and with Confucianism more generally. The stress is on politics *for* the people, but there's not much on politics *by* the people.[59]

DEMO (*frustrated*): Now you've really lost me. You keep on switching back and forth. You seem tempted by the J. S. Mill/Lee Kuan Yew proposal for granting extra votes to more sensible and public-spirited voters, but then you admit that selecting the relevant target group can be an arbitrary process subject to political manipulation. You seem tempted by Hegel's idea of a legislature

---

[58] De Bary also makes this point in ibid, 55. For a particularly harsh evaluation of Huang Zongxi's antidemocratic outlook, see W.J.F. Jenner, "China and Freedom," 84–85.

[59] The same criticism can be made of Sun Yat-sen's proposed constitution of five separate powers, which includes an independent branch responsible for setting civil service examinations. Under Sun's proposed scheme, all public officials, including those elected to the legislature, "must pass examinations before assuming office" (*Selected Writings of Sun Yat-sen: Prescriptions for Saving China*, ed. J. L. Wei, R. H. Myers, and D. G. Gillin [Stanford: Hoover Press, 1994], 49). Sun hoped to avoid "the corruption and laxity of American politics," where "those endowed with eloquence ingratiated themselves with the public and won elections, while those who had learning and ideals but lacked eloquence were ignored" (ibid.), but the effect would be to exclude from political power elected politicians who fail examinations. It is difficult to imagine that a government that completely excluded the "people's chosen leaders" could achieve much legitimacy in the "eyes of the people" (consider a situation where someone elected with 80 percent of the vote but who fails examinations is replaced by a successful examination candidate who received only 20 percent of the vote).

composed of representatives from community groups, but then you admit that in all likelihood this arrangement will unfairly benefit rich and powerful sectors, as it did in Hong Kong. You seem tempted by Huang Zongxi's proposal for a parliament of scholar-officials selected on the basis of competitive examinations, but then you admit that this political system deprives the people of any voice in politics. Sometimes you're a democrat, sometimes you're a Confucian. You want rulers of talent and character, but only in an overall democratic context. Can you have it both ways?

WANG: I guess you want to hear my own proposal.

DEMO: Yes! You've kept me waiting long enough.

3. THE PROPOSAL

WANG: Here it is. As I mentioned, the idea hit me one day in the Kentucky Fried Chicken outlet at Tiananmen Square. I was thinking to myself, if capitalism and communism can co-exist in the economic realm, then why not democracy and Confucianism in the political realm? And then, all of a sudden, it seemed so obvious, and I must admit this is the first time in my life that a sudden illumination still seemed quite persuasive several months after the fact. The solution: a bicameral legislature, with a democratically elected lower house and an upper house composed of representatives selected on the basis of competitive examinations. I call the upper house the "House of Scholars."

DEMO: Mmm . . . interesting . . .

3.1. Selection Procedures

(*A Beijing University graduate student named Li Xuedong*[60] *enters Professor Wang's office and stops, momentarily surprised to see Demo.*)

---

[60] Li is a common surname in China. Xuedong, which means "study the East," is a "revolutionary" name commonly given to children born during the Cultural Revolution.

WANG: Let me do the introductions. This is Mr. Demo, an American friend who works with the National Endowment for Human Rights and Democracy, and this is Li Xuedong, a doctoral student doing a thesis on Dzhaparidze's system of bimodel logic. (*Demo and Li Xuedong shake hands.*)

LI: Pleased to meet you. Is Professor Wang explaining his proposal for "democracy with Chinese characteristics"?

DEMO: Yes, what's your view?

LI (*turning red*): Well, you know, we never criticize our professors in China.

WANG: Please, Xuedong, tell Mr. Demo what you think.

LI: I generally support this proposal. My only concern is Professor Wang's idea that representatives of the House of Scholars be selected on the basis of competitive examinations. Here at Beijing University—the most prestigious university in China— many of our top undergraduates arrive fresh from the countryside. I'm not saying they're not smart, but they're good primarily at memorizing answers for the university entrance exams, and often they're not very sophisticated in other respects. Some of them change once they stay in Beijing for a few years, but I'd be worried about giving political power to narrow-minded young men and women.

DEMO (*smiles*): You, I presume, are not from the countryside.

LI: I'm from Shanghai, which helps a bit.

WANG: Xuedong, I share your concern about rewarding young persons "fresh from the countryside." But more generally I'd worry about being governed by overly clever young people no matter where they're from—imagine a House of Scholars full of arrogant and hot-headed twenty-year-olds![61] So I'd im-

---

[61] It is not uncommon in "Confucian" countries such as Japan and Korea, however, to be tried in court cases before judges in their twenties. In Korea, for example, judges need to pass the bar exam and then go through a two-year program at the Legal Training Institute run by the Ministry of Justice, with the effect that young persons in their twenties preside as judges in Korea's courts. However, this may be the result of having adopted the German-style civil law tradition (as opposed to the Confucian emphasis on examinations as a means for selecting

pose an age minimum for the examinations of, say, thirty-five or forty years.

DEMO: Perhaps I should also step in to defend the proposal. Professor Wang was telling me that he endorses Huang Zongxi's idea for examinations that test for both memorization *and* independent thought.

WANG: That's correct. I favor exams with an essay component, and I'd award high grades to those who can provide innovative yet plausible solutions to the questions we ask them. I'd also include one or two essay questions on ethics, to help filter out the brilliant but morally insensitive technocrats.

LI: Professor Wang, I don't want to criticize your proposal, but it may not be easy to test for the kinds of "moral" qualities you're looking for.

WANG: It's not easy, but we have to try. We're not just looking for professional competence, or the ability to implement goals handed down by others. We want people who can reflect upon the deeper purposes of public policies and who give attention to the claims, real and potential, of those who might be affected by those policies. Ideally, of course, we'd select those with a certain amount of civic virtue.

LI: But it's difficult to test for those qualities in an exam. For example, people can provide you with "moral" answers, but it doesn't mean they're sincerely held or that decision-makers would use them in actual situations.

WANG: Look, no system is perfect. At the very least, we could filter out morally obtuse people—for example, those who aren't even aware of the need to secure basic human rights. As well, we could eliminate political demagogues by asking questions that have people look at both sides of controversial questions[62]— most demagogues seem congenitally unable to articulate in a

---

decision-makers), and the Korean government is currently trying to mitigate some of the defects of this system by not allowing people to become judges until they serve some years as lawyers or prosecutors (I thank Hahm Chaibong for this information).

[62] Examinations for high-ranking members the civil service in Hong Kong similarly test for the ability to look at both sides of controversial political issues.

plausible way the kinds of arguments they hope to refute. In that sense, it's safer to rely on exams than the democratic process. And if we're lucky, we might get some really good ones.

Lɪ: But you can't guarantee that you'd come up with the most "moral" candidates.

Wᴀɴɢ (*raises voice*): Of course there's no guarantee! This is politics, not philosophy. It's a question of how this system compares to the feasible alternatives—we're not searching for iron-clad proofs. If you want to criticize my proposal, you have to suggest another method that's more likely to produce talented and public-spirited decision-makers.[63]

Lɪ (*somewhat taken aback*): Professor Wang, I guess I'm not against exams per se, it's just my concern that they should be as objective as possible. If you allow for subjective factors to intervene— testing for civic virtue and so on—the tests can be easily abused, with high grades being awarded on the basis of guanxi[64] rather than merit. At least the results of our multiple-choice university entrance exams can't be skewed by personal favoritism.

Wᴀɴɢ: I appreciate your point. At the first stage of the examination process, for reasons of efficiency I'd stick to multiple-choice exams. But after that, I think it's essential to include an essay component. I agree with you that the selection process must be seen as scrupulously fair and impartial—otherwise people won't accept the legitimacy of the House of Scholars. This isn't an insurmountable obstacle, however. The essay questions can be graded "blind," say, by a committee of experts in the field who are given scripts with numbers rather than names.

Dᴇᴍᴏ: Pardon the interruption, but wouldn't you want to interview the candidates as well? It seems to me that they should be tested for their ability to respond to oral questions. Some people are good at written exams, but they can't express themselves well or participate intelligently in a conversation with real-life

---

[63] Winston Churchill's (apocryphal?) quip about democracy—that it's the worst possible political system, except for all the others—can also be used to defend the examination system as a procedure for identifying decision-makers of talent and integrity.

[64] This can be translated as "connections."

310

individuals. This doesn't matter much if one is an academic, but it would be a serious weakness in a political ruler. And once you allow for oral interviews, you're back to Xuedong's point about potential bias in the selection process.

WANG: I agree about the need for oral interviews, but there's a neat solution to the problem of bias in oral interviews. Candidates can be interviewed behind screens, which is how musical examinations are sometimes administered.

DEMO: But screens can't block out everything. For example, it would still be possible to identify the sex of the applicant. That might be a problem, as the female applicants could find themselves at a disadvantage. After all, only males took the civil service examinations in the past, and some people might want to maintain the tradition of selecting male decision-makers.

WANG: Well, that's the past. East Asian countries today don't bar females from civil service examinations, and that's what I'd want for China. In fact, one of the virtues of examinations is that they're likely to increase the proportion of female decision-makers. You might even get 50 percent, which is better than the Scandinavian countries! And no need to rely on an artificial and unmeritocratic quota system.

DEMO: You didn't answer my point. If you allow for oral examinations, "informal" discrimination might take place at that stage.

WANG: Perhaps voices can be processed through a kind of synthesizer that masks the sex of the respondent. Or else they can be typed on a computer screen. I'm sure there's a technical solution to this problem.

LI: Professor Li, I have another problem with "blind" examinations. If we can't actually see the respondents, it means a person with *sanjiaoyan* might get through. Who would trust a ruler with *sanjiaoyan*?

DEMO (*interjecting*): I must admit, I do not quite understand.

WANG (*sighs*): *Ai ya*, this is quite complicated. You see, Westerners distinguish between different eyes colors—women look with envy upon Elizabeth Taylor's beautiful violet eyes, Frank Sinatra's pale blue eyes made him handsome, and so on. But

311

Chinese people all have brown eyes, so we hardly notice eye colors, distinguishing instead between different eye *shapes*. The most common distinction is of course between single and double eyelids. Few Westerners notice the difference, even after being told of its relevance for Chinese people—perhaps because nearly all of you have double eyelids—but in China it's quite important to have double eyelids, which make the eyes look bigger and supposedly more attractive. In fact, the most common form of plastic surgery in China—and in other East Asian countries such as Korea and Japan—is a slice above the eye to add a second eyelid.

DEMO (*slight twitch*): Really?

WANG: It's a painless operation, far less problematic than what you call "nose jobs," not to mention the infamous silicone "treatment" debacle. In any case, what's interesting is that a rich and subtle vocabulary has evolved in Chinese to describe different eye shapes.[65] There's a prejudice in Chinese society against *doujiyan*, or "fighting rooster eyes," but on the other hand *xingrenyan*, or "almond shaped eyes," are widely admired. I suspect that most Westerners wouldn't even notice a difference.

DEMO: This is interesting, but I'm not too sure how the topic of eye shapes fits into our discussion on "democracy with Chinese characteristics."

WANG: I was getting to that. It's not just that we've developed an aesthetic hierarchy of eye shapes. Sometimes eye shapes are said to express certain *personality traits* as well. For example, people with *sanjiaoyan*, or triangular, "three angle" eyes, are said to be untrustworthy. That's what was worrying Xuedong—my proposal for blind grading wouldn't be able to filter out people with *sanjiaoyan*, and he couldn't imagine that anyone would trust a ruler with this sort of eye shape.

Li: Thank you, Professor Wang. I should have made myself clearer.

---

[65] The Chinese also distinguish between different eyebrow shapes. For example, the term *jian mei* ("sword-shaped eyebrow") is used to describe the ideal "form" of male eyebrows, and the term *liu mei* ("willow-shaped eyebrow") is used to describe the ideal "form" of female eyebrows.

WANG: But let me add that I wouldn't want to modify my proposal to accommodate this cultural value. On the contrary, I think we should challenge this absurd tendency to rank people on the basis of eye shapes, in the same way that we challenge other harmful traditional values and practices such nepotism, the preference for siring male children, and the historical practice of excluding women from entry to the public service. At least from a political standpoint, it's important to distinguish between desirable and undesirable cultural traits. The government should try to promote only those cultural values appropriate for the modern era, like the tradition of respect for rule by an intellectual elite.

LI (*embarrassed*): You're right, Professor Wang. I'm not an expert in the field of political philosophy, and I should have deferred to your viewpoint.

WANG: No need to be so modest, Xuedong. I may face these questions tomorrow at the constitutional convention, and it's important to be prepared with persuasive answers.

LI: If you'll excuse me, I must return to my studies. Nice meeting you Mr. Demo. (*Li Xuedong exits from Professor Wang's office.*)

DEMO: Perhaps I can add that American political culture is also subject to harmful prejudices. If FDR had run for president in the age of television, voters would have been aware of his physical disability and he may have had difficulty getting elected. Many people still seem to judge political rulers on the basis of irrelevant physical characteristics.

WANG: Hence the need for blind evaluation of candidates for the House of Scholars.

DEMO: Let me return to the question of the *content* of the examinations. Even if your written examinations test for memorization, independent thought, ethics, and the ability to make good points in an actual conversation, it may still be that you're failing to test for the quality that really matters, that is, the capacity to deal with the problems of government. Don't you think it's also important to test for the ability to deal with actual political problems?

WANG: Yes, of course. Confucius himself was quite concerned with the need to identify those with know-how. He said, "A man may be able to recite the three hundred Songs; but, if when given a post in the government, he cannot turn his merits to account, or when sent on a mission to far parts he cannot answer particular questions, however extensive his knowledge may be, of what use is it to him?" (13.5). In the same vein, our exams could include questions covering a wide range of actual political problems. We could ask questions about pressing issues in domestic and foreign policy, for example.

DEMO: But you'd only succeed at identifying talented generalists. And this poses certain problems. The Federal Reserve Bank, for example, is composed mainly of professional economists. More generally, conceptions of meritocracy have changed since the days of Confucius. Under conditions of modern knowledge, with their vastly more specialized character, it's best to identify and appoint highly trained specialists to work on policies in their particular field. Your "Confucian" exams would be quite useless for this purpose.

WANG: I'm not sure about that. Knowledge may be more specialized, but many different types of knowledge are relevant for political decisions. If anything, things are becoming more interconnected. For example, economic forces drive foreign policy more than ever before; during the Asian economic crisis, we saw more of Robert Rubin than Madeleine Albright. On the other hand, it's difficult to make sense of economics without a good grasp of the underlying political forces—the World Bank was bullish about the Indonesian economy until the very end because they didn't factor in political issues like resentment against the Suharto clan or the concentration of economic wealth in the hands of the Chinese minority. So I don't think we'd want highly trained specialists deciding things at the very highest levels of government. What we're looking for are men and women of talent and integrity. They must be learned and sensitive to ethical considerations, as well as intellectually agile, in the sense of being able to take a "bird's-eye view" and adapt quickly to new situations in a rapidly changing modern world. Once these people are identified, it's my firm belief that they can learn to exercise wise and prudent political judgment.

DEMO: But this requires a veritable leap of faith!

WANG: I'd like to point out that what you call a "leap of faith" is already the practice in much of East Asia, and the results are quite positive overall. In Singapore, the ruling PAP favors top civil servants and ministers who have a "helicopter view," meaning that they can detach themselves from nitty-gritty details to focus on the big picture, put issues in their overall social and political context, and anticipate the likely impact of a changing environment.[66] Often these people have no political or technical background, but here too they learn to apply their wisdom to whatever problem comes up. In Hong Kong, administrative grade officers—the elite unit at the apex of the civil service pyramid—are generalists; they change departments every five years or so. The assumption is that they need to be broad-minded and wide-ranging, spotting changing trends in different areas and adapting to new situations. And in Japan—like I said—the top graduates from Tokyo University's law faculty, chosen on the basis of competitive examinations, are almost automatically given important posts in the Ministry of Finance and the Ministry of International Affairs. It's simply assumed that the top academic achievers will learn "on the job." . . .

DEMO (*interrupting*): But that assumption has run into problems of late. Japanese-style, meritocratically chosen bureaucrats may have been an asset in the early stages of development, but they've failed quite spectacularly to provide creative solutions to the problems of an advanced economy. Just about everyone agrees there's a need for more democracy and less bureaucracy in Japan.

WANG: First of all, China is still a relatively undeveloped country, so that objection isn't relevant for China's current situation. More importantly, I'm not saying that China should copy every aspect of the Japanese model of selecting political managers. The idea is to take what's worked and avoid the rest.

DEMO: But you're not answering my point. Even in a relatively undeveloped economy, it's better to rely on specialists than on

[66] See chap. 3, sec. 3.

generalists. China's central bank, for example, should appoint trained economists, not generalists from the House of Scholars.

WANG: Look, I'm not arguing against the need for expertise. Of course decision-makers need to rely on the views of experts, but they often need to rely on the views of different experts looking at different sides of public policy questions. Moreover, scientific "evidence" on important public policy issues is rarely conclusive. More often than not, it leaves lots of room for interpretation and judgment calls, and that's where we want decision-makers of talent and integrity to come in.[67] Even the Federal Reserve Bank might be better off if it included more noneconomists. After all, the Fed is often accused of favoring the interests of Wall Street over Main Street, and perhaps generalists could make a difference.

DEMO (*pause*): Maybe you're right. And come to think of it, the use of the examination system to select political generalists is not distinctive to East Asia. In France, students compete for entry to the Ecole Nationale d'Administration, and successful graduates are subsequently empowered to make decisions in the political and business worlds, often moving back and forth between the private and public sectors. In the United States, however, it's usually the private sector that draws on academically successful individuals with the ability to move from one domain to another and to develop the required skills "on the job." The leading business consultancy firm, McKenzie and Company, offers jobs to all Rhodes scholars who apply, no experience necessary. Investment banks like Goldman Sachs hire Ph.D.s from top universities in fields completely unrelated to banking, once again on the assumption that talent is transferable from one domain to another.

WANG: Exactly. So why shouldn't governments do the same? It would benefit society as a whole if the brightest minds were entrusted with the task of devising policies for the common good, rather than promoting the good of particular commercial en-

---

[67] This point is well articulated by Alan Blinder (see note 10), though he presents it as an argument for "the other side" (see "Is Government Too Political?" 126).

terprises. Those who succeed at rigorous and wide-ranging competitive examinations should be given the opportunity to work for the political community.

DEMO: There's another issue we need to discuss. Wouldn't you be worried about empowering people without any political experience?

WANG: I'm not saying they should immediately be given political power. Correct me if I'm wrong, but business consultants and brokers are usually trained for a year or so before they're given the power to make important decisions. I'd do the same with the House of Scholars. Once representatives are selected, they can choose an area of specialization (the top candidates get first choice) like economic policy or foreign affairs, and then they can work under the guidance of the previous batch of scholars for a transition period of a year or two. That should be enough time to get them to the point where they could make informed judgments aided by experts.

DEMO: Well, I hope you're right. But a lot seems to turn on untested hypotheses.

WANG: It's not completely untested. To repeat, this is already the practice in successful East Asian countries. However, what's distinctive—or perhaps I should say "superior"—about my proposal is that it would institutionalize the method of selection for political rulers, unlike the case of Japan where de facto rulers are chosen on the basis of an informal process. And unlike Japanese-style competitive examinations, which are frequently criticized for placing too much weight on memorization and rewarding those who show an excessive tendency toward conformity,[68] our exams would also test for independent thought and ethics. Moreover, the exercise of political power would be more transparent, compared once again with Japan, where top bureaucrats wield power in mysterious ways hidden behind the facade of democratically elected politicians. I expect

[68] According to Professor Onuma Yasuaki, however, Tokyo University is trying to improve the situation by placing more emphasis on creative answers to questions for the university entrance examinations.

that political deliberations in the House of Scholars, with the exception of debates concerning national security, would be televised and transmitted directly to the public.

3.2. The Problem of Corruption

DEMO: Even more important than ensuring transparency, however, is the question of *accountability*. And how can the representatives of the House of Scholars be held accountable if they're not subject to the electoral process? If they're given lifetime tenure, they may become arrogant, insensitive, and corrupt.

WANG: Not necessarily. Nonelected judges on the U.S. Supreme Court are given lifetime tenure, yet the Supreme Court is perhaps the least corrupt and most widely respected institution in the American political system.

DEMO: But you're proposing to give "scholar-officials" real power in the sense of the right to formulate their own policies, not just the power to enforce the constitution.

WANG: You're right. Judges at least in theory have less room to maneuver than political decision-makers, and it may be particularly important to institutionalize a check on the irresponsible behavior of the latter. But the electoral process is only one way of curbing power; setting term limits is another. In my view, deputies in the House of Scholars shouldn't be given lifetime tenure, but on the other hand they must be given enough time to learn about politics and work for the long-term good. A constitutionally enshrined term limit of, say, seven or eight years, seems about right.

DEMO: But how can you guarantee that "scholar-officials" would work for the common good, as opposed, say, to abusing their power for the sake of personal enrichment? If they know they'll be out of a job in seven or eight years time, they may use their period of tenure to plunder the treasury.

WANG: I am assuming, of course, that a free press will do its best to investigate and publicize incidents of corruption. Equally important, deputies should be paid handsome salaries to reduce

318

the incentive for corruption. Singapore pays the world's highest salaries to its top politicians and civil servants, and the result is an enviably low level of corruption.

DEMO: But civil servants in Singapore have a life-long career path. What would deputies from the House of Scholars do when they retire? If they retire at the age of, say, fifty, they may turn into behind-the-scenes power brokers with the ability to deliver access in exchange for cash.

WANG: Perhaps we can move up the minimum age for deputies by five or ten years, so that a stint in the House of Scholars could be seen as the final stage in one's career.[69] And I assume we'd pay them enough so that they wouldn't need more money after they retire. Also, I'd like to point out that this problem isn't distinctive to the House of Scholars—it's also a problem how to prevent corruption and "back-door influence" when elected politicians retire. I presume we'd use the same methods to prevent corruption, such as constraints on lobbying for interest groups that one dealt with as a politician. Actually, I'd worry less about deputies from the House of Scholars—the fact that they're chosen by exams and change often should make them less immune to ongoing connections with their former colleagues.

DEMO: You still seem to be placing a lot of faith in these "scholar-officials."

WANG: I don't think we should depend entirely on their honesty. I'd favor using the stick as well as the carrot. Singapore, for

[69] If the minimum age is moved too high, it can be argued that not many "senior citizens," particularly those successful at other careers, will be willing to sit through a rigorous examination process. One solution might be to let thirty-year-olds write the exams and to seal the results for the next quarter century, at which point the results could be made public and successful candidates could assume their posts as deputies in the House of Scholars as the age of fifty-five (this system has another advantage—it would give a wide range of persons hope that they might be successful later on in life, which can keep them going through rough patches experienced between the ages of thirty and fifty-five). Of course, there will be a problem with selecting the first few batches of scholars if this system is put into pratice immediately.

example, imposes stiff penalties for corrupt behavior. I'm also tempted by the Republic of Venice's anticorruption strategy. This republic, as you may know, endured for over eight centuries in the last millenium. The regime provided peace and prosperity to its citizens, had an excellent legal system, possessed an elaborate and closely observed constitution, and yet from the year 1300 onward it was legally governed by only 2 percent of its population.[70] So how, you may ask, did the Republic of Venice ensure that its rulers resisted the temptation for personal enrichment? An audit was performed at the end of their tenure, and if a financial discrepancy was discovered the ruler's children were penalized.[71]

DEMO: The ruler's *children*? But what if the children were innocent?

WANG: They rarely were, and the same is true in China. The sons and daughters of government officials are notoriously corrupt, more often than not relying on their family's political connections to strike favorable deals of dubious legality. No great harm would be done by penalizing the children. On the contrary, this "Venetian" method may help to secure the honesty of officials. It may also be worth penalizing government officials for the misdeeds of their children so that public servants have an incentive to monitor the dealings of family members.

DEMO: But how can you suggest penalizing some people for the actions of others?

WANG: This may be difficult to understand. You see, the Chinese conception of the self is quite different from the typical Western view. In the West, "the buck stops" at the individual. The individual is responsible for his or her own "chosen" behavior, no more and no less. In China, by contrast, the family is typically viewed as an indissoluble organism linking ancestors and descendants into a single unit. So it's seen as quite normal for family members to be treated less as individuals than as outcomes of family and clan lineage, and thus be held responsible for the misdeeds of close relatives. No doubt family-based punishment can be

---

[70] See Robert Dahl, *Democracy and Its Critics*, 64. See also chap. 2, sec. 1.1.
[71] I thank Robert Dahl for this information.

cruel. In the dynastic period whole families were executed for the crimes of one member, and torture and execution included the slicing of bodies into tiny pieces and the public exposure of offenders' heads, punishments meant not to maximize pain but rather to destroy the future lives of offenders and hence ending family lines. Other punishments, however, seem positively humane. Inspired by the best of Confucian values, some laws allowed for family members to stay in prison to care for sick relatives, and families could choose to rotate sentences among themselves, rather than imposing the burden of imprisonment all upon one individual.[72]

DEMO: But how much of this is still relevant in the contemporary era?

WANG: I'm not saying that we should try to reimplement every one of these practices in today's society. The value of family-based responsibility, however, is still very much with us in the Chinese world. One of most painful aspects of our experience with "communism" is that people were frequently punished for the "counterrevolutionary" acts of family members. Some of my friends were persecuted simply on the grounds that distant relatives had "bourgeois" backgrounds. And let's not mention the distasteful practice of charging families for the cost of bullets used to execute their relatives.

DEMO: As you say, these were painful experiences. So doesn't it follow that contemporary Chinese should *challenge*, rather than affirm, the traditional value of family-based punishment?

WANG: Yes, but my point is that the conception of the family as a single unit of responsibility can also serve to justify certain policies designed to address contemporary problems. You're familiar, for example, with China's overpopulation crisis. The Communists tried to improve the situation by implementing a one-child-per-family policy, which in practice meant that second children faced limited educational opportunities compared with first-borns. One might say that the children were punished for the misdeeds of their parents. This might seem unjust given

---

[72] See Michael R. Dutton, *Policing and Punishment in China* (Cambridge: Cambridge University Press, 1992), chap. 4.

Western conceptions of individual responsibility, but most Chinese—or in any case, most urban intellectuals[73]—support the one-child-per-family policy, as well as its publicly affirmed practical consequences.

DEMO: Come to think of it, the value of family-based responsibility also plays a role in legitimizing some policies in the United States. Some states withhold welfare payments from single mothers, and their children often pay the price. Voters in California supported Proposition 187, which punished the children of illegal immigrants by barring them from public schools. At one time the Clinton administration punished foreign companies operating in Cuba by barring both executives and their children from visiting or studying in the United States.[74] There have also been proposals to punish parents for the misdeeds of their children as a means of reducing juvenile delinquency. I must admit, however, that I feel uncomfortable with such policies.

WANG: So do I. Family-based punishment can easily be abused. But the problem of corruption is so serious in China—and much can be traced to the misuses of family connections in political circles—that I think it's worth thinking about the possibility of invoking family-based punishment as a means of minimizing corruption in the political system. I hope I'm wrong, however. If term limits work out in practice, and if a combination of publicity, public deliberations, high salaries, and harsh penalties directed solely at the perpetrator of financial misdeeds can successfully reduce corruption to a tolerable level, then family-based punishments may not be necessary. They should only be employed as a last resort.[75]

---

[73] See Link, *Evening Chats in Beijing*, 106–107. See also chap. 3, sec. 4.

[74] See, e.g., "The Cuba Boomerang," *New York Times* (editorial), 13 July 1996, 18. The *New York Times* is critical of this law, asking, "How far, one wonders, does guilt by kinship extend?"

[75] Another option more respectful of the value of individual-based responsibility might be a law requiring that the state closely monitor the business dealings of the sons and daughters of public officials, but that the children only be punished in cases of actual misdeeds (I thank Joseph Chan for this point).

3.3. The Question of Universalizability

DEMO (*pause*): Let's assume for the sake of argument that your proposal for a House of Scholars does indeed fulfill your expectations. It's composed of persons with the potential to act as "guardians" of virtue and knowledge governing in the interests of the common good, while various constitutional and anticorruption devices serve to curb the tendency to abuse power. Let's also assume that this system of "rule by an intellectual elite" is particularly appropriate for addressing the increasingly complex and interlinked political problems of modern societies. Now let me ask you the question—why do you seem to think that the House of Scholars proposal is only appropriate for China? Why shouldn't it be adopted by the political systems of all modern and modernizing societies?

WANG: I suspect that my proposal would be laughed out of existence in certain contexts. It seems appropriate in a Chinese context where most twentieth-century prodemocracy movements were initiated and carried out by the intellectual elite.[76] They weren't campaigning for pure democratic rule, but rather for "people's rule" constrained by the wisdom of a public-spirited intellectual elite. In other contexts, however, different groups played a greater role in democratization movements, and a House of Scholars–type proposal may not satisfy their aspirations. Equally important, the House of Scholars can seem legitimate in the eyes of Chinese people "on the bottom," because of our tradition of respect for meritocratically chosen scholar-officials. But things are different elsewhere. Think of the United States, with its deeply rooted anti-intellectualism, its tradition of popular resentment against "pointy-headed" intellectuals.[77] When I'm in East Asian societies built on a foundation of Confucian ideals and I tell taxi drivers I'm a professor of political philosophy, they almost invariably ask for my views on the burning

[76] See C. L. Chiou, *Democratizing Oriental Despotism*, 3. See also chap. 2, sec. 2.3.

[77] For several examples of the way politicians can use the anti-intellectual streak in American culture to their own advantage, see Bruce J. Schulman, "In America, Intellectuals Are Suspect," *International Herald Tribune*, 3 March 1999, 9.

political issues of the day.[78] In the United States, they typically scoff and proceed to inform me that I know nothing about the "real world." So I doubt that a House of Scholars could ever achieve much popular legitimacy in the United States.

DEMO: But there's more than one side to American popular culture. You yourself pointed out that the U.S. Supreme Court—composed largely of brilliant academic overachievers—may be the most respected institution in the American political system. And come to think of, at least one leading American intellectual has floated a proposal not altogether dissimilar from your own. Are you familiar with Daniel Bell?

WANG: You mean the distinguished American sociologist?

DEMO: Of course. About fifteen years ago Bell developed a highly imaginative proposal for political reform of the U.S. Congress. The main problem with this institution, as you may know, is that its members, particularly in the House of Representatives, are constantly scrambling to raise money for reelection, leading to the impression if not the reality that politicians are primarily beholden to financial interests instead of being committed to promoting the common good. So to "re-legitimize" the Congress in the eyes of the American public, Bell proposed setting a term limit for members of Congress—three terms for senators, and four terms of four (rather than two) years for representatives. Then retirees would be recruited into a third chamber, whose pension plus an additional income would give them financial security. This "House of Counselors," as Bell puts it, would be the pool for the commissions and independent bodies that evaluate policy and advise the government. The country would thus have a group of experienced and disinterested individuals ready to act for the common good, backed by a certain

[78] Kim Kwang-ok traces the value of respect for intellectuals in Korea back to its Confucian roots: "Since education is the most important mechanism by which people become proper human beings, jobs related to education, such as being a teacher or professor, are highly respected. The job of university professor is one of the most prestigious in Korea, as this represents the model of the noble man" (Kim, "The Reproduction of Confucian Culture in Contemporary Korea," 206).

degree of popular support.[79] I remember Bell's proposal well because my organization came close to endorsing the House of Counselors proposal a couple of years ago. We thought it was a better idea than, say, having the president's wife devise plans for long-term health care policy.

WANG: I don't fully understand the American political system, but wouldn't the implementation of this proposal require fairly radical changes in the U.S. Constitution?

DEMO: Yes, that's one reason we finally decided not to go along. But who knows, Bell's idea may come to fruition one day if the Congress continues to lose the trust of the American public.

WANG (*short pause*): Bell's idea is actually quite different from what I have in mind. The House of Counselors may still be composed of mediocre people whose sole qualification is that they succeeded in getting elected to Congress. I'm after truly disinterested men and women of talent who haven't had to demean themselves by pandering to the rich and powerful, or to the short-term concerns of the public. A closer Western analogue, though in a somewhat watered-down form, is the House of Lords in Britain.

DEMO (*surprised*): The House of Lords!

WANG: Yes. Contrary to popular belief, the House of Lords still has considerable impact on legislation. It has the power to delay bills passed by the House of Commons for one year, though it rarely exercises this power. More commonly, it operates as a revising body, refining bills from the lower chamber by filling in the details and closing the loopholes. And from what I hear, it performs that task with admirable competence and nonpartisanship. Its debates are elegant, nonadversarial, and informative, and sometimes lead to significant amendments. Many of its members have a depth of expertise from earlier careers that's often lacking in the relative youngsters occupying the House of Commons.[80]

[79] See Daniel Bell, "The Old War," 20–21.
[80] See John Darnton, "Labor Peers Into the Lords' Future," *International Herald Tribune*, 22 April 1996, 1, 8.

DEMO: But it includes hereditary peers, who inherit the right to sit there and vote on legislation simply on the basis of their aristocratic ancestry. That's not what you want for your House of Scholars, is it?

WANG: Of course not. But didn't Blair's Labor government get rid of hereditary peers?[81] Other peers are appointed by the queen on the recommendation of the prime minister, and this seems to be a relatively meritocratic process. The respected political philosopher Raymond Plant, for example, is a member of the House of Lords. But you're right, it should be reformed and made into a truly meritocratic body. I don't like the idea of political appointees either. If it were up to me, I'd convert it into a House of Scholars, composed of representatives selected on the basis of competitive examinations.

DEMO: Maybe your proposal is most appropriate for the United Kingdom?

WANG: I doubt it. There isn't a cultural base of support for a House of Scholars in the United Kingdom.[82] Of course there's an English tradition of deference to one's "betters," but the meritocratic idea of "rule of the best" is tainted with notions of property and class privilege in a way that hasn't been true in Confucian-influenced East Asia. I'm suspicious of sentimental readings of history, but generally speaking you did have a fair and open examination process in Confucian societies, and examinations have often been seen as a vehicle for upward mobility.[83]

---

[81] See Simon Macklin, "House of Lords to Oust Hereditary Peers," *South China Morning Post*, 11 June 1998, 14.

[82] The cultural terrain for a House of Scholars may be relatively favorable in France, given the social and political importance of French intellectuals (see Alain Touraine's discussion of the role of French intellectuals in *Comment sortir du libéralisme?* 147–154). If the Fifth Republic experiences a serious political or constitutional crisis, perhaps a House of Scholars can be considered as a constitutional proposal for a "Sixth Republic."

[83] According to He Huai Hong, this perception was often grounded in fact, i.e., civil service examinations did often serve as a vehicle for upward social mobility (and downward social mobility, for established families that could not produce successful offspring). See his paper, "Rujia de Pingdeng Guan Jiqi Zhiduhua" (Confucianism's equality and its institutionalization), presented at the confer-

DEMO: In that case, why not recommend a House of Scholars for Korea, Japan, Singapore, and Taiwan? You've already said, for example, that your proposal compensates for flaws in the Japanese system of de facto rule by powerful bureaucrats, such as the lack of transparency and accountability, so why shouldn't a House of Scholars be appropriate for Japan?

WANG: Maybe one day other East Asian societies will be attracted by my proposal. If the political status quo isn't seen to be working well, perhaps the House of Scholars can be considered as an option.[84] In China there's an obvious need for serious political reform, and people seem to be quite receptive to new political ideas.

DEMO (*pause*): I hope you're right. But I have a couple more questions, if you don't mind. I realize I've been asking about why you're limiting the scope of your proposal to China, but now let me suggest that you're being too ambitious by proposing to apply the House of Scholars idea to the whole of China. China, as you know, is not a culturally homogenous entity. This means, for one thing, that non-Han Chinese minority groups may not identify with a Confucian tradition of rule by a meritocratically selected political elite, and it seems unfair to ask them to participate in your scheme.

WANG: I have no objections to granting substantial self-administration to minority areas like Tibet and Xinjiang. With respect to the House of Scholars, minority groups can be guaranteed a certain number of seats. Hong Kong can be also be given a seat, and Taiwan, if it agrees to join, can be given three or four seats.[85]

---

ence on Confucianism and Human Rights, Beijing University, June 1998. Standardized (blindly graded) testing has also been an instrument of upward mobility in France, Britain, and the United States (see Adrian Woodridge, "A True Test," *New Republic*, 15 June 1998, 20–21).

[84] As it turns out, several persons (including myself) are currently involved in a project to draft a constitution for a Confucian democracy (with emphasis on the Korean context) which may include proposals similiar to this one. This effort is part of a multiyear series of workshops on Confucianism and Democracy,organized by Professor Hahm Chaibong of Yonsei University in Seoul, Korea.

[85] Minority groups can also be guaranteed representation in the democratic lower house, as in Yan Jiaqi's proposal for a federal system in post-Communist

DEMO: My point is that the practice of competition for political office on the basis of written examinations may seem foreign to some non-Han Chinese groups, and they may not support this method of selecting political rulers.

WANG: There are ways to accommodate the cultural particularities of minority groups. Minorities can choose a different selection process for their deputies. Or they can modify the content of examinations to better reflect their own traditions—for example, the examination for Tibetan representatives can include a component on Buddhism and the Tibetan language. These are details to be worked out at tomorrow's convention; or perhaps the delegates can appoint a commission with minority representation to work on this problem.

3.4. The Problem of Gridlock

DEMO (*pause*): One last question. So far we've only been talking about the upper house in your proposed bicameral legislature. The lower house, you said, should be composed of democratically elected representatives. But the two houses may not always agree on the same policies.

WANG: Of course.

DEMO: So my question is this: how would you resolve disputes between the lower house and the upper house? Is there a mechanism to break gridlock between the two houses of government?

WANG: A tough question. But the answer ultimately depends on which of the two houses has more power. Proponents of rule by a meritocratic elite—let's call them "Confucians"—would want to empower the House of Scholars.

China (see his article "China's National Minorities and Federalism"). More generally, it is worth emphasizing that the House of Scholars proposal is fully compatible with federal constitutional mechanisms regulating the relationship between national and provincial institutions—in fact, those favoring more local autonomy may have an interest in supporting a proposal for a House of Scholars, because deputies in the House of Scholars bound by term limits may be more likely to ensure that decisions at the local level are not usurped by national political institutions (in contrast to relatively "power-hungry" bureaucrats with lifetime tenure and ambitious politicians concerned about the next elections).

DEMO: If you really want to be a Confucian, then you'd want the top power-broker to be an emperor who stands above the fray. After all, the head of state in traditional China was a "divinely appointed" sage-king, and meritocratically selected civil servants had the role of advising, and perhaps admonishing, but they weren't the top decision-makers. So why not try to resurrect the monarchic Chinese tradition?

WANG (*laughs*): Don't be silly. That would never work—it's difficult, if not impossible, to resurrect a monarchical system that's been dead for nearly a century. It's not like you can make people believe in a divinely appointed ruler who emerges from a constitutional convention. And besides, nobody's pushing for that system now. What's more realistic, I think, is to select the head of state from the House of Scholars. Perhaps it can be the eldest member, or if you really want to be meritocratic it can go to the top achiever in the examinations. What's your advice?

DEMO: To be frank, I don't like either option. In my opinion, the House of Scholars should be constitutionally subordinate to the democratic lower house. Like Bell's House of Counselors, it could be the pool for the commissions and independent bodies that evaluate policy and advise the government. Like the House of Lords, it could play the relatively minor role of revising legislation passed on from the lower house, pointing out flaws and proposing small amendments. I don't mind if a symbolic, largely ceremonial, head of state comes from the House of Scholars, but the head of government—the one who *really* makes the political decisions—should come from the lower house. And so should the important ministers.

WANG (*face whitens*): But, but, I thought you were on my side!

DEMO: I am! Like I said, I'm not against a House of Scholars. I agree with your point that it seems to suit China's political culture and that it's better than alternative mechanisms for institutionalizing rule by an intellectual elite. But I can only go so far. I can't endorse a political system that gives unelected leaders the power to make final decisions. Elected politicians can—and should—rely on the advice of talented and disinterested individuals, but the people's chosen leaders should hold the ultimate trump cards.

WANG: But that would be a disaster in China! Democrats in the lower house—concerned primarily about the next election and heavily influenced by commercial interests—may favor rapid economic growth regardless of the long-term ecological consequences, whereas deputies in the House of Scholars—who arrive at their decisions following careful, nonpartisan deliberations, unconstrained by the need to accommodate particular interests—may opt for slower, ecologically sustainable development without the same immediate material benefits. Who should win? The democrats?

DEMO: It's hard to answer in the abstract. Policy disputes tend to be more concrete than that.

WANG: O.K., let's take the example of the one-child-per-family policy. Most peasants oppose this policy, partly due to the deeply held rural preference for siring male children. Those views would probably dominate the lower house—the large majority of Chinese still live in the countryside—and the democrats may well vote to repeal this policy, whatever the long-term consequences. But a House of Scholars—dominated by intellectuals, most of whom understand the need for this policy[86]—would probably vote to uphold it. And you think the democrats should get their way?

DEMO: You're presenting this as an "either/or" issue—the vulgar democrats versus the reflective meritocrats. But surely some meritocrats will side with the democrats in the lower house. Even if they're completely selfless, meritocrats won't necessarily converge on the same interpretation of the common good.

WANG: Of course not.[87] But conflicts can be resolved by majority decision-making, and the question is what to do when a majority

---

[86] See note 73.

[87] However, not every Chinese intellectual will readily admit the possibility that different persons can (justifiably) settle upon different interpretations of the common good. According to Thomas Metzger, many Chinese intellectuals, including self-described liberals, seem to believe that "specific normative problems can all be solved in an objective way based on "reason"; that the ultimate nature of all things . . . can be known; and that all knowledge can be organized to form a single unified system of thought which an enlightened elite can then use to guide society" (Metzger, "On Chinese Tendencies Resisting Democratization,"

in the upper house is opposed by a majority in the lower house. I'd favor—for example—a constitutional formula providing supermajorities in the House of Scholars with the right to override majorities in the lower house.

DEMO (*raises voice*): Well, I'd favor the opposite. And I doubt most Chinese would go along with a system that's designed to systematically override the wishes of the leaders they choose to represent their own interests! It's not like you're asking them to endorse an institution like the Supreme Court, which has carefully circumscribed powers. They're supposed to accept an institution that has overriding power, *in principle*, over all the decisions of democratically elected leaders!

WANG (*short pause*): Mmh, yes, you have a point. It would be hard to sell that part.[88]

DEMO: And you don't have to! Even a constitutionally subordinate upper house could play an important role in China. The country would have a group of relatively talented and disinterested individuals adding wisdom and long-term planning to the decision-making process. And if the House is legitimate in the "eyes of the people"—which is quite likely in a society with a tradition

---

paper included in folder distributed to participants in a workshop on Confucianism and Democracy, June 1998, Jirae, Korea, 6). This outlook can pose a problem for a political institution that depends on the willingness of members to abide by the decisions of the majority in cases of conflict between competing interpretations of the common good.

[88] Perhaps Wang could have suggested the possibility of a referendum, to gauge the people's support for a House of Scholars with the power to override the decisions of a democratic lower house. But this may be asking Wang to take a needless risk, since it may be preferable to settle for a purely advisory House of Scholars that is not put to a referendum. And even if the majority votes for a powerful House of Scholars, the system may not be stable for the long-term, as future (more educated?) generations may come to object to this political arrangement.

Another possibility is to give majorities in the upper house the power to override majorities in the lower house, but then allowing a supermajority (say, two-thirds of the representatives) in the lower house to override majorities in the upper house. This way, the upper house could exercise more de facto power, but the ultimate power would still lie with the people's representatives in the lower house. It is unlikely, however, that democrats would accept a proposal that effectively disempowers the lower house on most issues.

of respect for a meritocratically chosen politically elite—the House of Scholars can exercise a great deal of *moral* authority. Democratic majorities would find it hard to ignore the viewpoints that emerge from open deliberation among deputies in the House of Scholars. At the very least, politicians in the lower house who systematically disregard policy recommendations of the House of Scholars may find it difficult to get reelected.[89] What I'm trying to say is that you don't need much constitutional support to have a powerful House of Scholars!

3.5. Implementation of the Proposal

WANG (*pause*): Yes, you may be right. I guess I'd be satisfied with a constitutionally subordinate House of Scholars. The important point is that the House's decisions have real, practical impact in the political arena.

DEMO: Well, that would also depend on other factors, such as the relationship between the House of Scholars and the judiciary.[90]

WANG: Of course. There are many such details to be ironed out during the course of deliberations at the constitutional convention.[91] First, however, I have to deal with a more immediate

[89] This leads to the question of whether representatives of the lower house should also be subject to term limits. If they are not, an upper house whose members are limited to seven or eight years may not be able to stand up to a lower house whose members are long-time insiders.

[90] If the House of Scholars plays a purely advisory role, perhaps it should deliberate about public policies *and* legal judgments. But if it plays a more active decision-making role, there is more reason to worry about the need to separate the powers of the House of Scholars and the judiciary.

[91] Other important "details" include the questions of scale (perhaps the House of Scholars should be limited to two or three hundred seats, so as to allow for high-quality deliberations); of how to further insulate members of the House of Scholars from political pressure (perhaps they should be barred from joining political parties and be forced to publicly disclose memberships with interest groups, similar to the mechanisms that help to ensure the integrity of federal judges in the United States); of who should determine the content of the exams used to select deputies for the House of Scholars (perhaps a committee from the lower house should have the final say on the matter, which may help to alleviate the concerns of democrats); and of who should grade the exams (perhaps it should be a committee composed of representatives of different sectors of soci-

problem. I'm really worried about the possibility that I won't get enough votes for a House of Scholars, even one with minimal powers. The Communists—or the "Liberal Democrats," as they now prefer to call themselves—favor the electoral process, and they have no interest in a House of Scholars. They learned from the Russian case that their pervasive bureaucratic apparatus could easily be converted into a powerful electoral machinery. The ex-dissidents, especially the younger ones, also favor a powerful, democratically elected legislature. They're quite sure they can get elected, following in the footsteps of the Mandelas and the Havels. I don't blame them, mind you. I've always admired their courage over the years, and I think they deserve political payback of some kind or other. But meanwhile I have to deal with the fact that it's not in the interest of any of the major political forces to support my proposal. The only weapon I have at my disposal is rational argumentation.

DEMO (*smiles*): That's not very promising, is it?

WANG: No. This is real politics, unfortunately, not an academic seminar. Still, not all is lost. I think I can get some support from the women's groups—they like the idea of examinations that will have the effect of increasing the proportion of women in the political process. And there's one Marxist delegate—perhaps the only genuine Marxist intellectual in China—who may go along, because he's worried about the possibility that a democratically elected legislature will be captured by big business interests.

DEMO: That's it?

WANG: Well, I have to try to get more support from the democrats. If all else fails, I have one final argument up my sleeve—the "lesson" of Russia's transition to democracy. After the Soviet Union disintegrated, Russians were confronted with a stark choice—either Communist stagnation, or progress in the form of Western-style political practices. They may have gone along for a while if democracy had delivered material goods and provided social peace. But things didn't go according to plan, and

---

ety, to minimize the concern that one powerful group will select candidates relatively sympathetic to its interests).

not surprisingly it turned out that Western-style democracy had fairly shallow roots in the country. Can we really blame the Russian people? It's humiliating for a people—especially if they feel part of an old and proud civilization—to jettison the past as a whole, to be told that nothing valuable can be found in their national political history. So when things go wrong, when democracy fails to meet people's aspirations, the temptation will be to turn to a strongman who promises to restore national pride. But all this can be avoided if a democratic system incorporates an element of traditional political culture. Citizens will bear with the system even when things go wrong, and they can't put all the blame on the evil machinations of foreigners.

DEMO: So what you're saying is that Russian democracy was unstable because no serious effort was made to incorporate traditional political characteristics into its political system.[92] To avoid this mistake in the case of China, you're offering a middle way between Confucianism and Western democracy, a "democracy with Chinese characteristics."

WANG: Exactly! A House of Scholars designed to restrain democratic majorities can also have the paradoxical effect of securing a democratic system in China. Now let me ask you a question, if I may. I think it would help my case tomorrow if I can tell the delegates that your organization supports my proposal, at least the general idea of a bicameral legislature with a House of Scholars. I suspect that some of the "radical democrats" will try to portray my scheme as a reactionary plot concocted by sinister authoritarian forces. . . .

DEMO (*interrupting*): But that's ridiculous.

WANG: I know, but some of the younger ones are quite dogmatic— they won't even contemplate the possibility of a middle ground

---

[92] One exception is Solzhenitsyn's 1991 pamphlet "How We Are to Rebuild Russia," which sought to rebuild Russian national pride by drawing on prerevolutionary models (he proposed to re-create the elected district councils of prerevolutionary times and the Duma, the first Russian parliament in 1905, and to revive the Orthodox Church), but without some of the antidemocratic and colonialist elements of Russian nationalism. This proposal never did gain widespread support, however, perhaps because it was paired in people's minds with Solzhenitsyn's oft-displayed hostility to secular "materialist" modernity.

between traditional Chinese values and Western democracy. And for my proposal to pass even in its mildest form, I have to respond to all forms of criticism in an effective way. So if I say that even the U.S.-based NEHRD endorses my proposal, this can help to undercut the arguments of "radical democrats."

DEMO: Like I said, I can go along if the House of Scholars is constitutionally subordinate to the lower democratic house.

WANG: Fair enough.

DEMO: It's also in your interest to emphasize this part—you'd probably get more votes from the democrats if you make it explicit that the lower house has the ultimate say.

WANG: Yes, good point. I think I'll do that. (*Professor Wang rises from his seat.*)

CLOSING SCENE

DEMO: One last question . . .

WANG (*interrupting*): But you already asked your "last question"!

DEMO: One very, very final question—definitely the last one. I don't mean to suggest the presence of another agenda, but I was wondering if you saw any role for yourself in this House of Scholars. After all, I'm sure you'd ace those examinations.

WANG (*laughs*): Don't overestimate my abilities! There's a large talent pool in China, you know. But seriously, my sole concern is to improve the quality of China's governance. I'm not after political power.

DEMO: It would be nice to have both, wouldn't it?

WANG (*smiles*): I won't deny that. But let's move on to more important matters. (*Professor Wang proceeds toward the wooden statue of Confucius in the far corner of his office. Demo watches in amazement as Professor Wang gently unscrews Confucius's head, revealing a tray with a bottle of wuliangye[93] and two small porcelain cups. Wang fills the cups and hands one to Demo.*)

---

[93] A potent, high-quality Chinese rice wine.

WANG: In the famous opening passage of the *The Analects*, confucius says, "That friends should come to one from afar, is this not after all delightful?" (I.I)

DEMO (*lifting cup*): I'll second that: a toast to cross-cultural friendship. *Ganbei!*[94]

WANG: *Ganbei!*

[94] This can be translated as either "cheers" or "bottoms up."

* Select Bibliography *

Alagappa, Muthiah. "Democratic Transition in Asia: The Role of the International Community." *East-West Center Special Report*, no. 3 (October 1994).

Alford, C. Fred. "Koreans Do Not Believe in Evil—Should They?" *Korea Journal* (Autumn 1997).

Alford, William. "Making a Goddess of Democracy from Loose Sand: Thoughts on Human Rights in the People's Republic of China." In *Human Rights in Cross-Cultural Perspectives*. Edited by Abdullahi A. An-Na'im. Philadelphia: University of Pennsylvania Press, 1992.

Amar, Akhil Reed. *The Bill of Rights*. New Haven: Yale University Press, 1998.

Appiah, K., Anthony and Amy Gutmann. *Color Conscious: The Political Morality of Race*. Princeton: Princeton University Press, 1996.

Arneson, Richard. "Democratic Rights at National and Workplace Levels." In *The Idea of Democracy*. Edited by David Copp, Jean Hampton, and John Roemer. Cambridge: Cambridge University Press, 1993.

Asia Watch. *Silencing All Critics: Human Rights Violations in Singapore*. New York: Asia Watch, 1989.

Aung San Suu, Kyi. *Freedom from Fear and Other Writings*. New York: Penguin, 1991.

Baier, Annette. *Moral Prejudices*. Cambridge: Harvard University Press, 1994.

Barber, Benjamin. "A Mandate for Liberty: Requiring Education-Based Community Service." In *Rights and the Common Good*. Edited by Amitai Etzioni. New York: St Martin's Press, 1995.

Barkan, Joel. "Can Established Democracies Nurture Democracies Abroad? Lessons from Africa." In *Democracy's Victory and Crisis*. Edited by Axel Hadenius. Cambridge: Cambridge University Press, 1997.

Barrett, Thomas, ed. *China, Marxism, and Democracy: Selections from the October Review*. New Jersey: Humanities Review, 1996.

Barry, Brian. *Justice as Impartiality*. Oxford: Clarendon Press, 1995.

Bauer, Joanne R. "Three Years after the Bangkok Declaration: Reflections on the State of the Asia-West Dialogue on Human Rights." *Human Rights Dialogue* 4 (March 1996).

Bauer, Joanne R., and Daniel A. Bell, eds. *The East Asian Challenge for Human Rights*. New York: Cambridge University Press, 1999.

Befu, Harumi, ed. *Cultural Nationalism in East Asia*. Berkeley: Institute of East Asian Studies, University of California, 1992.

337

Bell, Daniel. "The Old War: After Ideology, Corruption." *New Republic.* 23 and 30 August 1993.

Bell, Daniel A. *Communitarianism and Its Critics.* Oxford: Clarendon Press, 1993.

———. "Minority Rights: On the Importance of Local Knowledge." *Dissent* (Summer 1996).

———. "The East Asian Challenge to Human Rights: Reflections on an East-West Dialogue." *Human Rights Quarterly* 18, no. 3 (August 1996).

———. "A Communitarian Critique of Capitalism: The Case of Singapore." *Political Theory* 25, no. 1 (February 1997).

———. "Hong Kong's Transition to Capitalism." *Dissent* (Winter 1998).

———. "A Confucian Democracy for the 21st Century." *Archiv fuer Rechts- und Sozialphilosophie.* Edited by Morigiwa Yasutomo. Beiheft 72 (1998).

———. "After the Tsunami: Will Economic Crisis Bring Democracy to Asia?" *The New Republic,* 9 March 1998.

———. "The Limits of Liberal Justice." *Political Theory* 26, no.4 (August 1998).

———. "Civil Society Versus Civic Virtue." In *The Freedom of Association.* Edited by Amy Gutmann. Princeton: Princeton University Press, 1998.

———. "From Mao to Jiang: China's Transition to Communism." *Dissent* (Summer 1999).

———. "Democratic Deliberations: The Problem of Implementation." In *Deliberative Politics: Essays on Democracy and Disagreement.* Edited by Stephen Macedo. New York: Oxford University Press, 1999.

———. "Democracy with Chinese Characteristics: A Political Proposal for the Post-Communist Era." *Philosophy East and West* 49, no. 4 (October 1999).

Bell, Daniel A., David Brown, Kanishka Jayasuriya, and David Martin Jones. *Towards Illiberal Democracy in Pacific Asia.* London and New York: Macmillan/St. Antony's College and St. Martin's Press, 1995.

Bellah, Robert, Richard Madsen, William Sullivan, Ann Swidler, and Steven Tipton. *Habits of the Heart: Individualism and Commitment in American Life.* Berkeley: University of California Press, 1985.

Benton, George, and Alan Hunter, eds. *Wild Lily, Prairie Fire: China's Road to Democracy, Yan'an to Tian'anman, 1942–1989.* Princeton: Princeton University Press, 1995.

Bergère, Marie-Claire. *Le mandarin et le compradore: Les enjeux de la crise en Asie orientale.* Paris: Hachette Littératures, 1998.

Bertrand, Jacques. "Growth and Democracy in Southeast Asia." *Comparative Politics* 30, no. 3 (April 1998).

Blinder, Alan. "Is Government Too Political?" *Foreign Affairs* 76, no. 4 (November/December 1997).

Bodde, Derk, and Clarence Morris. *Law in Imperial China.* Cambridge: Harvard University Press, 1967.

Brooks, Bruce. *The Original Analects.* New York: Columbia University Press, 1997.

Brown, Mark Malloch. "Why a Social Dimension to Foreign Policy Is Vital to U.S.–East Asian Relations." *Human Rights Dialogue* 11 (June 1998).

Buchanan, Allen. "Assessing the Communitarian Critique of Liberalism." *Ethics* 99, no. 4 (July 1989).

Buchwalter, A. "Hegel's Theory of Virtue." *Political Theory* 20, no. 4 (November 1992).

Buruma, Ian. *Behind the Mask.* New York: Pantheon Books, 1984.

Cahn, Doug. "Human Rights, Soccer Balls, and Better Business Practices." *Human Rights Dialogue* 9 (June 1997).

Calhoun, Craig. "Elites and Democracy: The Ideology of Intellectuals and the Chinese Student Protest Movement of 1989." In *Intellectuals and Public Life.* Edited by Leon Fink, Stephen Leonard, and Donald Reid. Ithaca: Cornell University Press, 1996.

Cerna, Christina. "Universal Democracy: An International Legal Right or the Pipe Dream of the West?" *New York University Journal of International Law and Politics* 27, no. 2 (Winter 1995).

Chan, Joseph. "The Asian Challenge to Universal Human Rights: A Philosophical Appraisal." In *Human Rights and International Relations in the Asia Pacific.* Edited by James Tang. London: Pinter, 1995.

———. "Hong Kong, Singapore, and 'Asian Values': An Alternative View." *Journal of Democracy* 8, no. 2 (April 1997).

———. "A Confucian Perspective of Human Rights." In *The East Asian Challenge for Human Rights.* Edited by Joanne R. Bauer and Daniel A. Bell. New York: Cambridge University Press, 1999.

Chang, Jung. *Wild Swans.* New York: Simon and Schuster, 1991.

Cheah, Hock Beng. "Responding to Global Challenges: The Changing Nature of Singapore's Incorporation into the International Economy." In *Singapore Changes Guard.* Edited by Garry Rodan. New York: St. Martin's Press, 1993.

Chee, Soon Juan. *Dare to Change: An Alternative Vision for Singapore.* Singapore: Singapore Democratic Party, 1994.

———. *Singapore: My Home Too.* Singapore: Chee Soon Juan, 1995.

———. *To Be Free: Stories from Asia's Struggle against Oppression.* Clayton: Monash Asia Institute, 1998.

Chew, Melanie. "Human Rights in Singapore: Perceptions and Problems." *Asian Survey* 34, no. 11 (November 1994).

Chiew Seen Kong. "National Identity, Ethnicity and National Values." In *In Search of Singapore's National Values.* Edited by Jon Quah. Singapore: Institute of Policy Studies, 1990.

Chiou, C. L. *Democratizing Oriental Despotism.* New York: St. Martin's Press, 1995.

Choate, Allen. "Local Governance in China: An Assessment of Villagers Committees." Working Paper no. 1, The Asia Foundation, February 1997.

Choi, Chongko. "Confucianism and Law in Korea." *Seoul Law Journal* 37, no.2 (September 1996).

Chomsky, Noam. *Language and Responsibility.* Sussex: The Harvester Press, 1979.

———. *Deterring Democracy.* London: Verso, 1991.

Chua, Beng-Huat. *Communitarian Ideology and Democracy in Singapore.* London: Routledge, 1995.

Cradock, Percy. *Experiences of China.* London: John Murray, 1994.

Crawford, James. *Democracy in International Law.* Cambridge: Cambridge University Press, 1994.

Crouch, Harold, and James Morley. "The Dynamics of Political Change." In *Driven by Growth: Political Change in the Asia-Pacific Region.* Edited by James Morley. Armonk, N.Y.: M. E. Sharpe, 1993.

Dahl, Robert. *Democracy and Its Critics.* New Haven: Yale University Press, 1989.

Dahrendorf, Ralf. "Can We Combine Economic Opportunity with Civil Society and Political Liberty?" *Responsive Community* 5, no. 3 (Summer 1995).

Davis, Michael. "Constitutionalism and Political Culture: The Debate over Human Rights and Asian Values." *Harvard Human Rights Journal* 11 (Spring 1998).

———. "The Price of Rights: Constitutionalism and East Asian Economic Development." *Human Rights Quarterly* 20, no. 2 (May 1998).

De Bary, Wm. Theodore. "Introduction." In *Waiting for the Dawn: A Plan for the Prince.* Huang Zongxi. Translated by Wm. Theodore de Bary. New York: Columbia University Press, 1993.

———. *Asian Values and Human Rights: A Confucian Communitarian Perspective.* Cambridge: Harvard University Press, 1998.

Detter, Ingrid. *The International Legal Order.* Aldershot: Dartmouth, 1994.

Diamond, Larry. "Economic Development and Democracy Reconsidered." *American Behavioral Scientist* 35, nos. 4, 5 (March/June 1992).

———. "Promoting Democracy in the 1990s: Actors, Instruments, Issues." In *Democracy's Victory and Crisis.* Edited by Axel Hadenius. Cambridge: Cambridge University Press, 1997.

Donnelly, Jack. "Post–Cold War Reflections of the Study of Human Rights." *Ethics and International Affairs* 8 (1996).

Donnelly, Jack. "Human Rights and Asian Values: A Defense of 'Western' Universalism." In *The East Asian Challenge for Human Rights*. Edited by Joanne R. Bauer and Daniel A. Bell. New York: Cambridge University Press, 1999.

Dore, Ronald. "Elitism and Democracy." *La Revue Tocqueville/The Tocqueville Review* 14, no. 2 (1993).

Doshi, Tilak. "Changing the Leviathan: A Public Choice Interpretation of Singapore's Elected Presidency." In *Managing Political Change in Singapore: The Elected Presidency*. London: Routledge, 1997.

Doyle, Michael W. "Kant, Liberal Legacies, and Foreign Affairs." *Philosophy and Public Affairs* 12, nos. 3 and 4 (Summer and Fall 1993).

Drucker, Peter F. "In Defense of Japanese Bureaucracy." *Foreign Affairs* 77, no. 5 (September/October 1998).

Du Gangjian and Song Gang. "Relating Human Rights to Chinese Culture: The Four Paths of the Confucian Analects and the Four Principles of a New Theory of Benevolence." In *Human Rights and Chinese Values*. Edited by Michael Davis. Hong Kong: Oxford University Press, 1995.

Dunn, John, ed. *Democracy*. Oxford: Oxford University Press, 1992.

Dutton, Michael. *Policing and Punishment in China*. Cambridge: Cambridge University Press, 1992.

Dworkin, Ronald. "Liberal Community." *California Law Review* 77 (1989).

———. *Freedom's Law*. Cambridge: Harvard University Press, 1996.

Ebrey, Patricia Buckley, ed. *Chinese Civilization: A Sourcebook*. 2nd edition. New York: The Free Press, 1993.

Elvin, Mark. *Another History: Essays on China from a European Perspective*. Canberra: Wild Peony, 1996.

Ely, J. H. *Democracy and Distrust*. Cambridge: Harvard University Press, 1980.

Emmerson, Donald K. "Singapore and the 'Asian Values' Debate." *Journal of Democracy* 6, no. 4 (October 1995).

———. "Americanizing Asia?" *Foreign Affairs* 77, no. 3 (May/June 1998).

Esposito, John L. "Political Islam: Beyond the Green Menace." *Current History* 93, no. 579 (January 1994).

Etzioni, Amitai. *The Spirit of Community: Rights, Responsibilities, and the Communitarian Agenda*. New York: Crown Publishers, 1993.

———. *The New Golden Rule: Community and Morality in a Democratic Society*. New York: Basic Books, 1996.

———. "The End of Cross-Cultural Relativism." *Alternatives* 22 (1997).

———. "Introduction." In *National Parks: Rights and the Common Good*. Edited by Francis Lovett. Lanham, Md.: Rowman and Littlefield Publishers, 1998.

Fairbank, John, and Edwin, Reischauer. *China: Tradition and Transformation.* Boston: Houghton Mifflin, 1989.

Fang, Lizhi. *Bringing Down the Great Wall.* New York: Norton, 1990.

Fitzgerald, John. "China and the Quest for Dignity." *The National Interest* (Spring 1999).

Fleischacker, Samuel. *The Ethics of Culture.* Ithaca: Cornell University Press, 1994.

Fukuyama, Francis. "Asian Values and the Asian Crisis." *Commentary* (February 1998).

Gandini, Jean-Jacques, ed. *Les Droits de l'Homme.* Paris: Librio, 1998.

Ganesan, N. "Democracy in Singapore." *Asian Journal of Political Science* 4, no. 2 (December 1996).

Gardels, Nathan. "Interview with Lee Kuan Yew." *New Perspectives Quarterly* 9, no. 1 (Winter 1992).

Ghai, Yash. "Hong Kong and Macau in Transition (I): Debating Democracy." *Democratization* 2, no. 3 (Autumn 1995).

Glendon, Mary Ann. *Rights Talk: The Impoverishment of Political Discourse.* New York: The Free Press, 1991.

Goldman, Merle. *Sowing the Seeds of Democracy in China.* Cambridge: Harvard University Press, 1994.

———. "Politically-Engaged Intellectuals in the Deng-Jiang Era: A Changing Relationship with the Party-State." *China Quarterly*, no. 145 (March 1996).

Goldstein, Steven. "Part 2: Politics (Introduction)." In *The Chinese: The Past, Facing the Future.* Edited by R. Dernberger et al. Ann Arbor: Center for Chinese Studies Publication, 1991.

Green, Philip, ed. *Democracy.* New Jersey: Humanities Press, 1993.

Gu, Edward X. "Elitist Democracy and China's Democratization: A Gradualist Approach towards Democratic Transition by a Group of Chinese Intellectuals." *Democratization* 4, no. 2 (Summer 1997).

Gurr, Ted. "Communal Conflicts and Global Security." *Current History* 94, no. 592 (May 1995).

Gutmann, Amy, and Dennis Thompson. *Democracy and Disagreement.* Cambridge: Harvard University Press, 1996.

Hadenius, Axel, ed. *Democracy's Victory and Crisis.* Cambridge: Cambridge University Press, 1997.

Hahm Chaibong. "The Confucian Political Discourse and the Politics of Reform in Korea." *Korea Journal* 37, no. 4 (Winter 1997).

Hall, David L., and Roger T. Ames. *Thinking Through Confucius.* Albany: State University of New York, 1987.

———. *Democracy of the Dead: Dewey, Confucius, and the Hope for Democracy in China.* Chicago: Open Court, 1999.

Han Fook Kwang, Warren Fernandez, and Sumiko Tan. *Lee Kwan Yew: The Man and His Ideas*. Singapore: Times Editions, 1998.

Hartcher, Peter. *The Ministry: How Japan's Most Powerful Institution Endangers World Markets*. Boston: Harvard Business School Press, 1998.

Hau Pei-tsun. *Straight Talk*. Taipei: Government Information Office, 1993.

He Baogang. *The Democratization of China*. London: Routledge, 1996.

———. *The Democratic Implications of Civil Society in China*. Basingstoke: Macmillan, 1997.

Helgesen, Geir. *Democracy and Authority in Korea: The Cultural Dimension in Korean Politics*. Richmond, England: Curzon, 1998.

Hill, Michael, and Lian Kwen Fee. *The Politics of National Building and Citizenship in Singapore*. London: Routledge, 1995.

Hsiao, Hsin-Huang Michael. "Political Liberalization and the Farmer's Movement in Taiwan." In *The Politics of Democratization*. Edited by E. Friedman. Boulder: Westview Press, 1994.

Huang, Mab. "Political Ko'tung and the Rise of the Democratic Progressive Party in Taiwan: 1984–1986." *Journal of Political Science* 5 (1996).

Huntington, Samuel. "Democracy's Third Wave." In *The Global Resurgence of Democracy*. Edited by Larry Diamond and Marc Plattner. Baltimore: John Hopkins University Press, 1993.

———. "American Democracy and Its Relation to Asia." In *Democracy and Capitalism: Asian and American Perspectives*. Edited by Robert Bartley et al. Singapore: Institute of Southeast Asian Studies, 1993.

———. "The Clash of Civilizations." *Foreign Affairs* 72, no. 3 (Summer 1993).

———. "The West Unique, Not Universal." *Foreign Affairs* 75, no. 6 (November/December 1996).

———. *The Clash of Civilizations and the Remaking of the World Order*. New York: Simon and Schuster, 1996.

Inoue, Tatsuo. "The Poverty of Rights-Blind Communality: Looking through the Window of Japan." *Brigham Young University Law Review*, no. 2 (1993).

———. "Liberal Democracy and Asian Orientalism." In *The East Asian Challenge for Human Rights*. Edited by Joanne R. Bauer and Daniel A. Bell. New York: Cambridge University Press, 1999.

International Council on Human Rights Policy. *Taking Duties Seriously: Individual Duties International Human Rights Law*. Versoix, Switzerland: International Council on Human Rights Policy, 1999.

Iokibe, Makoto. "Japan's Democratic Experience." In *Democracy in East Asia*. Edited by Larry Diamond and Marc F. Plattner. Baltimore: John Hopkins University Press, 1998).

Ishak, Lily Zubaidah Rahim. "The Paradox of Ethnic-Based Self-Help Groups." In *Debating Singapore.* Edited by Derek da Cunha. Singapore: Institute for Southeast Asian Studies, 1994.

Ivanhoe, Philip J. *Confucian Moral Self-Cultivation.* New York: Peter Lang, 1993.

Jenner, W. J. F. "China and Freedom." In *Asian Freedoms.* Edited by David Kelly and Anthony Reid. Melbourne: Cambridge University Press, 1998.

Jeyaretnam, Philip. "What Sort of Culture Should Singapore Have?" In *Debating Singapore.* Edited by Derek da Cunha. Singapore: Institute of Southeast Asian Studies, 1994.

Jones, David Martin. "Asian Values and the Constitutional Order of Contemporary Singapore." *Constitutional Political Economy* 8 (1997).

———. *Political Development in Pacific Asia.* Cambridge: Polity, 1997.

Jones, Eric. "Asia's Fate: A Response to the Singapore School." *The National Interest* (Spring 1994).

Josey, Alex. *Lee Kuan Yew: The Critical Years.* Singapore: Times Books International, 1968.

Kateb, George. *The Inner Ocean: Individualism and Democratic Culture.* Ithaca: Cornell University Press, 1992.

Kausikan, Bilahari. "Governance That Works." *Journal of Democracy* 8, no. 2 (April 1997).

Keith, Ronald. *China's Struggle for the Rule of Law.* New York: St. Martin's Press, 1994.

Keen, David. *The Benefits of Famine: A Political Economy of Famine and Relief in Southwestern Sudan.* Princeton: Princeton University Press, 1994.

Kennan, George. *American Diplomacy: 1900–1950.* Chicago: University of Chicago Press, 1951.

Kim Dae Jung. "Is Culture Destiny? The Myth of Asia's Anti-Democratic Values." *Foreign Affairs* 73, no. 6 (November/December 1994).

———. *Korea and Asia: A Collection of Essays, Speeches, and Discussions.* Seoul: Kim Dae Jung Peace Foundation Press, 1994.

Kim, Kwang-ok. "The Reproduction of Confucian Culture in Contemporary Korea: An Anthropological Study." In *Confucian Traditions in East Asian Modernity.* Edited by Tu Wei-ming. Cambridge: Harvard University Press, 1996.

Kim Young Sam. *Kim Young Sam and the New Korea.* Chicago: Bonus Books, 1992.

Kingsbury, Benedict. "The Applicability of the International Legal Concept of 'Indigenous Peoples' in Asia." In *The East Asian Challenge for Human Rights.* Edited by Joanne R. Bauer and Daniel A. Bell. New York: Cambridge University Press, 1999.

Kirk, Donald. *Looted: The Philippines after the Bases.* New York: St. Martin's Press, 1998.

Koh, Byong-ik. "Confucianism in Contemporary Korea." In *Confucian Traditions in East Asian Modernity.* Edited by Tu Wei-ming. Cambridge: Harard University Press, 1996.

Kohak, Erazim. "The Search for Europe." *Dissent* (Spring 1996).

Korsgaard, Christine. "The Right to Lie: Kant on Dealing with Evil." *Philosophy and Public Affairs* 15, no. 4 (Fall 1986).

Kukathas, Chandran. "Explaining Moral Variety." *Social Philosophy and Policy* 11, no. 1 (Winter 1994).

Kwok Kian Woon. "The Moral Condition of Democratic Society." *Commentary: The Journal of the National of University of Singapore Society* 11, no. 1 (1993).

Kymlicka, Will. *Liberalism, Community and Culture.* Oxford: Clarendon Press, 1989.

———. "Two Models of Pluralism and Tolerance." *Analyze & Kritik* 14, no. 1 (1992).

———. *Multicultural Citizenship: A Liberal Theory of Minority Rights.* Oxford: Clarendon Press, 1995.

Lacqueur, Walter, and Barry Rubin, eds. *The Human Rights Reader.* New York: Meridian, 1989.

Larmore, Charles. *Patterns of Moral Complexity.* Cambridge: Cambridge University Press, 1987.

———. *The Morals of Modernity.* Cambridge: Cambridge University Press, 1996.

Lawyers Committee for Human Rights. *Inhumane Deterrence: The Treatment of Vietnamese Boat People in Hong Kong.* New York: Lawyers Committee for Human Rights, 1989.

———. *Malaysia: Assault on the Judiciary.* New York: Lawyers Committee for Human Rights, 1989.

———. *Criminal Justice with Chinese Characteristics.* New York: Lawyers Committee for Human Rights, 1994.

Layne, Christopher and Schwarz, Benjamin. "American Hegemony without an Enemy." *Foreign Policy* 92 (Fall 1993).

Lee Kuan Yew. *Lee Kuan Yew on China and Hong Kong after Tiananmen.* Edited by Lianhe Zaobao. Singapore: Lianhe Zaobao, 1991.

Lee Kuan Yew. *The Singapore Story.* Singapore: Prentice Hall, 1994.

Lew Seok-choon. "Confucian Capitalism: Possibilities and Limits." *Korea Focus* 5, no.4 (1994).

Li, Xiaorong. "A Question of Priorities: Human Rights, Development, and 'Asian Values.' " Report from the Institute for Philosophy and Public Policy, School of Public Affairs, University of Maryland, 1998.

Lincoln, Edward J. "Japan's Financial Mess." *Foreign Affairs* 77, no. 3 (May/June 1998).

Ling, L. H. M., and Shih Chih-yu. "Confucianism with a Liberal Face: The Meaning of Democratic Politics in Postcolonial Taiwan." *Review of Politics* 60, no. 1 (Winter 1998).

Lingle, Christopher. *Singapore's Authoritarian Capitalism: Asian Values, Free Market Illusions, and Political Dependency.* Barcelona: Edicions Sirocco; Fairfax: Locke Institute, 1996.

Link, Perry. *Evening Chats in Beijing.* New York: Norton, 1992.

MacCormack, Geoffrey. *Traditional Chinese Penal Law.* Edinburgh: Edinburgh University Press, 1990.

McCormick, Barrett L. "Democracy or Dictatorship? A Response to Gordon White." *Australian Journal of Chinese Affairs* 31 (January 1994).

Macedo, Stephen. *Liberal Virtues: Citizenship, Virtue, and Community in Liberal Constitutionalism.* Oxford: Clarendon Press, 1991.

MacIntyre, Alasdair. *Whose Justice? Which Rationality?* London: Duckworth, 1988.

———. "Incommensurability, Truth, and the Conversation between Confucians and Aristotelians about the Virtues." In *Culture and Modernity: East-West Philosophic Perspectives.* Edited by Eliot Deutsch. Honolulu: University of Hawaii Press, 1991.

McKnight, Brian E. *The Quality of Mercy: Amnesties and Traditional Chinese Justice.* Honolulu: University of Hawaii Press, 1981.

Mahbubani, Kishore. *Can Asians Think?* Singapore: Times Books International, 1998.

Miller, David. "The Ethical Significance of Nationality." *Ethics* 98, no. 4 (July 1988).

———. *On Nationality.* Oxford: Clarendon Press, 1995.

Milne, R. S., and D.K. Mauzy. *Singapore: The Legacy of Lee Kuan Yew.* Boulder: Westview Press, 1990.

Miners, Norman. *The Government and Politics of Hong Kong.* Fifth edition. Hong Kong: Oxford University Press, 1995.

Muravchik, Joshua. *The Imperative of American Leadership: A Challenge to Neo-Isolationism.* Washington, D.C.: American Enterprise Institute, 1996.

Mutalib, Hussin. "Singapore's First Elected Presidency: The Political Motivations." In *Managing Political Change in Singapore: The Elected Presidency.* Edited by Kevin Y. L. Tan and Lam Peng Er. London: Routledge, 1997.

An-Na'im, Abdullahi A. "Toward a Cross-Cultural Approach to Defining International Standards of Human Rights: The Meaning of Cruel, Inhuman, or Degrading Treatment or Punishment." In *Human Rights in*

Cross-Cultural Perspectives: A Quest for Consensus. Edited by Abdullahi A. An-Na'im. Philadelphia: University of Pennsylvania Press, 1992.

————. "The Cultural Mediation of Rights: The Case of Al-Arqam in Malaysia." In *The East Asian Challenge for Human Rights.* Edited by Joanne R. Bauer and Daniel A. Bell. New York: Cambridge University Press, 1999.

Nathan, Andrew. "Sources of Chinese Rights Thinking." In *Human Rights in Contemporary China.* Edited by R. Randle Edwards, Louis Henkin, and Andrew Nathan. New York: Columbia University Press, 1986.

————. *Chinese Democracy.* London: Tauris, 1986.

Nathan, Andrew. "Chinese Democracy: The Lessons of Failure." *Journal of Contemporary China,* no. 4 (1993).

————. "China's Constitutionalist Option." *Journal of Democracy* 7, no. 4 (October 1996).

————. *China's Transition.* New York: Columbia University Press, 1997.

————. "Even Our Caution Must Be Hedged." *Journal of Democracy* 9, no. 1 (January 1998).

Nino, Carlos Santiago. *The Ethics of Human Rights.* Oxford: Clarendon Press, 1991.

Oh, Byung-Sun. "Cultural Values and Human Rights: The Korean Perspective." In *Human Rights in Asian Cultures: Continuity and Change.* Edited by Jefferson R. Plantilla and Sebasti L. Raj, S.J. Osaka: Hurights Osaka, 1997.

Okin, Susan Moller. *Women in Western Political Thought.* Princeton: Princeton University Press, 1979.

————. *Justice, Gender, and the Family.* New York: Basic Books, 1989.

Onuma, Yasuaki. "In Quest of Intercivilizational Human Rights: 'Universal vs. Relative' Human Rights Viewed from an Asian Perspective." Center for Asian Pacific Affairs, The Asia Foundation, Occasional Paper no. 2, 1996.

————. "Toward an Intercivilizational Approach to Human Rights." In *The East Asian Challenge for Human Rights.* Edited by Joanne R. Bauer and Daniel A. Bell. New York: Cambridge University Press, 1999.

Othman, Norani. "Grounding Human Rights in Non-Western Culture: Shari'a and the Citizenship Rights of Women in a Modern Islamic State." In *The East Asian Challenge for Human Rights.* Edited by Joanne R. Bauer and Daniel A. Bell. New York: Cambridge University Press, 1999.

Overholt, William M. *China: The Next Economic Superpower.* London: Weidenfeld & Nicolson, 1993.

Parekh, Bhikhu. "The Rushdie Affair: Research Agenda for Political Philosophy." In *The Rights of Minority Cultures.* Edited by Will Kymlicka. Oxford: Oxford University Press, 1995.

Patten, Christopher. *East and West*. New York: Times Books, 1998.

Paul, Erik. "Prospects for Liberalization in Singapore." *Journal of Contemporary Asia* 23, no. 3 (1993).

Peerenboom, Randall. "Confucian Harmony and Freedom of Thought: The Right to Think versus Right Thinking." In *Confucianism and Human Rights*. Edited by Wm. Theodore de Bary and Tu Weiming. New York: Columbia University Press, 1998.

Perry, Michael J. *The Idea of Human Rights: Four Inquiries*. New York: Oxford University Press, 1998.

Plantilla, Jefferson R., and Sebasti L. Raj, S.J., eds. *Human Rights in Asian Cultures: Continuity and Change*. Osaka: Hurights Osaka, 1997.

Putnam, Robert. "Bowling Alone: America's Declining Social Capital." *Journal of Democracy* 6, no. 1 (January 1995).

Quah, Jon. "Government Policies and Nation-Building." In *In Search of Singapore's National Values*. Edited by Jon Quah. Singapore: Institute for Policy Studies, 1990.

Ramesh, M. "Social Security in Singapore: Redrawing the Public-Private Boundary." *Asian Survey* 32, no. 12 (December 1992).

Rawls, John. "The Idea of an Overlapping Consensus." *Oxford Journal of Legal Studies* 7, no. 1 (1987).

Redlich, Norman, Bernard Schwartz, and John Attanasio. *Understanding Constitutional Law*. New York: M. Bender, 1995.

Reid, T. R. *Confucius Lives Next Door: What Living in the East Teaches Us about Living in the West*. New York: Random House, 1999.

Revel, François, and Matthieu Ricard. *Le Moine et le Philosophe: Le bouddhisme aujourd'hui*. Paris: NiL editions, 1997.

Rodan, Garry. *The Political Economy of Singapore's Industrialization: National State and International Capital*. Houndsmills: Macmillan, 1989.

———. "The Growth of Singapore's Middle Class and Its Political Significance." In *Singapore Changes Guard*. Edited by Garry Rodan. New York: St. Martin's Press, 1993.

———. "State-Society Relations and Political Opposition in Singapore." In *Political Oppositions in Industrializing Asia*. Edited by Garry Rodan. London: Routledge, 1996.

Root, Hilton L. *The Key to the Asian Miracle: Making Shared Growth Credible*. Washington: Brookings, 1996.

Rosemont, Henry Jr. "Human Rights: A Bill of Worries." In *Confucianism and Human Rights*. Edited by Wm. Theodore de Bary and Tu Wei-ming. New York: Columbia University Press, 1998.

Rosenblum, Nancy. "Civil Societies: Liberalism and the Moral Uses of Pluralism." *Social Research* 61, no. 3 (Fall 1994).

Roth, Kenneth. "Sidelined on Human Rights: America Bows Out." *Foreign Affairs* 77, no. 2 (March/April 1998).

Rozman, Gilbert, ed. *The East Asian Region: Confucian Heritage and Its Modern Adaptation.* Princeton: Princeton University Press, 1991.

Sandel, Michael. *Democracy's Discontent: America in Search of a Public Philosophy.* Cambridge: Harvard University Press, 1996.

Schacter, Oscar. *International Law in Theory and Practice.* Dordrecht, The Netherlands: Martinus Nijhoff Publishers, 1991.

Schaffer, Frederic. *Democracy in Translation.* Ithaca: Cornell University Press, 1998.

Schell, Orville. *Discos and Democracy.* New York: Pantheon, 1988.

Schlesinger, Stephen C., and Stephen Kinzer. *Bitter Fruit: The Untold Story of the American Coup in Guatemala.* Garden City, N.Y.: Doubleday, 1982.

Schmitter, Philippe, and Terry Lynn Karl. "What Democracy Is . . . and Is Not." In *The Global Resurgence of Democracy.* Edited by Larry Diamond and Marc Plattner. Baltimore: John Hopkins University Press, 1993.

Schwartz, Benjamin. *The World of Thought in Ancient China.* Cambridge: Harvard University Press, 1985.

———. *China and Other Matters.* Cambridge: Harvard University Press, 1996.

Sen, Amartya. "Human Rights and Economic Achievements." In *The East Asian Challenge for Human Rights.* Edited by Joanne R. Bauer and Daniel A. Bell. New York: Cambridge University Press, 1999.

Sennet, Richard. *Flesh and Stone.* New York: Norton, 1994.

Seow, Francis. *To Catch a Tartar: A Dissident in Lee Kuan Yew's Prison.* New Haven: Yale University Southeast Asian Studies, 1994.

———. *The Media Enthralled: Singapore Revisited.* Boulder: Westview Press, 1997.

Shih Chih-yu, *Collective Democracy: Political and Legal Reform in China.* Hong Kong: The Chinese University Press, 1999.

Shin, Doh Chull. "On the Third Wave of Democratization: A Synthesis and Evaluation of Recent Theory and Research." *World Politics* 47 (October 1994).

Shue, Vivienne. "China: Transition Postponed?" *Problems of Communism* 41, no. 1–2 (January–April 1992).

Sing, Ming. "Democratization and Economic Development: The Anomalous Case of Hong Kong." *Democratization* 3, no. 3 (Autumn 1996).

———. "Economic Development, Civil Society, and Democratization in Hong Kong." *Journal of Contemporary Asia* 26, no. 4 (1996).

Singh, Bilveer. *Whither PAP's Dominence: An Analysis of Singapore's 1991 General Elections.* Selangor, Malaysia: Pelanduk Publications, 1992.

Skinner, Quentin. "The Italian City-Republics." In *Democracy.* Edited by John Dunn. Oxford: Oxford University Press, 1992.

Smith, Steven. *Hegel's Critique of Liberalism.* Chicago: University of Chicago Press, 1989.

Spar, Debora L. "The Spotlight and the Bottom Line: How Multinationals Export Human Rights." *Foreign Affairs* 77, no. 1 (March/April 1998).

Spence, Jonathan. *The Search for Modern China.* London: Hutchinson, 1990.

Spence, Jonathan. *God's Chinese Son: The Taiping Heavenly Kingdom of Hong Xiuquan.* New York: Norton, 1996.

Su, Shaozhi. "Problems of Democratic Reform in China." In *The Politics of Democratization.* Edited by E. Friedman. Boulder: Westview Press, 1994.

Sugden, Robert. "Justified to Whom?" In *The Idea of Democracy.* Edited by David Copp, Jean Hampton, and John Roemer. Cambridge: Cambridge University Press, 1993.

Tamir, Yael. *Liberal Nationalism.* Princeton: Princeton University Press, 1993.

Tan, Kevin. "Economic Development, Legal Reform, and Rights in Singapore and Taiwan." In *The East Asian Challenge for Human Rights.* Edited by Joanne R. Bauer and Daniel A. Bell. New York: Cambridge University Press, 1999.

Tan, Kevin, and Lam Peng Er, eds. *Managing Political Change in Singapore: The Elected Presidency.* London: Routledge, 1997.

Tay, Simon. "Human Rights, Culture, and the Singapore Example." *McGill University Law Journal* 41 (1996).

Taylor, Charles. *Hegel and Modern Society.* Cambridge: Cambridge University Press, 1979.

———. "Conditions of an Unforced Consensus on Human Rights." In *The East Asian Challenge for Human Rights.* Edited by Joanne R. Bauer and Daniel A. Bell. New York: Cambridge University Press, 1999.

Taylor, R. H. "Delusion and Necessity: Elections and Politics in Southeast Asia." *Items: Social Science Research Council* 48, no. 4 (December 1994).

Teson, Fernando. "The Rawlsian Theory of International Law." *Ethics and International Affairs* 9 (1995).

Touraine, Alain. *Comment sortir du libéralisme?* Paris: Fayard, 1999.

Tremewan, Christopher. *The Political Economy of Social Control in Singapore.* Houndsmills: Macmillan/St. Antony's College, 1994.

Tsang, Steve. "The Confucian Tradition and Modernization." In *Democracy: The Challenges Ahead.* Edited by Yossi Shain and Aharon Klieman. Basingstoke: Macmillan/St. Antony's College, 1997.

———. "Transforming a Party State into a Democracy." In *Democratization in Taiwan: Implications for China.* Edited by Steve Tsang and Hung-mao Tien. Houndmills: Macmillan Press/St. Antony's College, 1999.

Tsuru, Shigeto. *Japan's Capitalism: Creative Defeat and Beyond.* Cambridge: Cambridge University Press, 1993.

Tu, Wei-ming. *Confucianism in a Historical Perspective.* Institute of East Asian Philosophies, Occasional Paper and Monograph Series, no. 13, Singapore, 1989.

———, ed. *Confucian Traditions in East Asian Modernity.* Cambridge: Harvard University Press, 1996.

Van Ness, Peter, ed. *Debating Human Rights.* London: Routledge, 1999.

Van Wolferen, Karel. *The Enigma of Japanese Power.* London: Macmillan, 1989.

Vogel, Ezra. *The Four Little Dragons.* Cambridge: Harvard University Press, 1991.

Walzer, Michael. *Interpretation and Social Criticism.* Cambridge: Harvard University Press, 1987.

———. *Thick and Thin: Moral Argument at Home and Abroad.* Notre Dame: University of Notre Dame Press, 1994.

———. "Comment." In *Multiculturalism: Examining the Politics of Recognition.* Edited by Amy Gutmann. Second edition. Princeton: Princeton University Press, 1994.

Ward, Michael D., and Kristian S. Gleditsch. "Democratizing for Peace." *American Political Science Review* 92, no. 1 (March 1998).

White, Gordon. "Democratization and Economic Reform in China." *The Australian Journal of Chinese Affairs* 31 (January 1994).

Wiredu, Kwasi. *Cultural Universals and Particulars: An African Perspective.* Bloomington: Indiana University Press, 1996.

Wong, Timothy Ka-ying. "The Ethnic and National Identities of the Hong Kong People: A Liberal Explanation." *Issues and Studies* 32, no. 8 (August 1996).

Woo-Cumings, Meredith. "The 'New Authoritarianism' in East Asia." *Current History* 93, no. 587 (December 1994).

Wood, Alan. *Limits to Autocracy: From the Sung Neo-Confucianism to a Doctrine of Political Rights.* Honolulu: University of Hawaii Press, 1995.

Wuer Kaixi. "New May Fourth Manifesto." In *Cries for Democracy: Writings and Speeches from the 1989 Chinese Democracy Movement.* Edited by Han Minzhu. Princeton: Princeton University Press, 1990.

Wu Hungyuk, Anna. "Why Hong Kong Should Have Opportunities Legislation and a Human Rights Commission." In *Human Rights and Chinese Values.* Edited by Michael Davis. Hong Kong: Oxford University Press, 1995.

Yan, Jiaqi. *Toward a Democratic China.* Honolulu: University of Hawaii Press, 1992.

———. "China's National Minorities and Federalism." *Dissent* (Summer 1996).

Yasuda, Nobuyuki. "Human Rights, Individual or Collective? The Southeast Asian Experience." *Archiv fuer Rechts- und Sozialphilosophie,* Beiheft 72 (1998).

Yokota, Yozo. "A Nation's Accountability and Responsibility: The Case of Comfort Women in Japan." *Human Rights Dialogue* 8 (March 1997).

Young, Stephen. "Human Rights Questions in Southeast Asian Culture: Problems for American Response." In *The Politics of Human Rights.* Edited by Paula Newberg. New York: New York University Press, 1980.

Zakaria, Fareed. "The Rise of Illiberal Democracy." *Foreign Affairs* 76, no. 6 (November/December 1997).

Zhao, Suisheng. "Chinese Intellectuals' Quest for National Greatness and Nationalistic Writing in the 1990s." *China Quarterly* 152 (December 1992).

* Index *